*More praise for th*

## The Madonna of 115th Street

"An imaginative and subtly written account of the development of Italian community life in New York. . . . It is an excellent analysis of a complex religious and domestic experience."—*Sunday Times*

"With the skill of a novelist, Orsi presents to the reader the smells, textures, and colors of the celebration. . . . *The Madonna of 115th Street* remedies a serious blind spot in contemporary studies of immigrant life in America."
—P. Joseph Cahill, *Journal of the American Academy of Religion*

"This is a beautiful book."—Peter W. Williams, *Church History*

"Orsi provides a sensitive portrayal of the agonies and hardships as well as the joys and hopes of the people of Italian Harlem."—Patrick W. Carey, *Records of the American Catholic Historical Society*

"A superb piece of work. Orsi makes a major contribution toward our understanding of popular religion, the experiences of immigration and community formation, and American Catholicism." —David O'Brien, College of the Holy Cross

# THE MADONNA OF 115TH STREET

*Faith and Community in*
*Italian Harlem, 1880–1950*

Second Edition

ROBERT ANTHONY ORSI

YALE NOTA BENE

YALE UNIVERSITY PRESS
NEW HAVEN AND LONDON

First published as a Yale Nota Bene book in 2002.
First edition published by Yale University Press in 1985.

Introduction to second edition copyright © 2002 by Yale University.
First edition copyright © 1985 by Yale University.

For information about this and other Yale University Press publications,
please contact:

|  |  |
|---|---|
| U.S. office | sales.press@yale.edu |
| Europe office | sales@yaleup.co.uk |

Printed in the United States of America

Library of Congress Control Number: 2001098541

ISBN 0-300-09135-4 (pbk.)

A catalogue record for this book is available from the British Library.

10  9  8  7  6  5  4  3  2

# THE MADONNA OF 115TH STREET

*Women carrying tiered structures of candles during the procession, ca. 1938*

This is dedicated to my parents, Mario Orsi and
Anna Cavallaro Orsi, and especially to
my grandmother, Giulia Orsi, who
immigrated to this country in
1951

# Contents

Introduction to the Second Edition                                    ix

Introduction: Popular Religion and Italian Harlem                   xxxix

1  The Days and Nights of the Festa                                    1

2  Italian Harlem                                                     14

3  The Origins of the Devotion to Mount Carmel
   in Italian Harlem                                                  50

4  The Domus-Centered Society                                         75

5  Conflicts in the Domus                                            107
   Conflict                                                          109
   Women in Italian Harlem                                           129

6  Toward an Inner History of Immigration                            150

7  The Meanings of the Devotion to the
   Madonna of 115th Street                                           163
   The Devotion and the Community of Immigrants                      163
   The Devotion and the People's Faithfulness to Italy and
   Southern Italian Traditions                                       168

The Devotion and the Domus                                        171
The Shaping of *Cara Harlem*                                      178
The Community Reveals Itself to Itself                            186
The Devotion and the Larger Collectivities of
    the City and Nation                                           188
Success                                                           191
Healing and the Sense World of the Festa                          193
The Italian Way of Being Human                                    195
The Festa and the World of Work                                   197
From Suffering to Sacrifice                                        202
Women and the Devotion to the Madonna of 115th Street             204
Power                                                             217

8   The Theology of the Streets                                   219

A Note on Abbreviations                                           233

Notes                                                             235

Selected Bibliography                                             271

Index                                                             283

# Introduction to the Second Edition
## Faith and Community in Italian Harlem, 1880–1950

When I climbed aboard Metro North in New Haven one day in the late 1970s, en route to New York to begin my research on Italian-American Catholicism in the city in the nineteenth and twentieth centuries, I understood myself to be a historian and I thought of my trip as being in search of archives where I hoped to find documents that would allow me to tell this story. I have heard historians proudly say that they study only dead people, and in those early days I, too, was looking for dead people. The archival moment—descent into moldy, poorly lit rooms heaped with filthy tattered documents, held tight in the clutches of vicious and venal caretakers in forbidding locations that the historian approaches at great personal risk—has been central to the production of the authority and status of history writing as a modern *profession*. The first practitioners of history as an academic discipline, anxious to distinguish themselves from the amateurs who preceded them, emphasized the arduousness of archival work and even its risks and dangers, grounding their authority in having met and overcome great obstacles on the way to truth. The new historians were men, the amateurs mostly women, and so also at stake in these origin myths was the gendering of the emergent historical profession as male. How much all this would affect me I did not yet know as I set out for New York. But somewhere in the back of my mind I am sure I was thinking or hoping that this trip to East Harlem was to be the foundation of my status as a real historian.[1]

## THE ANXIETIES OF A HISTORIAN IN THE FIELD

I found archives, and I had my share of archival moments. I encountered, as everyone studying New York Catholic history necessarily had to in those days, the much-feared gatekeeper of the city's archdiocesan archives, a nun who clearly understood it to be her job never to let anyone see the documents in her care. To this end she set impossible tasks for scholars. "I need the exact folder number of the document you wish to see," she told me the first time I contacted her, but there was no way of knowing this because there was no register or catalogue that I could ever discover. The forty days of Jesus' sojourn in the desert became the interval of our conversations. "It's Advent," she said; "call me after Christmas." "It's Lent—get back to me after Easter." Sacred seasons followed one another like the leaves of a calendar in an old movie. But in a much more welcoming archive, the Balch Institute for Ethnic Studies in Philadelphia, I found the papers of Leonard Covello, a beloved East Harlem educator and public figure. It was in his papers that I found the *festa* of Our Lady of Mount Carmel, and it was the discovery of the festa that got me to the streets of East Harlem.

It quickly became clear to me that although it was not the thriving community it once had been, *cara Harlem*, as the Italians had called it—beloved Harlem—continued to exist in a number of ways: in the remnant of old-timers in its northernmost sections; in the memories of the men and women who had left East Harlem only two decades or so before; and, most important, during the annual festa, when in an uncanny way memory took shape in the streets. On the Madonna's feast days, the neighborhood was (and still is) crowded with Italians again. Old neighbors meet in the streets as if they still lived in the surrounding tenements, and familiar faces fuss around the Madonna's procession float. These were not dead people. The border, indeed the firebreak, I had figured on between then and now, us and them, the past and the present, turned out to be porous. The precise configuration of the relation between the present and the past is not inherent in the nature of history but is constituted by historians and others engaged in the work of remembering (and forgetting) as they tell stories and write histories out of the needs, desires, and fears of their present circumstances. Even the pastness of the past—the quality of its being over, once and for all, that we tend to assume—is achieved, not given. The claim "oh, that's ancient history" is almost always a wish, an anxious attempt to put a boundary of time around some event that really is not over at all; it is a bid to silence the past. What I found in East Harlem made it impossible for me to establish the pastness of that particular past in any simple sense.[2]

So I began to do a kind of layered fieldwork in the fissure between the present and the past. Over a two-year period I traveled around New York City's outer boroughs and New Jersey, talking with people who had once lived in East Harlem; I spent many months in the old neighborhoods in northern Manhattan, meeting older and more recent residents and community leaders. This enterprise soon became a cause of real disorientation and anxiety. Was I still doing history? How would I cite my sources? What should I do with the specifics of my fieldwork? Women cooked for me when I stopped by their homes to talk with them and their families about Italian Harlem, for example, so that much of my research was conducted over long days of eating and drinking. I came to realize that I was learning as much from *how* people were talking to me as from what they were telling me, as much from what was going on around the stories as from the stories themselves. Was there a place for this information in my narrative? Were such interactions even appropriate for a historian? Did I have to validate everything I was told with a printed source? Was it necessary to archive my tapes so others could scrutinize them?

These questions seem naïve today, but they are revealing, too. I recognize all that anxiety about textuality, for example, about the absence of texts, as the fear of losing my own compass and authority as the interpreter of texts in a discipline (religious studies) wedded to textuality. The American Academy of Religion, the leading professional organization of scholars of religion in the United States, grew out of the National Association of Biblical Instructors, a pedigree that is emblematic of the enduring authority of the written word in the contemporary culture of religious scholarship and one of the grounds of the persistent uneasiness with ethnography in the discipline. My concerns about approaching the past through animated conversations in crowded, noisy kitchens, while everyday life went on around me— my tapes record grandchildren coming and going, neighbors dropping by, grocery deliveries, ambulance and police sirens, and the crash of pots and pans—were the enactment in my own experience, moreover, of gender anxieties attending and constitutive of history's emergence as a critical discipline in the modern era. Those descriptions by the earliest generations of professional historians of their struggles to overcome the conditions of archival work, to master and transcend the vicissitudes of the body, articulated an "antinomy of body . . . to spirit," according to the historian Bonnie G. Smith. Associated with the corporal end of this dichotomy—with body—were women and the various concerns of everyday life, while spirit represented the public, the political, and the masculine. This foundational body/spirit split determined what historians chose to study (war, politics, civic events, not the details of everyday domestic life), where they chose to study (in silent archives, alone, free of the multitude of the world's—especially women's—voices), and how historians carried and represented themselves, the discipline's emergent (and enduring) ethos. The intellectual and social authority of modern historiography was premised, indeed, on this antinomy. But here I was in women's kitchens, my body well-cared for, nourished by good food and surrounded by good company. I found myself, in other words, right in the vise of the antinomy that structured not only modern historiography but modern professionalism generally.[3]

Back in New Haven, meanwhile, I was asked one day what I anticipated the end date of my history would be. This was a problem, I confessed, because the festa still took place. Maybe I would go into the mid-1960s. The person I was talking to laughed. Right up to your own birth in the Bronx, she joked. The comment filled me with a hot professional shame. Not only was I not using traditional archives, but I had transgressed onto the time of my own being.

The issues raised by my experience in East Harlem have to do with the nature of historical knowledge, with the relationships between ethnography and historiography, between present and past, and between everyday life and academic knowledge and protocols; with the relative usefulness of text and practice as historical sources, with the appropriate positioning of the scholar of religion to his or her subject, and with the gendering of knowledge. And the insistence with which such issues pressed themselves upon me marks a moment in the history of the study of religious history. I had apparently stepped outside the borders of historiography—ironically, in search of history—and I was at a loss as to how to proceed. I was not completely conscious at the time that these were the stakes, but I knew this in my bones. The reality of such boundaries—which present themselves as matters of academic or professional limits or standards, but clearly involve much bigger existential and ethical dilemmas—is pressed not only into our professional consciousness but into our bodies, too. This is what it means to be trained in or acculturated to a particular intellectual discipline, to be disciplined by the expectations, orientations, limits, and fears of a field of inquiry, and to bear within oneself the history of the field's becoming. Transgression, even imagined transgression, registers as shame in the body and as intellectual uncertainty.

The intensity of feeling evoked in me and others by these questions—anxiety, disorientation, panic, humiliation—indicates that the borders between past and present, between history and ethnography, between scholar and subject were (and remain) closely guarded and defended, and that they are threatened by scholarship that looks outside archives and texts and proceeds intersubjectively in the spaces of everyday experience. I believe these to be issues of wide import in the contemporary practice of religious history and in the study of religion. There is broad interest among younger scholars of religion today in ethnographic approaches, at a time when the key terms in the discipline—including *religion*, *culture*, and *history*—are under intense critical scrutiny. We have gone well beyond the debates between intellectual and social history at this juncture to a rethinking of the very nature and practice of religious history and of the identity of the religious historian.

## THE DEAD END AND HIGH STAKES OF "POPULAR RELIGION"

I was tentatively making my way intellectually and emotionally in East Harlem, against these invisible obstacles and internalized authorities, to the study of what scholars have begun to call "lived religion": religious practice and imagination in ongoing, dynamic relation with the realities and structures of everyday life in particular times and places. This was the real battle, I can see now, not my efforts to get into a particular archive by outwitting a wily archivist. The study of lived religion explores how religion is shaped by and shapes the ways family life is organized, for instance: how the dead are buried, children disciplined, the past and future imagined, moral boundaries established and challenged, homes constructed, maintained, and destroyed, the gods and spirits worshiped and importuned, and so on. Religion is approached in its place within a more broadly conceived and described lifeworld, the domain of everyday existence, practical activity, and shared understandings, with all its crises, surprises, satisfactions, frustrations, joys, desires, hopes, fears, and limitations.[4]

This level of religious experience was all but invisible in the discipline at the time and absent from its critical lexicon. The only term available for it, *popular religion*, was unclear, misleading, and tendentious. Definitional debates over the meanings and implications of popular religion were endless and deeply frustrating. Did "popular religion" refer exclusively to the religious practices and imaginings of common folk? But then what becomes of "popular" religion when social or religious elites participate in it (as they almost always do)? Was popular religion distinct from "official" religion? Where did popular religion come from? Did popular religion represent a corruption or misappropriation of authorized teaching and ritual? Was popular religion even historically significant, or were such forms historically inconsequential curiosities, irrelevant to the main developments in religious history in any given period? Is the history of the feast of Our Lady of Mount Carmel absolutely essential to the story of the New York Catholic Archdiocese or of American Catholicism? Do students need to know about this to know about American Catholicism?

Rather than making it possible to study religious practice and imagination in relation to other expressions and forms of human activity—to legal or architectural idioms, for example, or cosmological speculations—the designation *popular religion* served to seal off certain expressions of religious life from an unspecified but obviously normative "religion" (without the qualifier *popular*). How were we to think about the social and cultural place of devotionalism (people's direct engagement with sacred figures amid the quotidian circumstances of life)? Where did domestic religious expressions (home shrines, for example, or the religious grounds or implications of intergenerational bonds or tensions) fit? What of highly emotionally charged religious idioms, and ritual practices that took place outside churches and temples (or at the intersection of inside and outside)? The term instituted unnecessary and confusing boundaries.[5]

These are issues of power—the power of our theories of "religion" to constitute some ideas and practices as religious and others not, some practices and perspectives as essential to a particular religious and cultural world and others marginal. Visitors from outside the community to the festa of Our Lady of Mount Carmel over the years have not always recognized what they saw (and see) there—people walking barefoot behind the Madonna, kissing the statues in church and penciling petitions for love or health on them, eating and gambling under the bright colored lights strung over the streets—as religious, and neither have many scholars of religion. Religious idioms like those associated with the Madonna's cult (the technical term for Catholic devotional practices) have been designated "magical," "superstitious," overly materialistic, and manipulative; they are deemed theologically incoherent, ambiguous amalgams of the sacred and the profane. There is also the question of what to do with the many different practices that surround a religious event—neighborly socializing, for example, or the family conflicts that may erupt on such occasions, or customs related to making and eating food. Are they to be included within the rubric *religious* in approaching such historical and cultural expressions? These are high-stakes matters that go well beyond issues of scholarly definition, or—put another way—scholarly definitions of religion are implicated in much broader social and cultural agendas. They inevitably entail what we are willing to tolerate as religion and what we find intolerable, what boundaries we insist on—between persons, for example, or between the living and the dead, or the past and the present—and what boundary transgressions frighten us, which behaviors are socially acceptable and which offend us, what postures we sanction and which we condemn, and so on.

The effort to contain and control religion by definition—by establishing some practices or experiences as authentically religious and others as perversions—has generated hierarchies in American popular and academic discourse. Sometimes a distinction is made between religion (which means the historically and culturally specific forms, rituals, moral prohibitions and permissions, and theological teachings of particular religious cultures, the things that separate one religious group from another) and spirituality (which refers to an ahistorical, interior apprehension of religious truth that is independent of culture), or between religion and faith (likewise defined as a matter of interiority, with an emphasis on the autonomy and individuality of believers). Spirituality and faith (in these pairings) are seen as superior to religion, more authentic because unbound by history and cultural contingency, above matter and free of particularity, essential rather than circumstantial, universal and transtemporal, not rooted in specific times and places. The term *popular religion* served to authorize religion, spirituality, and faith—defined and valued as I have just described—by standing as their necessary other. Sometimes a distinction is made between religion and "magic" or "superstition," in which case the latter two terms bear the onus of identification with the particular and contingent, with matter, emotion, and body, and with the ambiguous confusion of the sacred and profane.[6] Another way of containing what went on, and still goes on, in East Harlem is to call it premodern and to emphasize its disconnectedness from modern forms of religious experience and expression; from such a perspective, the festa represents the religiously atavistic. Popular religion, within the frame of these normative hierarchies, is the experience of dark, poor, alien folk, of children and women, of the colonized, enslaved, and "primitive," of the ignorant or uneducated. Modern societies enforce distinctions between good and bad, tolerable and intolerable religion in many different ways—by zoning regulations that prohibit certain forms of religious expression in particular places, for instance, by disregard for sacred places and objects not commonly recognized as such, and by ostracism and contempt—and these more overt prohibitions and constraints attain the sanction and authority of universal reason when they are restated in terms of religious theory. Thus the designations *magic, superstitious,* and *popular,* among others, are also ways of policing religion.

Such hierarchies are thoroughly cultural constructions, deeply implicated in the realities of power. Because distinctions among kinds of religious practice and imagination are so fundamental to contemporary culture, they appear normal and natural. They come to us as ever-present and without history—of course writing a petition on a saint's statue is an example of "magical" thinking; what else could it be? Of course it belongs under "popular religion" and not simply under "religion." But the basic nomenclature of religious studies is deeply and directly implicated in the history of Western racism and colonialism and in three centuries of divisive, bitter internecine Christian conflict. The words we use to categorize and rank religious phenomena are marked by this tumultuous history.

Two periods in particular emerge as crucial in the history of the Western conceptualization of religion: the religious conflicts of the sixteenth and seventeenth centuries, when Catholics and Protestants fought bitterly over territory, political authority, and the meaning and practice of Christianity, and the period of industrialization and of the colonization of Asia and Africa by Western powers in the nineteenth century. How we understand or construct the religious—which categories of persons and practices are seen as religious and which as superstitious or worse—reflects and encodes the politics, imperial ideologies, and religious conflicts of these periods. Theoretical accounts of religion in the modern era created, authorized, and sanctified social and racial hierarchies in Europe and the United States, and in the territories they dominated. Scholars of religion and apologists for empire both drew together—the one in theories, the other in practices of domination—African peoples and Irish Catholic immigrants in East London, for example, or Hindu practitioners and working-class children, in discourses of otherness that served the work of colonization and domination at home and abroad as it contributed to the construction of European authority as white, male, adult, Christian, "universal," "rational." The religious practices of exploited populations were reinterpreted as further indications of the necessity and inevitability of their domination, so that the languages of power and those of the critical study of religion converged. From South Africa to East Harlem, southern Italy to Mississippi, certain kinds of religious practice were theoretically construed in such a way as to deny the humanness of practitioners and to justify their oppression or marginalization.[7]

Setting the study of religion in its place in relation to political and social history, and understanding that the lenses with which we approach phenomena such as the festa of Our Lady of Mount Carmel are implicated in long and complex histories—understanding, in other words, that these lenses are not innocent or simple—allow us to unearth, for example, the deeply embedded anti-Catholicism in European and American religious studies. The designation *popular religion* in relation to American religion was, among other things, a code for Catholic-like ritual and devotional practices, deemed inappropriate and even incomprehensible on the religious landscape of the United States. Religious practices such as those associated with the feast of the Madonna of 115th Street were treated at best as a passing phase in the religious acculturation of premodern immigrants and migrants. "Popular religion" thus served to underscore what was un-American about such religious phenomena, and, as it did so, it contributed to the construction of a normative American religiosity that was the opposite of whatever happened on 115th Street. The term *popular religion* identified and cordoned off forms of religious expression that subverted or transgressed boundaries fundamental to the construction of modern religiosity and of modern society—for example, religious forms that blur distinctions between matter and spirit (as in the assumption by some of the faithful that the Madonna was really *there* in East Harlem, present in material representations of her), between the sacred and the profane (as in the gambling that took place within the Madonna's sight), between public spaces defined as free of religious presence and private religious experience.

My point here is not to defend or endorse such religious expressions. I do not share these practices or orientations (or I do not share all of them). I am deeply sympathetic to efforts to define and maintain a public space where citizens can meet and make necessary decisions for a common life without confronting or undermining each other with ontological or theological claims. Religious expressions like those called popular have been responsible for much personal, domestic, and social grief and turmoil. Religious practice and imagination may destabilize boundaries—of the self, for example, or in the social world—that are better left intact, as the Bosnian nightmare and the horror of September 11, among other instances, reminded us.[8] Rather, I am saying that we need to be aware of the history of the ways of seeing religion that we bring to religious phenomena such as the festa, that theories of religion are grounded in broader social agendas, and that they encode and enact fears of and desires for various forms of religious expression. This will better enable us to approach religion as it is in any particular social world, rather than religion as we want it to be or religion within the limits of our tolerance.

Sanitized, carefully bounded and contained notions of spirituality, religion, or faith are completely subverted by such phenomena as the festa on 115th Street. The festa was, and is, not about the cherished values of modernity or of normative, tolerable religion—not about individuality but about selves situated in social worlds, not about transcendence but about religion's place in everyday life, not about autonomy but about the ways that people come to be within the forms of their culture, not about empowerment but about living within the coordinates of the possible.

The major theoretical traditions of religious studies in the 1970s remained ahistorical, impatient with the contingent details of the quotidian, oriented primarily toward theology, and more interested in transcendence than in historical immanence. Mere historicity was treated with contempt. But historians, folklorists, and anthropologists, who were more comfortable on earth, began to clear the way past the simple and defeating dualities of the popular-religion debate in the 1970s and 1980s, creating an extraordinary body of compassionate, critical, closely observed, and richly textured ethnographic histories of religious practice and imagination in particular times and places, including Carlo Ginzburg's *The Cheese and the Worms; Person and God in a Spanish Valley*, by William A. Christian, Jr.; Emmanuel LeRoy Ladurie's *Montaillou*; the powerful chapter on religion in Eugene D. Genovese's *Roll, Jordan, Roll*; and Pierre-Jakez Helias's *The Horse of Pride*. Historians of the Reformation turned their attention to the ways that the religious upheavals of the sixteenth century registered in the everyday experience of local parishioners in towns and villages throughout Europe. This extraordinary efflorescence in the study of religious practice and imagination made a new, more capacious problematic of popular or vernacular religion possible.[9]

## THE STUDY OF LIVED RELIGION

The study of lived religion situates all religious creativity within culture and approaches all religion as lived experience, theology no less than lighting a candle for a troubled loved one; spirituality as well as other, less culturally sanctioned forms of religious expression (such as licking the stones of a church floor). Rethinking religion as a form of cultural work, the study of lived religion directs attention to institutions *and* persons, texts *and* rituals, practice *and* theology, things *and* ideas—all as media of making and unmaking worlds. This way of approaching religious practice as fundamentally and always *in* history and culture is concerned with what people *do* with religious idioms, how they use them, what they make of themselves and their worlds with them, and how in turn people are fundamentally shaped by the worlds they are making as they make these worlds. Religious practices and understandings have meaning only in relation to other cultural forms and in relation to the life experiences and actual circumstances of the people using them; what people mean and intend by particular religious idioms can be understood only situationally, on a broad social and biographical field, not within the terms of a religious tradition or religious language understood as existing apart from history.[10] Religion approached this way is set amid the ordinary concerns of life as these are structured at various moments in history and in different cultures, at the junctures of self and culture, family and social world, and on those occasions when the religious imagination (which itself is constituted both by culture and by personal experience and inheritance) takes hold of the world (as the world is said to be) in prayer, ritual, and theology, as it is taken hold of by the world.[11]

Culture is understood here to comprise the webs of meaning that humans spin and in which they are suspended, the ways that humans create and represent themselves and others. But culture is not a hermetic field of singular meanings. It is messy, contested, unstable, always in motion. The meanings of a single sign or practice may be multiple and inconsistent, and may change, moreover, as a particular sign is used to work on the world and the self. A particular practice— praying to the Madonna, for example—the meanings of which seem to be clear enough and discernible through Catholic theology, in fact may be caught in the tension between conscious and unconscious motivations and desire, or between now and then, here and there (in this case, between Italy and New York), hopes and memories. Because culture is always historically situated, human signs and practices bear within them the marks and tears of their histories; such signs are fundamentally historical creations.[12] Praying to the Madonna meant one thing to the older generation of immigrants, another when immigrants and their American born or raised children prayed together. Religion is always religion-in-action, religion-in-relationships between people, between the way the world is and the way people imagine or want it to be. The interpretive challenge of the study of lived religion is to develop the practice of disciplined attention to people's signs and practices as they describe, understand, and use them, in the circumstances of their experiences, and to the structures and conditions within which these signs and practices emerge.

People do not simply act, of course; they attempt to understand and narrate themselves as actors. So the study of lived religion includes the work of social agents/actors themselves as narrators and interpreters (and reinterpreters) of their own experiences and histories, recognizing that the stories we tell about others exist alongside the many and varied stories they tell of themselves. The study of lived religion is not about practice rather than ideas, but about ideas, gestures, imaginings, all as media of engagement with the world. It is pointless to study particular beliefs or practices—the Catholic teaching on the Virgin Mary, for example, or the Pentecostal theology of sanctification—apart from the people who use these ideas in the definite circumstances of their lives. Religion-in-action cannot be separated from other practices of everyday life, from the ways that humans do other necessary and important things or from other cultural structures and discourses (legal, political, medical, and so on). Nor can sacred spaces be understood in isolation from the places where these things are done (workplaces, hospitals, law courts, homes, and streets), from the media used to do them, or from the relationships constructed around them. The emphasis in the study of lived religion is on *embodied* practice and imagination, as men, women, and children exist in and move through their built and found environments. The material world is not inert background to cultural practice; it is its essential medium.

Because religion is so completely enmeshed in the structures of culture, issues of power become crucial. Indeed, power is fundamental to the very meaning of practice, generally, and of religious practice in particular.[13] By *power* I mean not only the power of some over others (although I do certainly mean to include this) but also the power that circulates through, as it sustains and vivifies, cultural forms, for example, aesthetics, ethics, kinesthesis, and architecture. These are the taken for granted aspects of a culture, the meanings of a particular world that are given the sanction of the natural, the inherently good, the commonsensical, or of the sacred. Ethnic ties, which are always contingent and fictive, are sanctioned by allusions to blood and mother's milk, for example; or stories are told about a people's sacred provenance. It is this power that makes us know in our bodies that certain ways of being are the only appropriate ones for the world, as we are taught the world is. The efficacy and effects of this form of power are manifest in the shame and terror we feel when we transgress the boundaries it establishes. This includes the intellectual world as well: a clear instance of this was the shame provoked in me when I felt I had failed to maintain the normative distinction between the present and the past as I found myself studying a history that was not over.

How is religion related to power? Religion is one of the cultural practices that constitute persons as particular kinds of beings in specific social worlds, and establishes, polices, and authorizes the boundaries of good and evil. As a person lives through religious idioms, as she prays in a distinct language, enacting certain ideas, arranging her body in the ways available in and mandated by her tradition—the women bent low, for example, to the stones of the church on 115th Street, bringing their bodies and petitions to the Madonna on the altar—she is also being enacted and created as a subject, with specific hopes and fears about herself and about the world. She is endowed, through these practices, with understandings of what is possible in life and what is not. What were women making of themselves at the annual festa? The celebrations on 115th Street and women's daily devotions to the Madonna del Carmine were not innocent. Religion is one of the more effective media by which social power is realized in bodies, just as religion shapes, orients, and limits the imagination, and it is pointless to study religion without reference to power (to both kinds of power)—pointless and irresponsible.

Understood this way, religion arises at the intersection of inner experience and the outer world. It does not belong completely to the self, because we inherit ways of thinking, feeling, and being, and because our culture's forms and expectations are pressed into our bodies and imaginations, establishing the grounds of comprehensibility and communication and the possibilities of creativity. A woman praying to the Madonna of Mount Carmel in the idioms of mid-twentieth century Italian-American Catholicism, for example—one of her inherited structures—was employing a decidedly poisoned medium in her quest for hope and consolation. Devotionalism taught that women were born to suffer, to suffer silently, to suffer on behalf of their kin, and that it was wrong to avoid suffering. Devotionalism, which women entered in times of dire need, often, and thus of great vulnerability, constructed women's interiorities, oriented their desires and hopes, and assigned them to the very suffering from which they were praying for relief.

But religion does not belong completely to culture, either. Devotionalism (as a Catholic idiom) has no life apart from people's experience of it. It is not possible, in other words, to tell the political history of Marian devotionalism, as some have tried to do, apart from the lives of particular women engaging the Madonna. Women took hold of the world in imagination when they prayed to the Madonna and other holy figures out of intense need, desire, hope, or fear, conscious and unconscious. In the company of the Madonna, within sight of her benevolent and encouraging gaze, women accomplished things for themselves that they might not otherwise have been able to do; at least they could reorient themselves to their worlds, directing themselves toward new, previously unimagined (or even unimaginable) horizons. Cultural structures, in this case devotionalism, *become* history precisely at such moments of engagement. This is the radical historicity of the study of lived religion. Many things may happen in this engagement: latent tensions in the structure might widen, contradictions emerge, hidden or unrealized possibilities surface, implicit and unintended interpretations become accessible, all presenting women with the possibility of using the structure against itself, even as they are shaped by particular dimensions of it. Religion, to borrow the British psychologist D. W. Winnicott's terminology for the situation of the imagination, exists "inside, outside, and at the border." As people pray to, worship, and plead with the gods, the culture acts on the imagination and the imagination works on culture, to the possible transformation of both. This is how I understand religious creativity.[14]

Some moments in social, domestic, cultural, and personal history are particularly open to the transformation of subjects and structures both—the hot spots of death, sexuality, pain, deep transformations in material reality, environmental disasters, occasions of contradiction or disruption. The designation *uncle*, to borrow Peter Berger's example, is not given in nature, nor are the responsibilities or the appropriate affect of this role; although uncles and their nephews and nieces approach these roles as given, they are made and sustained in the ongoing work of culture.[15] But in the circumstances I have just described, the taken-for-granted quality of "reality" is dissolved, and humans encounter the fictive nature of what they call real, in the sense that they apprehend the radical contingency of their worlds. This provokes in turn new uses of religious story, ritual, and metaphor, and new configurations of the real. Culture and self, inner and outer worlds are all in play at the same time. The challenge is to study religion dialectically, on the levels both of the self and of culture, tracking back and forth between structure and agency, tradition and act, imagination and reality, and, in the process, dissolving the solidity of such dichotomies.

I consider such a perspective one of realism, by which I mean understanding human imagination, creativity, and capacity as being situated at the intersection of necessity and choice, structure and agency, of the given and the hoped-for, and recognizing, moreover, that choice never exists apart from constraint, possibility without discipline, or desire without limits. We are shaped by our circumstances, but we shape them too; we are always both subjects and objects, acting and acted upon. Enraptured by notions of transcendence and by the fantasy of a spirituality that floats free of the contingencies of culture and the vicissitudes of the body, the study of religion and religious history (and especially such study in comfortable economic times) has often lost sight of this chastened view of human spiritual and historical capacities. But the study of lived religion might help us abandon simple notions that religion empowers people or makes them autonomous, that religion either sustains the world or transgresses it. Because it acknowledges the tremendous challenge entailed in using any religious idiom to work on the world in times of distress, the study of lived religion vividly opens out the tremendous creativity of religious practice and imaginings as it uncovers the limits of them.

## RESEARCH AS A RELATIONSHIP BETWEEN PEOPLE

I had been in the neighborhood for many weeks when Mount Carmel's pastor offered me one of the enormous cigars he smoked every day in his study after lunch. This kind interlude meant a great deal to me, and recalling it now brings back deep feelings of gratitude and relief. But at the time I did not quite know what to make of the pleasure I took in the gift. I did not yet understand what I was doing as fieldwork. My "research" was in the boxes of stored documents at the church, not in the quiet sharing of redolent cigars. I was a historian; the cigar was in the present; we were not in an archive. My exchanges with people in East Harlem were already pushing me past this static view of what I was doing, though—static and ungracious, because people were in fact inviting me into serious conversations about things that mattered to them (at my request)—and since these days in East Harlem I have become much clearer about this.

"Research is a living relation" between people, Jean-Paul Sartre says in *Search for a Method*, adding that "the *relationship* between them must be itself interpreted as a moment of history."[16] It took me a long time to understand that my research in East Harlem was taking place in and through the relationships I was forming there (in addition to the archival materials), that this is how I was learning about both the present and the past and about the relation between them. I imagined at first that I was doing a kind of oral history in the neighborhood, collecting information that was stored away in people's heads by asking good questions, the way one extracts information from a document. But this is not what was happening, I slowly realized, when I heard people say things like, "God, I haven't thought about this in years!" or "I probably shouldn't tell you this, but . . ." or when they looked away, unexpectedly moved or distressed or angered by a memory, by some piece of their lives that they had not thought about in a while, or perhaps never in this way. Fieldwork proceeds through relationships. This means that something that was not there before—understanding, memories, disappointments, and so on, hidden, unacknowledged, unformulated, or even unknown—becomes present in the exchanges as people tell their stories to another person who listens to them and responds. My sources reflected on their past, reinterpreted and reevaluated their experiences, discovered things about themselves and their histories that they had not previously realized or understood. A number of times, the interplay between present and past was acted out, when suddenly provoked by our conversation, people I was talking with who had grown up in Italian Harlem but had moved away suddenly decided to take me back to the old neighborhood for a tour. We piled into the car and made our way across one or another bridge that once upon a time had marked for these people the distance they had traveled from their childhood to their adult worlds—the George Washington Bridge, the Triborough, the Throgs Neck, or the Verrazano Narrows—headed back, in other words, toward the past, which existed only in the present. Italian Harlem, past and present, existed in between the present and the past in the relationships between me and the people with whom I was talking as we stood on their old blocks. Issues of trust became crucial. People tested me in various ways, making sure I could hold the stories they discovered they wanted to tell me.

My path to the realization that this kind of research is done not only among real people, struggling to make sense of themselves and of their worlds, but by real people too, also struggling to make sense of things, was slow. I held tightly to a poorly understood but deeply cherished notion of needing to be an objective, distant observer who brought a trained but socially unconnected rationality to the work. What did my experience, my childhood, or my hopes and fears have to do with anything? My first posture in the neighborhood was to insist on my difference: I did not have a devotion to the Madonna, these were not my people. (What on earth was I thinking? I am an Italian American, from the Bronx, and all my relatives pray to the Virgin Mary.) I would listen and record and then, later, back in New Haven, listen again and interpret, alone in my room. I was interested in the past, moreover, construed as unattached to the present, so it was only stories *about* the past that initially caught my attention.

But culture consists in the ongoing efforts of men and women to make sense of, to live more or less well within, and to represent and communicate their worlds, work that goes on in endless rounds of conversation, reflection, discussion, imagination, practice, gesture, and ritual. Culture itself is fundamentally and inescapably intersubjective. Language, perception, emotion, and imagination all take shape in and through relationships (including relationships with ancestors, gods, spirits, ghosts, and other such figures). Relationships are fraught with desire, fear, denial, and needs of all sorts, conscious and unconscious, which makes for ambiguity, confusion, and misinterpretation; they exist on crowded social and political fields and are implicated in domination, oppression, and exclusion. But the fact is that humans exist intersubjectively, that reality itself is intersubjective, and that fieldwork is intersubjective discovery.[17]

Ethnographers and the people they live and study among are alike involved in these processes of interpreting, arguing, communicating, and understanding. Scholars of culture step into these rounds, attend to them, and contribute to them as they in turn struggle to understand other people and cultures, to understand themselves in relation to other people, and to communicate what they know and feel. This realization drew me across the distance I had established between myself and the people I was talking to and began the process of liberating me at last to be present in East Harlem. My interlocutors did not let me be invisible, moreover, drawing me out with questions about my life and experience. It is not necessary to become the other in order to see, for a moment, the world through his or her eyes. The derogatory, and racist, accusation of "going native" is, like the term *popular religion*, boundary-setting rhetoric that seeks to preserve the utter alienness of the other. It is enough—and hard enough—simply to enter into real relationships with the other, in his or her environment, to engage their accounts of themselves and their worlds openly and attentively, with the willingness to disclose one's own world and imagination to them. I finally understood that this is what I was trying to do in East Harlem.

But what does ethnography have to do with historiography? What has a discipline based on sustained encounters with living people, usually in the circumstances of their everyday lives (not the ethnographer's) to do with a discipline grounded in the study of dead people whose remains have been moved to archives, often far from the places where they had once lived? On one level, it is useful to remember that the inert documents stored away in archives were once the living media of real people's engagement with the unfolding events of their times. The challenge for historians, as for ethnographers, is to figure out the relation between these archived pieces of a once-living world and the world from which they came, which they helped make, and to which they responded. My method in telling the story of the Madonna and Italian Harlem was to bring the voices from the archives and the voices from the streets into relation, allowing them to challenge, amend, deepen, and correct each other, to let the present inform the past and the past the present, and I could not have told this story without both kinds of sources. My listening-place was the juncture of past and present.

On another level, the oft-cited deadness of historical subjects and of the past itself has always seemed to me a form of license, not a natural given. "Dead" in this context means not simply that these subjects are no longer alive but that they cannot resist what is to be made of them. Deadness, and the accompanying silence, makes it possible, among other things, to locate figures of the past in *our* stories, to subsume their narrative into ours. Reference to the deadness of the past is a way of staking a claim on it. But historians must be open, as ethnographers try to be, to the shock of the unpredictability and difference of the past, which means open to the possibility of the past living in its insistence on telling its own story and so confounding us. Only in this way can the past teach us something new about ourselves, about the limits of our imaginings and ways of knowing, and even of our particular and distinctive ways of being human.

Although we have to begin with difference—and to this end it was a good thing that I was so preoccupied with distance and difference early in my East Harlem research, because this kept me from too easily analogizing from my Italian-American experience to theirs—we cannot end with difference. We cannot stop with otherness because then we turn the people we have gone among in the archives and in the field into curiosities. Historians need to be mindful of a common humanity with figures in the past—again, a bond that is denied by assertions of deadness. Figures in the past might be dead, but they lived once, and when they did, the fundamental impulses of their lives were probably not that much different from ours. Morally, we owe them and their heirs, whoever these heirs are, at least this recognition. If they remain other, or if we remain (or keep ourselves) other to them (out of some misplaced sense of academic propriety or epistemological caution), or if we even insist on their otherness, then we will tell bizarre and titillating stories about them, rendering their lives absurd and exotic. The political implications of this is that we open them up for possession and consumption by those to whom we represent them: if the people we study and write about are not recognizably human, they become available for appropriation by others, as inert objects of desire. The main existential point of all this, though, will be to establish the secure boundaries of our own worlds. The great payoff of otherness is the security of the givenness of our own experience.

So the other challenge of the journey to the past or to another culture is to recognize what people in these other times and places share with us, the ways our stories overlap, and the way in which a shared humanity creates the possibility for deeper understanding. This notion of shared humanity is not an assumption of mine. It has been both a discovery of fieldwork and archival research and a condition of them. The recognition of shared experience comes in exchanges in the field, when people ask me about my life or about my fears and needs, and I respond. On one level, this is simple human curiosity and indicates the sense that most humans appear to hold that they will find shared ground with others or with another. This is the hopefulness to asking someone else about their experience. But on another level this represents the refusal of otherness by the people we study; it is *their* determination not to be rendered alien. In the archives such moments are more subtle. They entail the surrender by the historian of the arrogance of the living. It requires understanding that people in the past have a story to tell about themselves that may not be congruent with the story we wish to tell about them and which is, at the same time, both like and unlike the stories we tell about ourselves. It means granting them the same authority for their voices that we demand in our own.

## TIME AND THE OTHER IN EAST HARLEM

I have returned to the festa almost every year since this book was published (I think I have missed two), and I am now recognized at the event. People seek me out to add to stories they have already told me. (At a festa about ten years ago some friends brought me over to a very old woman from the neighborhood who—my friends exclaimed—had tremendous stories to tell me about the history of the festa. I sat down next to the woman in church. "Who are you?" she asked me. I told her and she said, "Oh, you're the one who wrote that book." The stories she was telling my friends, it turned out, came from this volume.) I have been invited to participate in various aspects of the festa over the years—I read one of the Scripture passages during Mount Carmel's centennial Mass, for instance—and like returning Harlemites, which I am not, I visit with old acquaintances during the days before and after the celebration. I have made very good friends in the community, but everyone understands that my interests in and connections to Harlem are different from theirs. I "study" Harlem, and my acquaintances there know that when I talk with them I am, among other things, trying to better understand the life of the place. I am also catching up on what has been going on with them. Some are enthusiastic about this, others do not much care.

Every year at the festa—*every* year—a woman named Antoinette seeks me out. Antoinette is very tall, and she uses her height well on these occasions to tower over me. "So," she says, squinting down at me, "here you are!" Her enormous purse bumps between us. I stretch up so we can kiss each other hello. Then Antoinette sweeps her arm across the scene outside the church—every year she does this—taking in the crowds of people, the floats and banners, the boys and girls lined up for the procession, and the young men readying the racks of fireworks in the middle of the streets. Leaning over me, her voice dark with sarcasm, she asks, every year, "So you think the festa is dying out?" I say in the book that the festa is waning, Antoinette reminds me. "Looks pretty good to me," she goes on, "and next year, Father says. . ." Antoinette reports some new plan for the annual celebration, perhaps a bigger float, better rides or fireworks, more lights. Exhausted at the end of the long (and usually quite hot) night of marching through the streets we find each other again. "When are you going to take that out of the book?" Antoinette wants to know. She is very passionate about this.

Antoinette's accusation has long troubled me. The claim by ethnographers that the people one was studying were about to vanish from the earth was a standard trope of early anthropology. The anthropologist had just arrived in time to preserve a last glimpse of a primitive and disappearing world; he or she was the last person to behold the premodern paradise, before the fall. Ethnography became a series of prelapsarian postcards. Such claims still appear occasionally in contemporary work, but critics of anthropology have effectively uncovered the political implications of this salvage approach to the ethnographic enterprise.[18] The romanticism of the twilight elegies of the end of cultures obscured the historical forces that had contributed to changes in the local culture, including often enough the colonial activities of the researcher's own nation, but predating this too. The narratives also denied people the dignity of agency in their own history and experience, overlooking the ways that they were resisting or creatively adapting to changing social conditions. Indeed, the stories served to take these others out of history, situating them in a moment before time, before they descended into history (which is to say into our history). Ultimately, the myth of disappearing cultures served colonial interests, on the one hand, by presenting the end of a world as inevitable, and served to legitimate the presence and work of the ethnographer, on the other, as a kind of preservationist. Was I guilty of this? Now, with the prospect of a new edition, I had the opportunity to do what Antoinette had been asking me to do for years.

I can understand why Antoinette insisted that the festa was still as strong as ever. She had moved away from the community as a young woman, and the annual event was important to her as a homecoming. It had always been there, and since she was a girl her summers had been organized around these days. But I did have good reason in the early 1980s to think that the festa was not going to be around much longer. The crowds were dwindling. The old Italians in the neighborhoods were dying. Their children, who had moved away to the suburbs, seemed less and less interested in coming back, always more apprehensive about the safety of the neighborhood. Only occasionally were there Ferris wheels at the festa now, or outdoor food stands, and then they were pretty shoddy. The feast on 115th Street would not make it as a tourist attraction, I was certain, because it is one thing for out-of-towners to go to the San Gennaro festival in the middle of Greenwich Village, another to travel by the Lexington Avenue local to East Harlem. So I assumed the days of the festa to Our Lady of Mount Carmel were numbered.

I had not foreseen the arrival of the Haitians. How could I? A few Haitian pilgrims were already coming to East Harlem from Brooklyn in the 1970s, but their numbers sharply increased over the next decade. There is a church dedicated to Our Lady of Mount Carmel in Greenpoint-Williamsburg (founded as an offshoot of the church on 115th Street) and another one in the Belmont section of the North Bronx, and at first Haitian pilgrims traveled around the city visiting each representation of the Madonna of Mount Carmel, who is also the patroness of Haiti. But the migrants came to prefer Harlem's Madonna, perhaps because she most closely resembles the figure of the Virgin who is said to have appeared over a palm tree on the island as she is depicted in Haitian Catholic iconography. Haitian visitors who did not live in East Harlem journeyed to the festa in long pilgrimages from Brooklyn by car, chartered bus, and subway.[19]

More Haitians now attend the annual festa than do Italians. The priests at Mount Carmel open the church to Haitian groups by special request throughout the year and allow them to spend the night there in vigils. Haitian families move through the inner passageways of the church and rectory with easy familiarity during the festa. Haitian altar boys participate in official ceremonies at the event; the Haitian national anthem is played (along with the Italian and American) at the start of the processions of the Madonna; the Haitian flag is carried in the streets. The Madonna's older Italian-American devout are impressed by the newcomers' piety and by their ability to sing and pray "so beautifully" in Latin, in the words of one of Mount Carmel's priests. Haitian pilgrims walk behind the statue through the streets, reciting the rosary in French and raising their arms to the heavens during the fierce fireworks displays that greet the Madonna at various points along her route.

Mount Carmel's chroniclers treat the appearance of the Haitian pilgrims from Brooklyn as something of a mystery and a miracle, an uncanny event. Suddenly, one year, as Italian Americans at the church say, crowds of Haitians began coming, completely unexpectedly, to the annual celebration of the feast (from Brooklyn, no less, which in Harlem can seem as far away as Haiti itself). When they talk about this, Italian Americans use such phrases as "as far as I can determine" to mark the strangeness of this turn in Mount Carmel's history. The uncanniness of the moment is then used as a way of absorbing the surprising appearance of the Haitian pilgrims into another, older narrative, about Italian Harlem itself. The arrival of the Haitians, one church worker told me, is not really that surprising, for "this site has always been favored by heaven"; she went on to allude to some of the miracles worked at the church by Harlem's Madonna in recent years, a number of which la Madonna performed on behalf of Haitians. Haitians are thus called on as witnesses to the power of the Italian Madonna in what used to be (but is no more) Italian Harlem. Their presence confirms (as it embodies) the enduring presence of the Madonna and the enduring power of a place—in the memory of Antoinette and her friends—that had once been special because it was Italian.

Our Lady of Mount Carmel appears in Haiti's Vodou pantheon as the powerful figure Ezili Dantò, and a fair amount of Vodou practice takes place during the annual feast now. Some visitors from Brooklyn write petitions for help in thick gray pencil strokes on the statues in the church and leave offerings of burnt food in the plaster folds of the saints' garments; feasts of tropical dishes prepared in honor of the spirits or in thanksgiving for a favor granted (a way of relating to sacred figures that Harlem's Italians would certainly recognize) are shared with strangers on the streets in front of the church—indeed, one year, in the church's courtyard. Italian Americans deny that any of this is happening. Although they are deeply concerned about Puerto Rican *santeros*, practitioners of Santería, who occasionally visit the church and whom Italian Americans accuse of trying to steal power from the Madonna, Italian Americans at Mount Carmel steadfastly look away from the evidence of Vodou. They say that Vodou practices represent the handiwork of only a "few crazy ones." I was told by an Italian-American custodian that the writings on the statues were just expressions of teenage love, even though she could see as clearly as I could that they were entreaties for assistance from the spirits. All the evidence of their own eyes to the contrary, Italian Americans involved today with the festa flatly assert, as one priest told me, "Haitians are not involved in Vodou."

Such differences in the way Haitians and Puerto Ricans have been treated at the church have to do with the precise moments when Italians encountered the two different groups. Because they did not live in the neighborhood, the Haitians never posed a direct threat to the Italian sense of place, whereas the transformation of Italian Harlem into Spanish Harlem meant a profound recasting of the identity of the neighborhood and signaled the end of Italian-American dominance there. Italian Americans tend to hold Puerto Ricans responsible for the passing of Italian Harlem, which has been one way for the second and third generations to deny the fact that Italians—that they—chose to move away from Harlem when they could afford to, for better housing and schools for themselves and their children, not because they were pushed out. The moral force of the domus makes such choices hard to admit, though, so Puerto Ricans have been assigned blame for what the children of the domus cannot bear. Haitians, on the other hand, did not come into *Italian* Harlem but into a special place of cherished memory to which Italian Americans of the second and third generations were themselves "returning," even if they had never lived there, in order to express their respect for their grandparents' and great-grandparents' struggles, faith, and achievements. The Haitians were not seen as taking anything away. So the newcomers were not assimilated to a narrative of loss and betrayal—indeed, just the opposite, as the stories of their miraculous appearance made clear.[20]

This looks like the next chapter in the story of the Madonna of 115th Street.[21] During the July celebrations in Harlem, Haitian and Italian-American women wash each other's face with wet cloths, an Italian band plays the Haitian national song, Haitian pilgrims sing Latin hymns that the grandchildren of the immigrants never learned, Puerto Rican neighbors look down upon the Madonna from their windows and fire escapes, and Italians are moved by Haitian piety. I hope it makes Antoinette happy that I have included this coda. The festa is not disappearing. But the Madonna's world has changed. She hears requests now that are at once both familiar to her from the earlier days in cara Harlem—because all people want to be happy in love, to have work, to enjoy peace at home and an end to family quarrels, to be well in mind and body—and specific to the needs and history of the Haitian migrants. She learns about children and grandchildren back in Haiti, in addition to the woes of elderly Italian Americans and their worried middle-aged children. So it turns out that the Madonna is as exposed as the rest of us are to the unexpected and unforeseen in life and in history, that her world changes, and that even her identity—she who is now both Madonna and Ezili Dantò—is not singular or stable. This is what joins the Madonna and her pilgrims into a common lot, this is the ground I stood on with the people with whom I spoke, and this is what makes us all recognizable to each other, in heaven and on earth.

The ideas in this new introduction were all talked through with Amy Koehlinger, and it is to her that this second edition of *The Madonna of 115th Street* is dedicated, in gratitude and love.

NOTES

1. These comments on the discourse of the dangerous archive in the self-representations of the early generations of professional historians draw on Bonnie G. Smith, *The Gender of History: Men, Women, and Historical Practice* (Cambridge: Harvard University Press, 1998). Smith writes, "Descriptions of archival practices added a sense of forbidden knowledge and images of middle-class sexual prowess to the configuration of historical study as work and civic virtue" (120). Archives, she says, "provided a place where scenarios of pollution and danger might be envisioned" (119).

2. "The past," says philosopher of history Michel-Rolph Trouillot, "or more accurately pastness—is a position": *Silencing the Past: Power and the Production of History* (Boston: Beacon, 1995), 15. My thinking about these questions has also been helped by David William Cohen, *The Combing of History* (Chicago: University of Chicago Press, 1994).

3. Smith, *The Gender of History*, 138. Accounts of agonies in the archives stressed the work's "isolation, alienation, separation from friends . . . early hours, the scarcity and poor quality of documents . . . exhausting schedules for research trips, difficult relations with archivists," all cast in metaphors of "endurance, access, and control" (125).

4. My understanding of this rich and necessary term—*lifeworld*—owes much to the anthropologist Michael Jackson's discussion of it in "Introduction: Phenomenology, Radical Empiricism, and Anthropological

Critique," *Things as They Are: New Directions in Phenomenological Anthropology* (Bloomington: Indiana University Press, 1996), 7–8.

5. For a helpful review of the discussions surrounding the term *popular religion*, see Leonard Norman Primiano, "Vernacular Religion and the Search for Method in Religious Folklife," *Western Folklore* 54, no. 1 (January 1995): 37–56. An excellent example of how far the study of popular religion has come in terms of its theoretical apparatus (with some trenchant observations about the old theoretical impasses) is Paolo Appolito, *Apparitions of the Madonna at Oliveto Citra: Local Visions and Cosmic Drama*, trans., William A. Christian, Jr. (University Park: Pennsylvania State University Press, 1998). The preoccupation within religious studies with textuality has been challenged in recent years by new interests in ritual, image, and material culture, in all the various areas of study.

6. Because the normative distinction between spirituality and religion—with all that this means for marking the border between good and bad, tolerable and intolerable forms of religious practice and expression—is so embedded in our languages and so ubiquitous across the culture, it is both easy and difficult to cite particular instances of it. Two rich and highly influential examples are Robert Coles, *The Spiritual Life of Children* (Boston: Houghton Mifflin, 1990), and James Fowler, *Stages of Faith: The Psychology of Human Development and the Quest for Meaning* (San Francisco: HarperSanFrancisco, 1995, orig. pub. 1981).

7. This section of the introduction draws on a number of recent reviews of the history of the modern study of religion, including David Chidester, *Savage Systems: Colonialism and Comparative Religion in Southern Africa* (Charlottesville: University Press of Virginia, 1996); Richard King, *Orientalism and Religion: Post-Colonial Theory, India, and the "Mystic East"* (London: Routledge, 1999); Bruce Lincoln, *Theorizing Myth: Narrative, Ideology, and Scholarship* (Chicago: University of Chicago Press, 1999); Donald S. Lopez, Jr., *Prisoners of Shangri-La: Tibetan Buddhism and the West* (Chicago: University of Chicago Press, 1998); Donald S. Lopez, ed., *Curators of the Buddha: The Study of Buddhism Under Colonialism* (Chicago: University of Chicago Press, 1995); Tomoko Masuzawa, *In Search of Dreamtime: The Quest for the Origin of Religion* (Chicago: University of Chicago Press, 1993); Ashis Nandy, *The Intimate Enemy: Loss and Recovery of the Self Under Colonialism* (Delhi: Oxford University Press, 1983); Mary Louise Pratt, *Imperial Eyes: Travel Writing and Transculturation* (London: Routledge, 1992); J. Samuel Preus, *Explaining Religion: Criticism and Theory from Bodin to Freud* (New Haven: Yale University Press, 1987); Leigh Eric Schmidt, *Hearing Things: Religion, Illusion, and the American Enlightenment* (Cambridge: Harvard University Press, 2000); Jonathan Z. Smith, *Imagining Religion: From Babylon to Jonestown* (Chicago: University of Chicago Press, 1982); Jonathan Z.

Smith, *Drudgery Divine: On the Comparison of Early Christianity and the Religions of Late Antiquity* (Chicago: University of Chicago Press, 1990); Michael Taussig, *Shamanism, Colonialism, and the Wild Man: A Study in Terror and Healing* (Chicago: University of Chicago Press, 1987); Ann Taves, *Fits, Trances, and Visions: Experiencing Religion and Explaining Experience from Wesley to James* (Princeton: Princeton University Press, 1999); Mark C. Taylor, ed., *Critical Terms for Religious Studies* (Chicago: University of Chicago Press, 1998); Steven M. Wasserstrom, *Religion After Religion: Gershom Scholem, Mircea Eliade, and Henry Corbin at Eranos* (Princeton: Princeton University Press, 1999).

8. On the religious roots of this horror, see Michael A. Sells, *The Bridge Betrayed: Religion and Genocide in Bosnia* (Berkeley: University of California Press, 1996). Sells comments that "the human capacity for acknowledging religiously based evil is profoundly tenuous" (11). This incapacity seems to me less a human constant than a matter of how the religious landscape has been mapped in the West over the last two centuries—a matter of theory and history, in other words, not a dimension of the human soul.

9. Carlo Ginzburg, *The Cheese and the Worms: The Cosmos of a Sixteenth-Century Miller*, trans. John and Anne Tedeschi (Baltimore: Johns Hopkins University Press, 1980); William A. Christian, Jr., *Person and God in a Spanish Valley* (Princeton: Princeton University Press, 1989, orig. pub. 1972); Emmanuel LeRoy Ladurie, *Montaillou: The Promised Land of Error*, trans. Barbara Bray (New York: G. Braziller, 1978); Eugene D. Genovese, *Roll, Jordan, Roll: The World the Slaves Made* (New York: Vintage, 1976); Pierre-Jakez Hélias, *The Horse of Pride: Life in a Breton Village*, trans. June Guicharnaud (New Haven: Yale University Press, 1978). For useful reviews of developments in the field of American religious history in the past two decades, see Harry S. Stout and D. G. Hart, eds., *New Directions in American Religious History* (New York: Oxford University Press, 1997), and Thomas A. Tweed, ed., *Retelling U.S. Religious History* (Berkeley: University of California Press, 1997).

10. My thinking here has been influenced by Michael Jackson's reading of William James's notion of "radical empiricism." Jackson describes radical empiricism like this: "Lived experience overflows the boundaries of any one concept, any one person, or any one society. As such, it brings us to a dialectical view of life which emphasizes the interplay rather than the identity of things, which denies any sure steading to thought by placing it always within the precarious and destabilizing fields of history, biography, and time. . . . Lived experience encompasses *both* the 'rage for order' *and* the impulse that drives us to unsettle or confound the fixed order of things. . . . [Such a] conception of experience avoids narrowing down the field of experience to *either* the subject *or* the object, theory *or* practice, the social *or* the individual,

thought *or* feeling, form *or* flux." Michael Jackson, *Paths Towards a Clearing: Radical Empiricism and the Ethnographic Inquiry* (Bloomington: Indiana University Press, 1989), 2. See also Jackson's introduction to *Things as They Are*, 1–50. In James's words, "To be radical, an empiricism must neither admit into its construction any element that is not directly experienced nor exclude from them any element that is directly experienced. For such a philosophy, *the relations that connect experiences must themselves be experienced relations, and any kind of relation experienced must be accounted as 'real' as anything else in the system.*" "A World of Pure Experience," in William James, *Writings 1902–1910* (New York: Library of America, 1987), 1159–82. Sentences quoted are from p. 1160.

11. I am not sure who first used the term *lived religion*. The first collection with this title (that I know of) is David D. Hall, ed., *Lived Religion in America: Towards a History of Practice* (Princeton: Princeton University Press, 1997). If Hall did not invent the term, he certainly is responsible for making it a major part of the contemporary conversation about religion.

12. As the anthropologists John Comaroff and Jean Comaroff write, "Culture always contains within it polyvalent, potentially contestable messages, images, and actions. It is, in short, a historically situated, historically unfolding ensemble of signifiers-in-action, signifiers at once material and symbolic, social and aesthetic." *Ethnography and the Historical Imagination* (Boulder: Westview, 1992), 27.

13. The anthropologist Sherry B. Ortner writes, "any form of human action or interaction would be an instance of 'practice' insofar as the analyst recognized it as reverberating with features of asymmetry, inequality, domination, and the like in its particular historical and cultural setting. . . . Human activity regarded as taking place is a world of politically neutral relations is not 'practice.'" *High Religion: A Cultural and Political History of Sherpa Buddhism* (Princeton: Princeton University Press, 1989), 12. See also James C. Scott, *Domination and the Arts of Resistance: Hidden Transcripts* (New Haven: Yale University Press, 1990).

14. For Winnicott's discussion of this intermediate or transitional space and of the quality of creativity that takes shape within it, see the essays collected in *Playing and Reality* (London: Tavistock/Routledge, 1971).

15. Peter L. Berger, *The Sacred Canopy: Elements of A Sociological Theory of Religion* (Garden City, N.Y.: Anchor, 1967), 17–18.

16. Jean-Paul Sartre, *Search for a Method*, trans. Hazel E. Barnes (New York: Vintage, 1968), 72.

17. The spirit of this paragraph was profoundly shaped by Daniel N. Stern, *The Interpersonal World of the Infant: A View from Psychoanalysis and Developmental Psychology* (New York: Basic, 1985).

18. See, for example, Johannes Fabian, *Time and the Other: How*

*Anthropology Makes Its Object* (New York: Columbia University Press, 1983), as well as the various essays in James Clifford and George E. Marcus, eds., *Writing Culture: The Poetics and Politics of Anthropology* (Berkeley: University of California Press, 1986).

19. The next several paragraphs borrow from Robert A. Orsi, "The Religious Boundaries of an In-between People: Street Feste and the Problem of the Dark-Skinned Other in Italian Harlem, 1920–1990," in Orsi, ed., *Gods of the City: Religion and the American Urban Landscape* (Bloomington: Indiana University Press, 1999), 257–88; my discussion of the arrival of Haitian devout in East Harlem is on pp. 273–76.

20. Ibid., 269–73, for a more extended discussion of relations between Italian Americans and Puerto Ricans in East Harlem, especially around the figure of Mount Carmel.

21. Haitian participation in the annual feast of Our Lady of Mount Carmel is the subject of an excellent essay by Elizabeth McAlister, "The Madonna of 115th Street Revisited: Vodou and Haitian Catholicism in the Age of Transnationalism," in R. Stephen Warner and Judith G. Wittner, eds., *Gatherings in Diaspora: Religious Communities and the New Immigration* (Philadelphia: Temple University Press, 1998), 123–60.

# Introduction:
## Popular Religion and Italian Harlem

This is a study of religion in the streets. It is the story of a religious celebration, the annual *festa* of the Madonna of Mount Carmel on East 115th Street in New York City, and of the devotion to this Madonna which flourished among Italian immigrants and their American-born or -raised children who lived around her. It is also, necessarily, a study of the community in which that celebration took place—the troubled, poor, constantly changing, culturally isolated and neglected community of Italian Harlem.

It is the central assumption of this history that the celebration cannot be understood apart from an understanding of the lives of the people who took part in it. The annual festa was a very complex religious drama that began days before the solemn celebration and procession on July 16 and continued for days afterward. During this long religious event, men and women performed certain rituals, behaved in particular ways toward each other and toward the divine, adopted certain postures, moved and knelt in specific ways—all as though they were part of an intricate dance. Each of these gestures and postures, as well as the kinds of prayers said and the way they were said, had specific meanings; and these meanings were rooted deep in the inner life of the culture, demanding a close and prolonged analysis.

One ritual in particular will illustrate what I mean here. Until the clergy at the church finally put a stop to the practice in the 1920s, it was a common occurrence at the annual festa for members of a family

to drag one of the central women of their household down the aisle of
the church. As they went along, the woman stuck her tongue out so
that it touched the stones of the church floor, licking them as she was
borne toward the Madonna. This disturbing ritual, which was deplored by visitors to the church in the early years of this century,
clearly poses certain explicit questions about the role of women in the
culture and in the family. Why was a woman dragged this way by her
family up to the figure of a divine and powerful woman? What was
being expressed here of the inner life of the community? What were the
community—and the women—learning as they observed this scene?
To answer these questions, we must study the lives of women in the
community, the nature of family life, relations between men and wom-
en, and attitudes toward the sacred woman on the altar on 115th
Street.

This is a study of popular religion then. But "popular religion" is a
term badly in need of definition. Among detractors of the idea, popular
religion means all those crazy religious things that people do and all
the crazy ideas they have outside the structures of an organized and
properly ordered church. Among its defenders, popular religion too
often means the nostalgic evocation of peasant spirituality or the angry defense of magic and folk practices. When used to describe popular
Catholic religiosity, the term conjures up images of shrouds, bloody
hearts, bilocating monks, talking Madonnas, weeping statues, boiling
vials of blood—all the symbols which the masses of Catholic Europe
have found to be so powerful over the centuries and which churchmen
have denigrated, often while sharing in the same or similar devotions.
When southern Italians are the group in question, popular religion
takes on particularly luxuriant meanings, referring to practices that
range from rituals to ward off the evil eye to the custom of destroying
the statue of a saint who has not kept his or her promises. All of these
practices and symbols are worthy of serious study and attention, but
this is not completely what I mean by popular religion.

This study began in a sense of the limitations of the meaning of
popular religion and a desire to broaden and deepen our understanding of the phenomenon. The religious life of southern Italian immigrants to the United States and their children has always proved difficult to understand and to study. Right from the beginning, official
Catholic observers criticized Italian religiosity for being exotic and
pagan. In 1888, just after the beginning of the great migration of south-

ern Italians to the United States, a Catholic priest in New York City sought to explain these "dark-eyed, olive-tinted men and women" to his—and their—fellow Catholics.[1] They were certainly not Catholics, this observer wrote: "The fact is the Catholic Church in America is to the mass of Italians almost like a new religion." Their own "peculiar kind of spiritual condition" was strange and exotic, "fed on the luxuries of religion"—their devotions, pilgrimages, shrines, holy pictures—but completely uninformed by "the great truths which alone can make such aids to religion possible."

So the great discussion of Italian American religion and spirituality was under way, and it continued throughout the first half of the twentieth century. The debate was still on in 1953 when an Italian American priest writing in *The American Ecclesiastical Review* pleaded with his readers for a "more intelligent understanding" of Italians. He went on: "Italians in [the United States] have not perhaps 'arrived' in material affluence and rightful prestige. But their patriotism in two wars and their marked growth in Catholic living is becoming more and more impressive."[2]

When Father Zema here refers to a "marked growth in Catholic living," he means that Italian Americans were becoming more like Irish Americans and that in only a little while the transition would be complete. This was the only institutional opportunity held out to Italian immigrants and their children: to become American Catholics. In 1943, an Italian American priest and an expert on the "Italian Problem" of American Catholicism, proudly pointed to his own methods as the way of solving the problem: "Briefly, my plan of action has been to conduct a parish which is composed of Americans of Italian descent in the same general manner as one conducts a well-organized, highly efficient American parish."[3] He went on to note that most young Italian Americans were ashamed of the religiosity of their grandparents and parents:

> the average American Catholic of Italian descent prefers his devotional life in the church building, not on the city streets; and in a solid, serious and dignified manner. [He prefers, for his entertainment, the theater] to watching, with mingled feelings of amusement and shame, a haphazard and dishevelled group, tramping over the hot, traffic-burdened streets of the modern city, dodging trolleys and automobiles, while a few perspiring "contadini" carry the statue of the favorite saint. We know also, that the average American of Italian descent prefers to give his contribution for the

support of the church in a monthly collection envelope rather than by showily pinning a dollar bill on a flashy ribbon suspended from a saint's neck. . . .[4]

Father Tolino, the author of this piece and an American of Italian descent, wanted his fellow Italian Catholics to behave properly because he too suffered by association with all this flashy street religiosity. But historians and scholars have also been waiting for Italians to get into church and start behaving like other American Catholics. In 1946, Henry Browne wrote an influential article in the journal of the United States Catholic Historical Society in which he discussed and canonized the reality of the "Italian Problem" in the American church.[5] Silvano Tomasi, in his study *Piety and Power*, sees a slow but inexorable movement of Italian Americans into the mainstream of American Catholicism and, through that, into American society.[6] Even historians suspicious of this development, such as Rudolph Vecoli, insist on seeing Italian religiosity only from the perspective of the church. Vecoli has portrayed Italians as fierce anticlericals, angry at the church and looking for leadership to the radical political thinkers who emigrated with them and took up residence in the Italian colonies.[7]

It is true that Italian Americans have not made good American-style Catholics, as the many comparisons of their giving habits with those of Polish Catholics have demonstrated. But neither perspective—neither the one that waits for them to become American Catholics nor the one that insists that they rejected the church—is adequate or accurate. The study of Italian American religion must begin with the people themselves, and they invariably insisted that going to church was not so important to them but that they considered themselves good and faithful people, and Catholics. They went to church, of course: many observers, even the most hostile, admitted that Italians were faithful attendants at baptisms, weddings, and funerals, and no one denied that they went to church on the days of their *feste*. But in other ways, they were not good American Catholics.

The popularity of baptisms, weddings, and funerals begins to point us toward the meaning of Italian popular religion. If we look at this without judgment and without waiting for Italian Americans to start showing up in church at other times too, then we can ask why these events were so important. Why be so faithful about baptisms and not about Catholic schools? Why weddings and not Sunday mass? The people themselves are willing to answer these questions. My informants in Italian Harlem continually made a distinction between religion and church. A person could be a good man or a good woman—a *cristiano* or *cristiana* in the language of the immigrants—in other words, could be religious, without this having anything to do with how often he or she went to church. What determined the quality of a person then?

In this study the word *religion* will be used in two ways. First of all, and more traditionally, it will be used to describe the sacred rituals, practices, symbols, prayers, and faith of the people. The immigrants' religion, in this sense of the word, was deeply Catholic; it also expressed the consciousness born in centuries of oppression and colonization in the *mezzogiorno*, the part of the Italian peninsula south of Rome that Christ, as Carlo Levi was told, never reached. But *religion* will also mean something more comprehensive. I will be concerned throughout with the people's religion defined as the totality of their ultimate values, their most deeply held ethical convictions, their efforts to order their reality, their cosmology. This could be called their "ground of being," but only if this is understood in a very concrete, social-historical way, not as a reality beyond their lives, but as the *reason* that, consciously and unconsciously, structured and was expressed in their actions and reflections. More simply stated, *religion* here means "what matters."

There are at least two ways of finding and studying this latter meaning of religion. First of all, if this is possible, one can ask the people themselves. This is what previous students of Italian American religion have not done, and this is where I began. There are endless possibilities for distortion here, but a careful examination of what people say in light of what they do, and particularly in light of how and whom they worship, can give a historian a fairly good idea of the foundations of their culture. Second, the people reveal who they are and the qualities they value in religious celebrations like the annual festa of the Madonna of 115th Street. In the sacred theater of the festa, at which they were both the actors and the audience, the men and women of Italian Harlem revealed their deepest values and perceptions, their cosmology—the way they understood the world to work. By attending this drama we can better understand the people themselves.

The two meanings of religion, then, come together in an event like the festa on 115th Street. Religion in the first sense, the rituals, symbols, prayers, and practices of the celebration, is unintelligible apart from religion in the second sense, as the people's deepest values and perceptions of reality. This integration is what I mean by popular religion. I will be interested in the people's feelings about saints, in the reasons why they lit candles, in their practice of carrying heavy wax models of parts of the body in the annual procession; but my concern will be with these as symbols and gestures that have meaning only in the entire religious world of Italian Harlem. We will see, from this perspective, that the Italian American attitude toward institutional Catholicism is explicable as other than sheer perversity: when church-going is approached as normative in itself or as indicative of a people's spiritual quality, then the people's own perceptions and values will be lost; but if we begin with the latter—with the people's perceptions, values, needs, and history—then we can better understand their religious practices and attitudes. The people of Italian Harlem went to church when they did because only at those times did it make sense according to their religious values.

This is a study of popular religion in this broadest sense. We will explore the moral values and attitudes of the men and women of Italian Harlem, their perceptions of reality and meaning, their understandings of the good life and the good person and the bad, of destiny and providence. And the study will be organized around the annual celebration in honor of the Madonna of 115th Street, the occasion on which the Italians of Harlem revealed to themselves and to others who they were, introduced their children to their most fundamental perceptions of reality, and attempted to deal with the many tensions and crises that arose because they were immigrants in a strange land and because of the particular nature of their deepest values.

The festa, described in the first chapter, is presented in the way that the people themselves discuss it. They did not make a distinction between the "religious" aspects of the festa—the praying and penitential devotions, the religious sacrifice—and what outside observers felt were the inappropriate, "profane" characteristics of the celebration—the food, noise, dancing, partying. All the many different moments of the celebration had an integrated meaning. The annual religious celebration in honor of la Madonna del Carmine began when the residents of Italian Harlem set about preparing to welcome visiting friends and relatives to their homes and ended days and weeks later when the scapulars given out on the altar on July 16 were wound around distant bedposts in homes in Pennsylvania and New Jersey, as well as in Harlem.

It was my assumption that nothing about this celebration was irrelevant. For example, it is important to know that the procession wended its way through traffic and beneath the clatter of elevated trains, that the air of Harlem smelled of sausage and peppers and incense on these days, that women marched closest to the Madonna. Religious symbols and rituals take on their many meanings in these dense contexts, so it is essential to see them as densely as possible.

I am concerned almost exclusively with the Madonna's life in New York City. The devotion to la Madonna del Carmine has a venerable history in southern Italy, where the annual festa is celebrated in much the same way as it is in New York. What is important for the purposes of this study, however, is that the immigrants sought to reproduce the devotion in their new home, introduced and integrated their children into it, and marched through the streets of New York behind their Madonna. This book is about the American expression of the devotion.

There is another reason to study the devotion to the Madonna of 115th Street independently of similar devotions in southern Italy and, for that matter, throughout Catholic Europe. The Italians of Harlem came from many regions and towns of southern Italy, and they brought over with them many different devotions. In the church of the Madonna on 115th Street, for example, there are statues of Saint Ann, Saints Cosmos and Damian, Saint Rocco, the Infant of Prague, the Madonna of Montevergine, and many others. Each of these saints had a smaller devotion in Italian Harlem, but none of them ever even remotely attained the kind of local power and centrality the Madonna did. Clearly, this was a special devotion for the immigrants, with particular meanings, meeting particular needs. Although she was an immigrant, the Madonna we will be studying was truly of 115th Street.

In order to approach the inner meanings of the festa, we must also explore the moral world of Italian Harlem. We need to identify and study what it was that the people themselves claimed, implicitly or explicitly, as the foundation of their understanding of the good and the basis of their moral judgment. Without exception, the Italians of Harlem identified this as the "domus." I have borrowed this word from Emmanuel LeRoy Ladurie, who defines it in his study of Montaillou, as:

That unit, the *ostal* or *domus*, was at once building and family, the unifying principle that linked man and his possessions. It was thus the thing that counted most for the peasants, not yet obsessed, like their modern counterparts, with the problem of land. . . . The *domus*, in Montaillou as elsewhere, constituted a formidable reservoir of power and counter-power which could hold out with some degree of success against the external powers surrounding it.[8]

The family, in this broad sense encompassed by the idea of the domus, was, Ladurie says of Montaillou, the "chief unit of social relationships and cultural transmission."[9] I use the word in the same way, although I am talking about a landless urban proletariat. I decided to use it largely because this seems to be what the people of Italian Harlem themselves meant when they referred to their families. They had a very inclusive understanding of family—besides mothers and fathers and siblings, family comprised aunts and uncles, cousins, *comari* and *compari*, the latter being nonblood members of the domus. As Ladurie observed, the term is also meant to include the actual physical home, in this case the apartments of Italian Harlem.

Many students of Italian American culture have identified the family—although it is important to see that the domus means more than the family—as the center of that culture. There has not been similar unanimity about the troubles and conflicts in the Italian American family. The task of the fifth chapter is to study the way in which this foundation of Italian American culture was profoundly cracked, not merely by the strains of immigration, which the domus survived, but by the very nature of Italian American life. In order to understand the role of the Madonna in this context, we need to be as specific as possible about the precise sorts of tensions and conflicts the members of the domus had to live with. In chapter 6 I briefly consider some of the other inner struggles and difficulties, specifically related to the challenges of immigration, that the men and women of Italian Harlem had to confront.

Chapters 4 through 6 represent an attempt to delineate the religion, defined in the second sense noted earlier, of the people of Italian Harlem, their cosmology, definitions of the good, needs, and deepest aspirations, and to show the severe strains that developed on this level in the new world. It is also an effort to follow Robin Horton's excellent dictum, "Before ever he attempts to say what a given religious system does or does not reflect, the anthropologist must soak himself thoroughly in the every day preoccupations of the believers themselves." This immersion is followed by an extended exegesis of the devotion. At the center of both the devotion and the annual celebration were the many hopes and fears, conflicts, expectations and disappointments, and ambivalences in the lives of the people of the community. The symbol of the Madonna and the rituals associated with the devotion to her derived their meanings from this dense and complex context, and so they open out and disclose on many levels—personal, familial, communal, political, cosmic. I will explore many of the meanings of the devotion to the Madonna of 115th Street, although not nearly all of them, because it is impossible to exhaust the meanings of a popular religious symbol.

The main subject of this study, then, is the history of the devotion to and the festa in honor of the Madonna of 115th Street and its place in the religious life of the people who lived in the tenements, shopped in the stores, courted in the parks, and walked the streets around *la casa della Madonna* in Italian Harlem. I also had some secondary interests and concerns as I prepared the study. First of all, I was interested in analyzing a modern, urban religious experience and in exploring the ways in which such an analysis might be done. Urban popular religion is a phenomenon of a world of parks, stoops, alleyways, hallways, fire escapes, storefronts, traffic, police, courtyards, street crime and street play, and so on. The Madonna was taken out into this world and asked to bless it, and so it seemed necessary to study the intricate and particular meanings of the streets. I think this method would be useful in studying other urban street faiths, such as the popularity of Father Divine in Central Harlem during the Depression, faith healers in Spanish Harlem, or storefront churches. The ecologies of these devotions and experiences must be explored in all their particular details before they begin to make sense to an outside observer. What does an abandoned building mean to the community? How does the community feel about the new housing project? How do members of the community perceive the streets, hallways, rooftops, and alleys of their neighborhood? Only as the inner meanings of the urban landscape become clear does an analysis of urban religious ritual and myth become possible.

Second, I wanted to make a contribution to the project of understanding what *Catholicism* is. Popular devotions such as the one to the Madonna of 115th Street—or to the Madonna of Lourdes, Padre Pio, the Shroud of Turin, and many others—are not very popular among those who articulate the meanings of Catholicism. Usually such devotions are not even mentioned by theologians in their discussions of the nature of Catholicism. But I think that in the sensuous, graphic, and complicated piety of the people of Italian Harlem—and of other people who walk with difficulty and hope to Lourdes or who are moved by the impression of a face they believe is Christ's—we see an expression of something primitive and essential in Catholicism itself. The people have their own ways, authentic and profound, of being Catholic. As we explore the devotion to the Madonna of 115th Street and consider the theology of the streets, I hope we will also get a glimpse of something of the inner meaning of Catholic faith.

Third, this is a social history of a religious symbol. It is an attempt to understand as intimately as possible why a particular religious symbol meant what it did and how it came to acquire this meaning. I was interested in the shaping power of religious symbols. A powerful relationship existed between the Madonna of 115th Street and the community surrounding her. The meanings of the Madonna were rooted in the history and conflicts and struggles and expectations of the people—they shaped the meaning of the Madonna. But they also inherited the Madonna. The devotion bore the marks of southern Italian history; in the new world, as the immigrants integrated their children into the devotion, the celebration became the expression of the needs and values of the community and a means of confirming and enforcing these perceptions and orientations. The Madonna, in other words, was both of the community, unintelligible apart from it and independent of any single member of the community, each of whom was forced to confront her (and what she represented manifestly and latently) as a reality in his or her life. Finally, we will also have an opportunity to see what happens to a religious symbol when the community in which it found meaning disperses.

Fourth, the annual festa allows us to observe how popular religion serves as the sacred theater of a community like Italian Harlem. The people who came to the festa assumed well-defined roles and watched others assume well-defined roles. There was almost no flexibility here: a man was never carried down the aisles of the church toward the Madonna, according to my informants. The drama that then took place was the drama of the inner life of Italian Harlem. The streets became a stage and the people revealed themselves to themselves. The immigrants' deepest values, their understandings of the truly human, their perceptions of the nature of reality were acted out; the hidden structures of power and authority were revealed. Within the confines of this sacred street theater, people expressed their rage at the implicit assumptions and demands of their culture, but they did so in a way that was approved and contained. The festa, which at certain moments was marked by great hysteria and frenzy and a mood of mourning, allowed people to purge themselves of the many difficult emotions of the domus-centered society while it reinforced the cosmic inevitability of that particular ordering of society. Purged, cleansed, healed, and returned to the domus, the people set out to live another year.

A word is in order here about sources. I was extremely fortunate in having at my disposal the transcripts of the interviews Leonard Covello and his friends conducted in Italian Harlem in the late 1920s and 1930s. These transcripts, along with the many letters, memos, notes, and sketches that comprise the Covello Papers at the Balch Institute in Philadelphia, allowed me to ask the people themselves about their values and perceptions.[10] The Covello Papers, used with other important collections relating to the life of Italian Harlem, permitted a real immersion in the culture. The other major collections included the papers of Marcantonio and LaGuardia. Both men were very popular in the community and people took their problems to them; letters from their constituents also enabled me to hear the voices of the people. The women of Italian Harlem wrote to the Madonna to request graces, and many of these letters were printed in the parish bulletins at the Church of Mount Carmel. Finally, I supplemented these written primary sources with about eighty interviews of my own with former or present residents of Italian Harlem.

## CHAPTER I

# The Days and Nights of the Festa

S HORTLY after midnight on July 16, the great bell high in the campanile of the church of Our Lady of Mount Carmel on 115th Street announced to East Harlem that the day of the festa had begun. It was a solemn moment; the voice of the bell seemed more vibrant and sonorous on this night. The sound touched every home in Italian Harlem. It greeted the devout already arriving from the other boroughs and from Italian communities in Connecticut, New Jersey, Pennsylvania, and even California. The sound filled Jefferson Park, where pilgrims who were not fortunate enough to have *compari* or family in East Harlem were camping out. In the church, the round of masses had begun and would continue until the following midnight, each mass expressing either gratitude for a grace bestowed or a plea for comfort and assistance.[1] Italian Harlem was ready and excited: "In alto i cuori, oggi è la grande, memorabile, solenne giornata del XVI Luglio."[2]

The Italians of East Harlem had been preparing for the festa for weeks. They had a special responsibility to host friends and relatives who came from out of town. The homes of Italian Harlem had been scrubbed clean, the windows had been washed and the floor polished. Residents had bought and cooked special foods in anticipation of the arrival of their guests. One participant described the scene in the homes like this:

I remember my father, every year, people came from Paterson, New Jersey, there was a group of these people from our *paese* who lived there, they would come every time, they would sleep in our house, and eat and drink for four days, five days, going on. And everybody in the neighborhood had to clean their house that week, the week before, new curtains, and everything; it was the feast of Mount Carmel.[3]

The time of the festa was long and undefined. Some people say it lasted two or three days, others say a week, even two weeks. It was a celebration that knew no time. As one participant expressed this, "It started July 16th and went on for about a week. . . . These things went on and on, for hours and hours."[4]

Italian Harlem slept little during the days of the festa. Children played with their cousins from New Haven and Boston and then fell asleep in the laps of the adults, who stayed up all night talking and eating. People went out into the crowded streets at two or three in the morning to go to confession or to attend a special mass at the church that had been offered to *la Madonna* for the health of their mother or in the hope of finding a job. When they returned, there was more eating and talking and visiting.

Then sometime in the early afternoon of July 16, people would begin walking over to the church. They were dressed in their finest clothes, particularly the children, whose new outfits their families had bought at considerable sacrifice but also with the fierce determination that the family should make *bella figura* in the community and show proper *rispetto* for the Virgin on her feast day.[5] According to Garibaldi Lapolla, "the whole colony had emptied into the thoroughfares, jostling, guff-awing, shouting, shuffling back and forth."[6] Italians living in relative isolation in West Harlem made their way eastward. The crowds walked beneath fire escapes decorated with crepe, American flags, and the Italian tricolor, and under arches of colored lights. Colorful blankets were hung out of the windows. The streets of Italian Harlem had been especially cleaned for the occasion, and local restauranteurs had set up tables outside where the people could stop for some refreshment at, in the words of advertisements in the parish bulletin, special festa prices, though we are not told whether this meant they paid more or less for their food.[7]

Italian popular faith in both Italy and America sought the streets to express itself, and the street life of the festa was dense. Men stood in groups in front of storefront regional social clubs, getting ready to march in the procession, proud of their regional identification and secure in the company of their fellows. Boys from the different neighborhoods within East Harlem went to the church in groups—the Pleasant Avenue crowd, the guys from 109th Street. Girls went with their families. The day held the promise of flirting and meeting, furtive in the earlier history of the celebration, much more open in the 1930s and 1940s. Men and women gambled during the festa, privately and publicly playing games of chance. During the 1920s an old Jewish man wandered through the crowd with a Yiddish-speaking white parrot on his arm; the parrot had been taught to say in Italian, "Come, Italians," and predicted fortunes by drawing cards from a deck.[8]

Vendors of religious articles set up booths along the sidewalks, competing for business with the thriving local trade in religious goods. The booths were filled with wax replicas of internal human organs and with models of human limbs and heads.[9] Someone who had been healed—or hoped to be healed—by the Madonna of headaches or arthritis would carry wax models of the afflicted limbs or head, painted to make them look realistic, in the big procession. The devout could also buy little wax statues of infants.[10] Charms to ward off the evil eye, such as little horns to wear around the neck and little red hunchbacks, were sold alongside the holy cards, statues of Jesus, Mary, and the saints, and the wax body parts.[11]

The most sought-after items were the big and enormously heavy candles that the faithful bought, carried all through the blistering July procession, and then donated to the church. There was a wax factory at 431 East 115th Street, and candles were available at several stores on the block near the church.[12] According to one of my informants: "They sold candles. They did a *tremendous* business in candles for years."[13] In the June 1929 issue of the parish bulletin, in time for that year's celebration, Nicola Sabatini, who owned a religious articles shop at the prime location of 410 East 115th Street, advertised: "The faithful who need candles of any size, votive articles of wax and silver, and other religious articles can get them here directly at reasonable prices and made to their specifications."[14] The weights of the candles chosen by the people corresponded to the seriousness of the grace they were asking, and this was carefully specified in the vows made to the Madonna. A bad problem or a great hope required an especially heavy candle and weights could reach fifty or sixty pounds or more.[15]

Sometimes the candles weighed as much as the person for whom prayers and sacrifices were being offered. In 1923, for example, Giuseppe Caparo, sixty-nine years old, who had recently fallen from the fifth floor of a building without hurting himself, offered the Madonna a candle weighing as much as he did, 185 pounds. If, as often happened, the candles were too long or too heavy to be carried by one person, other family members and friends would share the burden.[16]

The most characteristic sensuous facts of the Mount Carmel festa were the smell and taste of food. In the homes, in the streets, and in the restaurants, the festa of Our Lady of Mount Carmel had a taste. Big meals, *pranzi*, were cooked in the homes, and after the festa, family, friends, and neighbors would gather for long and boisterous meals.[17] During the day, snacks of hard-boiled eggs, sausage, and pastry were ready at home. But it was in the street that the real eating took place. From the street vendors the devout could buy beans boiled in oil and red pepper, hot waffles, fried and sugared dough, boiled corn, ice cream, watermelon, sausage, "tempting pies filled with tomato, red pepper and garlic," bowls of pasta, dried nuts, nougat candy, raisins, tinted cakes, and "pastry rings glistening in the light."[18] Beer and wine were drunk, to the horror of those who came from New York's better neighborhoods to watch the lower classes at play.

The crowds slowly made their way to the Church of Our Lady of Mount Carmel on 115th Street between First and Pleasant avenues. The front of the church was decorated with colored lights that traced the outline of the facade and spelled out "Nostra Signora del Monte Carmelo." It was on the steps of the church that the intensity and diversity of the day were at their extreme. Penitents crawled up the steps on their hands and knees, some of them dragging their tongues along the stone.[19] Thousands of people were jammed onto 115th Street in front of the church in the crushing July heat and humidity. Nuns and volunteers from the parish moved through the crowd to help those who succumbed. Many of the pilgrims stood barefoot on the scalding pavement; many had walked barefoot to the shrine through the night from the Bronx and Brooklyn—a barefoot and wearying trek through the long hours of the morning. They took off their shoes as an act of penance, as a demonstration of rispetto for the Virgin, and because they considered the place holy.[20] The crowd had been gathering since midnight, and as the time of the procession neared—la Madonna would soon leave the church and come out among her people—the excitement sizzled like the heat.

*The facade of the Church of Mount Carmel on 115th Street during the annual celebration, ca. 1930–34*

There were outsiders in the crowd in front of the church. Irish and German Catholics, who dominated the neighborhood in the early days of the festa and still maintained a presence in East Harlem during the years of Italian ascendency, came to watch. It is likely that in the late nineteenth and early twentieth centuries many of these Irish and German onlookers were the men and woman who supervised and bossed the Italians on the job. The wealthy strolled over from West Harlem to enjoy the exotic spectacle. Jews came both from the East Harlem working-class community and the wealthier Jewish community on the West Side. In the earliest period, in the late nineteenth and early twentieth centuries, blacks came from West Harlem, some of them to pray at the shrine. Irish police kept the peace.[21]

In the afternoon, after the solemn high mass, parish and neighborhood societies began to take their places in front of the church in preparation for the procession.[22] The members of the Congregation of Mount Carmel were there, together with the women of the Altar Sodality and the girls of the Children of Mary; also represented, until they gradually faded away after the Second World War, were the regional societies from the neighborhood that held their annual, smaller feste at Mount Carmel. Bands lined up at intervals in the procession, and throughout the march they played Italian and American music. Behind the societies, a large statue of the Madonna—not the one from the high altar, which left the church only on very special occasions, but a second statue—was mounted on a float which had been decorated with flowers and white ribbons. An honor guard of little girls and young unmarried women clothed in white surrounded the Madonna. Dressed in their best suits or, later in the history of the devotion, in rented tuxedos, the young men from the Holy Name society who would be pulling the float through the streets of East Harlem—a task that was viewed as a great honor and privilege—lined up in front of the Madonna. When everyone was in place, the banner of the Congregazione del Monte Carmelo was carried out by male members of the congregation. Then, at a signal from the priests and with an explosion of music and fireworks, the procession began.[23]

The great Mount Carmel parade, with thousands of marchers, several bands, trailing incense and the haunting sounds of southern Italian religious chanting, made its way up and down every block in the "Italian quarter" of Harlem. Until the late 1940s, the banner was carried down to 102d Street and up to 124th Street, passing under windows filled with the devout. Two processions were necessary to reach all the streets of Italian Harlem: the first went south from the church; the second, on the evening of the 16th, went north. As the neighborhood shrank, so did the procession, gradually withdrawing to the blocks around the church itself. It weaved in and out of the blocks between Third Avenue on the west and Pleasant Avenue on the east. Immediately behind the banner walked women chanting; men and women walked in segregated groups in the procession until at least the 1940s. People of all ages marched. Children helped support the old, who marched on, grimly fulfilling vows made perhaps decades before. Daughters walked arm-in-arm and barefoot with their mothers, sharing the responsibility of the vow.[24]

At the head of the procession marched *i prominenti*, members of the East Harlem and New York elite. This group included judges, lawyers, doctors, local politicians, and prominent funeral directors.[25] Before this elite emerged in the 1920s, the festa was presided over by local merchants and businessmen—men of material success who had "made America," in the popular expression—who valued the prestige and rispetto that came from being known as a sponsor of the procession. These merchants paid for the fireworks that were set off on street corners near their stores when la Madonna passed.[26] As soon as economic capacity matched social aspiration, which allowed Italians to send their children to school, the entire grammar school of Our Lady of Mount Carmel marched in the procession by grade.

As la Madonna slowly made her way through the streets of East Harlem, the devout standing on the sidewalks in front of their tenements kicked off their shoes and joined the procession. Fireworks that had been strung along the trolley tracks were lit as la Madonna approached, making a carpet of noise and smoke for her. In the days before the community was powerful enough to make arrangements, the procession was forced to stop while the trolley cars rumbled past. Above the procession, as it moved down Third Avenue, the thunder of the elevated train drowned out the music. Pushcart vendors saluted as the Madonna was carried past the great outdoor Italian market on First Avenue. Women and girls shouted entreaties over the heads of the crowd to their patroness; others cried aloud, arms outstretched, fingers spread. Noise, smoke, people shoving to get closer, the city's public transportation bearing down on them, children lighting firecrackers—all this, and men and women were still able to kneel on the gritty sidewalk as the statue or banner passed and, pulling a shawl of silence and respect around themselves, bow to la Madonna.[27]

From time to time la Madonna was forced to stop in the street by her faithful. Lapolla tells of one woman who threw herself at the base of the "wandering shrine" to beg help for her family. Before the community, she identified her need, described the details of the situation that had brought her to the feet of la Madonna, and made her request.[28] Others pushed their way through the crowd, or pushed their children through the crowd, to pin money onto the banner. In front of the image was a small box into which people threw money and jewelry. The contributions of the faithful on the day of the festa, even in the days of poverty, were considerable; it was this money that permitted the frequent beautification of the church.[29]

At the very rear of the procession walked the penitents. All of them walked barefoot; some crawled along on their hands and knees; many had been walking all night. For the most part, it was the women who walked barefoot on the searing pavement, though one of my informants told me that men would do this if their wives insisted. In his words, "You do that, or you don't get any food."[30] Women bore huge and very heavy altars of candles arranged in tiered circles ("like a wedding cake," one of my East Harlem sources told me) and balanced on their heads with the poise that had enabled them and their mothers to carry jugs of water and loaves of bread on their heads in southern Italy. Sometimes white ribbons extended out from the tiered candles and were held by little girls in white communion outfits.[31] Some of the people in the rear had disheveled hair and bloodied faces, and women of all ages walked with their hair undone.[32] Some people wore special robes—white robes with a blue sash like Mary's or Franciscan-style brown robes knotted at the waist with a cord; they had promised to wear these robes during the procession, though some had promised to wear their *abitini* for several months, or even a year.[33] Although the rear of the procession was the area designated for these practices, a penitential motif characterized the entire procession and, indeed, the entire day.

This behavior was governed by the vows people made to la Madonna. The seriousness with which these promises were made and kept simply cannot be overemphasized. All my East Harlem sources told me, matter-of-factly, that people did all this, that they came to East Harlem—and kept coming even when Italians grew frightened

*Women carrying tiered structures of candles during the procession, ca. 1938*

of Spanish Harlem and knew that the neighborhood was no longer theirs—because they had made a vow. One of my sources described the promise like this:

> You see, these elderly women would make a vow, you know, they would pray for something, say, if I ever get what I'm praying for . . . you know, a son was sick or someone had died [at this point, another former East Harlem resident interjected, "Like some kind of a penance"], and they would make a vow . . . they'd say, maybe for five Mount Carmels we would march with the procession without shoes. In other words, do some sort of a penance to repay for the good that they'd gotten.[34]

In later years, as the older generation passed away or became too sick to come to the festa, their children came and kept their promises for them.[35]

When the tour of Italian Harlem was over, the procession returned to the doors of the church, where la Madonna was greeted with a round of fireworks and, in the earlier days, gunshot.[36] Then the people lined up to wait for hours for their turn to enter the sanctuary and present their petitions or express their gratitude to their protectress, who waited for them on her throne on the altar of the downstairs church until 1923 and then in splendor on the main altar of the newly built sanctuary. Around her, hundreds of candles blazed and, until the late 1930s, the altar was piled high with wax body parts melting in the heat.[37]

The people had come to be healed. The mood in the sanctuary was tense and charged, the crowd dense but quiet, the heat overpowering. Frequently the pilgrims broke spontaneously into hymns and prayers in the Virgin's honor. One man who witnessed this moment of the festa in 1939 wrote that the people were weeping when they came to the altar and that they spoke "with incomprehensible words and deep sighs."[38] Others laughed at the altar in joyful and uncontrollable gratitude for a grace received.[39] The lame were carried in and the old were helped to the front. Men and women lit vigil lights for the intentions of their family and friends, in the United States and in Italy.

When, after the long wait outside and then the difficult passage to the altar, the pilgrims, predominantly women, were able to push through to la Madonna's throne, they lay at her feet the burdens they had been carrying during the procession. They gave the heavy candles and the body parts to the priests and nuns waiting at the altar; they also gave gifts of money and gold. The 1939 souvenir journal saw these gifts in the context of the people's lives: "Every offer represents a sorrowful tale of great sufferings, of unexpected joys and of eternal gratitude. Each heart is enclosed in that offer. Tight in their trembling hands it represents the fruit of their labour [sic], and for many it probably represents their daily sacrifice."[40]

Occasionally the following scene would be enacted. A woman (this penance was never undertaken by men, according to my sources) would begin crawling on her hands and knees from the back of the church toward the main altar, dragging her tongue along the pavement as she went. If she got tired or was unable to bend over far enough to lick the floor, members of her family would come and carry her along. The clergy discouraged this practice, and it seems to have disappeared for the most part by the 1920s.[41]

Men and women from the neighborhood volunteered to help the pilgrims, an involvement which they viewed as their annual responsibility and privilege. One woman, who has participated in many feste at Mount Carmel, told me: "Naturally, when you're in a family you want to be as helpful as you possibly can, so where the help was needed, we went. It isn't that, nothing is forced, it was all voluntary, and if you're going to do something voluntary, you have to do it with all your heart, otherwise don't do it."[42] She and her friends in the Children of Mary used to greet the pilgrims as they came into the sanctuary, they took their names and addresses for the parish records, ran the church's religious article shop, and handed out scapulars. Others moved through the crowd outside making sure that all went well.

These volunteers also accepted the small bundles of clothing thrust over the altar rail by women. In the earliest years of the devotion, it was customary for a woman who had had a child healed by the Madonna to bring that child to the festa dressed in the best clothes she could afford, often straining family resources to buy a new outfit especially for the occasion. Sometime during the day, the woman would find a private place in the church and change the child into more ordinary clothes, which she had carried along with her. Then she would make her way to the altar and offer the new clothes as a gesture of gratitude to the Madonna and an offering to be distributed to the poor of the parish.[43]

The pilgrims had only a moment at the altar because others were pushing up behind them. From the priests on the altar they received a scapular, which they valued as protection from all harm. They paused for a brief moment to say a prayer to la Madonna, and then they made their way back outside.[44] The line waiting in the July night stretched down 115th Street to First Avenue, where it went along for blocks.

The day of the festa did not end with the visit to the sanctuary. At night there were concerts, at first in Sulzer Park on 126th Street and Second Avenue and then, after 1902, in Jefferson Park, and people danced in the streets of Italian Harlem until early morning. Meat, donated by local butchers, was raffled off in the evening in the park. The residents of the neighborhood prepared feasts for their visitors, and all night family and neighbors dropped by to eat and celebrate. Men and women who grew up in East Harlem but left it in the 1940s and 1950s still remember the feast day of Our Lady of Mount Carmel as a very special time, a time of gaiety and parties that lasted for a week, but also a time of serious religious dedication.

At the heart of this joy and longing was the figure of la Madonna del Carmine. The statue that still stands high above the main altar is a lifelike representation of a young Mediterranean woman holding a small child. The Madonna's first gown, which she wore until her coronation in 1904, was decorated with rings, watches, earrings, and chains, all given to her by men and women who believed she had helped them in a moment of terrible difficulty or pain; and her statue, until it was moved into the upper church, was surrounded by canes, crutches, braces, and wax body parts left there as signs of their gratitude by people she had healed.[45] Both mother and child have real hair, long, thick, and very beautiful; la Madonna's hair flows down over her shoulders. The woman's figure is full. She has broad hips and an ample bosom. Her face is round, though not heavy, and her neck is delicate. She wears pendant earrings. The child she holds is the Infant Jesus. His hair resembles his mother's, thick and very long, as Italian women would often keep their sons' hair until they were four or five years old. Both mother and son are holding scapulars. The statue resembles those in Salerno, Naples, Avellino, and in small towns throughout southern Italy.

The questions we must now ask are: What did this devotion mean to the immigrants and their children in the new land? What role did it play in the history of East Harlem? How could this devotion not only survive the sea change but take on a new and powerful life in New York

City? What does the devotion reveal about the immigrants' values and hopes? What does it teach us about the nature of their religious faith?

And how was it that a beautiful peasant woman not only presided over a community along the East River but every year summoned thousands of Italians to Harlem?

## CHAPTER II

# Italian Harlem

T HE story of Italian Harlem begins in work—or in the realities of work as these were experienced in the burgeoning period of American capitalism at the end of the nineteenth century. The first Italians arrived in northern Manhattan in the 1870s. They were brought there from Italy and from the Italian colony in lower Manhattan by an Irish American contractor, J. D. Crimmins, as strikebreakers to work on the First Avenue trolley tracks. An Italian workers' shanty town developed along the East River on 106th Street in an area called Jones Woods, once used as a picnic ground by New Yorkers. This little community was just north of the Irish shanty towns that stretched from 74th to 104th streets along the waterfront.[1]

Harlem quickly became a destination of Italian immigrants. Italian workers trudged north from lower Manhattan. They came in search of work on New York City's expanding rapid transit lines and in the booming construction industry in central Harlem; they also came in search of the relatively cleaner air and more open spaces of northern Manhattan, much less congested in this period than the area of Italian settlement around Mulberry Bend. Other immigrants came directly from southern Italy, summoned by family and friends who had already established themselves in Harlem.[2]

The Italian population of Harlem grew slowly and steadily. By 1884, there were approximately four thousand Italians in northern

*View of East Harlem, ca. 1940*

Manhattan. A significant increase took place after the depression of the 1890s and as reformers in lower Manhattan were finally successful in their efforts to convince the city to clean up the Italian colony around Mulberry Bend. By 1899, the Italian community in Harlem had scattered west to Third Avenue and was pushing north of 110th Street. This northward movement continued into the 1920s, as Italians reached 116th Street and beyond.[3]

As the community developed, it began to generate its own sources of economic growth. Italian merchants came from lower Manhattan to service the growing Harlem community. In 1885, a small private Italian bank was opened in East Harlem, an indication of the much-praised thrift of Italian workers. By the turn of the century, Italian Harlem had its own funeral parlors, produce merchants, specialty shops offering an array of Italian goods, and even its own intellectual elite of doctors, lawyers, journalists, musicians, and translators.[4]

The Italian population of Harlem, reflecting the general pattern of Italian immigration after 1880, came almost exclusively from southern Italy. (There was a small community of Genovese living below 106th Street in 1881.)[5] Neapolitans lived on 106th to 108th streets; immigrants from Basilicata lived on 108th Street to about 115th Street. A large contingent of workers arrived in the 1890s from Calabria. Throughout the history of Italian Harlem, southern Italians and their children dominated the culture and life of the community.[6]

East Harlem was already an ethnically diverse and complex community, and Italian Harlem took shape amid this diversity. Irish and German Catholic workers lived along the east side of Harlem up to 116th Street. A working-class Jewish population entered the community along with the southern Italians at the end of the nineteenth century. Puerto Rican migrants began arriving after the First World War, and there were small enclaves of black residents throughout the history of the area.[7]

The older residents resented the intrusion and competition of the newer groups. Irish gangs attacked Jewish immigrants on the streets of East Harlem in 1900.[8] Conflict between the Irish and the Italians seems to have been particularly fierce. As the Italian community grew westward toward Third Avenue in the 1890s, it displaced the Irish community there. The new immigrants were not welcomed either by the Irish Tammany Club on 116th Street or by the Catholic churches of the area. Italians resented what they perceived as the arrogance of their Irish supervisors in the construction industries and envied the greater access the Irish had to jobs; Irish (and Jewish) workers accused the Italians of being strikebreakers, which is how they were sometimes used. This conflict was frequently given a religious definition as well: the Irish held the Italians responsible for the "imprisonment" of the pope by the forces of the Italian revolution.[9]

By 1920, a large part of East Harlem had become an Italian community. The Irish and Jewish populations had begun to leave in the first decade of the twentieth century, moving up to the more pleasant areas of the South Bronx. This exodus continued after the First World War.[10] By the end of the 1920s, social workers at Union Settlement were noting that their neighborhood at the southern end of East Harlem had become Italian, and in the same period the Italians finally took over the attractive area on 116th Street from Third Avenue to the river.[11] At its peak, Italian Harlem extended to about 104th Street on the south, Third Avenue on the west, north to about 120th Street, and east to the river.[12]

Looking ahead for a moment, even at the time when Italian Harlem was mostly Italian—in the years 1920 until the Second World War—East Harlem remained an ethnically complex community. As late as 1930, only three municipally designated health areas in Harlem had a majority of Italians, the 21st, 22d, and 26th, which together roughly comprised the area from 119th to 104th streets and from Third Avenue to the East River.[13] In these areas, Italians constituted, respectively, 79.6 percent, 78.6 percent, and 84.3 percent of the population. Beyond these borders, however, Italians were confronted with the full diversity of New York's population; and even in the areas of highest Italian concentration, the immigrants lived with thirty-four other ethnic and racial groups, according to a count made by Leonard Covello in 1938.[14]

Italians crowded into tenements with or near Jews, Germans, and Irish at first, and then blacks and Puerto Ricans in increasing numbers. At no time in the history of Italian Harlem did Italians not compete with members of other ethnic groups. This ethnic mix invariably resulted in conflict when boundaries were violated. As a result, the residents of Italian Harlem—and their neighbors—were acutely conscious and respectful of borders. There was no doubt in the 1930s, for example, that Lexington Avenue marked the boundary between Italian and black Harlem; if the boundary was crossed, it was done intentionally.[15]

The southern Italian men and women who came to Harlem in the

1880s and 1890s came to work hard. They had traveled by steamship away from the world of *la miseria*, the great suffering of southern Italy, best translated as a slow dying, an emptying of hope and ambition in the face of oppression and neglect. The immigrants themselves knew the spiritual consequences of this economic disease—a numb posture of hopelessness and despair.[16] The world they left was characterized by unemployment, overpopulation, disease, overtaxation, and internal colonization. They left to save themselves and their families. Their plan was not necessarily to settle down;[17] rather, they wanted to make enough money to return and enable their kin to live as "Christians," the word they used to name their deepest aspiration.

Immigration to East Harlem followed a number of patterns identified by historians for other Italian American communities. The decision to emigrate was a family decision, taken as part of a broader family strategy for survival.[18] Some member or members of the family would leave home and travel to America to make money and send it back to the family. A Sicilian resident of Italian Harlem recalled his decision to emigrate in these terms:

> We young men used to hear about America from people who had been there. We used to get together and dream about the kind of life we could have, and compare it to the life we had. Some of us would talk it over with our families. They liked the idea of our emigrating and bettering ourselves and often made tremendous sacrifices in order to give us the chance to come to America. Of course, it was understood, that we would send money to them, and either come back to Italy to live with them or send for them.[19]

Italian immigrants in the early years of the Harlem community considered themselves family members working far from home. In many cases, emigration was the only way a young family could hope to preserve itself as a family. This sketch of a husband and wife on the eve of departure for Italian Harlem is typical: "Maria was an expectant mother. Felix found himself hard pressed to keep up the family's accustomed scale of living or to make any living at all. On account of these causes—poverty and the general hope of bettering themselves, the young couple decided to leave their old home and come to America."[20] The goal of emigration, then, was usually to strengthen and preserve the family, and the decision to emigrate was taken on its behalf.

Immigrants to Italian Harlem traveled along well-established transatlantic kinship networks. Men in Italy heard about work in Italian Harlem from relatives who had already established themselves there. These advance guards secured jobs for their arriving kin. Immigrants were met at the port by relatives, who then ushered them up to Harlem and usually to a huge celebration of welcome.[21] From this perspective, Ellis Island can be seen as a point of reunion, a moment in a larger family strategy.[22] As one young Italian Harlemite wrote of his arrival in New York, "The spirit of the hour having descended upon them [his New York kin], they proceeded to welcome us warmly to the land that was to be our home."[23] Family members also served as mediators between the newly arrived immigrants and American culture and institutions, squiring their kin around and interpreting American life for them.

Once in Italian Harlem in the late nineteenth and early twentieth centuries, and uncertain about how long they were going to be there, first-generation southern Italians remained deeply preoccupied with and loyal to their families back in Italy. This was a family-centered loyalty, despite the patriotic rhetoric and celebrations of *italianità* of Italian journalists in Harlem. As long as important segments of an immigrant's family remained in the mezzogiorno, Italy absorbed that immigrant's attention; as more and more of the immigrant's closest family members emigrated (or died), the immigrant's gaze shifted to the new world. It was a common observation in Italian Harlem that the decision to bring family members over was better than naturalization as an indication of an immigrant's desire to stay.[24] When there was no more family in Italy, the ties to the old country were cut. According to a second-generation Italian in Harlem:

> My parents express no desire to travel to Italy for the sake of visiting the native place. My mother who has a few relatives in Italy lets out an occasional sigh but never my father. He says that since all close branches of his family are in America, he sees no need to expend money on foolishness. "One goes to Italy," he says, "only because of family reasons."[25]

But as long as these "family reasons" remained, the immigrants' attachments to Italy persisted. This faithfulness was expressed in the remittances that workers in Italian Harlem, like Italian immigrants elsewhere, sent back regularly to southern Italy. Men and women in Italian Harlem often served as the main source of support of their family in the mezzogiorno.[26] Contact with Italy was also more direct.

Even in the earliest days of the community there was travel back and forth between Italian Harlem and southern Italy. One worker in the late nineteenth century, for example, went back to Italy to attend his daughter's wedding; another went back after his first year in Manhattan to celebrate Christmas with his family.[27]

Many workers committed themselves to the hard struggle to bring their families over from Italy. This was often accomplished only by fierce determination and after years of strict self-denial on the part of immigrants, who acquired the reputation of being willing to endure almost any conditions on behalf of their families in Italy. One immigrant worked steadily for four years after his arrival to pay his sister's passage to Harlem. Others were preoccupied with bringing over wives and parents to their new community.[28]

The old picture of immigrant colonies as places where women leaned out tenement windows, men sat on fire escapes, and everyone sighed for the old *paese*, simply will not do. The reality of Italian Harlem right from the beginning was much more complex, with numerous interrelated levels of conflict, ambivalence, and desire. Some immigrants, to be sure, pined for the old country and longed to be back in familiar surroundings. This desire was particularly acute in times of crisis or loss. It could be strong enough to kill: Edward Corsi's mother died after a long depression brought on by the dislocations of immigration.[29] This powerful nostalgia was alive among the first generation, and those who felt it most acutely served as revealing mirrors to those who were trying to still this longing.

But the emotional possibilities were varied. The lives of many immigrants were driven only by the keen desire to have their families with them in the new world. Others were glad to have shaken at last their family's influence over them.[30] Many others, perhaps the majority, were undergoing a gradual distancing from their old lives, and from Italy, as their families came to join them or passed away in the mezzogiorno. These immigrants would soon be finding themselves Americans by attrition.

All of this was made yet more complex by the arrival of the second generation in Italian Harlem. The first generation, in its uneasy and often unconscious process of transition, wanted to introduce its children to Italian culture—not to Dante and the Renaissance, as Italian culture was defined by the middle-class journalists in Italian Harlem, but to traditional patterns of respect, familial obligations, and social behavior. First-generation parents wanted their children to know their dialect. But the first generation seems to have given very mixed signals on the subject of Italy and the old paese. The working-class immigrants in Italian Harlem before the 1920s did not get swept away by the rhetoric of italianità. They remembered and told their children stories of the poverty and exploitation of the mezzogiorno. The first generation passed on very conflicted attitudes toward Italy to their offspring.[31]

Young people in Italian Harlem, however, grew up in the complex world described earlier; if their parents had lost contact with Italy, there were plenty of other adults in the community who retained a deep loyalty. So the second and third generations in Harlem knew about Italy and about the attachments that still bound their parents or grandparents or neighbors to the old paese. Italian Harlem's younger generations after 1920 also had the services of a man determined to introduce them to Italian language and history. Leonard Covello saw to it that later generations knew something about the world of their parents. With his encouragement, Italian American young people formed clubs like the Italian American Students League, which was organized in 1936 on 116th Street.[32] Finally, there is plenty of evidence to suggest that immigrants discovered that they were Italian after they had lived in Italian Harlem for a number of years. They responded loyally to the campaigns to collect gold and jewelry for Mussolini's campaign in Africa; and after the Second World War, they expressed real concern for the plight of Italy.[33]

These complexities and ambiguities were sharpest in the lives of the men and the smaller number of women who came to Italian Harlem in its earliest days. Men significantly outnumbered women in the first decades of Italian Harlem, a pattern that reflected the general trend of Italian immigration in the late nineteenth and early twentieth centuries.[34] They lived in a largely male world. After their arrival in Italian Harlem, the immigrants could choose from among a number of possible living arrangements. They could live with family members who had already established themselves in Harlem or they could board with friends and paesani. Many set up familylike households with other male immigrants in rooming houses. Few seem to have chosen to live alone in rented rooms in boardinghouses, in part because of the cost, but also because of fear of social isolation.[35] Sociability in Italy was family-based, and these first male immigrants seem to have wanted to recreate familiar family structures in the new world.

The men who lived in rooming houses set up small households. They lived with their paesani, pooled expenses for food and rent, and shared household responsibilities. They cooked for themselves to save money, washed their own clothes, even made their own wine. Other immigrants lived as boarders with relatives and friends, a practice which Italians valued for the extra money it brought the family and Americans excoriated because of the imagined moral abuses that such close living was said to have encouraged. The women of the house frequently washed and cleaned for the boarders as part of the financial arrangement. The boarders might be included to a greater or lesser extent in the life of the family, though full board was probably the exception. Usually, the boarder prepared his own food and ate with the family only at the important Sunday afternoon meal.[36]

The earliest male immigrants to Italian Harlem, therefore, who came on behalf of their families and traveled along family-based networks, could live in familylike settings in their new community. They inhabited in this way a continuous moral and social world with southern Italy. As visible symbols of this moral continuity, they filled their rooms with sacred images of the family and the holy; or to put this another way, they reminded themselves of and celebrated this continuity by surrounding themselves with sacred images of it. The popularity of household shrines is a well-documented feature of the lives of the earliest Italian immigrants in New York City, in both the uptown and downtown communities. A Protestant home visitor affiliated with Calvary Church on Worth Street in lower Manhattan noted in 1882 that many immigrants kept small statues of the Virgin with vigil lights burning in front of them in their homes.[37] Jacob Riis commented in 1899 that the "real Italian man" was glimpsed "when he is 'at home' with the saint in the backyard, the church or wherever it may be." Riis noted that the saint's statue was the "rallying point" of the Italian immigrant's civic and domestic life. The saint, said Riis, meant "home and kindred, neighborly friendship in a strange land, and the old communal ties."[38] Garibaldi Lapolla, East Harlem's novelist, has drawn powerful pictures of the rooms of early male immigrants, aglow with vigil lights burning before pictures and statues of the Virgin and hometown saints.

The immigrants obtained these images in ways that linked them directly to the old paese and to the many emotions of the ocean crossing. They might have been given the image in a ceremony of departure in their hometown, such as that described by Broughton Brandenburg in 1903.[39] Or they could buy familiar images from friars who moved among the crowds at the points of embarcation.[40] In these cases, the image traveled as a companion and protector with the immigrants as they journeyed from their old home to their new. Other immigrants sent for a statue or card of their hometown patron after they had settled in their new community; this is how the statue of la Madonna del Carmine of 115th Street came to Harlem.

There were real continuities, then, between the moral world of southern Italy and the emerging moral world of Italian Harlem. We must now make this picture more complex and complete by turning to the immigrants' deeply felt pain of separation. There was continuity, but it was continuity within the context of disruption. Continuity and disruption cannot be separated or understood apart from each other. For our purposes, it is important to call attention to this tension because it was precisely in the interstices between continuity and disruption that the devotion to the Madonna of Mount Carmel emerged in Italian Harlem. We must turn here to the troubles of the early immigrants. In the words of a Calabrian folksong of immigration, which can serve as an introduction to our consideration of the pain experienced by the early immigrants, "You'll go far away, and then you'll remember / Calabria *bella*, where have I left you?"[41]

The decision to emigrate was a family decision, but the pain of separation—on both sides of the Atlantic—was no less real for this. In 1921, Leonard Covello took a trip back to Italy, and the emotional intensity of his encounters with his family in Avigliano, which he had left some fifteen years before, are revealing. On his last night in Avigliano, Covello wrote of his uncle: "As we were going to bed, the hon[orable] old man said that he did not want the sun to rise. Separation is terrible. Heaven is the reunion of loved ones." At the train station the next day, as Covello was about to leave Avigliano for a second time, his uncle gave him a picture of his sister—Covello's deceased mother—and a school book which Covello had used as a child in Italy. Covello notes in his journal, "He has kept them these many years."[42] One of my informants recalled that in 1914 his mother took him and his brothers back to Naples from Harlem "because my grandfather was broken-hearted. He wanted to see his grandchildren."[43]

Italian Harlem in the period under consideration was a community in separation: men separated from their wives and children, men
and women separated from their parents and grandparents. The memories of the community include many variations on distance. One man
came to Harlem in the early twentieth century after three months of
marriage and endured a five-year separation from his wife, who stayed
behind in Naples to take care of her mother-in-law.[44] Another man
worked for about ten years to secure the eventual passage of his seven
brothers.[45] The same preoccupation was true of other Italian American communities as well: Virginia Yans-McLaughlin discovered that
early arrivals to Buffalo sent back for their relatives as soon as possible.[46]

This separation and the accompanying desire to end it created
unique and powerful pressures in the lives of the first residents of
Italian Harlem. One student of the community, working with information gathered in interviews with residents, has described the pressures
in these ominous terms:

> the immigrants . . . labored harder in order to be in a position to
> bring their families from abroad. In many cases they were suc-
> cessful. . . . there were very painful instances, however, whereby
> the immigrants, through no fault of their own, failed in their at-
> tempts and the tragic consequences of such failures are too well
> known to be mentioned in this short compass.[47]

Covello has written that it took his father six difficult years after his
arrival in 1889 to make enough money "to pay the debt to get over,
maintain us in Italy, live here, and make enough money to create a
home for us here."[48] Guilt that they were not doing enough, pressure
to work harder and faster, and fear that they would be unsuccessful
haunted the early arrivals.

There were other anxieties. American observers, certainly over-
emphasizing the point for their own reasons but still calling attention
to an important reality of immigrant life, noted a moral confusion
among new arrivals to New York's Italian colonies. One commentator
saw an initial excess followed by very severe self-restraint and discipline.[49] Among the immigrants themselves there was an anxiety, however ill-founded, that family structures and norms would be eroded in
the experience of migration. There were undoubtedly fears among the
women in Italy that their men would be unfaithful, fears of which the
men themselves were probably aware. One of Carla Bianco's infor-

mants told her that a woman from the Abruzzo flew to Roseto one night as a witch to check out rumors that her husband was sleeping with his sister-in-law.[50] Finally, another, more subtle but possibly also more troubling fear is expressed by one of Garibaldi Lapolla's characters, Gennaro, who wonders whether this separation from his family will make them unrecognizable to him when they finally arrive in New York:

> She [his wife] seemed the living proof of another life from which he had fled. He had come into new ways and new thoughts, and she would be filled with the old notions . . . though he would send for his family, he trembled to think that between them and him was now a great gap. The ocean that separated them was as nothing to the change that had come about in their outlooks. Even their bodies must have been transformed.[51]

These manifold anxieties and pressures dogged the earliest immigrants and shaped and fired their lives. The first residents of Italian Harlem endured severe economic hardship, depriving themselves of even basic necessities to end the separation from their families. They took whatever work was available—this was not a matter of choice. They accepted close and unpleasant quarters in order to save money. Their discipline and self-sacrifice became an essential part of the community's understanding of its own history, and tales of the hard early years, Italian Harlem's foundational myths, were still being told and collected in the 1930s.[52]

To the ordinary troubles of unemployment and the difficulties of finding work in the new environment—and the immigrants in Italian Harlem were familiar with both of these realities—were added the pressure and guilt of knowing that this was time lost in the struggle to bring families over or to support them in Italy and in Harlem. The hunger for work became all-consuming in the context of the family strategy of immigration.[53] This hunger had two consequences. First, it left Italian workers vulnerable to exploitation by *padroni* and bosses. The *padrone* system flourished in the early years of Italian Harlem.[54] Italians were often unwilling to challenge the authority of the bosses because they needed the work and they realized how easy it was for the padroni to find other workers to replace them. Other ethnic groups were harshly critical of this apparent docility, which they saw as constituting a real threat to the nascent labor movement in New York City in the late nineteenth and early twentieth centuries.[55] Although the

Italian hostility to labor organization has been both exaggerated and misunderstood,[56] Italians were willing to keep quiet to keep their jobs. Italian workers, male and female, tolerated the most awful conditions as long as they found work.

Many of the inner complexities and trials of immigration are illustrated in the work-biography of Vincent Scilipoti. His story was written down in 1934 by Marie Lipari, a resident of Italian Harlem who was doing research on the community.[57] Scilipoti came to Harlem from Nicosia in the province of Catania in 1888. He was thirty years old. He left behind him in Nicosia a wife and two small children.

Scilipoti was working as a small merchant—he owned his own grocery store—and was making "just enough to live" (all quotations are Scilipoti's own words, translated from Sicilian by Lipari), when two paesani who had immigrated to Harlem returned to Nicosia looking "prosperous and well-dressed." They told him "tales of prosperity in America" and he decided to emigrate. When he left, "I thought that work was plentiful and I could get a job easily." The reality proved to be quite different. He was met at Castle Garden by a paesano who took him to his own apartment on 110th Street and First Avenue. Three days later, Scilipoti found a room in the same neighborhood for two dollars a month. He then began a long and difficult odyssey in search of work through the terrible labyrinth of late-nineteenth-century American capitalism.

His first job, which lasted two weeks and which he got by simply joining the men already at work, was on a building under construction in West Harlem. His second job, laying pipes on Morningside Heights, also lasted two weeks, but this one had some expensive strings attached to it. The boss of the job demanded and received a three-dollar commission and an additional fifty cents for medical insurance. None of this was refunded, of course, when Scilipoti lost the job. As he observed: "This boss never kept men longer than 2 weeks; after he had collected his $3.50 he discharged the workers and hired others, who were again asked to pay $3.00 in order to get the job."

His next job came courtesy of a padrone named Emilio, who had emigrated a few years before from Basilicata. Emilio, who worked for the Banca Garofalo, was gathering a thousand men to work on a dam in Cincinnati. This is how Scilipoti describes his trek westward:

> I joined the group, which started out in the night. Emilio had told us we would reach our destination before morning, so none of us

took any food. Instead we were kept one night and one day on a boat with nothing to eat. We were taken to Norfolk, Va., where a special train was ready for the 1,000 workmen. We were promised that we would get to our destination in an hour so we were not given time to eat. But the train took all night. When we arrived the construction company had trucks ready at the station, which was four miles from the place of work.

The workers had been told that the company was paying for their transportation; instead, ten dollars was deducted from their pay for the journey.

Scilipoti settled in to what he expected would be regular labor. But he was in for yet another surprise. The workers were given $1.25 for a ten-hour day, but they worked only irregularly. The rest of the time they sat around in the shacks the company had provided for them—one hundred to a shack. The only place to buy food was from Emilio, and "Emilio overcharged." Living conditions in the shacks were terrible. As Scilipoti described them: "We slept on the second and third floors. The floor space was divided into spaces about 4 or 5 feet wide with boards. Two or three men slept in each of these spaces. . . . There were no beds even for the sick, and the only bedding we had was a little straw." Emilio was armed to ensure that none of the men he had brought from New York would try to escape; when a group of workers did flee one night, Emilio went after them with a company crew, caught them, and "beat them unmercifully."

Scilipoti eventually made his way back to Harlem, which he used as a point of reorientation, where he found work digging cellars in West Harlem. After two days on this job, he hurt his leg and was unable to continue working. His boss refused to pay him for his two days' labor, and when Scilipoti insisted the boss called the police. Scilipoti, terrified of arrest and possible deportation, fled without his pay. A number of other jobs followed, including one in Louisiana planting beets, and Scilipoti had several more experiences with Italian padroni in Harlem. Finally, in about 1891, Scilipoti, who was "disgusted with bosses" by this time, began to sell lemons on the streets of Italian Harlem. In 1893, five years after his arrival, he was at last able to go back to Italy for his family. They returned together in 1894.

Scilipoti's experience was quite typical of early immigrant life in Harlem in its general outline of exploitation, endurance, unemployment, difficulty, and separation. The work experience of Italian women in Harlem in this period was no less oppressive. Working for small contractors in the garment trades or in small tobacco or candy factories, the women of Italian Harlem labored under atrocious conditions at unreasonable speeds. Flower-making a.id dressmaking, both in the home and in factories, were conducted on a piecework basis until the labor reforms of the New Deal. Piecework is always frenzied, particularly when it is driven by want, as it usually is. The workshops were dark and poorly ventilated, and women were frequently made ill by the glue in paper-box factories, by inhaling feathers in feather factories, and by the dyes used in artificial flowers. In the garment trades, women hunched over their work, staring for nine hours in dim rooms at the rapidly moving needle of a sewing machine. The shops were dirty and dangerous, the work exhausting, the environment oppressive. The women of Italian Harlem also labored under an enormous load of work in the home, cooking and cleaning for their families—which often included brothers and brothers-in-law, parents, cousins—and their boarders.

The world the Italians entered in Harlem was recognizable to them—it was a world of unemployment, overpopulation, disease, and exploitation. There is no evidence, however, that familiarity made these conditions any easier to bear. Indeed, the discrepancy between the immigrants' aspirations for their lives in the new world and the realities encountered here created one of the more serious inner problems of immigration. The lives of Italian immigrants and their children in New York City demanded a constant and hard struggle. Italian neighborhoods in New York, and East Harlem in particular, had among the highest infant mortality rates, usually considered a helpful index of the health of the general population of a neighborhood, in the city at the end of the nineteenth century, and these remained high until the late 1930s.[58] In the summer of 1880, an epidemic of diphtheria ravaged the Italian community in Harlem. The *New York Times* noted that the death rate among Italians in northern Manhattan was "truly terrible."[59] The health of the community remained poor at the other end of its history as well: in 1938–39, doctors at the East Harlem Health Center deplored the high rates of contagious diseases in the community.[60]

Disease flourished in large part because population density was so high in Italian Harlem, another problem that plagued the community throughout its history.[61] Anna Ruddy visited one home in 1907 that

housed a family of eight and ten boarders.[62] In 1932, a researcher for
the Boys' Club study of Italian Harlem gave this picture of community
congestion:

> On one "social block," two facing sides of one street, for the dis-
> tance of one block, there are three thousand individuals, and no
> tenement in this block is over four stories high. Other blocks in the
> study area range from this inconceivable congestion down to nine
> hundred sixteen individuals per block, the lowest estimate for any
> block in the area which has a total population of forty-six thou-
> sand one-hundred thirty-one families within thirty square blocks,
> according to the new figures of the 1930 Census.[63]

Former residents of Italian Harlem invariably comment on the density of life in their apartments.

Housing stock in Italian Harlem was deteriorating from the moment it was built. Unlike West Harlem, which was constructed with
the care lavished on luxury neighborhoods, East Harlem was always a
working-class community, and the immigrants inhabited substan-
dard buildings from the first days of the community. The condition of
East Harlem's housing deteriorated further just before and then during the First World War.[64] In 1913, a Charity Organizations Society
report, cited by Jeffrey Gurock in his study of Jewish East Harlem,
observed of housing in East Harlem, "All tenements in the area are
narrow and thickly populated with a poor class of people."[65] During
the war, landlord neglect, a housing shortage, and restrictions on
building intensified deterioration. Even in the 1930s, when Italian
Harlem had become a politically sophisticated community and its
residents were more skilled at securing services and improvements in
the neighborhoods, housing remained a local problem. In 1936, a student in the community summed up the housing conditions like this:

> Unfortunately, the housing problem has always been one of the
> most crucial in East Harlem. As a rule the types of houses are
> nothing very desirable; on the contrary they need a great deal of
> improvement. The common type of house is "walk-up" to five or
> six floors. Bath tubs are more of an exception than a rule; in many
> cases toilets are located in the hall-way or on the corridor of each
> floor. The tenants on each floor keep a key to such places where
> sanitary measures are very much needed. Radiators are almost
> unknown as the houses are not supplied with steam heat equip-
> ment. The old system of the coal stove is still predominant. . . . As
> a whole, the housing conditions are very lamentable and very

*The back of an East Harlem tenement, ca. 1935*

unhealthy, so much so that a great many families have already moved away to better homes in the Bronx, Brooklyn or Astoria.[66]

Throughout the 1930s, the Italians in Harlem organized a number of public campaigns for better housing.[67] But the residents of Italian Harlem who wanted to improve their housing simply had to leave the community.[68]

From its earliest days as a workers' shanty town, Italian Harlem was plagued by crime and juvenile delinquency. Norman Thomas, who spent many years there as a pastor at the beginning of his career, offered this description of the community to a friend in 1915: "We live in a part of the city which has rather more than its share of problems. Gangs of all sorts flourish and crimes of blackmail and violence are disgracefully common. When business conditions are poor our people, very many of whom never earn enough properly to support their families, are the first to suffer."[69] Sophie White Wells, the daughter of Union Settlement's Headworker, Gaylord White, who worked in Italian Harlem from 1901 until 1923, recalls that an organization called "the Black Hand," specializing in extortion, flourished on Second Avenue between 104th and 105th Streets.[70] The homicide rate in Italian Harlem at the turn of the century was high.[71] Again, these were problems which troubled the community into its maturity. Former residents of Italian Harlem note that the neighborhoods were carved up into little territories by local gangsters, who maintained a visible public presence.[72] In the 1930s, Covello was disturbed by the persistently high crime rates in the area, which he attributed to the "filthy conditions . . . of slum areas."[73]

Perhaps more troubling than this serious crime, however, was the nagging problem of juvenile delinquency, which affected the lives of the people of Italian Harlem more intimately than the activities of gangsters did. All my informants emphasized that the "racketeers," as they called them, kept to themselves and usually left most of the residents of Italian Harlem alone. But they were all equally insistent that juvenile delinquency was a real threat. Thomas and other religious social workers worked against gangs in the earliest history of the community, and they preoccupied Covello and his staff at Benjamin Franklin High School in the closing years of Italian Harlem. Covello and other local Italian American leaders campaigned in the mid-1920s to bring a Boys' Club to Italian Harlem to offset the attraction of the gangs.[74] Researchers for the Boys' Club, which was opened in 1927

*Boys hanging out in an alley, ca. 1939–40*

and grew quickly to a membership of six thousand, noted that problems of delinquency persisted into the 1930s.[75]

The existence of the gangs posed problems for the community on a number of different levels. Gang fights in the streets and parks were disturbing and unpleasant local events. The gangs intimidated local merchants. Boys who did not belong to a gang were often terrified of entering certain neighborhoods and would go far out of their way to avoid certain blocks. The gangs frequently established control over public recreational facilities in the neighborhoods, making it difficult for others to use them. In the 1940s, the existence of the gangs exacerbated deepening racial tensions between the Italians and both the Puerto Ricans and blacks, who were moving into the community in greater numbers as the Italians were leaving.[76]

But there were also inner meanings to the existence of gangs in Italian Harlem. There is an iconography of the streets in dense urban communities like Italian Harlem: the street is a text composed by the people, though their composition is shaped and constrained by the social and economic facts of their lives. The people of Italian Harlem lived on the streets almost as much as they lived in their homes: the streets became extensions of their homes. The street life of Italian Harlem was dense with symbols that adumbrated the inner structures of community life and the inner meanings of the people's lives. Women leaning out windows, young men gathered on corners, girls sitting on stoops, older men gathered around folding tables in front of social clubs—in these ways the community revealed itself to itself and to others.

The gangs were there on the streets of Italian Harlem as a model and an opportunity for all the young men of the community, for those who joined them and for those who would not. They revealed one pole of their possible destinies. To those who resisted the temptation, the gangs on the streets were a reminder of what could have happened to them. One of my informants struggled with the temptation of the gangs for many years. He was a boxer and an athlete, so he was a much-sought-after recruit. He was attracted by the prestige, power, money, and authority of the gangs. Sixty years later, this man remembered that the gangs offered what was almost a career choice: "You could do two things when we were kids—you either became a thief and eventually go to the rackets or you could go to school." He chose the latter—a fact which still astonished him.[77]

As the extreme territoriality of the gangs suggests, Italian Harlem was a segmented community. In the earliest history of the area, immigrants from the same towns and provinces in southern Italy clustered together whenever they could. A spirit of regionalism, or *campanilismo*, prevailed, although this must not be over-emphasized—immigrants from the same town might inhabit the same tenement or the same floor in a building, but they were also forced to have constant contact with people from other areas of Italy and even with non-Italians. Nevertheless, regional hostilities persisted in the early days of Italian Harlem.[78] The rivalry between Neapolitans and Sicilians was particularly fierce. Sicilians had the reputation of keeping only to themselves.[79] Older immigrants were accused of confining their social cooperation to others of the same paese.[80] Special devotions to regional saints remained popular in Italian Harlem through the 1930s. On the feast day of their saint, immigrants from a particular town would gather at the church of Mount Carmel or another church in the community for a special service and homily followed by a huge meal in someone's apartment.[81] In 1934, Covello made a partial list of regional societies in Italian Harlem; his total came to sixty-four.[82] Different neighborhoods within Italian Harlem, where more immigrants from a particular town were gathered than elsewhere, held local celebrations.

Extreme regional consciousness began to fade in the 1920s and 1930s, only to be replaced by an equally extreme neighborhood focus. Campanilismo was translated into a more American, urban idiom as intense neighborhood loyalties developed. Little communities formed within Italian Harlem, each with its own traditions and sources of authority and maintenance. Strictly defined borders marked out the neighborhoods within Italian Harlem, and people tended to keep to their own blocks, choosing friends and spouses only from the immediate vicinity.[83] As one of my informants expressed this: "Each block has its own crew, each block has its own personality."[84] Class differences identified some blocks: the local elite of doctors and lawyers, for example, lived on 116th Street from First Avenue to the river. Poorer Italians lived at the southern edge of Italian Harlem, on the boundary between Italian and Spanish Harlems. Other blocks were set apart by racial and ethnic factors.[85]

Finally, each separate neighborhood was presided over by a powerful local club that was part social club, part political organization, and part athletic association. Club leaders secured political favors for their blocks and provided the funds for local recreational activities.[86] Community leaders found they had to deal with the clubs if they hoped to accomplish anything. In 1936, for example, Covello contacted the local clubs to secure their cooperation in a campaign against vandalism at Benjamin Franklin High School and violence against the students there.[87] The appeals produced some results, but Covello's staff at Franklin was frustrated by the refusal of the block clubs to think in community-wide terms.

The structured street life of Italian Harlem was male-dominated. Women, of course, were frequently seen on the street—Italian women were sheltered, but not imprisoned. They went to work and returned, they talked to their neighbors and friends, they disciplined their children in the streets when necessary, sometimes they even entertained guests there; later in the history of Italian Harlem, young girls socialized on the stoops of their buildings and little girls played on the sidewalks. Older women, resting their arms on pillows, leaned out of tenement windows and watched the life of the streets below. But the streets were predominantly a male place. Men hung out in front of their regional and social clubs, they played cards on folding tables set up on sidewalks, they played *boccie* and socialized in the street. More importantly, the streets were the public arena of male authority. The gangs and the clubs, the local bosses and neighborhood leaders were all male. Boxing matches and other sorts of athletic competition were held by men in the streets. Except for a short period in July, men used the streets to display their power and authority; the exception was, of course, the festa of the Madonna, when women took over the streets.

Although neighborhood boundaries were so clearly defined, people moved around a great deal in Italian Harlem, sometimes within their old neighborhood, but frequently to other sections of the community or even out of it altogether. The men who came to Harlem in the late nineteenth and early twentieth centuries were ready to travel in search of work, though in many cases they used Harlem as a home base. People seemed to be moving in and out of the community and up and down within it, depending on their changing fortunes, throughout the history of Italian Harlem. They moved in search of larger and better apartments; they moved up from the less attractive area at the southern end of Italian Harlem toward the very desirable northern end.[88] Sometimes they went back to Italy for a while. Later, in the

*Members of a social club in an Italian neighborhood on a summer day*

1930s and 1940s when they could afford to, they moved out to the Bronx, the ultimate in geographical attainment. Italian Harlem was a community always in flux, in motion, a fact observed of the downtown community as well.[89]

Italian Harlem was never a physically attractive place to live. The streets were crowded, filthy, and dangerous. In the 1880s, refuse tar was dumped into the East River at 116th Street; garbage was unloaded on 97th and 98th streets between Second and Third avenues. The gas works on the river burned and belched flames and fumes all day and into the night. There were stockyards on 99th Street and Third Avenue at the end of the nineteenth century. The noise of public transportation was unrelenting throughout the history of the community, and vehicle traffic in the streets was extremely high.[90]

The immigrants were troubled by the noise and hurry of New York, by the absence of trees and the difficulty of finding even a moment's quiet. Leonard Covello remembered his earliest impressions of New York in this way: "The sunlight and fresh air of our mountain home in Lucania were replaced by four walls and people all over and under and on all sides of us, until it seemed that humanity from all corners of the world had congregated in this section of New York City known as East Harlem." Fifty years later, Covello could still recall the traffic noises, first the sound of horses' hooves on the stones and then the rumble of the elevated train (and later still, the streams of traffic heading for the newly built Triborough Bridge),[91] the sirens wailing all night long, the reek of the toilet in the hall, and the stink of the East River at ebb tide.[92] He also remembered that his stepmother stared with dazed and tear-filled eyes at the countryside in upstate New York when Covello brought her there for an afternoon's outing after she had been in East Harlem for twenty years. She could not believe she was still in America.[93]

The depth of the sadness and sense of dislocation that could overcome the immigrant newly arrived in the steamy chaos of northern Manhattan is glimpsed in the story of Edward Corsi's mother. Corsi writes that his mother was bewildered by the "din and bustle" of Harlem; "they were in startling contrast to the peaceful routine of life back in Abruzzi." The apartment they moved into in Harlem, for which they were forced to pay an exorbitant rent, was in a "sordid" tenement. There was only one outside-looking window, which opened on the "dingy street" below. Corsi recalls, "My mother was discour-

*Children playing in gutter water, ca. 1935*

*Children playing in the gutter and on stoops, ca. 1934*

*An outdoor market on 121st Street between Second and Third avenues*

*Children wading through refuse in the East River, ca. 1935*

aged by the sight of the apartment the moment she stepped into it, and she never overcame that repulsion." She loved quiet and hated noise and confusion; and so she almost never went out into the streets of Italian Harlem: "She spent her days, and the waking hours of the nights sitting at that one outside window staring up at the little patch of sky above the tenements." She lasted in this environment for three years, then she returned to Italy, where she died a year later.[94]

Three decades later, the community looked much the same. A researcher for the Boys' Club left the following description of Italian Harlem in 1932, a description that is useful despite the undisguised ferocity it directs at the neighborhoods:

> Old brick buildings, row on row, dingy, dreary, drab; wash flying like strings of pennants from the fire-escapes, garments of a none-too-selective choice; streets littered with rubbish from push carts, busy curb markets of the district; "mash" in dark heaps in the gutter, silent evidence of a flourishing illegal industry; garbage in piles, thrown from kitchens where heavy, oily fare is prepared for gluttonous gourmands; pencilled or chalk lines on walls and side-walks, indecent expressions of lewd minds; ground floor shops, unattractive warehouses of dusty stock; cellar pool rooms, "drink parlors," many curtained or shuttered, suggestive of their real business; human traffic busy about nothing in this squalid congestion.[95]

Italian Harlem remained a congested community of people living in inadequate housing. The ethnic complexity and tensions of the neighborhood became sharper through the 1920s and 1930s as the area suffered acutely from the effects of the Depression and as migration from Puerto Rico increased.[96] The health of the community remained poor.[97] Its streets were still filthy and dangerous. In the early 1940s, a group calling itself "the mothers of East 114th Street" wrote to Covello to ask his assistance in their campaign against pushcarts. This is their description of their block: "Not only are these pushcarts causing accidents, they are also very unsanitary. The streets are full of flies and at night when they leave, there are about thirty ashcans on the sidewalk full of garbage. Now that school is over, we dread having the children around in such a filthy street and most of us cannot afford sending them away."[98] Population mobility and flux intensified through the 1930s and 1940s. Some Italians moved back into the community at the start of the Depression, returning for cheaper or shared housing.[99] Some in the community returned to Italy during the Depression. Then, in the late 1930s and throughout the 1940s, Italians began leaving Harlem in greater and greater numbers.

Italian Harlem was hit hard by the Depression. Skilled and unskilled workers lost their jobs. Evictions were common sights. According to Helen Harris, who was the Headworker at the Union Settlement during the Depression: "Evictions were going on right and left. Landlords not being able to collect their rent were putting people on the streets."[100] One of my informants told me this story as soon as I asked her about the Depression in Italian Harlem: "I was dispossessed, oh yeah . . . they took my furniture out into the street . . . I didn't pay that rent, they took all the furnishings, put a lock on my door, and put all the furniture in the street. . . . I was pregnant, and I had a baby on my lap."[101] Other people remember that storekeepers gave their customers credit as long as they could, often until their businesses collapsed.[102] Helen Harris summed up this time, "Without the Home Relief Bureau, people would have starved."[103]

The residents of Italian Harlem did not need outside researchers and statisticians to inform them about the plight of their community. They could see Italian Harlem crumbling around them; they inhabited its primitive housing and walked its dangerous streets. Leonard Covello, the community's most sympathetic and well-informed observer, distributed a fact sheet to the teachers at Benjamin Franklin High School who had volunteered to serve on a speakers' committee during the Depression to represent East Harlem to the rest of the city. Among the many problems identified were these:

1. Heterogeneity of the population—Mobility of population
2. Congestion of population
   a. 200,000 persons living within less than a hundred city blocks.
3. Poor housing, aggravated by congested living in the community and in the family
4. Handicaps imposed by low incomes and economic restrictions . . .
7. Lack of modern school buildings and facilities
8. Large numbers of persons who either do not speak English or have no fluent command of English . . .
10. Second-generation problems
11. Factionalism engendered by differing cultures and differing political allegiances
12. Lack of general understanding of the particular problems of the foreign minority groups constituting the population of the community

13. Isolation of East Harlem community from the larger life of city, state, and nation

14. Pathological community situation induced by unwise exaggerated publicity as to crime and delinquency and political allegiances, radicalism.[104]

Covello's last two points must be emphasized. Throughout the history of Italian Harlem, a great deal of bitter, hostile, and frightened attention was directed at the community by outsiders. In 1893, the *New York Times* published a little story about the Italians in Harlem which bore the following headline:

> MAFIA CODE IN NEW YORK. ITALIANS WHO AVENGE THEIR GRIEVANCES IN BLOOD. CONTEMPT FOR PROCESSES OF LAW. ASSASSINATION A FAVORITE PENALTY FOR REAL OR FANCIED WRONG. METHODS CONDEMNED BY ITALIANS. RECENT CRIMES WHICH ILLUSTRATE THE LAWLESSNESS AND VINDICTIVE IMPULSES OF MANY IMMIGRANTS FROM SOUTHERN ITALY. SICILIAN AND NEAPOLITAN PRACTICES COMPARED. NATIVES OF OTHER ITALIAN PROVINCES PEACEFUL AND INDUSTRIOUS AS A RULE. JAILBIRDS DETAINED.[105]

At the other end of its history, Italian Harlem endured this bit of alliterative acrimony from the writers at *Time* magazine:

> The core of Manhattan's sprawling 18th Congressional District is a verminous, crime-ridden slum called East Harlem. Its hordes of Italians, Puerto Ricans, Jews and Negroes have traditionally voted Republican. [Republican because that was LaGuardia's party.] But in the last decade a new force came into power: the patchwork patronage machine of shrill, stooped, angry-eyed, pro-Communist Representative Vito Marcantonio. The little *padrone* was the passionate 18th's new-style ward boss and idol. . . . Taut, 43 year old Vito Macantonio was born in the congressional district he lives in and represents. To its gunmen, madams, policy and dope peddlers, he is "The Hon. Fritto Misto" (Mixed Fry), the man who began as a Republican with the blessing of East Harlem's Fiorello LaGuardia, the man who ladles out jobs, pocket money, speeches—anything for votes.[106]

The men and women of Italian Harlem were well aware of the reputation their community had among outsiders. They were forced to organize at several points in Harlem's history against such economically dangerous and culturally offensive calumny.

Italian Harlem's problems, then, from its earliest history until its close, fell into four general categories: an urban pathology located in the streets (crime, filth), neighborhood isolation (within East Harlem and from the greater city), degradation in the eyes of the surrounding community, and persistent conditions of poverty in the neighborhoods. There was certainly change and development over the years. Slowly but steadily, many of the Italian residents of the community improved their lot. When they did, they usually left the neighborhood, though frequently they left behind close relatives who chose to stay in the familiar world of Harlem despite the persistent deterioration of the area. A second important change was the gradual assumption of power and control in East Harlem by Italians, a control that lasted long after Italian Harlem had become Spanish Harlem. This maturation of Italian Harlem into a self-aware and politically and socially sophisticated community took place between the years just after the First World War up until the late 1920s. It was in this period that young Italian Americans of both the first and second generations assumed leadership positions in prominent local social and religious institutions. For example, in 1917 Edward Corsi became the headworker at Haarlem House, where not too many years before he had played as a tough and lonely youngster; in 1922, LaGuardia began his long career as East Harlem's Congressman; in 1925, a group of young people in the area, including Vito Marcantonio, all of them Covello's students at DeWitt Clinton High School, began teaching night classes in civics and American history at Haarlem House for the working men and women of the area.[107] In 1920, Marcantonio, working with the Tenants League recently founded at Haarlem House, organized Italian Harlem's first successful rent strike. Nevertheless, the problems that had plagued the community in its beginnings persisted throughout its history.

Despite this continuity of trouble, however, many came to love Italian Harlem. They may have moved when they could afford to, but while they lived in the neighborhood they found it a secure and supportive community where neighbors helped each other in times of trouble and shared in each other's celebrations. It was a recognizable and familiar world—not static, not particularly stable, but dependable enough. Because Italian Harlem no longer exists, we must be wary of the powerful distortions of memory; but testimony of the love of men and women for the neighborhood is there in all Covello's interviews from the 1920s and 1930s; it appears in the handbills prepared for the various community campaigns, such as the sanitation and housing campaigns of the 1930s; it is there in compositions that students wrote about their neighborhood; and it is most powerfully present in the memories of people who left the world of Italian Harlem long ago.

Former residents always emphasize the solidarity of neighborhood life, stressing that people "looked after each other," helped each other in times of trouble, cooperated. One of my informants used this story to summarize his memories:

> You know, at that time it was a different life entirely in Harlem . . . you lived in a different life there . . . It's not like this here, not cutthroat . . . Everybody was friendly . . . you helped one another . . . Christmas Eve, maybe there were five floors over there, and you would make the rounds, and each apartment they would give you a drink and spend Christmas together. . . . Everybody, they all invited you in.[108]

This emotion characterizes the memories of Italian Harlem, even though people do not forget the problems and sufferings of the area. One man still living in the old neighborhood told me that the Italians loved Harlem and that many came to regret leaving it.[109] Many of those who left returned frequently to shop in local stores or attend the devotion to Mount Carmel. Some of the first generation insisted that no matter where they moved to, they wanted to be buried by the neighborhood's funeral directors.[110] Others kept in touch through the active alumni associations of institutions like Haarlem House.[111]

An example of this community solidarity and affection is the journal of the "Service Boys' Fund of East 104th Street," a newsletter printed for the men of Saint Lucy's parish who were in the services. The first issue of the journal came out in 1943. The newsletter was mainly a celebration of life and community on 104th Street. It was full of news about marriages and baptisms in the parish, assuring the servicemen that life back in Harlem was going on much as usual. The journal also printed testimonies from the servicemen to 104th Street. For example, one soldier wrote in: "All my life I have lived in 104th Street and a better group of people who are willing to help one another I've yet to meet." Another observed: "I was very glad to get the paper and I proudly showed it off. Not many neighborhoods can boast of cooperation, like we have in 104th Street. I am proud and glad that I was born and raised in 104th Street."[112] Several servicemen commented that the arrival of the newsletter prompted them to brag about life in Italian Harlem to their fellow soldiers, giving them what was undoubtedly an unexpected perspective on life in a New York slum. As was true throughout the United States, the Second World War was lived as a community reality in Italian Harlem, with frequent gatherings for prayer and consolation.

Other groups in the area shared this love of East Harlem. A black social worker who had lived in East Harlem since 1929 told an interviewer at Union Settlement that "I get disturbed when East Harlem is referred to as a slum." Then she continued: "I chose to stay here because I grew up in this community. I know I got a kind of richness in my life here that I wouldn't have gotten in Central Harlem or other areas. I got to learn about people and their differences and respect them and they respect me and mine."[113] In 1939, a young Puerto Rican man, in an essay titled "My Community," celebrated the diversity of life in East Harlem, the "pleasant vistas" of the area, the apartment houses which are "human in scale, suggesting the ease of the country rather than the pressure of the city." Although he was not blind to the social problems of his community, still he concluded that East Harlem was a good place to live.[114]

A recognition of this love of place in poor urban neighborhoods is essential for understanding such communities. It could be quite a sensuous love, an intense sensitivity to the sounds, smells, and tastes of the neighborhood. Italian Harlem had a taste for its residents, the taste of good bread and sausage sold in the local stores; and it had a smell of grapes and tomatoes and peppers and Italian cooking which survives in memory longer than the polluted air of the place.[115] The author of "My Community" recognized neighborhoods by the smell of food; these sensory clues were very important in establishing the boundaries of the different communities within East Harlem. At times, people expressed their love of Italian Harlem in anthropomorphic terms, personalizing the community and then celebrating the secrets of its personality.[116] One of the most intimate expressions of this love of place is Piri Thomas's frightening evocation of life in Spanish Harlem, *Down These Mean Streets*. Without minimizing the suffering of his world at all, Thomas displays a passionate love for Harlem, a passion that is nicely symbolized in his emotion toward his apartment building: "I wondered why I always looked at her [his building] as an old *novia* [lover]."[117]

The solidarity and community spirit of East Harlem is not only a memory. Italians living there today together with their black and Hispanic neighbors still speak of the community in these terms. An Italian American woman told me:

> We got a lot of growing pains on 115th Street today, a lot of growing pains. If there would be a way of soothing them out, it's just by talking them out. This is why I think the Legion of Mary [at Mount Carmel] is so helpful . . . because you go house to house and get to talk [to Hispanic people] . . . get to really know them and say, you know there's a God who loves you everywhere and bring them forth.[118]

The strength of the community in East Harlem received a rather bizarre confirmation during the urban riots of the late 1960s. The New York press reported that the racial confrontations that occurred on the East Side would have been much worse had it not been for the nature of community life in Spanish and Italian Harlem.

So Italian Harlem was a theater of extremes. It was a place of separation where people came to work on behalf of those from whom they were separated. Italian immigrants came to Harlem with great hopes and found there a world often not very different from the one they had left. It was a place of hope and ambitions, where fear of failure, despair, and uncertainty were just as great. It was a poor, densely populated, and physically deteriorating place, troubled by crime and juvenile delinquency, but it was also a place that people came to love, a place where—against the odds—Italian immigrants and their children created a community life. It was *Italian* Harlem, but it was populated by many other peoples as well. It was a place of hard work and exploitation, however willingly endured. It was a world of distances: the distance between Harlem and southern Italy, between Harlem and the rest of New York City, between the values and perceptions of the old world and those of the new, between generations, between hopes and realities. People feared the streets of Italian Harlem, but they also lived in them. It was a world of gangs as well as a place where parents hoped that their children would do better in life than they had done—but not so much better that they would be unrecognizable. It was a fragmented community of isolated neighborhoods and separate groups, but people always knew that they were also a part of the larger world of Italian Harlem. It was a proud community with its own leaders and traditions, and it was a community scorned by the outside, so that young Italian Americans from Harlem looking for work often had to lie about their addresses. It was a beloved place that people struggled hard to leave and then returned to whenever they could, to visit, to shop, or to be buried.

The devotion to the Madonna of 115th Street grew amid these extremes. It is to the origins of that devotion in the early history of Italian Harlem that we must now turn.

## CHAPTER III

# The Origins of the Devotion to Mount Carmel in Italian Harlem

THE Madonna of 115th Street shared the history of the people of Italian Harlem. She journeyed to the new world with the immigrants and lived among them in their neighborhood. She shared the poverty and ostracism of their early days. When Italians were relegated to the basements of churches in East Harlem, so was she; like the immigrants, she was an embarrassment to the Catholic church in New York City. The Madonna left the basement of the church on 115th Street at the same time that Italians and their children were beginning to take control of political and social life in Italian Harlem: just at the time when the Italian language was accepted by the Board of Education for study in New York's public high schools, when LaGuardia took his seat in Congress and Corsi began his long career at Haarlem House, and just at the time of Italian Harlem's first successful rent strike, the Madonna took her place on the main altar of the church.

She heard the changing needs of the community. First she heard prayers for families left behind in Italy and then she began to hear prayers for families sinking roots in the new world. She was asked for help in finding jobs during the Depression. Her protection was sought for the men of Italian Harlem who went off to fight in the Second World War, and she was taken out of the church to greet them when they returned. In the years after the war, she heard younger voices pleading for assistance in school and in finding homes and success outside of Harlem; and she heard the voices of older men and women pleading with her to keep their children from forgetting them and the ways of life of Italian Harlem. Like these older men and women, she waited in her home in Harlem for those who had left to come back and visit, which they did at least once a year. Images of the Madonna were taken away by those who left and set up on bureaus in the Bronx and Westchester next to pictures of the folks still in Harlem and of themselves when they had lived there too.

The story of the devotion to la Madonna del Carmine in East Harlem begins in the summer of 1881, when immigrants from the town of Polla, in the province of Salerno, formed a mutual aid society named after the Madonna, who was the protectress of Polla. Mutual aid societies, which were quite popular in Italian American colonies, were regional organizations composed of immigrants from the same Italian town who gathered together to provide some unemployment and burial benefits and to socialize.[1] They allowed paesani to get together and enjoy each other's company; they also encouraged and enabled the immigrants to remember and preserve traditional customs in the new world. One of Covello's informants described the meaning of mutual aid societies in these terms: "the Italian feels safer when he pays homage to the patron saint of his hometown or village who in the past was considerate to the people. . . . Our Italians, and I mean the old folks, feel that without with guardianship of their former patron saint, life would be next to impossible." These interwoven themes of protection, mutual support, and faithfulness to the values and history of the paese are expressed in the most important function of the societies, according to the immigrants—the assurance of support for burial in accordance with southern Italian customs. Covello's informant emphasized this function of the mutual aid societies:

> The older Italians, even while in good health, are never overlooking the event of death. Preservation of funeral rituals is sacred to the old folks. Prospects of a "potter's field" fills them with terror. . . . To bury one without proper customs is hurtful to the pride of every Italian. And so the Mutual Aid Societies are fulfilling their probably most important role in assuring a member of a dignified funeral.

But the deep need for this assurance was also indicative of a profound mistrust of the effect the United States might have on Italian faithfulness and tradition: "I personally also think that the main motive of joining a society for burial reasons is the man's constant suspicion that here in America his relatives may skip on their traditional duties and be negligent towards him when he dies."[2] So the formation of the mutual aid society by Pollese in East Harlem in 1881 expressed the immigrants' commitment to their past but also their uncertainty and unease in the present.

The members of the new society determined to organize a festa in honor of their patroness.[3] The first celebration took place in 1882 in the courtyard of a house on 110th Street near the East River; in the following year, the festa was held on the first floor of a house on 111th Street and the East River in a rented room that measured eight by thirty feet. The other rooms in the building were let out to poor Italian workers, and in the back courtyard, right behind the altar of the little chapel to the Madonna, there was a rag-sorting yard where local rag pickers brought their daily hauls to be sorted, washed, and packed.[4] Such celebrations were common among Italian immigrants. One Catholic observer noted in 1900 that when immigrants from the same town managed to take over an entire tenement, they would transform the building's backyard into the setting of their religious celebrations.[5] Another Catholic commentator remarked in 1899 that Italians seemed to prefer outdoor devotions to entering a church.[6]

During these earliest years, the festa was intimate and intense and intensely Neapolitan, and there is no indication of any ecclesiastical supervision; it was a popular, lay-organized celebration—as these feste usually were, to the consternation of both the American and Italian Catholic clergy. The first celebrations were quite simple. The immigrants knelt in someone's apartment or behind a tenement, in a courtyard—though this euphemism undoubtedly obscures the real conditions of the setting—especially decorated for the occasion, before a small printed picture of the Madonna that had been sent for from Polla.[7] They said the rosary, prayed the Magnificat, and then sat down to a huge meal together. In 1883, for the first time, an Italian priest, Domenico Vento, was present at the festa. He said mass, joined in the procession, and delivered, as was the custom, a moving panegyric on the life of the Virgin and on the wonders she had performed for the people of Polla. Father Vento remained in the community throughout 1883, saying mass and administering the sacraments on the first floor of a house on 111th Street and the East River. Then he disappears from the story.

By 1884, the official history tells us, the devotion to the Madonna del Carmine in northern Manhattan had already become a great popular celebration. By this time, the Confraternity had sent for and received a statue of the Madonna from Polla, a transaction which, together with the acquisition of benches for the chapel and rent, put the group in serious debt.[8] In a historical sketch on the devotion prepared for the church in the mid-1920s, it is noted that thousands gathered for the celebration in 1884, coming from far and wide, both immigrants and their children.[9] This proved to be an important year in the history of the devotion to Mount Carmel in East Harlem for a number of reasons. It was, first of all, the year that the Pallotine fathers arrived in the community. Slowly awakening to the "problem"—as it would be called for the next thirty years—of the religious life of Italian immigrants, the New York Archdiocese, at this time under the actual direction of Bishop Michael Corrigan ruling on behalf of the dying John Cardinal McCloskey,[10] invited the Pallotine order to New York to work with the growing Italian population. The Pallotines had been conducting a ministry among Italian immigrants in London, where Cardinal McCloskey had met them and been impressed. The first Pallotine priest, Father Emiliano Kirner, arrived in New York in May 1884 and was soon given care of the little chapel on 111th Street in East Harlem.[11]

The ecclesiastical history of the devotion to Mount Carmel also begins in 1884 with the completion of the church on 115th Street and the formation of the official "Congregazione del Monte Carmelo della 115ma strada."[12] The latter, which was a church society more or less under the authority of the parish clergy, replaced the regional society of Pollese as the official sponsor of the church celebration. Both the erection of the church and the formation of the society mark an official change in the public life of the devotion, which was now officially associated with a church. The members of the society were all male, as was customary with such organizations. For the entire history of the devotion, this celebration of a woman, in which women were the central participants, was presided over by a public male authority.[13]

Finally, two events took place in 1884 that served as the background against which the devotion to Mount Carmel developed in the Italian colonies in New York City. First, Bishop Corrigan fought to prevent the confiscation of the North American Seminary in Rome by the Italian government. Corrigan's participation in this struggle proved important in shaping his attitude toward Italians. The Third Plenary Council of the American hierarchy also met in 1884; it was at this council, as we will see, that American prelates managed to offend the Vatican by their high-handed treatment of the Italian "problem."[14]

Father Kirner encountered on 111th Street the powerful devotion of the people for la Madonna and discovered that they were eager to build a suitably beautiful and dignified residence for their patroness. Soon the plans were ready for a church on 115th Street near the river, a church, in the words of the official history, "built by Italians, the first church which would be called, 'the church of the Italians in New York.'" So committed were the immigrants to this project that many of them came home after terrible and exhausting days of work and with their own hands dug the foundation of the new church and laid its bricks. Junkmen and icemen lent their carts and horses to carry building materials and people in the community prepared refreshments for the workers. When organizers from the masons' union objected to the free work being done by Italian men on the church, Italian women from the neighborhood tied back their hair and took over the job. Kirner's expenses were considerably reduced by this labor.[15]

Despite this participation of Italian immigrants, the Church of Our Lady of Mount Carmel was built just outside, although close by, the Italian neighborhood, which ended at the time at about 113th Street. After this, the blocks became a mixture of German and Irish, and it was mainly from these groups that funds for the building came.[16] Kirner's original intention was to name the church after Saint Vincent Pallotti, the founder of the order he belonged to, but the Italians in the community begged him to put the church under the protection of their patroness, and he agreed.[17] When the work was completed, in the same year it was begun—the first mass was celebrated at the church on December 8, 1884—Italians were sent into the lower church to worship. They remained there until Gaspare Dalia became pastor in 1919. They remained in *la chiesa inferiore* despite the fact that, in 1884, 86 out of 90 children baptized at Mount Carmel were Italian; in 1885, 229 out of 302; in 1886, 345 out of 511. By 1898, although they were still worshiping in the basement, Italian baptisms numbered about 1,600.[18] The Italian community resented this basement exile and remembers Dalia as the man who rescued their devotion from indignity.

La Madonna, her gown covered with precious stones, signs of gratitude for the graces received by the people of the community, was in the basement too. In order to put the statue in the crypt of the church, Kirner had to make a donation to the Mount Carmel society of the considerable sum of one hundred dollars.[19] The location of the statue in the church has several meanings, and to understand it properly we must pause here to consider it in the much broader context of Catholicism in New York City.

Feste were the most obvious declaration of what was unique and different about Italian Catholicism. They were held more frequently in the United States, where any Italian neighborhood could boast dozens of festa societies, than in Italy, and they quickly became the representative characteristic of Italian American communities. Throughout the 1890s, the upper-class residents of West Harlem would stroll over to the East Side on Sundays and holidays to observe the festivities in the "foreign village" along the East River.[20] The Irish American church also took note of these feste, which were held by their fellow Catholics, after all, as non-Catholics were happy to remind them. An Irish policeman standing by and watching a festa in Brooklyn told Antonio Mangano, an Italian Protestant clergyman, that he thought all the money Italians spent on these frequent and violent festivals would be better spent building churches and orphanages.[21]

Irish American Catholics could not understand Italian popular spirituality. In a bitter attack published in *The Catholic World* in 1888, the Reverend Bernard Lynch excoriated "the peculiar kind of spiritual condition" of the Italian immigrants, fed on pilgrimages, shrines, holy cards, and "'devotions'" but lacking any understanding of "the great truths of religion."[22] The feste provided some American Catholics with material for ridiculing Italians. In an abusive article published in the prominent magazine *America* in 1935, H. J. Hillenbrand told his readers that an Italian workman he knew, whom he calls "Spot"— "one smelly old workhorse"—had told him that feste are really just "street carnivals" for old men and women.[23] If the American church was going to tolerate feste it would only be if they were conducted under the control of the parish clergy and only if they functioned as a means of getting Italians into church and accessible to the authority of "their Cardinal Archbishop."[24]

The New York archdiocese, first under Archbishop Corrigan and then under Cardinal Farley, was ambivalent in its policies and attitudes toward Italian popular devotion. Both prelates were concerned about the welfare of Italian immigrants and sympathetic to their problems. But both were afraid that any official encouragement of feste would delay what they considered the necessary assimilation of Italians into American culture, though both also knew that any prohibition of these religious celebrations would alienate the Italian community.[25] Their policy, then, seems to have been to tolerate feste as a way of keeping Italians in the church and away from the blandishments of Protestants, but only as a transitional stage in their progress toward a more American Catholicism and only under the careful supervision of the clergy. All of this, however, was worked out in the context of a resentment by New York City's Irish Catholics, lay and clerical, of their Italian neighbors so fierce as to constitute a Catholic nativism.[26]

When Archbishop Farley wrote to Leo XIII in support of the popular aspiration to have Mount Carmel elevated to the dignity of a sanctuary under the special protection of the Virgin, he managed to transform his support into a critique of the very immigrants on whose behalf he was writing. He argued that the elevation of the devotion would help prevent Italians from converting to Protestantism (which they were not doing in any significant numbers) and would help get them into church. Neither of these comments was likely to soothe Rome's anxieties over the reception of Italian immigrants in the United States.[27]

A priest who spent his whole life in East Harlem and at Mount Carmel told me that he always knew the Irish clergy were "against" the Mount Carmel devotions, viewing them as pagan superstitions: "They thought we were Africans, that there was something wierd. They didn't accept it at all. . . . We were always looked upon as though we were doing something wrong . . . and I knew from my own experience . . . [that] they looked down on us."[28] At one point in the late 1940s, archdiocesan officials tried to forbid the use of candles in popular devotion at Mount Carmel. American Catholic officials also objected to the practice of holding high masses with the panegyric in honor of the various patron saints and suspected the Italian clergy of charging too much for these celebrations. On one occasion, when the feast of la Madonna fell on a Friday, the Chancery—"the Irish clergy"—refused the request of Mount Carmel's pastor for permission for the faithful, who were crowding into East Harlem by the thousands, to eat meat during the festivities. The faithful were "very disturbed" by this denial, though it did not keep them from eating meat. New York Catholic officials also tried, at various times in the history of the devotion, to ban the outdoor activities of the festa, which they viewed as "sacrilegious."[29]

Besides being an embarrassment both to American Catholicism and to the Italian American clergy, who at times longed for their people to behave in ways more acceptable to the American church within which they had to function too,[30] feste challenged the authority of official Catholicism over the religious lives of the immigrants. Italians make a rather clear distinction between religion and church, and they often view the latter with critical cynicism.[31] The feste and the festa societies competed successfully with the clergy for the people's loyalty, devotion, and money. Jacob Riis saw this clearly in 1899, when he wrote of a festa on Elizabeth Street:

> Between birthdays . . . the saint was left in the loft of the saloon, lest the priest got hold of him and get a corner on him, as it were. Once he got into his possession, he would not let the people have him except upon the payment of a fee that would grow with the years. But the saint belonged to the people, not to the church. He was their home patron, and they were not going to give him up.[32]

Italian and American clergy in Italian parishes knew that they were financially dependent on the festa societies; Italian people might not contribute to the church or toward the building of a Catholic school, but they contributed extravagantly to the festa societies.[33] Beyond this, they also realized that they were pastorally dependent on the feste. It was a widely accepted fact in East Harlem that people who would not set foot in church on any other occasion attended with fervent devotion on the feast day of the Madonna.[34] This religious competition could take a more direct form. An American Catholic observed in 1913 that Italians would hold their feste on the steps on the local church, crowding the streets, while inside the priest said Sunday mass before empty pews.[35]

Kirner's transfer of the statue of la Madonna must be understood in the context of these manifold conflicts and embarrassments. By moving the statue and the devotion out of the apartment on 111th Street, it is likely that Kirner was trying to contain this dramatic and embarrassing expression of unwashed faith which had become so visible on the streets of northern Manhattan. There is a hint of remembered tension between the Mount Carmel festa society and the clergy in the official history of the church.[36] In an account of the founding of the church written in the late 1920s by a graduate student living in East Harlem and working from interviews with members of the community, it is noted in a rather harsh phrase that, several years after the founding of the regional society in honor of the Madonna, "a priest who came from Rome proclaimed it a sacrilege to house the statue in a squalid tenement and proceeded to raise funds for a church."[37] Kirner noted in a letter to his superiors in Rome that the New York Archdiocese was displeased with the little chapel on 111th Street and wanted him to move the devotion out of there to 115th Street—out of the Italian neighborhood, in other words, to the more respectable world of Irish and German East Harlem.[38] Throughout the story of this festa—and this is true for other feste held in other Italian American communities—it is clear that the clergy and the people understood the celebration in different ways. The priests minimized the importance of the merrymaking of the festa, insisting that all this noise and the smell of food were secondary to the real purpose of the event, which was religious.[39] This criticism of the street life of the devotion—the parties, food, games, noise, and dancing that are an inseparable part of the religious meaning of feste—intensified at Mount Carmel as the church became more of an American parish in the 1940s and 1950s.

By separating the devotion to la Madonna del Carmine from its Neapolitan identification, Kirner opened the way for it to become an Italian American devotion, belonging to all the immigrants and their children regardless of their regional origins in Italy. The people of East Harlem themselves acknowledged the importance of this triumph over divisive regionalism, a triumph that prepared the way not only for a universal devotion but also, through this, for the strength and coherence of community life in East Harlem.[40]

The establishment of the Neapolitan statue in the basement of the church on 115th Street initiates the double history of Mount Carmel: the history of the church and the history of the faith that flowed out the open doors of that church into the parks and streets and homes of Harlem, a flood bearing on its crest the beloved figure of la Madonna. This is not to suggest that the people were not devoted to the church; it was, after all, their mother's house. The conflict between the two histories lay dormant while the people's enthusiasm and love for la Madonna inspired them to build and beautify her house and while the clergy participated enthusiastically in the devotion. But it would be a mistake to assume at any point that popular enthusiasm for the festa is indicative of popular attitudes toward church Catholicism.

There were really three feste on 115th Street, three different spheres of jurisdiction and action—interrelated, never completely separate, but distinct nevertheless. One festa took place inside the church under the authority of the clergy, who distributed scapulas, received the candles brought by the faithful, and collected the people's offerings to the Madonna. A second festa took place in the streets. Control here was in the hands of the members of the Mount Carmel society. They sold concession rights to the street vendors and collected a share of the considerable proceeds of many days of celebration, out of which they would make a donation—always too small, according to the clergy—to the church. A severe and bitter struggle raged between these two authorities for most of the history of the devotion, culminating in the late 1930s in a lawsuit by the clergy against the society. As a result of this legal action, the clergy took control of the street festa, and its proceeds, as well. It was during this battle that the fresco over the main altar was removed by the pastor. The painting was of the coronation of the Madonna and depicted prominent members of the local community and of the society approaching the Madonna's throne with gifts. It is said that the pastor was anxious to remove from the ceiling of his church images of men who had gone on to notorious criminal careers, some of whom were involved in collecting the revenues of the street festival; it is also possible, however, that the pastor wanted to eliminate an icon of his lay rivals. The third festa, of course, was the celebration of the popular devotion to the Madonna, which existed and developed apart from the struggle between the clergy and the society, the church and the street, and which expressed itself in both the church and the streets.[41]

When the church was finished, Kirner set about building a school for Italian children. In 1887, the pastor and several workmen were killed when the wall of an addition to the school collapsed on them. Kirner was the victim both of his own eagerness to complete the school and of a trend in cheap and dangerous construction practices that plagued the Upper East Side during the real-estate boom of the 1880s.[42] The legend of the church's founding which was preserved in the community transformed this harsh fact into the image of a church "cemented with its founder's blood."[43]

The faith of the people continued to burn in the streets of Italian Harlem. The community was fortunate in the years after Kirner's death to have the services of two Italian Pallotines, Don Scipioni Tofini and Don Gaspare Dalia, sympathetic and capable enough to tend this flame. With the Virgin now reigning in at least relative dignity in the church basement on 115th Street, and with the cult annually attracting thousands of Italians who came to the shrine to be healed and comforted by la Madonna, Don Tofini, a Roman-born priest assigned to Mount Carmel for the first time in 1892, was possessed by the dream of having the shrine elevated to the status of a sanctuary. In this ambition Tofini was driven by his own devotion to Mount Carmel and by the intensity of the people's love for la Madonna.[44]

The process of crowning a particular statue of the Virgin and elevating a shrine to the officially recognized dignity of a sanctuary is a formal ecclesiastical procedure with specific rules and requirements. The custom was initiated during the Catholic Reformation by a Capuchin, Padre Girolamo Paolucci. Between 1681 and 1954, fewer than three hundred statues of the Virgin had been granted this dignity, and only three of these were in the new world: Our Lady of Perpetual Help in New Orleans, Our Lady of Guadalupe in Mexico, and the Madonna of 115th Street. All three of these new world coronations had been decreed by Pope Leo XIII. This procedure held several advantages for Rome. It provided first of all an occasion for a diplomatic gesture of good will toward the nation that housed the shrine. It also enabled the church to assert its authority over popular devotions, which are always potentially disruptive and independent of official control.

The priests and people of Italian Harlem, on the other hand, desired the dignity and legitimation that such official recognition and blessing would convey. Early in 1903, Tofini, who had returned to Mount Carmel in 1896 after a year-long tenure as Vicar General of his order, went to Rome to present the people's plea for a crown directly to the pontiff. He had collected from the residents of Italian Harlem sworn testimony concerning the graces granted by la Madonna. Tofini presented his case to the Holy Father and to the canons of Saint Peter's. The latter decided that the devotion met two of the requirements for coronation—evidence of favors granted the devout by the Virgin and popularity of the cult—and then Leo himself intervened and waived the third criterion, antiquity of the cult. According to the official history, this was the first time a pope had ever taken such a step in this matter. An official vote was taken in Rome on April 19, 1903; the result was announced in New York on July 16, 1903; and the Virgin was crowned before an enormous concourse of people on July 10, 1904. This was the first communal event of Italian Harlem.[45]

It was Pope Leo XIII's decision to accept Tofini's argument about the relative antiquity of the cult, so it is necessary and appropriate to consider what some of his motivations may have been. Tofini found the pope a kind and receptive listener. Not only did the aged pontiff have special devotions to the Virgin and to Saint Vincent Pallotti, he was also especially concerned about the welfare of his Italian children, as he referred to them in his interview with Tofini, living in America.[46]

But there may have been other reasons for the pope's ardent support of the devotion to Mount Carmel in New York, which can only be suggested here in a tentative and somewhat speculative reflection on the story. These other reasons are rooted in the Vatican's relations with American Catholic hierarchy in this period and in the international crises of nineteenth-century Catholicism. The American Catholic hierarchy had offended Leo in the early 1880s by suggesting that Italian immigrants came as pagans to the United States. Before the meeting of the Third Plenary Council of American bishops in 1884, Leo and *Propaganda Fide* had sent Bishop Michael Corrigan of New York City a list of topics they wanted to see on the council's agenda. Prominent on this list was the suggestion that committees be formed in the United States for the care of Italian immigrants.[47] The Americans, particularly some members of the hierarchy who were afraid that the Vatican would use the council as a way of insinuating its own authority into the affairs of the Catholic church in the United States, diplomatically agreed with the agenda suggestions.

At the discussions on the agenda, however, the hostility of the American church to the threatening waves of Italian immigrants broke through and the bishops cast diplomacy to the winds. Corrigan, into whose diocese both the immigrants and la Madonna were coming: "contended that inasmuch as Italian immigrants did not ordinarily frequent the churches, that they tended to dwell in scattered clusters within cities and normally made no offering to maintain parishes, they could hardly have their own parishes."[48] Corrigan used the council itself as a platform to criticize the immigrants, going beyond his comments at the agenda meeting. He urged the council to ignore the chapter on Italian immigrants prepared by *Propaganda* because: "It assumed that Italians were somehow their own masters when, in reality, they were notorious for their subservience to bosses or padrones. It passed over the poor quality of faith and religious practice that Italian immigrants brought with them and the poor lot of Italian priests that were here administering to them."[49] If these references to the inadequacy of the church in Italy and the faith of the immigrants were not enough to hurt and anger the pope, Rome was reminded of what Americans thought of the faith of Italian immigrants in the letter Farley sent along with Tofini in support of the Mount Carmel devotion.

Also in the background at the time of Leo's support of the devotion to the Madonna of 115th Street was the complex of circumstances and controversies known as the Americanist crisis. Rome's attention was kept focused on the Irish American hierarchy throughout this period by powerful German prelates at the Vatican who resented what they perceived as the mistreatment of their compatriots in the United States by the American church.[50] In 1880, an international conference of Saint Raphael societies published the Lucerne Memorial, calling for the organization of American Catholicism along multiethnic and multilingual lines. This drew from Corrigan a bitter letter to the founder of the Saint Raphael Society, elaborating the dangers of appearing foreign in the United States.[51]

This ethnic conflict provided the setting for Rome's denunciation of the various religious emphases thought to be characteristic of American Catholicism, which were grouped in Europe under the designation "Americanism." The denunciation came first in the papal encyclical to the American church, *Longinqua oceani*, in 1895 and again in a letter from Leo to Cardinal Gibbons in 1899.[52] The central point of the encyclical was the gentle admonition that the American Catholic way of doing things, admittedly a necessary compromise, must not be suggested as the best possible ordering of the church universal.[53] Though Leo was discussing polity here, the background of ethnic conflict suggests and permits a broader cultural interpretation of the encyclical. In his letter to Cardinal Gibbons in 1899, the pope addressed what were thought to be the theological and even spiritual errors of Americanism, emphasizing in particular that, in Robert Cross's summation of the argument, "supernatural virtues were superior to natural virtues by the element of divine grace which alone made them possible."[54] Leo also emphasized the necessity of obedience, humility, and abstinence and condemned "discussion" with heretics, which included American Protestants. Leo had very definite—and very definitely Roman—ideas about how American Catholics should live.

One final piece needs to be in place before the crowning of the Madonna of 115th Street can be understood in its proper position in late nineteenth- and early-twentieth-century Catholicism. At least since 1870, the American hierarchy had feared the appointment of a papal delegate to the United States, as much out of jealous regard for their own authority as in the legitimate fear of nativist hysteria. In 1882, Patrick Reilly, a priest from Newark, New Jersey, wrote anxiously to Corrigan from Rome that Propaganda was "thinking seriously of sending a papal delegate to the States, and I fear an Italian."[55] The pope was quite aware of the hostility of the East Coast bishops to the appointment of a delegate. Just before the delegate was sent in 1892, the pope, using a significant turn of phrase, asked Denis O'Connell, rector of the American College, "Why don't they want the pope there?" As a result of this tension over the appointment of a papal delegate, Corrigan was in trouble with Vatican officials.[56]

This was the context, then, within which Leo and his advisors approved the devotion to the Madonna of Italian Harlem by waiving the requirement of antiquity. With this approval, Leo was able to put a symbolic seal on the actions he had taken toward the American church in the preceding decade. His action may have been the final Roman move in the Americanist controversy. Rome affirmed a distinctly and embarrassingly obvious non-American devotion, a devotion, moreover, which was resolutely supernatural in its impulse. The cult of la Madonna del Carmine was by its very nature opposed to what the Americanists were thought to cherish. With his action Leo was also able to give his blessing to his much-maligned compatriots abroad and to reassert thereby the dignity, integrity, and exemplary stature of Italian Catholicism. Italian American Catholics now had tangible evidence of their special friendship with the pope.[57]

When Leo approved the crowning of the Madonna of 115th Street, he was asserting the triumph of Marian Catholicism over modernism and he was sealing the presence of a Rome-centered Catholicism in the United States. The church which had argued that a papal delegate would seem foreign in modern America was given la Madonna del

Carmine in the nation's most modern city. The crown was there on
115th Street as the symbol of papal power and the authority of Rome
and of a particular kind of Catholicism. The cult of the Madonna del
Carmine was the simple, sensuous, passionate, and loyal expression of
popular faith that seemed the refuge of Catholicism in the troubled
nineteenth century.

Finally, the coronation was also a gesture of good will toward the
Italian government, which was slowly turning its attention to the
escape of much of its southern population from government-enforced
poverty and indignity. Leo was interested in tentative rapproache-
ment with the Italian government. His concern for the immigrants
provided him both with an opportunity to demonstrate that the Vatican cared about the Italian people and with a chance to embarrass the
government in Rome by showing that it cared for them more than the
government did.[58]

The crowning of the Madonna of 115th Street thus had both a local
and an international context. This double meaning is symbolized by
the crown placed on the Virgin's head in a ceremony held in Jefferson
Park because the church could not contain the crowds. The crown was
made in New York of gold donated by the immigrants in gratitude for
the graces they had received, and it was set with precious stones donated by Leo XIII and his successor, Pius X, and by Archbishop
Farley.[59] The gold that the immigrants had to give was family gold—
rings and brooches and the family heirlooms that southern Italians
cherish; their gift to the Virgin was a most intimate one, a great sacrifice made at the center of their moral world. Of the ceremony itself, we
are told by the official history that "it seemed as though all the Italians
in America had poured into Jefferson Park for the privilege of witness-
ing such an event."[60]

In the years that followed, the church and the devotion grew and
changed with the community of Italian Harlem.[61] When poor men and
women are asked to tell the story of their lives, if they have been
fortunate enough to have built a house, they make the event of this
building the centerpiece of their autobiographies.[62] This is particularly true of Italians, for whom the home is a shrine and who value so
highly the construction of a house. The centerpiece of the history of
East Harlem is the building and constant beautification of the church
of Mount Carmel, which the immigrants identified explicitly as *la casa
della nostra mamma*.[63]

The next significant event in the public life of the devotion after the crowning of the Madonna was the renovation of the interior of the church. In 1919, Gaspare Dalia became the Provincial Superior of the Pallotines. He was determined to establish la Madonna in her rightful place in the main church. On Christmas Day, 1920, he shared his dream of rebuilding the interior of the church into a proper home for la Madonna, and the people responded generously. Work was finished in 1922. On June 23, 1923, the statue of la Madonna del Carmine, the Neopolitan queen who had become the protectress of all Italian Harlem, was moved to a throne on the main altar. In 1927, after Dalia had returned to the church as pastor, the bell tower of the church was completed; the first notes were heard on Christmas Day.[64]

The way the history of the campanile is told in the parish records illustrates how Mount Carmel reflected and symbolized—and by symbolizing helped to shape—the life of Italian Harlem. The bell tower was rich in meaning for the people of Italian Harlem. They were still very poor, and at first, we are told, the campanile, like the church and the crown before it, had seemed a distant dream. Yet the people made the necessary financial sacrifice, so great was their love and respect for the Madonna.[65] Just as the poor insist on dignified and even costly public funerals as a demonstration of respect and loyalty, so the people of Italian Harlem wanted their divine mother's house to be beautiful. There was certainly more money in Italian Harlem by this time, and the campanile reflects this hard economic fact. But the bad times were not over, and for the people the real significance of the tower was that it revealed their continuing love and faithfulness to their protectress by their financial sacrifice.

It was also emphasized in the souvenir journal that the bell tower was built by all the Italians of East Harlem, not by immigrants from any one region of the mezzogiorno. Italian Harlem, as we have seen, eventually attained a real sense of community identification, solidarity, and loyalty transcending the campanilismo that the immigrants brought with them from Italy. The cult of Mount Carmel and events such as the construction of the bell tower and the inevitable celebration that followed it contributed to the redirection of the people's loyalties to Italian Harlem. The church and the devotion belonged to the entire community, not to any particular neighborhood or region of Italy.

The construction of the bell tower was also a celebration of the community's Italian heritage. With the campanile, the church—and the neighborhood—looked more Italian. The street in front of the church now had the feel of an Italian village square. Significantly, now that it looked more Italian, the author of the souvenir journal prepared for the celebration of the bell tower was moved to compare the facade of the church to the face of a woman. The face of the church, he tells us, is as beautiful as a bride's.

On July 16, 1929, just a few months before the financial crisis that was to throw the community back into hardship, East Harlem cele-brated the fifteenth anniversary of the coronation of the Madonna. At 5:30 in the afternoon, the statue of la Madonna was carried out into the street, where she was greeted by a volley of fireworks, the pealing of the church's bells, and by the tears and hymns of the crowd surging up the steps of the church. The windows and fire escapes of Italian Harlem were decorated and the streets were lit by arches of colored lights. The hot night was redolent with the familiar festa smells of food and incense and gunpowder. Those who could not march in the proces-sion leaned out their windows to see la Madonna high above the shoul-ders of her massed followers. The parish journal tells us that at sunset, particularly beautiful on this day, excitement reached its peak as Dalia stood weeping on a raised platform in Jefferson Park. Italian Harlem was celebrating and creating itself as it celebrated la Madon-na. Fifty-seven years after the first celebration of the festa of Mount Carmel in a tenement on the East River, the Madonna was presiding over a strong and real and troubled community of immigrants and their children in northern Manhattan.

During the period of Italian Harlem's maturity, the Church of Our Lady of Mount Carmel—the church as Italian and Italian American shrine, not as an American Catholic parish—came to occupy an important and unique place in the history and life of the community. Mount Carmel became the village church of Italian Harlem and one of the centers of community life. The front doors were kept open wide all the time, and people dropped in throughout the day on their way to or from work and while they were going about their daily chores.[66] From the street, passersby could see the main altar, glowing with the warm light of hundreds of candles, each representing a plea or the gratitude of some member of their community. The Madonna herself stood high above the altar, watching over Italian Harlem. Men and women in the community preferred to have their significant rites of passage enacted at Mount Carmel even if they were members of other parishes.[67] These rites of passage—baptisms, weddings, requiems—which incorporated individuals into the community or sent them on their way, did not seem legitimate unless they were performed at the symbolic center of that community.[68]

The women of Italian Harlem turned to the Madonna during the difficult years of the war, imploring her to watch over their men on distant battlefields. They promised their protectress special devotions and penances if she answered their prayers, promises that were still being kept throughout the 1950s and 1960s.[69] One woman gratefully observed after her son had returned from the Pacific, "I know that only through the aid of Our Blessed Mother was it possible [for him] to escape without a scratch."[70] Another woman brought her grandson, on the eve of his departure for the war, to the little *Cappella dei Soldati* which had been set up in the lower church and made him promise that, if he survived the war, he would faithfully attend the annual festa with her.[71] Women went to the Madonna for solace and peace of mind for themselves too, for comfort during the long wait for the war's end. One woman expressed the tension felt by others in the community: "Many times, in this long period of four years, I was without any news, and my heart suffered terribly. But I never gave up—instead, I kept on praying."[72] These fears and prayers were expressed directly to the Madonna in letters written to her by the women of Italian Harlem and published in the parish journal.

Soldiers from the neighborhood went into battle wearing scapulars with the Madonna's image on them around their necks. They too turned to her in times of need. One man, among the first to land in France toward the end of the war, was blinded by a wound in his eyes. As he lay sightless, he "remembered the scapular of the Madonna of Mt Carmel and I began to pray." He attributed recovery of his sight three months later to the intercession of la Madonna.[73] Some in the neighborhood still believe that the scapulars turned away bullets.[74] The Madonna was also called upon to heal the harrowing, intimate wounds of war. The soldiers of Italian Harlem called on her in moments of terror and confusion. One young private wrote to the church after the war from an institution where he had been committed for emotional troubles. He thanked the Madonna for setting him on the road to recovery, "My condition now is almost normal and I am feeling much better."[75]

Deep in the war years, the Madonna was asked to heal a different kind of Italian American pain in a service of reconciliation at the church. In 1944, after Italy's surrender to the Allies, the pastor of Mount Carmel, Father Fiore, heard from a friend of his serving as the chaplain at an army base just outside of the city that there were five hundred lonely and disoriented Italian "ex-prisoners" of war at the base. After preparing the community by preaching a sermon of forgiveness, in which he reminded his listeners that "God gave us a commandment: Love your neighbor," Fiore brought the five hundred former prisoners to Italian Harlem for the festa.

A woman in the neighborhood who participated in the event recalled some of the emotions of the day: "It was so beautiful because, you see, they were actually considered our enemies. Nobody of the mothers who had their sons overseas didn't know out of their guns came the bullet that killed their sons. They didn't know. It was a beautiful way of forgiveness."[76] Fiore asked the people of Italian Harlem to take the men into their homes and share Sunday pranzo with them. This act of hospitality to Italians who had been enemies constituted the way of forgiveness. "They took them into their homes for that one day, fed them, was kind to them, and treated them as guests. Now that was one beautiful way of those mothers who had lost their sons or whose children came back wounded or disabled in such a way, as a sign of forgiveness. Love your neighbor." The former prisoners were not sure what kind of welcome they were going to get in this Italian American neighborhood and they were frightened. After all, as my informant emphasized, "they were enemies—we come from the same home town, but they were enemies." But the people of Italian Harlem gave the men "a beautiful day." Friendships were formed, and some of the Italian men married neighborhood women.

On this day in Italian Harlem's history, the Madonna was asked to heal many different kinds of pain. Women who had lost sons or brothers or husbands in the war came face-to-face with young men who looked all too familiar and who reminded them of their own losses. Italian Americans were confronted by men who had been enemies of the United States but who were also their people, a vivid encounter with this particular wartime anguish. But perhaps the deepest sorrow to be healed was the pain of the first generation—and of many of their children—of having to go to war with Italy. According to my informant, it was this pain that many brought to the Madonna:

> Father was very wise in doing that. It covered a lot of hurts. The Italians were so proud of being Italian. The people would take their wedding bands and send them to Mussolini. [I interrupted

here to ask how Italian Americans felt about fighting in Italy against Italians.] Not too hot, no, because it was their own [pause]. . . . But we couldn't do anything about it. [Italian American men] had to go, they were drafted.

The act of forgiveness by hospitality allowed the immigrants to express their love for Italy again and to be relieved of the burden of having to see Italy as an enemy nation. The event, my informant concluded, changed the lives of many in Italian Harlem.

The voice of Mount Carmel's bell calling from the campanile announced the end of the war in Europe to the community.[77] Men and women gathered in great numbers in front of the church to pray and sing and to thank their protectress for peace. During this spontaneous celebration, the statue of the Madonna was carried out into the street among her people. The festa drew a huge crowd in 1946, as "countless mothers, wives, sisters, brothers came back to give thanks for a safe and sound return of a loved one, or to pray for the eternal rest of a soul."[78] In the same year, the Catholic War Veterans of Italian Harlem held a communion breakfast at the church on Mother's Day and then marched through the streets in a great procession.[79] Several months before this happy occasion, the Cappella dei Soldati was closed and the names of the men of Italian Harlem who had been killed in action were "recorded in a special album and kept near the Miraculous Image of Our Lady of Mount Carmel."[80] The community turned again to the tasks of peacetime.

In the years after the war, Mount Carmel increasingly became an Italian American Catholic parish eager to conform to the styles and values of American Catholicism. This represents the fulfillment of a trend that had been under way in the official life of the church since at least 1930. But in the earlier period, the power of the popular devotion to the Madonna in the community overwhelmed this official Catholicism of the parish and kept it to tentative statements in the parish journal. After the war, however, the festa itself was slowly overwhelmed by the church. In part, this reflected the changing social and economic position of Italians in the United States, in part the passing of the first generation. Its result was clear: by the 1950s, Mount Carmel had become a church with an annual festa rather than a festa housed in a church.

One conduit of this change was the fervent mood of patriotism that gripped the nation—and Italian Harlem—after the war.[81] The church blessed and rode the waves of postwar fervor. Fiercely patriotic Italian American veterans, whose parents and grandparents had been on the receiving end of American xenophobia, expressed their own xenophobic love of America in the pages of the parish journal. In 1946, the Head Commander of the local Catholic War Veterans urged his fellow veterans to support the organization—which, it was noted, had the encouragement of Cardinal Spellman—because "the necessity of a well-organized, militant Catholic group has been recognized by the clergy and laity alike. The Red enemies of the church are making their progress felt with every passing year."[82] In another article in the following year, an effort was made to integrate the local veneration for the Madonna with the new anti-Communist offensive by detailing Communist disrespect for the Virgin.[83] Two years later, a comparison of Lenin's social ethics with those of Pius XII appeared in the bulletin.[84] Anticommunism proved useful as a source and public proof of the second and third generations' identification with American society in a community that went for Robert LaFollette in 1924 and had given the nation two of its most progressive Congressmen.

The parish journal registered the changing nature of the church in other ways. Throughout the 1940s and 1950s, more and more space was devoted to the activities of the parish clubs and societies. In place of news about Italian regional organizations, the journal now printed information about the Holy Name Society and the Children of Mary. Parishioners were invited to PTA meetings, "coffee and cake" evenings, and communion breakfasts. Articles about the school became common after 1946, praising the success of Mount Carmel's children in taking exams, urging the parents to get involved in the life of the school, and boosting for more school spirit.[85]

Reports of the activities of the parish's athletic teams came to dominate the journal. In 1948, an article entitled "Competitive Sports Help Make Good Citizens" informed the community that sports are essential to the moral education of the young and that "sports activities are found to be of great moral and social value also in the field of parish and parochial school life."[86] The church's popular basketball team received great attention, and in 1949 Italian Harlem's mothers found themselves urged to send their children for basketball coaching, an experience that would make their sons better "Catholic Citizens."[87] There had always been a passionate interest in sports among the young people of Italian Harlem—despite their parents' insistence that sports were just an American way of wasting time. But until the postwar years this passion was not shared by the editors of Mount

Carmel's journal, whose main concern was to report the graces bestowed by the Madonna.

Just as anticommunism served as a lightning rod between the Italian American veterans in Harlem and the sentiments of the rest of the nation, so all these parish activities and sports teams, indicative of changes in the people's values and needs, served to bring Mount Carmel more into the mainstream of New York Catholic life. Diocesan officials came to 115th Street to address meetings of the parish societies, and representatives of these societies appeared at diocesan meetings.[88] In 1954, parishioners from Mount Carmel traveled down to Saint Patrick's Cathedral for a special "Italian Sunday" in honor of the Marian year. The parish journal proudly notes, "The Cathedral was crowded with Italian lovers of Mary." In the same year, Cardinal Spellman's picture appeared on the front cover of the September-October issue of the journal, replacing the picture of either the Madonna or the church that usually adorned the cover.[89]

Italian Harlem itself was changing rapidly in this period.[90] Former residents speak of this as the time when they were forced out of Harlem by the growing Puerto Rican community at the southern end of East Harlem and by public housing, which they say disrupted the settled life of the entire neighborhood. But Italian Harlem began to disappear because Italian Americans left its inadequate housing and congested streets for better areas of the boroughs and Westchester. As they left, poor people took their places in the bad housing, beginning a cycle that would eventually whittle Italian Harlem away. These changes were soon reflected in the life of the parish and the devotion to la Madonna and contributed to the shaping of the postwar lives of both.

In 1953, this notice appeared for the first time in the parish bulletin: "Moving? Don't you do it unless you and your entire family join first the Mt. Carmel Catholic Apostolate Society. Through this association you will be forever connected with the Church you love so."[91] (It is significant that this promises a continuing connection with the church, not with la Madonna.) In the same period, as the journal begins to entreat its readers to pray for the troubled neighborhood of East Harlem, many of the accounts of and requests for graces are sent in from the tristate area.[92] In 1948, those faithful who could not make it to Harlem for the festivities were urged to listen to them on the radio.[93]

In the postwar years, religious power waned on 115th Street;

strength and meaning drained from a figure who was once most powerful indeed. Her power faded as her community disappeared: as the Italians left Harlem and as later generations believed they were moving out into the mainstream of American economic and social life, the intimate connection between la Madonna and *the place*, a place made sacred by her presence, was snapped. The holy, which had been localized, no longer has a place, a community, and so its power seems broken—it can be listened to on the radio, it is no longer necessary to approach on bare feet the holy in its place. New themes of distance and loss began to characterize the portrayal of the festa in the parish press. In 1953, the pastor reflected: "Many people who were once living in the neighborhood but now are far away will remember the Church which is associated with the earliest memories of their life, will remember the Statue of the Blessed Mother at whose feet they poured their hearts at the time of their first joys, their first sorrows.[94] The tone here is the one used to talk about deceased relatives; the mood is nostalgic. People will remember not the Madonna in all her power but her statue. Throughout the 1950s, the Madonna's power seems to be diminishing. There are fewer reports of graces in the parish bulletin, and many of those which are printed have a crude quality of bartering about them. In 1947, for example, a woman wrote into the church from Brooklyn asking the priests to light one candle in gratitude for a grace received and another "because I am expecting another favor."[95] The fear and trembling before the holy in its place is gone, replaced by a wager.

Italian Americans still came to the festa in great, although ever-diminishing, numbers throughout the 1950s and 1960s, but these were very different Italian Americans coming to a very different festa.[96] They had left the neighborhood and had become more American; they returned to an Italian American Catholic parish that had an annual feast. The church was now described as the Pallotine order's most important parish rather than as *la casa della nostra mamma*.[97] Throughout the postwar period, the parish clergy redefined the nature of the festa. A greater emphasis on order and decorum appeared, as the clergy attempted to control what they saw as the less acceptable features of the devotion; and there was at last a chance of their succeeding in this. In 1953, the pastor urged all those who were planning to attend the celebration to make sure they went to confession and communion during the festa. Then he warned: "The Mt. Carmel Feast is not a feast of games, orgies and outside pastimes. Although there will be some moderate outside signs of joy, yet the Mt. Carmel Feast, the real and true feast will be in the Church, at the feet of the Miraculous Statue of the Virgin, it will be in your HEARTS."[98] The meaning of the festa is interior, controlled, a matter of the heart and not the street. The people have come not to march and eat and cry in the hot streets, but to go to church.

For some, of course, the festa seemed not to change: for older Italians, and especially for those still living in East Harlem, which would soon more accurately be called Spanish Harlem, and for the younger people who were essentially rooted in the perceptions and ways of their parents and grandparents, the festa held something of its old power. This is reflected in the two completely different accounts of the annual feste, in English and Italian, that began to appear after 1947. The English-language versions emphasize the importance of proper behavior and "perfect order" at the celebration. In 1954, the pastor urged the people of the neighborhood to clean their sidewalks and be courteous to visitors to the community, but above all to "give good example, refraining from vulgar noise and foul language."[99] The Italian accounts, on the other hand, continue to be cast in the passionate language of devotion to *la Mamma celeste.*

The difference between these two conceptions of the festa is quite sharp in the parish journal of 1947. The English discussion of that year's festa begins by noting that a "huge and hectic" crowd had attended the celebration. It observes that the festa "brought back a touch of local color to the festivities." The author hopes that the Madonna will grant her children all "necessary graces" and concludes on a hollow and perfunctory note, "July 16th, ever memorable in the annals of our parish, had passed round the corner into the realm of its many historical predecessors." Expressions of gratitude follow to all those "whose loyal and generous cooperation was largely instrumental for the smooth and efficient manner in which all arrangements were handled."

The Italian version appears to be describing another event; it speaks from another culture, another experience of the festa. Written in the familiar, impassioned prose of the earlier days of the devotion, the Italian account celebrates the fervor of the people's faith, which kept them before the throne of the Madonna all day and night. The author recounts what he saw and heard in the sanctuary: passionate expressions of joy and grief, faces bathed in tears, the sounds of sighs and sobs. Then he builds to a fervent conclusion: "The Sanctuary of the Madonna of Mt. Carmel of 115th Street is the eternal flame which lights the difficult paths of our lives, it is the safe port for those shipwrecked by society and it is the inexhaustible font of graces and blessings."[100]

Like the old Italian women in East Harlem living in a changed world, their children off in New Jersey or the Bronx, the Madonna lost her power in the postwar world. Not completely, of course: the old folks in Harlem still commanded the respect, devotion, and attention of their children and so did the Madonna. But she no longer possessed her awesome power of the past. This is strikingly revealed in an exchange in the parish journal in January 1954. A sick man wrote in to say that at the festa of the previous summer he had prayed for Saint Vincent Pallotti to be his doctor in this illness—and the Madonna to be his nurse. The pastor of the church comments, "What a happy idea! Vincent the doctor, the Madonna the nurse."[101] The triumph of church over cult is complete. The Madonna has been relegated to a subordinate position, the handmaid of the priest who founded the order in charge of the church on 115th Street. Is this the same figure men and women begged to heal them, to enter their lives and sufferings? Did the Madonna of 1882 and 1925 need the assistance of a male church official? Is Saint Vincent's assistant really the woman who once presided over the people of Italian Harlem? The days of power were over.[102]

Once that power had been great. The Madonna of 115th Street did not work miracles in any spectacular sense. There are stories of children healed after tumbling out of third-floor windows, but these are rare. Instead, the Virgin's power was intimate; the graces she granted were intensely private, rooted in the daily lives of the people. Her power was in the family; it was into this setting that she was most often asked to come to help with problems that could be quite mundane. She was asked to heal the minor burns that women received while cooking, or to help someone recover quickly from a cold so she could get back to her housework. She was also asked for help in breaking painful emotional ties or for success in love. These intimate affairs of everyday life were the source and locus of the Madonna's power. So if we hope to understand her power, we must study the intimate lives of the people of Italian Harlem.

## CHAPTER IV

# The Domus-Centered Society

THE source of meaning and morals in Italian Harlem was the domus. Men and women in the community defined and determined who they were according to the standards of the domus. This is how they knew what was good and what was bad, how they defined the good life, how they understood what it meant to be human. An Italian American's most intimate perceptions about the nature of reality and about the bonds that exist among people originated in the domus. The people of Italian Harlem distinguished themselves from Americans with reference to the domus. This was the heart of Italian Harlem, the foundation of its culture.

In 1912, an Italian American priest, Louis Giambastiani, tried to explain his community to an American Catholic audience.[1] He began with a conundrum: "It is in a way difficult to reconcile the deep religious sentiment of the Italian people with their attitude toward their church and priests. It is a puzzle which is not easy to solve." But, he insisted, Italians are nonetheless "naturally and essentially a religious people." Directing attention away from Italian ecclesiastical prejudices, Giambastiani offered a solution to this troubling and embarrassing problem in a meditation on the location of this religious sensibility: "It is not far from the truth to say that for many Italians, whatever religion they possess is narrowed within the walls of the home; for the home of the Italian is essentially religious." "Even the

*Women of Italian Harlem marching for cleaner streets and better housing, ca. 1935*

elements of the family," he adds, "are deeply religious." Father Giambastiani does not mean that Italians bring their religious devotions into their homes, although there are times in this complex article when he does intend this more conventional idea. Rather, in this meditation written to assure American Catholics that Italians were not utterly irreligious, he means that in some way the Italian home and family, what I have been calling the domus, *is* the religion of Italian Americans.

The people themselves quite clearly identify the domus as the center of their lives and culture. The topic is the focus of their recollections of Italian Harlem and the core around which they organize their self-presentation. They talk about the domus with affection, awe, and fear; they also talk about it quite sternly and seriously, because this is what differentiates the good person and community from the bad. The domus is what matters to them. One former resident of the community entitled his novel, which was at least in part a fictionalized account of growing up in Italian Harlem, "The Family and Some." Attempting to summarize life in Italian Harlem for me, he insisted time and again, "The family was everything. The family was everything."[2] Another of my informants characterized his essential education in Italian Harlem—his introduction to the community's understandings of human worth—like this: "We were taught two things: religion and we were taught family life. That was it, that was it. We weren't taught family—we just picked it up. We were very close. Sunday was the meal you had to be there." Asked for clarification, he explained that the "religion" he was taught was attendance at Sunday mass. Although his mother and father never went to church, they insisted that he go weekly until he was a teenager, when this practice dropped away without protest. Family values, on the other hand, which occupied most of his memories of Italian Harlem, were so deep in the culture that they were "picked up," not explicitly learned. At the end of two days of discussion about Italian Harlem, this man said he wanted to conclude with just one thought: "The biggest emphasis was family."[3]

The American-born generations learned this respect for the domus from their immigrant parents, who celebrated the unique characteristics of the southern Italian domus as that which made them distinct from Americans and that which made them good people. The immigrants presented life in the paese as domus-centered. One immigrant woman remembered: "The family provided for everything. . . .

We ate as one family. We had no use for money as individuals."[4]
Another woman painted this cultural icon as a warning to her children
to be faithful to Italian ways: "So when you marry we shall have a
house like my grandfather had in Italy. He had four sons and there
were four houses all joined together. . . . *La famiglia* often ate together
and in the cool autumn evenings or cold winter nights would gather
around a tremendous fire-place and talk over the events of the day."[5]
The immigrants often constructed such proud and evocative images of
the domus in the mezzogiorno for their children."[6]

Indeed, the immigrants' memories of Italy were really memories
of the domus. These people could not understand the proud italianità
of Italian Harlem's middle-class immigrant professionals who had
managed to find some identification with the Italian nation. The immigrants did not know an Italian nation—they only knew the domus
in their paesi. So their memories and images of Italy were memories of
strict family order and discipline, of family loyalty and mutual support. One immigrant from a small town outside Naples observed that
for him Italy was "the little village, my family and my relatives, and
the celebrations we had either in the home of my parents or at my
relatives."[7] Another man, recently arrived from Brindisi in the early
1930s, praised the italianità of the people of Italian Harlem, but he
defined this value not with reference to Dante or the traditions of the
Renaissance, but to the domus:

> I was proud to see families gather together on Sundays; their
> preference for the good old Italian cooking. And when I saw how
> industrious the Italian girls in the community were, how they
> brought reverently the weekly paycheck to the mother . . . I was
> willing to forgive their layers of lipstick and marry one of the
> American Italians.[8]

What was valuable about the mezzogiorno and what needed to be
passed on to the younger generations in Italian Harlem was the
domus.

Both generations felt that their love and respect for the domus
marked them out as a distinct and different people in American
culture, and they frequently compared Italian and American family
values—to the great detriment of the latter. When the immigrants
wanted to criticize their children's new ideas about themselves and
the ways they wanted to organize their lives, they accused them of
being American. One man noted about his sons, who wanted to choose

their own dating partners, "My two boys have gone along the American way."[9] A woman told Covello that she had heard a story about a young Italian American man who went off to City Hall to get married without his parents' permission. His bride must have been "Irish, German, Polish, Jewish," this woman concluded, since "no decent Italian girl of good family would do such a thing."[10] The younger generation shared these family values and took pride in the maintenance of the domus, although as we shall see in the next chapter, they also chafed and rebelled under its constraints.[11]

A well-raised child, then, a young member of the community who was *ben educato,* was not one who had successfully completed the course of American schooling, for example, but one who had been successfully taught the values of the domus. This is clearly revealed in one of Covello's interviews.[12] A forty-two-year-old immigrant, who arrived in Italian Harlem when he was three years old, notes that he would not object if one of his five daughters wanted to marry an American. Indeed, "I even would feel very proud if they married into good American stock." But, he quickly adds, none of his daughters would want to marry an American. "They somehow feel strange among non-Italian people."

It soon becomes clear that this man is proud that his daughters will marry only Italians because this reveals how well they have been educated in respect for the domus. His oldest daughter, Tessie, is sure to marry an Italian, not because of parental pressure, but because "she feels much more at home among Italians." Tessie is a good woman of the domus: "She likes Italian cooking and knows herself how to cook. She is eighteen years old now, and by now has made up her mind what her own home should look like. And I bet, she knows that it is safer to marry an Italian, because she knows in advance what to expect; and she knows—she learned it from her mother—how to go around one's husband." Significantly, Tessie's imagination, her anticipation of the future, has been assimilated to the domus: she already knows what she wants her home to look like, already envisions the next generation of the domus. Of course, Tessie is acquainted with and even admires some fellows "with blue-green eyes and red hair." But she would never choose such a man for a husband, her father insists—and at the heart of his insistence is the fear that such a choice would represent the failure of fundamental education: "She would do that if she were educated to consider marriage a gamble or should I say, an adventure." Tessie's father repeatedly compares his daughter's domus-centered virtues with what he perceives as the immorality of American women: "American women are quite willing to take chances, always figuring on the possibility of a divorce. But Italian girls are not adventurous. They believe in marrying only once." So low is the American respect for the domus that American women can anticipate the prospect of shattering it without much anxiety.

There was a sense in the community, a kind of popular arrogance, that only southern Italians really knew how to raise families. A second-generation grandmother put this bluntly to an interviewer in 1943: "It is very good to be Americans, it is not even a great fault not to be able to speak Italian. But I know of only one way of bringing up a family in a decent manner, and that is the Italian way."[13] In the 1930s, a recently arrived immigrant, whose husband had already been living a long time in the United States, sent her small daughter to Italy to be raised by her mother and father. Her husband strongly objected to this; but twelve years later, when his daughter returned, he was pleased with the way she had been educated into the values of the domus and he doubted that this could have been so well accomplished had the girl grown up in this country.[14] Especially difficult situations could result when a son or daughter married someone who was not Italian. Could this American be trusted to raise the children according to the standards of the domus? One grandmother, who had been living in this country and observing its ways since she was six years old, feared not: she felt that her son, by marrying outside the domus-centered society, would fail to prepare his children for life. The interviewer noted of this woman:

> She is delighted at the sight of her children and grandchildren eating good and healthy Italian food, and being brought up in the good Italian tradition. She quite openly dislikes, therefore, the way in which the two blond children are being brought up. In her estimation, the children may be wealthy, have good jobs, they may have the respect but she believes that they, in turn, will never be able to raise a family properly.[15]

They might have all this, but without a southern Italian mother they would not be integrated into the values of the domus.

A person so fundamentally and essentially uneducated would be bereft indeed: he or she would hardly be a person. The self took shape in the domus. According to the values of the domus-centered society,

*A summer street scene near Jefferson Park, ca. 1942*

there were no individuals in Italian Harlem, only people who were part of a domus. Italians had a very intimate sense of the way a person was formed in and according to the values of the domus. Many in the first generation believed that a mother's blood was mixed in with the milk her child suckled. This blood-sharing was thought to be the essential foundation of personal identity and morality.[16] "Blood" was the symbol of this deepest intimacy: it was the spiritual expression of value placed on family solidarity and loyalty in the domus-centered society.

Individuals were warned that to violate the blood bonding of the domus meant disaster. There were a number of levels to this blood unity. It referred, first of all, to the blood-bond existing between mother and child, the essential blood tie; it also meant the special bonds that exist among siblings: the brother-sister relationship or the brother-brother relationship was thought to be closer than the father-son or father-daughter relationship because brothers and sisters were of the same blood, had suckled their mother's blood.[17] But a blood-bond was also thought to exist among Italians. According to one of Covello's sources: "Italians must marry Italians. They may be Sicilian, Calabresi, Neapolitans—but they have the same blood. They belong to the same nation. Hungarians should marry Hungarians. Jews marry Jews. Everyone in his blood."[18] If one married outside the blood, one might not be able to incorporate his or her children into the domus and this meant that the blood violator and his or her offspring would be doomed to living like "animals."

The individual thus located in the world by blood ties was not, and could not be, an isolated self: the self in Italian Harlem was a self-in-connection. In a very fundamental way, the individual could not exist apart from the domus and remain a human being. He or she could not make plans or take steps apart from the priorities of the domus. The men and women of Italian Harlem spoke not of their own success or progress but of that of the domus.[19] All were expected to forego personal satisfaction on behalf of it. Important decisions were made by its members, not by the individuals involved in a particular situation. There are frequent references in Covello's interviews to "family councils" and "family conclaves," important gatherings of the domus to make decisions affecting the lives and plans of individuals.[20] Children were the responsibility of all members of the domus, not just their parents. Successful education of the young into the values of the domus was far too important a cultural task to be left to two people who might or might not be able to handle it. One young man in Italian Harlem was frustrated in his attempts to skip school by the vigilance of the domus. He complained that his mother had alerted all his relatives "that it is their duty to squeal on me if they learned that I keep company with truants."[21]

In an exercise apparently undertaken during the preparation of his dissertation, Covello attempted to list the principles that governed the life of the domus.[22] Among them he included:

10. One should stand by blood relatives in any situation whether they be right or wrong.
15. Married couples should never sever their relations with their parents.
17. Children should respect the friends and relatives of their parents and in their behavior conform to the opinions of these friends and relatives.
21. Husband and wife should represent the union of two blood groups, and not a union of two people who mutually arouse each other's emotions.

Covello emphasized the powerful demands of family loyalty in the community, the insistence on shared responsibility in the domus, and a concomitant insistence on self-sacrifice. In all cases, the individual was called upon to make important personal decisions with reference to the domus and not to his or her wishes.

The most serious punishment that could be inflicted in the domus-centered society was expulsion from the domus.[23] The individual so excluded would truly be an exile: alienation from the domus meant expulsion from the deepest sources of the self and exclusion from the human community. The exile would no longer be a "Christian." One of Covello's informants quoted an Italian proverb: "He who does not obey father and mother lives and dies like a dog."[24] One of the most desolate feelings a man or woman in Italian Harlem could suffer was the feeling of having been abandoned by the members of the domus.[25]

The community could be quite cruel to those who by circumstance or choice found themselves outside the domus. Two groups in particular were the focus of especially intense ridicule and hostility, a combination of responses which signals that we are on the borders of a culture. These were unmarried women and priests. I will discuss the former in a subsequent chapter; for now, let us consider the sources of Italian American popular anticlericalism. Italian anticlericalism is usually understood as the result of the alliance between the church and the wealthy oppressors of southern Italy; but an additional source for this popular animus is the fact that priests are not necessarily linked to a domus.

A common expression of popular anticlericalism is the tale of the cuckolding priest. One man told me that in its earliest history, Italian Harlem had enjoyed the services of a priest with a notorious sexual appetite. He could frequently be seen slipping out of women's apartments in the middle of the day, since—an additional goad to anti-clerical sentiment—priests did not work. This libidinous priest walked with a limp, I was told, which he acquired when he fell out of a window while trying to escape the scene of one of his trysts on a day when a husband had come home unexpectedly. The priest's leg had gotten tangled in a curtain.[26]

The story could be true: there were a number of renegade Italian clergymen in Harlem in the late nineteenth and early twentieth centuries.[27] But the story's real significance is as a myth of the domus-centered society, a myth which by its bitter humor defines the community's boundaries of value. This priest was a violator of the domus. Free of the domus-centered constraint of having to work and standing outside the life of the domus by vocation, the priest is a threat to the domus, an outlaw to popular values. Southern Italians were not always pleased when their sons decided to become priests; the church in this way became too intimate a rival to the domus.[28] In this story, though, the domus took its revenge: it reached out and grabbed the priest as he fell, putting a temporary end to his sexual adventures.

There are two exceptions to this spirit of anticlericalism. First, according to one knowledgeable commentator writing in the 1920s, Italian immigrants would willingly go for advice and spiritual care to men who belonged to a religious order.[29] Second, it was also noted that Italian nuns were welcomed into the homes of Italian colonies in the United States, even by people who could not tolerate priests.[30] Both of these exceptions must be understood with reference to the values of the domus. Religious orders resemble the domus: individual members are parts of a larger whole, and they must sacrifice their own intentions and desires to the wishes of the community. Vowed religious could be trusted because they too were located in a domus.

The sisters, who enjoyed some of the authority which Italians ascribed to women in the home, may have been accepted for other reasons as well. First of all, they did not pose a sexual threat to the domus, a threat which was, of course, always understood as a threat against its women. Second, in their submission and obedience to their orders, in the absorption of their selves into the larger identity of the order—publicly symbolized by the enfolding and enclosing garment they wore—the sisters embodied and revealed the posture valued in the domus. Finally, as strong and untouchable virgins, they were also symbols of the inviolability of the domus. For all these reasons, sisters were welcomed at crucial moments in the life of the domus, moments of transition, definition, or vulnerability. They cared for the sick, nursed the dying, prepared children to receive their first communion, and took care of the poor.

The self that thus took shape in the domus, nurtured and formed most fundamentally by its values, was also revealed there. This is where people declared who they were, where they identified themselves as human beings. The domus in Italian Harlem was a theater of self-revelation: on this stage, a person showed the world his or her worth and integrity, responsibility, and devotion, the respect they gave and the respect they were due. One of Covello's informants, for example, proudly described himself as a man who respected his parents.[31] The behavior of children was most closely watched, since the quality of their education into the values of the domus would determine the continuity of the domus-centered society.[32] Young women were expected to reveal the kind of wives and mothers they would be on the stage of the domus.[33] One young woman who was born in Italian Harlem explained the meaning of dowries in terms of the revelation of the self in the context of the domus:

> Here in America, my mother insists, the dowry itself amounts to little since everything can be bought cheaply; many things even at Woolworth's. Yet when a girl works on her dowry, when she sews and crochets, when she acquires kitchen utensils and little things that make a home beautiful—she shows her serious disposition toward married life. Such a girl has reason to advertise her dowry for it characterizes her as a dependable wife and mother.[34]

Another young woman wanted her boyfriend to see her doing housework so that he would know she was "a good worker who thinks of the family. A man is sure of this kind of girl."[35]

The meaning of the words *good* and *bad* were determined by the domus. The immigrants in Italian Harlem spoke of their deepest and most fundamental aspiration as the desire to be "Christians." (The opposite of living like a Christian was to live like a Turk.)[36] A Christian was defined as a person rooted in and responsible to the domus. One woman explained the word to her children: "When you all grow up and are earning money and are married, we must buy or build a house which will hold our whole family together. That's the only way to live like Christians. The American way is no good at all for the children to do as they please and the parents don't care."[37] Another woman held out as an example of Christian living the insistence of a young woman that an importuning suitor come and meet her family before she allowed him to walk her home from work. The old woman emphasized her point: "He came three times and then both families got together to arrange for the engagement. They were ready to be married when the war came along. This girl will marry and be blessed because she revered her parents and did the right thing. I call that living like a 'cristiano' not behaving like a Turk."[38] A Christian had a domus sensibility; he or she was ready to sacrifice without question for the good of the domus.

Holy figures were also celebrated by the people for their place in the domus: the most cherished and important Catholic figures in Italian Harlem were sacred figures in domus relationships. The Madonna held her infant in her arms; Saints Cosmos and Damian were brothers who died together; Saint Ann was loved as the mother of the Madonna. Covello discovered that southern Italians conceptualized the Trinity as the Holy Family, with Sant'Anna, Jesus' *nonna* (grandmother), always in the background as an additional figure.[39]

One of my informants, whose name is Anna, demonstrated the meaning of being a Christian according to the very severe standards of the domus-centered society.[40] Her mother had had a number of serious strokes. She was completely paralyzed and had slipped irretrievably into coma. For four years, Anna visited her mother daily at the nursing facility in which the family had placed the older woman. The trip from Anna's house to the hospital took about an hour and a half each way, and Anna often made this trip after working all morning at a part-time job. She never thought of skipping a day: for four years, she traveled to her mother's bedside, even though her mother never recognized her, never knew she was there. When she returned from the hospital, she set about doing the housework and preparing dinner for her husband and children. She did not question what she was doing: this was, quite simply, what was expected of her. This daily sacrifice was a powerful demonstration to her children and to the community of the qualities of self-sacrificing loyalty and devotion demanded by the domus.

Anna bitterly resented Saint Anthony, however. The saint had been her mother's favorite, her special protector. Anna had prayed to him to heal her mother—but the saint had done nothing. She was surprised at his cruelty and now wanted to have nothing more to do with him. Saint Anthony had violated the expectations and values of the domus: although Anna did not say it, what she meant was that Saint Anthony was a Turk.

A common term of opprobrium in Italian American communities is *cafone*. The word literally means "peasant" but carries the further connotations of "boor" and "clodhopper." When used seriously, however, it referred to someone who disregarded the values of the domus. The word was not used in reference to non-Italians: it was used only to describe people within the domus-centered society from whom more could have been expected. It described a deep failure of human quality: cafoni were selfish, uncaring, crude. They had no respect for the domus, and as a result they had no respect for anything else. One of Covello's informants defined a cafone as a person without "any sense of dignity, ill-mannered, shiftless, with no interests in life." Another emphasized that a man or woman who did not revere the domus could not be trusted in any other context:

> [A cafone is] rough, ill-mannered. He showed no respect for the customs and traditions of the family and society. When he could get away with it he did not consider the rights or feelings of other people. He had no ideal to rise to. He was an unfeeling clod, too dull to think of the finer things in life. He was engrossed merely in material pursuits. Nothing was sacred to him. A man with no soul.[41]

Another person added that cafoni did not respect their wives or children.

It is important to see here that these people perceived a connection between the way a person behaved in the domus and the way he or she behaved in society. A Christian was expected to show the same qualities of respect and consideration outside the domus as within; and a cafone would behave no better in society than in the domus. It was in the domus that the men and women of Italian Harlem learned values for living in society. Although these values were based on the primacy of the demands of the domus, they also mandated a code of conduct toward people outside of it: the values of the domus extended outward to include all of society and all social dealings.

A man or woman in Italian Harlem would see all things and make all their moral choices on the basis of the domus. For example, a stranger encountered on the street had to be treated with respect—a word that means both wariness and consideration—because that stranger might be a member of a domus. As it was explained to me: "If your sister walked down the street, and someone got out of place, they would always say, 'Hey! That's Danny the Milkman's sister' or 'That's Sally's sister.' And that was it, that was it." Another informant told me that Puerto Ricans should be treated well by the Italians of Harlem because, after all, they have families too.[42]

Leonard Covello and most other scholars who have taken up this question of the relevance of domus-centered values to the outside community claim that domus-centrality rendered Italians unconcerned with the world outside the domus.[43] Covello comments: "Such ethical qualities as honesty, a sense of justice, kindness, if they developed among southern Italian youths, were developed outside any communal intercourse." Different standards obtained outside the home from inside; outside, he says, one could do whatever one wanted.

This is a harsh and not completely accurate judgment, which reflects in part Covello's difficult position as an apologist for Italian Harlem. Apologists begin on the ground marked out by their adversaries; Covello set out to "explain" the widely held perception of crime and trouble in East Harlem. He was particularly disturbed by what he perceived as the absence of abstract ethical principles that referred not to the self or the domus but to transcending ideals. Citing an example similar to the one I have quoted above, Covello complained that the individual respected as a member of a domus was not respected "as a person," and this seemed to constitute a failure of moral sensibility.[44]

But the people of Italian Harlem did not see "individuals as individuals"; they saw individuals in relation to the domus. It was on this basis that they could be expected to make their moral choices. Covello himself, in his work as principal of Benjamin Franklin High School and as a leader of the Italian community in Harlem, recognized that the values of the domus could be extended outward. In 1938, at a time of some tension between the Italian and Puerto Rican communities of East Harlem, a young Hispanic man was killed by a truck.[45] Covello used the occasion to try to ease some of the hostilities in the community. He wrote an open letter to the boys of Franklin describing the great sorrow of the boy's mother and grandmother. He told the students that the two women were deeply moved by the flowers sent from the high school. Then Covello concluded with a plea for neighborhood harmony: "Let us strive to live on a family basis with all our neighbors—remembering that the gesture of sympathy is more manly and noble than a gesture of hate."

Covello here was addressing people raised in the domus. By evoking the powerful image of the sorrowful women mourning their lost son, he was depicting the Puerto Rican community in a way that Italians could understand. Covello wanted to show Italian Harlem that Puerto Ricans are people just like Italians, and he did this with an icon of the domus. Then he called for a response rooted in the domus: Puerto Ricans must be respected too. Covello used this strategy of extending the values of the domus whenever there were interracial troubles in East Harlem. In 1945, to cite another example, following a clash in the community between white and black youths, he delivered an address in Italian on WOV, a local Italian radio station.[46] He opened by celebrating the "calm and tranquil" neighborhood of Italian Harlem. The Italians of Harlem, he said, "have always given without doubt proof of industry, of calm, of order and of kindness and respect [*rispetto*] towards all"—all values connected to the domus. Then, addressing his comments to "my dear listeners, fathers and mothers of families, to all of you who live only for the future of your children," Covello finished by calling for an end to racial disharmony in East Harlem. It is clear in both these examples that Covello, who in his dissertation wondered whether southern Italians had any extra-familiar sense of responsibility, assumes that the values of the domus can be extended to serve as the foundation of social ethics.

There were a number of ways in which the people themselves extended the reach of the domus to include people who were not blood kin. The individual domus was linked to others in the community by the complicated networks of aunts and uncles that bound the domuses of Italian Harlem together with strong, invisible cables. One man told Covello that he had "millions of relatives" all over Italian Harlem.[47] Another informant, an American-born teenager whose parents came from Apulia, responded to a question about members of his family with this reflection on the extension of the kinship network:

> I don't get you. Do you ask me about my own family or my whole family? My whole family consists of all my uncles and aunts and their children—both on my mother's and father's side—my grandmother and my godmother. As to my godmother, her husband also belongs to the whole family. He has been made our relative after he married my godmother. To correct myself, I should say that to our family belong quite many godmothers and godfathers.[48]

Another young man, complaining about the rounds of respect he was forever going on, told Covello that even a cousin in the "nth degree" commanded respect because "no matter how remotely, I am still related to him."[49]

There were many other ways of extending the scope of the responsibilities of the domus. As one of the young men quoted above indicated, every family included a number of comari and compari, women and men who were treated with special respect and affection by members of the family.[50] Comari and compari may have served as godparents for the children of the family or they may have been old friends or *paesani* of the family. But the designation of a man or woman as *compare* or *comare* was quite flexible. As one man explained:

> If my mother needed something, like a dollar at that time, she would borrow the money from my *comare* downstairs. As you got close to people, they became *comari* and *compari*, even though they weren't involved like with confirmation or nothing, or no blood was involved, the affection was so strong with one another that you called them *comare* and *compare*.[51]

This tradition served the domus-centered society well as a way of incorporating members of the outside community into the domus. The families of the comari and compari were due the respect and devotion of members of the domus.

Close friends of young Italian Americans would be welcomed into the domus in some cases and accorded a special status.[52] Hospitality, which was treated very seriously in the community, was another way of welcoming outsiders into the protective embrace of the domus. The people of Italian Harlem made sure to welcome those visitors they wanted in their homes properly and with great attention, although they could also be quite direct and even rude to those they wanted to keep out of the domus. One of my sources described hospitality as the way members of the community came to accept responsibility and to show concern for each other. Discussing tensions between Puerto Ricans and Italians, she noted that the way to respond to this problem was through hospitality: "If I come to your place and I'm hungry, I can be sure that if you have a piece of bread you'll share it with me. You're not going to let me go hungry, you're not going to let me sit for a couple of hours and not give me anything." This sharing of bread, she concluded, would lead to a sense of shared lives as well: "They [the people of Italian Harlem] extended themselves in more ways than one. They took a real interest in a person once they got to trust them, got to know them. And that's the thing. If you're a stranger, you're going to be kept a stranger unless you say, 'Hey! I'm here.' "[53] It is helpful in this context to recall that Italian Harlem's great moment of reconciliation with the Italian prisoners of war took place in the domus: the soldiers were forgiven and accepted by welcoming them into the domus according to the standards of hospitality.

Apartment houses also occupied an important place in the ecology of the domus in Italian Harlem. It appears that the men and women of the first generation treated their neighbors with great respect, though also formally and somewhat aloofly, according to southern Italian traditions.[54] This formality broke down in later generations. It is clear that the apartment building could be considered an extension of the domus. All my sources emphasized that the doors of their apartments in Italian Harlem were always open, a symbol of the fluid relationship between domus and apartment. Families would choose their comari and compari from the other families in the building. A spirit of cooperation and mutual support characterized relations in the extended domus of the apartment house. One woman kept her front door open, and whenever she saw one of her upstairs neighbors going home with an armful of groceries, she would invite her in for a cup of coffee and send her children up with the packages.[55] One of my informants recalled: "I can never remember my mother closing the door of the apartment we lived in; we never closed the door. Neighbors came in and out and however they could help one another, they would."[56] This spirit of shared responsibility and support in an apartment building was celebrated on Christmas, when neighbors would spend part of the day going from floor to floor, visiting and eating in each other's domus. One family's baptism became a day of celebration for the whole building, as neighbors and comari and compari got involved in the festivities and preparations. Funerals were also times of shared duties as neighbors gathered to cook and clean for the bereaved and to pay their respects to the domus.[57]

Life in Italian Harlem was very public. Although there was, as we will see, a strictly maintained core of privacy in the domus itself, the life of the domus spilled out into closely watched streets and hallways. Women leaning out of windows, men sitting on stoops, children playing in courtyards—all served as a kind of urban chorus surrounding the intimacies of the domus. The self-revelation that began in the domus continued in the streets. Young men and women preferred to choose their spouses from among neighbors because they had seen them in action and knew their qualities from the neighborhood stage. Neighbors were expected to watch the behavior of each other's children. Grandparents watched to make sure that the younger generation was being raised properly.[58]

One man characterized the intensity of neighborhood intimacy like this:

> Everybody knew each other. Their fathers lived there, their mothers lived there, you all went to the same school. You got to know everybody. You married your friend's sister or somebody in the neighborhood who you knew all your life. And you married and where did you live? A block away from where your parents lived, two blocks away.[59]

The lines between neighborhood and domus were not sharply defined. People had to be very careful how they behaved in the streets because these too were a theater of the domus. This could be intimidating and threatening: the men and women of Italian Harlem were intensely concerned with their reputations. They also knew how attentive and critical their neighbors could be.[60] But all of this insured that the standards and values of the domus would be maintained in the streets as well.

Perhaps the most effective channel between the values and standards of the domus and the world outside the domus, however, was the popular insistence that individuals in the streets and in the domus show each other respect. *Rispetto* was the essential and fundamental social value of the domus-centered society. The men and women of Italian Harlem talked and thought about rispetto constantly. They insisted on it in all their dealings with people, and it was the most serious criterion they used to judge the quality of another person. All the complexity of southern Italian history, its centuries of oppression and humiliation as well as of resistance, and all the aspirations of Italian Americans, are contained in the concept of rispetto, which means both love and fear, intimacy and distance.

Fundamentally, rispetto is a value of the domus. One of my informants defined it as submission and obedience within the domus: "Respect means that you listen to your folks, what they say. And you listen to them. And if they think that something is wrong, right? and you don't think so, you go along with it, because you say, 'Well, we respect what he has to say because he knows what he has to say.'"[61] The word embraced all the attitudes that Italian Americans valued as appropriate in the domus: courtesy, attention to the desires and commands of the older people, deference to authority, a sense of mutuality. The quality of respect was founded on an individual's relations with his or her parents. I was told: "They were intransigent of respect for the father and the mother. I mean, we couldn't answer the way the kids answer today. Never could we use foul language in front of our parents. Never could we talk about sex in front of our parents. This is out of respect."[62] Rispetto meant listening to and obeying the older people in the community, and above all it meant a posture of obedience to authority as this was defined in the domus.

It also meant love, but in a very complicated way. As one of my sources put this: "Respect to them . . . love was respect to the Italian people. Their definition of love is respect. When you respect somebody you love them, you don't want to hurt them, you'd think twice before you'd do something to hurt them."[63] Rispetto was clearly a deeply ambivalent term. It meant love, as all my informants insisted, but it was always clear that fear was an intimate part of the love expressed by the respectful. It was a love that acknowledged certain inescapable realities of power; it was also a love, as is suggested in the last quote above, by which the lover refrained from doing the harm that the entire community believed could be done by individuals so intimately related. A rather brutal sense of the possibilities of interpersonal relationships and impersonal forces underlies the meaning of rispetto.

Rispetto is a dark and complex concept, then. All of my sources acknowledged this—usually right in the middle of celebrating the centrality of rispetto in Italian American life. One woman added this to the definition of rispetto as obedience: "I think some of it was fear too; that's the way I feel. Fear of parents. I was afraid of my mother. I mean, this was it. She was boss. There were no two ways about it."[64] Another person made this important connection: "We had the fear of God in us and we had the fear of our parents, because our parents demanded respect and demanded obedience and we gave it to them."[65] He went on to say that rispetto also meant love, but that if parents could not get this love from their children, they would resort to fear to secure respect. This man would not separate respect from fear; he finally offered this as a conclusion of his understanding of the meaning of the word, "It's fear-respect, respect-fear."

Because it was in large part a way of dealing with power and with the irrational possibilities of the world's working (and the working of the domus), rispetto also functioned as a means of subversion. It was a public posture, a face Italian Americans assumed in the streets and in the domus that was useful in placating the necessary powers. But the wearer of the mask might have been intending something quite different from what his public behavior suggested. As one of my sources suggested, right after he had been discussing the severe and serious meaning of rispetto in Italian Harlem: "And, in a roundabout way, you got your own way, but you made them believe that you went along. Because—they weren't authorities on everything."[66]

Nevertheless, it remained the expected public posture of Italians in Harlem right through its history. Families demanded rispetto of each other: if there was a crisis or a death in a family, or a celebration like baptism or marriage, or even if two families simply met for some occasion, great care was taken to maintain the canons of rispetto. Men and women in Italian Harlem were careful to demonstrate rispetto to their families in Italy. Hard work was seen as an expression of rispetto—to the family, of course, but here especially a deeper meaning was also involved: hard work was human destiny, inevitable and therefore to be respected. It was the public quality expected of community leaders such as Marcantonio or the Farenga brothers, who ran Italian Harlem's most prestigious funeral parlor. Covello, when he wanted to evoke a deep response from the community, presented it to itself as a community of respect, a self-presentation seconded by one of my sources: "All of it [life in Italian Harlem] added up to one word: respect. That's the one word that was there in East Harlem: respect."[67] Rispetto was the public acknowledgment of the world as it was, of power and of those relationships which the culture defined as central and authoritative.[68]

The verdict of *vergogna* (shame) was pronounced by the community when the canons of rispetto had been violated. The denunciation of a person or action as shameful was one of the ways the community policed its borders. A family might be shamed if the proper hierarchy of the domus was not maintained: for example, if a younger brother was either allowed or was compelled to usurp his older brother's pre-eminence in the home.[69] It was considered shameful for children to relate to their parents with too great a familiarity.[70] In this case, the necessary distance demanded by rispetto, the appropriate posture of fear and love, would publicly appear to be missing in a family's relations. An immigrant woman explained the meaning of vergogna to Covello by contrasting the stability and devotion to hard work of the domus in Italy with American customs: "That's where you really worked. There was no playing. In America it's all play and I see young men [*cazzoni*] who should be married and have families of their own playing ball in the streets—*che vergogna!* Games are the invention of the devil! Even children did their share when they were five years old, watching the little lambs."[71] These young men were not behaving according to the appropriate standards for the maintenance and continuity of the domus, and they were flaunting their disregard in public. This woman called attention to this risk and explicit challenge to the authority of the domus by pronouncing the verdict of vergogna.

American laws were deemed good or bad by members of the community according to whether or not they maintained the authority of the domus.[72] Relations between the sexes and between the races in Italian Harlem were governed or explained by reference to the domus. A favorite explanation, for example, of hostilities between blacks and Puerto Ricans on the one hand, and Italian Americans on the other, was that the two former groups did not respect their families, a well-used rationalization for a reality that, as we have already seen, was economic and social in origin.[73] On the other hand, there is some evidence that Italians and Jews got along better than Italians and Puerto Ricans because, according to the Italians, Jews were also a domus-centered people. One of Lapolla's characters, for example, condemns an Italian immigrant's efforts to seduce a young Jewish woman of the neighborhood by observing of the woman: "Such a good family she comes from, so hard working, they mind their own business. For shame on the man."[74] These are the values prized in the domus-centered society, and they were to be respected when they were met in another community.

Italian political motivations, perceptions, and loyalties also originated in the domus. The campaigns that generated the most intense
local support were those for better housing—campaigns in defense of
the domus. The standards and values of the domus could impel people
into a larger quest for social justice. One young Italian American activ-
ist described the roots of his social vision in the moral education of the
domus: "The family ties have been a dynamic force which has made
me strive for greater goals and fused with that characteristic a sympathetic understanding and humanness towards my fellowman."[75]
Popular utopian thought imagined and longed for a world of peace for
the domus, peace in which men and women could fulfill completely
the requirements of the domus. One of my informants, an older woman, expressed this as a longing for "peace and onions."[76] The good life
meant the condition in which the domus could function well and happily: the family, old and young, gathered around the fireplace after a
day of work, the older people on chairs, the children on mats on the
floor, talking over the events of the day in the cool evening. This is as
fine a prelude as any to political action.[77]

For much of its history, Italian Harlem supported radically progressive congressmen: first Fiorello LaGuardia and then his protégé,
Vito Marcantonio. Both men were known for their progressive social
legislation—for their struggle for better housing, full employment,
safer working conditions. Political pundits assumed that these men
were elected because they ran good machines or because they were
effective at doing favors for the people in the community. They did
both of these things, but this rather cynical view of the democratic
process posits an electorate without values. We are now in a position
to see that these leaders themselves reflected, in their social programs,
the values of the domus. Marcantonio came to LaGuardia's attention,
for example, when he was a student of Covello's at DeWitt Clinton
High School. The young man gave an address on the need for social
welfare programs, an advocacy that won him LaGuardia's notice and
a real popularity in the community.[78] Marcantonio and LaGuardia
both were especially adept at expressing rispetto for the domus: the
people who lived in Italian Harlem remember these politicians for
their efforts on behalf of the working class and the poor, but also for
their availability to deal with problems that arose in the domus and
their willingness to enter the domus to eat and talk.[79]

The priorities of the domus also shaped—or were expected to

*Mayor LaGuardia defending the domus in a speech delivered at the site of the East River Houses*

shape—personal choices concerning the way an individual organized his or her life. Family members were expected to live near each other in the same neighborhood, even in the same apartment building.[80] If a young man or woman after marriage decided to leave Italian Harlem for the Bronx in the 1930s, before the general exodus, they were risking scandal and neighborhood outrage.[81] Even when it became common to leave Italian Harlem, the decision to do so could cause real pain in the domus. The norms of the domus also demanded that desires for upward mobility on the job be tempered by consideration for the stability of the domus. Covello identified as one of the principles of Italian American family life: "It is better to be happy with one's wife and children and have a small income than to be wealthy and have all kinds of trouble with the wife and children."[82] One commentator at the turn of the century noted that Italians seemed more easily contented with their lot on the job than other ethnic groups.[83]

In order to understand the dynamics of life in Italian Harlem, it is important to take a position in the middle of the debate over whether culture or economics determines the life of a community. Several scholars have suggested that the family orientation of Italian Americans led them to choose against rapid upward mobility: an Italian American worker might not accept a higher position if this meant spending less time with his family or moving out of the community.[84] Others have warned against such an exclusively cultural interpretation. Stephen Steinberg, for example, has argued that Italian mobility on the job reflected less the priorities of the family than it did the condition of the first generation, which entered the country without the skills that might have assured them a rapid climb in New York's manufacturing economy; when they acquired these skills, Steinberg demonstrates, they moved up. Along the same lines, Miriam Cohen has suggested that the decision to send Italian women out of the home to work paralleled the changing nature of employment opportunities in New York City: when homework in the garment trades was the work most readily available for women, Italian American women worked at home; but when New York began to shift toward becoming a financial center, at which point clerical positions became most abundant for women, Italian Americans had no objection either to educating their daughters to fill these jobs or to sending them out of the home to work.[85]

The interaction of culture and economics, however, is not always straightforward and rational, if "rational" means that culture will reflect economic realities. Culture does not always keep pace with economic change, and a particular community may find itself with a set of cultural norms that do not neatly legitimate (and may even condemn) their economic aspirations and possibilities or allow them to cope with economic failure. Success was publicly esteemed in Italian Harlem when it aided the task of supporting and maintaining the domus; but individuals were *publicly expected*, whether they actually did so or not, to refuse promotions that threatened the domus. The realities of economic change, in other words, had to be explained and justified to the self and to the community according to the standards of the domus-centered society. Occasionally, individuals did relinquish occupational success because they would not (or could not) violate the expectations of the domus. But even those who went ahead and began their move up kept one eye on the domus as they climbed.

The way domus expectations and values worked in an individual's life is most clearly seen in the matter of marriage. Until late in the history of Italian Harlem, marriage was viewed as a relationship between two domuses. When a young man or woman brought a girlfriend or boyfriend into the domus, this was almost enough to constitute an announcement of engagement: the members of the domus did not welcome mere dates, as *americani* understood this relationship, into the home.[86] All members of the domus then took great care to ascertain the suitability of the prospective spouse: aunts, uncles, cousins, and comari were all responsible for getting as much information as they could on the young man or woman.[87] After the couple was married, husband and wife were expected to live as close as possible to the woman's former domus. One man, not a resident of Italian Harlem, explained to Covello how he had arranged for his children's postnuptial proximity: "But they somehow stick to our neighborhood. My married children live close to us. I even built some years ago an eight family apartment house so that there would be no need for them to live elsewhere."[88] A couple that failed to conform to this requirement risked causing a real scandal in the community and bringing shame on the name of the domus. One woman told this story to Covello:

> A cousin of mine was the oldest of a family of five—two boys and three girls. He married and set up a separate household in the Bronx, much to the consternation particularly of the mother who

wanted her son to take over the direction of the family. The father was getting old and there were younger children in the family. The relatives and *paesani* were also much concerned. Gossip was rife. The comment was: [from here on, the woman spoke Italian] They left them without spending even a night under the roof of the family. He gave a nice gift to his mother who gave him her blood. They'll cry too someday when they have children. If there's a God, he'll be the one to punish them. They're really bold-faced and arrogant. It's the air of this damn country.

Marriage was meant to strengthen the domus, not shatter it.[89]

Great care was taken to maintain the domus as the strong and visible center of life in Italian Harlem. Family gatherings—convocations of all the members of the domus—were frequent, and attendance was a serious requirement.[90] The members of the domus got together for religious holy days, secular holidays, weddings, baptisms, and funerals, and all these events were given a meaning with reference to the domus. One of Covello's sources explained, discussing family gatherings, that at such events all four generations of his domus "were tied up and kept together." At celebrations of the domus, the members affirm that "they are Italian; they live in the Italian manner, and they will die and be buried in the Italian manner."[91] Members of the domus also patronized each other's businesses, even if this meant long trips out of their way.[92] Children were given the names of older members of the domus in a carefully defined sequence: usually the names would be drawn from their grandparents and aunts and uncles.[93]

The invisible cables of rispetto which bound the members of a domus together and which bound one domus to another in Italian Harlem were revealed, celebrated, sanctified, and maintained on the sacral occasions of weddings, baptisms, and funerals. These events, clearly important in the life of the domus, were the central public events, along with the religious feste, of Italian Harlem. On these occasions, men and women who ordinarily kept away from church entered it willingly on behalf of the domus. Ecclesiastical institutions and personnel were valued when they served to sanctify the domus; otherwise, they held no intrinsic interest for the people.[94] On these public, sacred occasions, a domus revealed its quality and the success of its efforts to integrate all its members into itself; and its members expected signs and gestures of respect from members of other domuses. These were moments when Italian Harlem revealed itself and its inner workings and expectations to itself.

Funerals were particularly important and threatening occasions.[95] Death had different meanings at different times in the history of Italian Harlem. In the earliest period, when Italian Harlem was a society of people in transition a great distance from their place of birth, death suggested the finality of their decision to emigrate and occasioned painful reflection on whether it had been a good decision or not. The distance that all felt from their domuses in Italy was cast into sharp relief by the burial of one of their community in American soil.[96] Later, as the older generations passed, death raised the possibility that the values they had represented and maintained would not survive them. So the community needed to reassure itself of its strength in times of mourning—in particular of the strength and depth of the values of the domus; the men and women at the funeral needed to see that the domus would survive.

"Death in a family far surpasses all other social events in importance," according to one of Covello's sources in 1940.[97] Rispetto was expected from members of the domus of the deceased and from all the domuses which had some connection with him or her. One young man noted in 1934 that if he skipped the funeral of a relative, no matter how distantly related, "I would be ostracized and actually hated by all East Harlem residents who know me."[98] If a family for some reason wanted to express bitter rejection of another domus, according to Italian Harlem's leading funeral director, it would not send anyone to a funeral.[99] People were expected to contribute to the expenses of the funeral in amounts relative to their intimacy with the deceased, a custom that allowed for the expression of the priority of relations among family members and between the domus of the deceased and the other domuses of the community. Death provided a moment of exceptional clarity in social relations, illuminating the private hierarchies and structures of loyalty and commitment in the community.

There were many moments during a funeral for the clarification and definition of social relationships. Friends of the family were expected to come and prepare food during the wake and after the trip to the cemetery. Throughout the days of the wake and then at the side of the open grave, women keened the good (and sometimes bad) qualities of the deceased, creating a public biography of the good life for all to hear and learn.[100] After the funeral, the members and friends of the domus gathered for a huge meal in the home of the deceased. People ate heartily, according to a young commentator on Italian ways in

Harlem.[101] It was in this moment, of course, that members of the community could convince themselves, in the domus of the deceased, that the community and its values would indeed survive: how better to attest to this than to eat Italian food prepared by loyal friends of the domus?

We must now make our understanding of the relationship between the domus and the world outside it a little more complex. We have seen that the values and standards of the domus could be and often had to be extended to include parts of the outside society. It must also be said, however, that the domus could be quite exclusive and self-contained, and that domus-centered values could lead to strange moral perceptions outside the domus. The error of earlier students of this question has been their preoccupation solely with the exclusivity of the domus. But the reality cannot be simplified to an either/or dichotomy: the dynamics and tension of Italian American popular ethics is precisely the conflict between the extension and the exclusivity of the domus.

Members of the domus frequently tried to surround it with a dense screen of privacy, refusing to allow any public expression of its inner life.[102] One student of life in Italian Harlem observed, "Family life . . . was . . . a kind of sanctuary, wherein were allowed only officiating members and strangers constantly kept at a distance from its walls."[103] Friends of younger members of the domus were often sharply excluded from its life. American-born generations had to wage battles simply to convince their parents that it was good to have a friend: Their elders could not understand why the domus was not society enough for their children. Loyalty to the domus could result in a perception of everyone else as "strangers," worthy of no consideration or attention.[104] The values of the domus were used to legitimate, and may even have been partially responsible for, the intense rivalry and hostility between Italians and blacks and Puerto Ricans in East Harlem.

Loyalty to the domus could at times take on a real ferocity. One man told me, in an ominous tone of voice, that Italians in Harlem were peaceful and quiet people who preferred to keep to themselves—until their families were "crossed"; then they would stop at nothing to defend themselves.[105] If this ferocity was internalized it could become a deep rage against the world outside the domus, a rage fired by the constant suspicion that the domus was threatened. The priority of the domus was also not always an infallible guide to social and moral decisions. The domus could eliminate the importance of any other social group, such as the nation or the city or even the community.[106] Covello frequently had to confront families that had lied to truant officers to keep their children out of school, deeming their salaries more of a contribution to the life of the domus than their education.[107] A double standard could prevail in the community: Italians were to be treated one way and everyone else could be treated in any way they would endure. As one young man put this: "I feel myself free to use my hands when in company with non-Italian girls. When it comes to Italian girls, I am somehow subdued."[108]

The difficulties and complexities of extending the priorities and values of the domus outward are clearly revealed in the prevalent myth of the Mafia in Italian Harlem. For many Italians who grew up in East Harlem, gangsters are romantic figures, characters like those in southern Italian legends and folktales. They are said to have helped keep the community safe, looked after poor people, and watched over the women of the community. They made sure that people coming home from work late at night were safe in the streets, according to the legend. They insured that the strict canons of rispetto were observed in the streets. The racketeers are especially remembered for protecting the sisters and daughters of the men in Italian Harlem: they walked the women home and made sure that no rude comments were made as they went about their chores in East Harlem. A popular tale about the Mafia in Italian Harlem concerns the recovery of the Madonna's crown after it had been stolen by thieves "who were not Italian—they were Irish or Jewish, something like that." As the story is told, after the jewels were stolen sometime in the mid-1930s, word went out on the streets that the mob would not tolerate this disrespect for the Madonna and wanted the jewels back. The jewels were recovered, I was told triumphantly, in two weeks.[109]

The racketeers, in the community's mythical restatement of their identity, were the enforcers of the values of the domus. The gangsters were familiar, and the people believed that these tough men also belonged to the domus-centered society. One of my informants denied that anyone had ever feared the gangsters because, "You knew [their] mothers, you knew their fathers."[110] Another source pointed out, "You were brought up with these fellows."[111] The racketeers came from the domus-centered society and protected its codes.

Of course, no one talked about what these men might have done outside the community: according to the narrowest interpretation of domus morality, they were good because they "wouldn't touch anybody in the neighborhood."[112] The gangsters were not judged or criticized, indeed they were idolized, because they were members and protectors of the domus—the rest of their behavior was irrelevant. This refusal to see the criminal activities of the racketeers in a broader perspective emphasizes how the domus fixation could profoundly isolate the community: all that really mattered here was what took place inside the domus or in the community into which the domus had been extended. A different code of values obtained outside the domus-centered community; the absolute priority of the domus, narrowly conceived, could lead Italian Americans to respect what was disrespected by the rest of society and to disrespect what was valued—an inversion that could transform criminals into heroes as well as it could conduce to progressive political action on behalf of poor families. Frank Costello and Fiorello LaGuardia came out of the same world of the domus.

The myth of the Mafia further illustrates the isolation that Italian Americans could accept as their lot in the larger society. One man, discussing the community's respect for racketeers, revealed the way the myth enclosed the community: "The law's going to disagree with you on this. But the law didn't live there—we lived there."[113] The members of the domus-centered society were on their own. The surrounding society could not only not understand this code but might even, in its disrespect and misunderstanding, seek to subvert it. The man's comment on the law illustrates the adversarial spirit often assumed by Italian Americans in defense of the domus in American society. The image of the domus surrounded by armed enforcers, men who were willing to put their considerable cruelty at the service of the domus, is a frightening image of one possibility of domus-centrality.

The shrine of the domus-centered society, its central sacred space, was the home. This is the place Italian Americans speak of with real reverence. They tended their homes carefully and took deep pride in the cleanliness and beauty of them. The men and women of Italian Harlem continually called attention to the fact that, no matter how extreme their poverty and regardless of how squalid the tenement house they lived in, the insides of their homes were always clean, a perception echoed by outside observers of the community.[114] The people of Italian Harlem surrounded their homes with gardens of flowers and vegetables, planting whatever tiny strip of soil was available in alleyways and courtyards. They grew tomatoes and grapes in the mean soil of Manhattan, so that the smells of autumn there along the East River, next to sewers and factories, included the sharp smell of tomato sauce being readied for canning and the sweet smell of grape pulp fermenting.[115] The neighborhood children did a thriving business collecting and selling horse manure for all this agricultural activity in northern Manhattan.

People were expected to behave respectfully and somewhat formally in the home. Swearing was strictly forbidden, a taboo that was rigorously enforced.[116] Southern Italian parents could be quite stern and formal with their children. Modesty and decorousness were expected at all times. One of my informants recalled that he had never seen his parents any way but completely dressed, which he contrasted with his own habit of walking about his home in his shorts.[117] Parents demanded postures of deference from their children.[118] This formality and deference were in particular evidence during the Sunday meal, a central occasion in the domus and one that no one was allowed to miss. The central figure of authority at this ceremony was "the father," as fathers are always called by the people of Italian Harlem. Covello collected an account of a Sunday dinner in which "the father" sat at the head of the table, his wife at his right hand, the children ranged about them, silent and expectant.[119] The father served food and conversation was kept to a minimum. The kitchen, the theater in which this value-enforcing drama occurred, was the most important room of Italian Harlem.[120] At these weekly rituals, which defined the public hierarchy of the domus in the sacred space of the home, the people of the domus gathered to eat only traditional foods, prepared by women in ways that were unique to every family but also generations old; this was the sacrament of the domus, a corporate act of communal self-definition, bonding, celebration, and maintenance.

The sacredness of the domus was emphasized by the profusion of sacred objects and figures with which it was filled, although by now we can understand that the home was not sacred because these figures were there, but, rather, these figures were there because the home was sacred. Shrines to favorite saints and to the Madonna were set up in the bedrooms of Italian Harlem; candles, statues, holy cards filled the homes, and lighting the candles before the saints was an important ritual of the domus.[121] The saints constituted a chorus in the home, a sacred parallel to the chorus of neighbors and friends in the streets, watching over the behavior of the members of the domus and ensuring the proper codes of conduct. The shrines and sacred figures linked the domus to the divine: the candles burning in the domus recalled those burning in the church of Mount Carmel, for example, establishing a connection between the two.

Important religious holy days, finally, were celebrated as events of the domus. On these occasions and during the street feste, a fluid interrelationship and a real intimacy were initiated between the domus and the church: church and domus merged in the celebration. But the members of the domus could also sponsor private religious feste outside their domus, which had nothing to do with the local churches, reminding us that what was sacred, even in the more traditional religious celebrations like Easter, was the day's meaning in the domus.[122]

The sacred never exists without a demonic counterpart, however. The domus could become voracious in its demands, cruel in its insistence on its own primacy. When this happened, as it always did, the men and women of Italian Harlem reacted with bitterness, confusion, and pain. Their rage was often turned inward, because it was too threatening to turn these emotions against the domus. It is to this idolatry of the domus and the pain it could evoke, to the inner complexities and confusions of the domus-centered society, that we must now turn.

## CHAPTER V

# Conflicts in the Domus

A LOUD and unceasing lament rose from the streets and apartments of Italian Harlem throughout its history warning that the domus was in danger in American society. Although there was little evident reason for this dirge, since the domus remained the essential focus and source of the culture of Italian Harlem, still it persisted. The intensity of these expressions of fear and threat seems to have been in inverse proportion to the success of the maintenance of the domus in the community. One man, an immigrant from Sicily who had been in East Harlem for about fifty years, told Covello that in the United States, Italian "children run wild and are not taught to have any respect for their parents." They are allowed to "play in the streets and make friends." Italian American women "no longer tend to their household duties but run here and there all day long and at night too." They can "get away with" being seen in public with men other than their husbands, while they neglect their homes and undermine the authority of their husbands. A grandmother in Italian Harlem complained, "In this country it is the young who rule. Older people don't count for anything." Another person wondered, "What good are the laws of this country if a child is given liberty to talk back to his parents?" Many of the immigrants were haunted by the fear that their entire social order would collapse in the new world; their fears led them to suspect that the very air and water of the United States were weakening the domus.[1]

Immigration, even when motivated by the desire to make money in order to strengthen and preserve the family, was a traumatic experience. These persistent apprehensions of subversion and decline may have been the consequences of that trauma. In Italian Harlem, this lamentation was the background against which conflicts in the domus were experienced. Efforts to maintain the domus in all its authoritarian purity at the center of the culture were driven by this dread of its imminent collapse. But the domus did not collapse, nor did it ever seem close to doing so in the history of Italian Harlem; so we must consider whether the persistent sense of its fragility was not the expression of deep conflict within and ambivalence toward the domus itself. Perhaps the fear that it *might* lose its power was the articulation of a subliminal hope that it *would*.

The domus in Italian Harlem was the scene of bitter conflict and profound struggle. Its stability and the popular (and scholarly) celebrations of its place and importance in the culture of Italian America have masked its dark side. Rage and rebellion, rivalry and resignation frequently characterized the relations between the individual and the domus within the context of the continuity of the latter. The source of conflict were many, and they changed as the historical circumstances of the community changed. One source was the subtle but real alienation that existed between the Italian-born generations and their Italian American children, a conflict that was always exacerbated by the extreme demands for conformity and submission within the domus. Other conflicts arose out of the nature of the structure of the domus itself. Individuals felt suffocated by the unrelenting demands for intimacy and self-sacrifice made by its members. Intense rivalries for power raged in the hierarchically ordered domus, rivalries paralleled by equally intense competitions for affection and devotion. The carefully monitored sexual lives of young men and women in the community were fraught with tensions and confusions.

All of this occurred in the wings of the closely watched public theater of the domus. Individuals were under enormous pressure not to reveal their anger against the demands and constraints of the domus; such indiscretion would signal to the community the failure of their domus to educate its members, as well as their own private failure to be good human beings. So the people of Italian Harlem had to find other outlets for their rage, other ways of expressing their confusion and of living with the complete power of the domus.

## CONFLICT

The immigrants who came to Harlem from southern Italy in the last years of the nineteenth and the first years of the twentieth centuries and their American-born children inhabited different worlds. At times the worlds collided, resulting in conflict and hostility, but mainly the generations seemed to exist in subtle and quiet alienation from each other. The immigrants wanted their children to remain faithful to their customs and perceptions and often did not realize that these were not completely relevant in the new world. One Sicilian immigrant, for example, wanted her daughter, a well-educated young schoolteacher, to marry a barber, whom the older woman considered, according to Sicilian standards, a professional. Her daughter's exasperated comment on this incongruity of perception was, "There is nothing strange to her if a teacher, meaning myself, marries a barber."[2] This situation is indicative of the distance and subtle misperceptions that set in between the generations.

The men and women of the first generation kept up a relentless, demanding pressure on their children. They continually accused them of abandoning the traditions and values of the domus. One immigrant told Covello:

> I was born in Lucania [Basilicata] in a small town called Spinosa—some of its traditions are beautiful, and it gripes me when I have to listen to unappreciative misunderstanding young people who could never in a million years live up to such fine customs and home life that is carried on in these little towns hidden up in mountains or down in the valleys.[3]

The clear implication here is that there is almost nothing the younger generation, not privileged to have been born in Italy, can do to meet these high standards. "Good children," according to a young man in Italian Harlem, were defined by the immigrants as children faithful to their parents' traditions.[4] But many parents wondered whether their children could be so faithful. One worried immigrant told Covello that although his children tried to please him and his wife "by doing some things in the Italian manner," still he was afraid that they were "thoroughly American, for good or bad."[5] These worries were echoed and amplified throughout the 1930s by "Donna Lydia," the writer of a popular personal-advice column in *Il Progresso Italo-Americano*.

Donna Lydia expressed only unrelieved scorn for "the American way."[6]

Community leaders and outside observers frequently called attention to the distance between the first and second generations. Covello devoted much of his professional life, first at DeWitt Clinton High School and then at Benjamin Franklin, to constructing bridges between the immigrants and their children. Edward Corsi, who did the same at Haarlem House, was afraid that the differences in perception between the two generations were irreconcilable.[7] Dorothy Reed, a researcher for the Boys' Club, noted a lack of trust and confidence between generations.[8]

Often enough, however, the worlds collided, and then there was open friction between the generations in Italian Harlem. Friendship was a troubled area: the immigrants wanted their children to choose their companions from among the members of the domus and often resented the "strangers" their children socialized with. One young women, born in East Harlem, complained to Covello:

> My husband and I always craved the inspiration, satisfaction and fun that can be derived from sincere friendship. Before our marriage, we were forced to meet our friends and acquaintances outside of our respective homes, because we knew that if we did arrange small gatherings at home, we would always be under the direct supervision of our elders; instead of understanding and cooperation, destructive criticism and ridicule would be our lot.[9]

The immigrants were afraid that close loyalties outside the domus would threaten its integrity and stability. They also found it more pleasant to socialize with their family and paesani and could not understand why this did not also satisfy their children. The young people of the community were frequently challenged by their parents to choose between the domus and their friends.[10]

Conflicts also erupted when the American-born wanted to do the things they believed other American adolescents did. Sports became a symbolic focus of the conflicting perceptions of the generations. The young people of Italian Harlem were intensely interested in sports, in particular basketball, baseball, and boxing.[11] The immigrants thought such games were a pernicious waste of time that distracted young men from their primary responsibility, the maintenance of the domus. An Italian-born mother told a New York juvenile court judge: "Nick [her son] no wanta work. He big man, 14 and wanta play ball all day. Father say, 'you go today and work in restaurant with your un-cle'—He makes faces, cusses, laughs and runs out to play ball. . . . He get up at noon and go out to play. I go out to the ballgame and say, 'Nick, come home from these bad boys and work.' "[12] Nick's side of the story was somewhat different. He complained that his parents "fight me and hate me" simply because he wanted to spend part of his day with his friends on a baseball diamond.

The immigrants and their children clashed over many seemingly trivial issues; the picture that emerges is one of persistent misunder-standing and bickering within the domus. In one family, a young man's parents made fond plans to send him to Italy to find a wife while at the same time he was secretly dating seriously a non-Italian. A young woman every week proudly handed her parents what she called her "salary," but only after she had quietly set aside half of it. Young women wondered how they were going to explain their newly bobbed hair to their parents, who believed that only "bums would do such a thing." Children were scolded for playing with non-Italians, for play-ing in the street, for staying out late. Immigrant parents were not always sure they saw the point of working hard in school, since that might not necessarily result in the security of the domus. Often the two generations did not even speak the same language to each other: the immigrants might speak to their children in dialect and be answered in English, because their offspring could understand but not speak the tongue of the paese. As one young woman confided to Covello in the late 1930s, immigrants and their children seemed not to respect each other's values.[13]

From the perspective of the young men and women born in Amer-ica, all of this confirmed their sense that they and their parents inhab-ited different worlds. The young people saw themselves as American: on one level, perhaps not the deepest, their sense of prestige, the way they wanted to look and talk, their goals, were shaped by what they saw and heard in the streets, in the movies, and in school. A young man summed up the difference between himself and his parents for Covello with the observation, "I was born in America."[14] Covello himself, who was born in Italy but raised in East Harlem, recalled of his own youth, "I removed myself emotionally, intellectually, socially and almost physically from my family and what my family stood for."[15]

Covello was not alone in this quest for distance: in a variety of ways, the young people of Italian Harlem called attention to the difference between themselves and their parents. Sometimes they made harsh and unflattering public comparisons between Italian and American culture. They publicly resisted the imposition of Italian standards on their behavior.[16] They tried to build a wall between the world of Italian Harlem and their outside worlds. One young man sat in the dining room of one of his American friends anxiously wondering whether this meant he would have to reciprocate by inviting his friend into Italian Harlem, a prospect he dreaded.[17] Reflecting on the failure of a father-son dinner he had organized while he was teaching at Clinton, Covello concluded that the Italian American boys, although they wanted to be friendly with their fathers, were ashamed to be seen with them outside of Italian Harlem.[18]

Of course, this effort to keep the worlds apart was never completely successful. Again, Covello's experience is indicative: although he tried to keep the American world of school and and world of Italian Harlem as far apart as possible, still he always realized that for him (and for all those shaped by the domus-centered society) "the real world was Italian Harlem."[19] Austin Works, chairman of the English department at Franklin in the 1930s and a well-informed observer of Italian Harlem, noted that young Italian American men seemed confused, caught between the conflicting values of the home and the streets.[20] A young woman from the community studying education at New York University told Covello that she felt American in school and Italian in Harlem, a conflict she could not reconcile.[21]

At the same time, the two generations were deeply dependent on each other. For most of the history of Italian Harlem they were economically interdependent. The first generation relied on the second to translate American culture for them: it was widely recognized among medical professionals in Italian Harlem, for example, that the first generation would not appear at a clinic until the second generation had approved the facility.[22] But the deepest bond between the generations was their shared life in the domus: the younger generations had been well-assimilated into the culture of the domus and had internalized its perspectives and values. The struggle between generations, therefore, was a most intimate one, not easily avoided by rebellion or departure. It took place within the well-maintained confines of the domus, as well as deep within the individual consciences and psyches of the second generation; however tempted they may have been by American styles and values, they would eventually have to answer to their own domus sensibilities. This is what made the struggle so explosive, but also so subtle.

The second major source of conflict at the foundations of Italian Harlem was the structure of the domus itself. The life of the domus was lived very closely and with an intense inward preoccupation: its members insisted on living close together, visiting each other frequently, and socializing with other members of the domus. Individuals had no privacy, which reflected in part the economic realities of Italian Harlem, but also the priority of the domus, which interpreted privacy as hostility and rejection. In the cramped and crowded apartments of Italian Harlem and within the equally cramped boundaries of the domus, the lives of men and women could become quite claustrophobic.[23]

The claims of authority in the domus were strict, hierarchical, and total, and elders demanded submission and complete obedience. Covello listed as one of the principles of southern Italian family life, "Parents have a right to feel that they own their children."[24] He also noted that punishment and reproof could be "severe and harsh . . . measured in strong language and blows."[25] Parents in Italian Harlem were strict with their children, a severity that was motivated in part by their fears of the bad and ubiquitous influence of local street life. A young woman painted this picture of parental severity:

> The Italian parents consider it a most serious duty to bring up their children properly. They must know who their companions are. Are they Americans or are they Italians? Have they been brought up in the Italian manner? If not, immediately the child is forbidden to associate with them under the threat of severe punishment. The child must tell the parents where he is going, besides telling them with whom he is associating. If this does not meet with the parents' approval, the child cannot go. Then if the child is allowed to go out, woe betide him if he comes home at a late hour.

She recalled that one evening she came home fifteen minutes late from a friend's house, two buildings away from hers. For this infraction, she was punished severely because "any number of minutes after [the specified time] was deliberate disobedience and terribly wrong."[26] Often younger children were not allowed outside of the house to play. One young man recalled: "My first playmates were my sisters. I was always wondering why I couldn't go outside with other children. One day my mother forgot to close the door. At last I had a chance to go outside and play with the other children."[27] But such absent-mindedness regarding the door of the domus was rare. Punishment of children, though almost never brutal, was often public, a humiliating encounter with the authority of the domus in the important public theater of the streets.[28]

Insistence on complete submission to the authority of the domus intensified as the children became old enough to threaten the domus seriously by making their own choices concerning how they were going to live their lives and whom they were going to marry. At important moments in the life of the individual, which of course were also very important moments for the continuity and security of the domus, the members of the domus crowded close, anxious to maintain the integrity of the domus and frequently unconcerned for the wishes of the individual. One young man was forced to capitulate to his family's insistent demands that he surrender his new job, which would have required him to live away from home, even though he had hoped that by taking this particular position he would "learn to be a 'man,' learn to take care of myself."[29] A young woman was compelled to wage a protracted and bitter struggle, in the days before her wedding, against her Sicilian parents' insistence that she supply the mattress for her new home, a custom that angered and embarrassed her.[30] And the price of resistance could be very high indeed. This young woman's parents refused to attend her wedding. One man told Covello that his wife would not welcome their son into their home because he had defied her and married a Polish woman. "My wife does not want to hear about the child. If he had married an Italian girl, we would have at least no doubts as to the child's father. But by marrying a Polish girl, we are not even sure whether this is our grandchild."[31] Another woman refused to enter her son's home because he had married a Scottish woman.[32] The refusal to offer or to accept hospitality, particularly from one's blood kin, was a very serious punishment in the domus-centered society. These parents believed that their children had behaved like Turks and so did not deserve to be treated like Christians.

Although the younger people knew the standards of the domus-centered society, still, such hard punishment hurt them. One young woman ended an interview with Covello on the subject of relations between parents and children:

Oh, if only our Italian parents were a little more loving and much less dutiful! I know of many Italian boys and girls who have never known the touch of a loving arm around them or a sweet voice that would give real advice and solace. What the child hears instead is a series of commands and orders as if taken from a long-ago written manual of child duties.[33]

Although this picture is perhaps too harshly drawn and needs to be balanced by the equally fervent appreciation often expressed by the young people for the closeness and joy of their family lives, still the same sentiment was echoed by this young woman's peers: the structure of the domus was too inflexible, too unrelenting in its demands. Covello noted of himself and his students at Clinton that they longed to be "pals" with their fathers, a desire all knew to be a little ridiculous. But they also chafed at and rebelled against the authoritarianism of the domus and resented their parents. A student ended a family history he had prepared for Covello with an angry coda: "On the whole, peace has come to the Bruno family. But it is a peace that came only after many years of arguments, beatings, wailings and disagreements. Though there is peace—the parents still think they were absolutely right in whatever they did."[34]

Times of dating and courting were fraught with special anxieties and tensions for the young people and their families. The residents of Italian Harlem were discomfited by the subject of sex, and sexual discussion was not encouraged in the domus. The immigrants had very strong and well-established notions regarding behavior between the sexes. They expected formality and distance between young men and women until they were engaged. They wanted their children to marry members of the domus-centered society, and they expected to be the primary and final authority in choosing a spouse for their son or daughter. So they carefully watched and unhesitatingly participated in their children's courting.[35]

The community assisted the domus in policing the sexual activities of the young people of Italian Harlem, adding more voices to the chorus the adolescents were expected to heed. Dating and courting, properly conducted, were the most public moments of a young person's life. The community, in the persons of comari, aunts, uncles, cousins, and friends, was the repository not only of certain essential information about the prospective spouse but was also the source of approval. Was the young woman pure? Was the young man good, ben educato, respectful of his family? Would this be a blessed union or an unfortunate one? The community presumed to have the answers to these questions. So the young couple was surrounded by the scrutinizing eyes of the extended domus. As one young man observed:

> Our Italian boys brag a lot about their indifference to the reputation of the girl they intend to marry. But the truth is, if they find out that the girl had in the past, several boyfriends, they drop their sweetheart as easy as a piece of wood. . . . If a boy's steady sweetheart permits herself even some trifle liberty with another boy, you can be sure that the fellows in the neighborhood will not omit to make it known to the girl's boyfriend.[36]

If young men and women did not proceed very carefully here, they could find themselves with damaged reputations, and they could endanger the rispetto of their domus.

As a result, there was a great deal of fear associated with dating. One standard in particular seems to have caused special agonies: a young woman was expected to marry the first man she dated. One woman told Covello: "Italian girls try to carry on their social life like American girls but can't really do it. They have boyfriends, change boyfriends, but do not dare bring anyone home because the family feels that if a girl invites a boyfriend to the house that the matter is serious."[37] A woman who dated more than one man was considered frivolous and irresponsible, if not worse; likewise, if a couple dated four or five times and did not get engaged, a procedure carried out with great formality in Italian Harlem, both the man and woman—but especially the woman—were in danger of doing permanent harm to their reputations.[38] There was no such thing as puppy love, in other words, no casual dating; these young affairs were treated very seriously. A sixteen-year-old boy had been dating a sixteen-year-old girl for a couple of months when "the detective agency," as he called his extended domus, got to work and discovered that when the girl was a child, she had gotten sick with an illness that none of the doctors in Italian Harlem could identify. His family insisted that he break off his relations with her.[39]

This enormous social pressure on dating had a number of consequences. Young men seem often to have dreaded their dates. According to a nineteen-year-old student at Franklin in the 1930s: "No, you can't do it with Italian girls. If you kiss them or even touch them, they think you want to marry them. So they tell their mama and the whole tribe is on your neck in no time. Everyone lays off Italian girls unless he invites trouble—or unless he really means to marry her."[40] The "tribe," the "detective agency": these metaphors are indicative of the tensions and anxieties young people felt dating in the domus-centered society. The pressures forced many of them to carry on their affairs clandestinely, in the parks and schoolyards of Italian Harlem and even outside the neighborhood, in places like Central Park. There was much talk of elopement among young people, and occasionally a couple would brave the wrath of their families and wed privately. The pressures also forced many boys outside of the community in search of their first girlfriends, girls they would not have to propose to after their first date.[41]

But these various solutions were not very satisfying or comforting to young people who had internalized the values of the domus. Those who chose secrecy and elopement found themselves in internal exile from the domus, outside the community's canons of respect and worth. Boys who left Italian Harlem in search of girlfriends entered an uncomfortable moral twilight zone where they had to encounter aspects of themselves otherwise successfully sublimated and controlled. One young man observed: "Our Italian boys get 'hot pants' quicker when in company with Irish, Jewish or Polish girls than with Italian girls. . . . I would not say I am afraid, but something just bangs me on the head—I think the main reason is that Italian girls don't provoke me; Irish and especially Jewish girls are just inviting me."[42] These young men had to reap the discomfort of their double standard; they found themselves uneasily wondering whether or not these Irish and Jewish girls were, after all, girls of loose morals, since they did not expect, as the young men themselves assumed girls would, to get engaged after the first date.[43]

But the internal conflicts generated by the structure and demands of the domus extended into other areas besides the sexual and involved other struggles than those between generations. Fierce rivalries raged among particular members of the domus for power and authority. The oldest brother was the dominant male in the household, actually superior to his father, although usually the latter made a public claim to superiority. One of my sources said that his oldest brother was the family's "god."[44] Covello was told by a young man who lived in Harlem: "My family consists of 10 members. Everyone is very friendly to each other. My oldest brother Anthony—now 26 years old—bossed the family until he was married. Now Freddie, my next oldest brother, who is 24 years old, bosses the family."[45] Sometimes a married woman's oldest brother would serve as the primary authority in her household until her oldest son came of age. A boy told Covello that his mother was forever pleading with him to show deference and respect to her oldest brother who, according to this young man, "at family gatherings talks the loudest and is a kind of counsellor. They all listen to him and think everything he says is smart."[46]

The source of the oldest son's authority was his especially close relationship with his mother. Mother and son often acted together as family disciplinarians. A young man told Covello that his mother always turned to her oldest son, and never to her husband, to punish the other children.[47] One of my informants, emphasizing that his brother represented all that was good and orderly in his family, told me: "He was the apple of my mother's eye. In other words, he was the main man. Whatever he said, goes."[48]

But the priority of the oldest son provoked powerful conflicts within the domus. The other sons of the household often resented and felt oppressed by his authority. Sometimes the second oldest son responded by rebelling against authority, both within the domus and in the community. For example, in one family in Italian Harlem, the oldest son had his way paid through college by his sister while at the same time his younger brother was presenting the faculty and administration at Franklin with real disciplinary problems. Characteristically, when the school asked that someone in the family come in to discuss the problem, the oldest son was sent, a further blow to his brother's pride and self-esteem. Another second son, brother of the family god already mentioned, "went his own way" and took to living in his car.[49]

Fathers and their oldest sons also frequently engaged in bitter competition for authority in the domus. Sometimes the older men withdrew. Covello was told by a young man at Franklin:

> My father leaves everything to my mother, and she relied quite a deal on Frankie, especially where it concerned our doings outside the home. When I or my sister did something bad, our mother did not squeal to our father for fear that he would beat us up too much. So she let Frankie do the beating, which was no joke. But since he was a brother, he never beat us as hard as my father would.[50]

In other cases, the older men chose to fight their sons and exert their authority over them. One father went into Covello's office to rage at the airs his oldest son was affecting. He told Covello that he was thinking seriously about throwing his son out of the house because: "This behavior on the part of the boy is breaking down my wife's health. She stays up half the night waiting for this boy to come home."[51]

One of Covello's sources, a fifteen-year-old boy whose father emigrated from Apulia, explained that most Italian fathers "are simply mad." They rage against their wives, whom they perceive as rivals for the respect of their children. The boy told Covello:

> In my family, I have no reason to side with my mother against my father because he is nice to her. But I don't think I would keep quiet if my father maltreated my mother. She is anyway the underdog, and if he tried to be more bossy than is necessary, or if he tried to beat her, I would certainly not hesitate to jump on him. I am not a child and I know what's what.

This young man also claimed that the wrath of Italian fathers was often directed against all the women in the domus, extending to their daughters as well as their wives, and that their sons, in imitation of them, also tried to tyrannize over the women, though they would do this only when the older men were around.[52] This account is a succinct expression of the nuances of relations between fathers and sons in Italian Harlem. The father is presented as ferocious, almost mythically wrathful. He lords his power over his women and encourages his sons to do the same. But the central focus of the boy's discussion is his oedipal fantasy; he imagines himself jumping on his father in defense of his mother, a fantasy followed by the enigmatic claim to knowledge of dark secrets, "I know what's what." What does he know? The implication here is that he knows something deep about his father, something that is not apparent in his father's public posture.

As these anecdotes suggest, oedipal rivalries raged right on the surface of the life of the domus. In the incidents described above, competition between father and son is total. There can only be one victor: either the father withdraws, leaving the field to his wife and her son, or he fights back and expels his rival from the domus. The angry father quoted above reveals the underlying sexual tensions in this struggle within the domus. He refers to his son's mother as "my wife," establishing his claim to the coveted woman in a sentence in which "his mother" would seem more appropriate. He goes on to express his anger at this wife's nocturnal vigils. Like a lover, she waits through the night for the return of her "main man." She is giving her nights to her son when they really belong to her husband, who is now enraged and determined to win his wife back.

The father clearly occupied a highly ambiguous position in the life of Italian Harlem. Reflecting traditional southern Italian values and perceptions, the community was a public patriarchy.[53] Its residents helped to create and present a public image of their fathers as stern authoritarian figures, demanding and frequently harsh. A non-Italian observer in the community noted that fathers wanted to appear as "blustering, loud and angry" disciplinarians.[54] A young Italian American professional women living in East Harlem provided this angry sketch of the authority and power men claimed for themselves in the domus:

> But he! oh, he can come home, eat, dress up, go out with his friends, come home at any time he pleases, in whatever condition he chooses, and mind you, nothing must be said about it. The husband wants to be accepted as the head of the house at all times. . . . I remember an incident which occurred when I was about ten years of age. . . . Mother had commanded me to visit one of our neighbors who had just come home from the hospital after a serious operation. When I got there, I found her lying in bed because she felt too weak to do otherwise. Her father happened to call at the same time. She greeted him in a casual, matter of fact way and the old man was highly insulted. She should have kissed his hand as a sign of respect for him.[55]

The men themselves, as this account indicates, made a great show of demanding formal and public rituals of respect from the members of their families. The streets in particular were a theater of male posturing and demand; children dreaded to encounter their fathers in the streets of East Harlem because they knew some sign of submission would be demanded of them.[56] A young man recalled of his youth in Italian Harlem, "At that time to be reprimanded by my father in the street was like having a knife pierced through my heart."[57] In their homes, fathers remained aloof and formal, insisting not on love but on deference and respect, imagining themselves emperors of the domus. One young woman told Covello:

> In the majority of Italian homes the father is the dominating force in the family. He is the one who says what must be done and what must not be done. The wife and children must go to him when they want permission to go somewhere. In many cases respect for the father is borne more out of fear than out of love. In order to main-

tain this reverence he goes about with a countenance of severity and because of this fails to develop the love and friendship of his offspring.[58]

A striking symbol of the self-demanded and communally maintained role of fathers in Italian Harlem is the tendency for people to refer to their father as "the father," suggesting that the individual has been absorbed by the role.

The authority of the southern Italian father was highly theatrical in nature. The man who demanded that his daughter kiss his hand, for example, did so in the presence of a visitor; fathers who insisted on displays of submission in the streets were acting out their assigned and expected role before the eyes of the entire and understanding community. Often there was a melodramatic quality to this paternal posturing, as though the men were trying to make themselves grander and more fearsome than they knew themselves to be. The reason for this public extravagance becomes clear when we consider other recollections and presentations of fathers which invariably accompany the insistence on their authority and power. Men and women do not seem to talk about or remember their individual fathers—as opposed to "the father"—with any precision or detail. One of my sources, who spent about half of a four-hour conversation talking about his mother, could offer only the vaguest memories of his father, whom he presented as both gentle and distant and harsh and demanding.[59] The same fathers portrayed as stern and powerful are depicted as silent in the domus, distant, uninvolved.[60] As we have seen, some even believed that fathers were not really members of the domus because they did not share in the blood-bond between mother and children. Despite public protestations to the contrary, fathers seem indistinct figures in the domuses of Italian Harlem, although the same men might have great authority as oldest brothers or sons.

There was a great deal of resistance to the imperious claims of fathers in Italian Harlem. Sometimes this took the form of a subtle, corrosive mockery of paternal posturing. One man, whose family was from Apulia, gave Covello a sardonic picture of the family's evening meal. He noted that his father distributed food to his silent children (who were in fact repressing giggles) "in a manner a ruler would dispense his favors or wrath over his subjects." He kept the best portions for himself and gave the next best to his sons. Then the family ate in silence, an "unpleasant ordeal" for the children. But at last, when the meal was over, "the acting was unnecessary; the father went out into the street and suddenly behaved as his real self."[61] Often resistance could be more direct. Children found ways of subverting or ignoring paternal commands. In one family, a man's daughters spoke Yiddish in front of him to make plans that violated his wishes.[62] Sometimes children called on their mother to overrule their father, although usually this was never done so directly as to violate the public authority of the male. One man complained that his wife and children had formed a quiet alliance against him.[63] The conflicted position of fathers in Italian Harlem contributed to the complexity of struggles within the domus. Publicly, fathers claimed the status of domestic emperors and lords of the streets; privately, they and their children knew that real authority and power in the domus resided elsewhere. One of my informants insisted most strenuously on the preeminent authority of "the father" in Italian Harlem (though characteristically he spoke very vaguely of his own father), but when I asked what role his mother played in the life of the domus, he replied, with no awareness of contradiction, "Oh, she was the boss."[64] Perhaps this is what the young man quoted earlier was referring to when he claimed to know "what's what" in the domus.

All of these conflicts—and others not considered here, such as the competition between husbands and their oldest brothers-in-law—took place within the rigidly guarded and maintained communal boundaries of propriety and appropriateness. A great deal of energy and anxiety was devoted to the delicate task of maintaining the reputation of the domus in the community. But the obsession with reputation worked as seriously within the domus as without. Members were expected to contain their anger and hostility against other members of the domus so as not to give a picture of instability and disrespect to the outside community. Individuals longing to live their own lives were warned that their actions would endanger the reputation of the domus. Although such fears were probably not exaggerated, the rigidity of the boundaries of respect and submission intensified pressures within the domus.

There were ways of escaping—at least temporarily—the pressures of the domus, particularly for young men. Italian Harlem had a geography of rebellion: subways, elevated trains, buses, and social clubs were some of the spaces people inhabited apart from the domus. Pretending to share their surprise and outrage, a young woman explained her newly bobbed locks to her parents by suggesting that someone must have cut her hair while she was asleep on the subway.[65] The parks were good for romantic assignations. Young men escaped into the world of close friendships and street gangs. Friendships among young men seem to have been especially close and satisfying in Italian Harlem. Friends were useful confidants and allies against the demands of the domus; friends could also adopt each other like "brothers" without the rivalry and competition that existed among brothers in the domus. A young man explained to Covello: "I still go with men I used to play with as a child. We respect ourselves like we are brothers and are always together whenever we can get a chance."[66] Street gangs, which fostered an intimacy, security, and mutual regard similar to those demanded in the domus, offered a recognizable world for young men to escape into. A young gang member told Covello, "The lure of my gang was stronger than my father's shellacking."[67] The older men had regional clubs and societies of mutual aid. Movie houses offered shorter, less satisfying periods of flight.[68] Sometimes marriage was thought of as a way of escaping the demands of one's domus.[69] It was also very tempting to see the streets as a locus of freedom where children and young men could roam free. Norman Thomas noted early in the century that Italian American youth seemed to delight in insulting their parents and elders in the streets, although not to their faces, shouting out that the older members of the domus were "wops" and "dagoes."[70]

Subtler forms of evasion were also attempted. An individual might try drawing a sharp distinction between what in his or her private life was subject to the authority of the domus and what was to remain private. A New York University student from Italian Harlem explained to Covello: "I find the old custom of all relatives meeting together a very beautiful custom. It makes sense to me. So I accept it wholeheartedly. But there are other things which are a trifle old-fashioned; these I don't follow, especially if they make me look ridiculous in other people's eyes."[71] An individual might try to limit, in advance of any major decision, which members of the domus he or she would listen to and obey, and then, when the time came, skillful diplomacy might insure the cooperation of these specially designated relatives with one's own plans.[72]

But it was not really possible to escape the domus. Almost all the gestures of rebellion cited here and earlier in the chapter actually

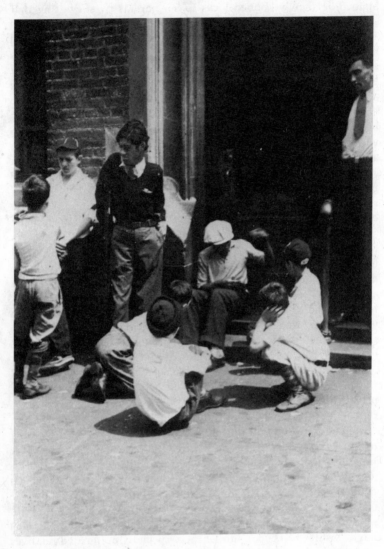

*East Harlem boys playing on a stoop, ca. 1935*

strengthened its power, which was like an oriental finger trap—the more one struggled to get out, the more entangled one became. The young woman who secretly withheld part of her paycheck was acknowledging the power of the domus over her. The same is true of the young man who dreaded his parents' matrimonial plans for him but would not tell them he was dating a non-Italian woman. In both cases, the public power of the domus remained unchallenged. It was impossible to escape into the streets and parks of Italian Harlem because these too had been incorporated into the extended domus. The more serious challenges to the authority of the domus, such as choosing one's own spouse or deciding for oneself where to live, required an exhausting and debilitating struggle that bound the individuals involved to the domus by the deep ties of bitterness and frustration.

The most profound bond between the individual and the domus, however, the link that frustrated all efforts to escape, was the fact that the men and women of Italian Harlem had deeply internalized the values and perceptions of the domus. They could not free themselves, however much they may have wanted to, because they bore the domus within. So they surrendered, a capitulation that seemed inevitable even when attended by the fiercest struggle.

A twenty-eight-year-old man named Tony, whose parents came from a small town outside of Naples, fell in love with and decided to marry a German-American woman. Anticipating the trouble this would cause at home, Tony began a long and careful period of "diplomatic activity" to prepare his parents to meet his fiancée. He reminded them that things were different here in America. Finally, he gathered enough "courage" to bring his fiancée home, and the reaction was all he had feared. "My mother was nasty to the girl, and coaxed my father, who kept himself rather at a distance, to exert his authority as a father." In the weeks following this unpleasant visit, Tony's mother pressured her son relentlessly to give up his girlfriend, emphasizing the questionable behavior of American women, "the way they obey a husband, their use of lipstick, their smoking cigarettes, etc." At last, Tony broke under the pressure and surrendered his own plans for what he believed was the good of the domus, "I finally had to give in—to preserve peace in our home and the good relationships with my other relatives." Tony's capitulation was complete; having lost this battle for autonomy, he was ready to give up the struggle to obtain his own desires. He says of himself, "How it came about I don't know, but somehow today I share my mother's viewpoint." His mother wants him to marry one of his cousins in Naples, and Tony is prepared to go all the way with his surrender and accede to her wishes. "My mother works on me for several years, suggesting that I should marry any of the girls. They don't look to me like great beauties, but I gave up long ago to be attracted by good looks. . . . As my mother says, any of the girls would make a good wife; besides my marriage would greatly help the family." The note of resignation is clear; Tony has decided to sacrifice himself completely to the demands of the domus.[73]

Miss S., a twenty-year-old student born in Italy but raised in East Harlem, was prevented from sharing any of the pleasures and activities of her peers by her stern father. She recalled, "One of my father's chief purposes in life was to safeguard the morals of his children." S. desired in particular to go to the movies, but her father would absolutely not hear of this. She and her brother never rebelled, though; indeed, they internalized their father's values, "Filled with chagrin by our schoolmates' conversations and subdued ridicule, we adopted father's theory: Movies were demoralizing. We were proud of the fact that we had never seen one." She and her brother suffered under their father's regime but remained silent. After his death, however, S. felt free to express years of growing bitterness, "the many restrictions imposed in order to achieve ideal purity, however, cannot but be condemned."[74]

A sixteen-year-old boy at Franklin told Covello that he would never disobey his oldest brother, Frankie, his mother's favorite and her enforcer in the home. "I do not prefer to do things that are contrary to his wishes." Frankie's power was considerable: "If Frank wants to be mean to me he can do many things. He can put me in trouble with my mother or father who will believe every word he says but who will disbelieve me because I am the younger brother. He can also spread all kinds of rumors about me, and everybody will believe him." Despite all this potential and actual cruelty, however, this student not only did not rebel against Frankie, but managed to convince himself of the legitimacy of his brother's authority. "Maybe that is the right way, for there would be no order in the family if everybody did the way he felt." For the good of the domus, as he thinks it is being defined by his mother and oldest brother, this young man will submit to his brother's tyranny. "And if he told me not to do something, I usually obeyed for

he would beat me up, and my mother always took sides with him."
Then Frankie joined the army and this student, physically free from
him at last, dreaded his return, when he would judge whether his
younger brother had maintained the standards of the domus in his
absence. The student ended his account to Covello by celebrating and
forgiving (and indirectly expressing his anger against) his oldest
brother: "My mother and aunts think he is a great guy. I think so too, in
spite of the many bruises he deliberately put on my skin."[75]

In each of these stories, the men and women involved repressed
their own needs and emotions, and submitted themselves to the authority and hierarchy of the domus. This is how the life of the domus
was lived in Italian Harlem. Hostility was deflected away from its
genuine objects—the older brother who oppressed, the mother who
would not let her son marry whom he wanted—by the insistence on
the "good of the family." This became the epitaph of the self in Italian
Harlem. Certainly people expressed anger often; there was a great deal
of free-floating rage and anxiety in Italian Harlem: younger brothers
struck out with powerful and uncontrollable anger at their sisters'
boyfriends; fathers publicly disciplined their children with unusual
severity for minor infractions; sons imagined fistfights with their fathers. As we will see, bitter tensions, which often erupted into angry
confrontations at family gatherings, existed also among women: between sisters-in-law, mothers and daughters-in-law, women and their
sons' girlfriends. As these intimate contexts suggest, the source of this
rage was the absolutism of the domus, its many conflicts and its inevitable triumph over the individual. This anger was rarely expressed
against the domus itself: more often, it was internalized and directed
against the self, or it was focused on certain symbols of the domus,
leaving the domus itself unchallenged and unchanged.

Two kinds of stories were popular on the streets and in the living
rooms of Italian Harlem: tales of the domus in all its complexity, and
tales of the Mafia. But the most popular tale of all combined the two
genres. These were the stories, discussed in the previous chapter, of the
Mafia defending the domus: tales of gangsters who walked young
women home when they came from work late at night, protected older
women going about their chores in the neighborhood, gave food to the
poor and elderly in hard times, and watched over the Madonna. A
variant of this genre concerned the good family man who, when his
family was threatened, revealed himself as capable of going to ex-

tremes of violence, which often included seeking the assistance of professionals, in its defense.[76]

Everyone in the community knew that local mobsters spent most of their time in Italian Harlem extorting Italian merchants and running numbers games that took money away from the community. The mobsters were never presented as *banditti* who took from the rich and gave to Italian Harlem. In other words, when the storytellers of Italian Harlem told Mafia tales, they and their listeners were holding together two conflicting perceptions of the heroes of the tales: as men of violence and greed and as men who protected the domus. This leaves us with several questions. Why did the domus need to be surrounded and the Madonna rescued by violent and cruel men? Why did the community make heroes out of these mobsters, if only in the tales they told, when they knew full well the reality of their crimes? Why did anger and violence assume such central places in the fantasies of Italian Harlem? And what was the threat to the domus that could be repelled only by such extreme measures?

These tales articulate some of the rage and confusion the people in the community felt toward the domus but were unable to reveal publicly without disguise. The violent men (whom the community knew to be violators but chose to represent as protectors) surrounding the domus represent both the violence that individuals knew they had to do to their own aspirations and plans in deference to the domus, and the violent fantasies they sometimes entertained against the domus itself. The guns of these cruel men are aimed against violators of the domus: in this way, the mafiosi also articulate the rage that people inevitably turned inward in their struggles against the demands of the domus and the guilt they suffered for struggling. In the tales, the domus is always successfully defended: these myths allowed the people to express their rage against it while both assuring them that the domus was safe against that rage and reminding them of what was necessary for their submission. It is significant that in the way they tell these stories, the people are not frightened by the mafiosi. This may be a further indication that the storytellers and their audiences knew that the domus would survive because they would never do anything to provoke the gangsters into shooting. But the mafiosi did become frightening outside the community—to men and women who were not Italian, to outsiders who invaded the neighborhood. The message here was that as long as one stayed inside the boundaries of the community and the domus, all would be well. Symbols of aggression and repression, the mythical mafiosi embodied the complexity of feeling and anxiety which the people of Italian Harlem bore toward the domus.

Although the American-born generations loudly proclaimed that they were Americans, no longer bound by the customs and traditions of the paesi of their grandparents and parents, they always remained bound by the demands and values of the domus. Just as the real link between the immigrants and the old country was the domus, so the real continuity in the history of Italian Harlem was the continuity of the domus. But the success of the domus came at an enormous cost, which historians of Italian America have long overlooked. The persistence of the domus as southern Italians understood it generated terrible burdens of guilt, anxiety, anger, and frustration in the lives of the men and women of Italian Harlem. They simply could not escape or change the domus—they were trapped. The survival of the domus also meant the survival of a kind of historical, culturally institutionalized neurosis, a domus obsession, which the Italians of Harlem had to suffer along with other Italian Americans. All was not well in the domus of Italian Harlem.

## WOMEN IN ITALIAN HARLEM

In 1940, a young woman in Italian Harlem, Marie Concilio, told Covello that she really had only begun to understand herself after her parents died, an unusual unchecked expression of hostility. Then she launched into a fierce and bitter attack on the role of women in the domus. Young women were reduced to silence and subservience. "A girl can have no voice or opinion. She is taught to speak only when addressed." She had to obey all male relatives, even those only distantly related and much younger than she. The only future imagined for women was marriage, a union that must be approved first by all the men in the family. "Girls should work all the time. Reading is a waste of time." Concilio concluded that the real mission of women in the domus-centered society was to "help the mother in spoiling the father and the brother by waiting on them and by making them helpless around the house."[77] Concilio points us deep within the heart of Italian Harlem here. The domus was the center of the life of the community, and women were the center of the domus; the burdens and complexities of life in the domus-centered society fell most heavily on

*Women and children of East 114th Street celebrating their victory in a sanitation campaign*

them, and it is to their lives and roles in the domus that we must now turn.

Italian Harlem was a private matriarchy. Married women with children were the source of power and authority in the domus and in the intimate private matters of people's lives; they were the hidden center of the domus-centered society, the fountainhead of the blood which bound together members of the domus and connected it to the rest of the community. It was in a woman's power to define who belonged to the domus and who did not, who was to be excluded. They identified the comari and "cousins" to be respected by their husbands and children.[78] A woman's relatives were also closer to her domus after her marriage than were her husband's relatives. Women tended to live close by their mothers after they were married, for example, and a woman's oldest brother was a recognized authority in her household because he was related to her.

Married women were the guardians of traditional mores in Italian Harlem. If a person wanted to know what the appropriate forms of behavior were in a particular situation, he or she would not go to the old men sitting in front of their regional clubs in East Harlem, but to old women, grandmothers and comari, revered in the neighborhoods. There were many of these powerful women in Italian Harlem, figures to be reckoned with in the daily life of the community. They were treated with special respect and consulted on all important family decisions. A young woman explained to Covello that although her grandmother "is very feeble and her mind is a little hazy," still "she occupies a position of great respect; the children and grandchildren are waiting on her hand and foot."[79]

Rose Marello Tiano immigrated to East Kingston, New York, from Calabria in 1906. By the time of her death in 1939 at the age of one hundred and two, Rose Tiano was presiding over a huge domus, a "prolific tribe," in the words of one of her grandchildren, which included some three hundred members spanning four generations. Rose's authority over this domus was total. She never learned how to speak English and insisted that all her grandchildren and great-grandchildren be taught the Calabrian dialect, which they were, out of respect and fear of Rose. No family decision could be taken without her participation. Her grandson recalled: "She was representing a dynasty, for her influence over the Tiano clan was supreme. Her children, grandchildren and great-grandchildren were brought up in a particular world where nothing could have been undertaken without the knowledge and consent of the old woman." Rose's death provoked profound anxiety among the members of her domus. It was feared that the passing of the "matriarch," as her grandson called her, would bring Italian life in East Kingston to an end. Her sons and daughters and her grandchildren were terribly frightened: "now that the *genetrice* (progenitor of a tribe) is dead, we know nothing will keep [the younger generation] from marrying Irish girls and moving to New York. Our grandmother was keeping us together. From now on everybody will go his own way." The cosmos of the domus was about to explode because the matriarch was gone.[80]

Some of the older immigrant women in the community were respected for their skill in healing with traditional cures and for their knowledge of southern Italian magical rituals, in particular rituals of protection against the evil eye. In the earliest days of the community, these women also served as midwives. Until the 1940s, men and women, though usually women, sought out local women healers to cure them of a variety of ailments and to protect them against curses. One of the central figures in "The Family and Some" is an old woman named Julia Russo, called a "witch" and respected in the community despite her "freaky ways." When she dies toward the end of the novel, "the neighbors and friends respond and give Julia a funeral befitting a queen."[81]

Women played a number of important roles at funerals in Italian Harlem. They were assigned the task of keening a biography of the deceased, both at the wake and the gravesite, which served as a public definition of the way good people of the domus lived. They sat next to the body at wakes while their male relatives stayed toward the back of the room or in the kitchen, a powerful reversal of the usual allocation of public and private roles. The sight of women, symbols of power and the durability of the culture, gathered around the corpse, symbol of the culture's fragility, was a reassuring diptych. Women were called upon to express the grief of the domus while their husbands stood by mutely, and they bore the public burden of mourning, even for their husbands' relatives. It often seemed that women in Italian Harlem were always in mourning.[82]

Mothers were the centers of power and authority in the household as well, a reality acknowledged by the greeting most commonly used when acquaintances met on the streets of Italian Harlem, "How's your mother?"[83] "Mother," wrote one of Covello's students in an auto-biographical sketch, "retiring and self-sacrificing, was the keystone of our family."[84] Mothers dominated the life of the home. They were the disciplinarians of the family, either meting out punishment themselves or instructing their husbands or older sons to administer it. They controlled the family finances, and the various members of the household were expected to hand their paychecks over to them. Women greeted their children's dates and determined whether or not they were acceptable to the domus.[85] An outside observer characterized the organization of power and authority in the households of Italian Harlem like this:

> The (Italian) father retains his attitude of a desire to establish himself as head of the family. This sometimes takes on the character of a blustering, loud and angry disciplinary action towards the children. Underneath this exterior manifestation which is donned to impress everyone as to who the boss is, you are likely to find a kindly, gentle and even affectionate disposition. . . . The mother is the peace-maker, family advisor and nurse. Actually, many an Italo-American family might be considered matriarchal. She is inconspicuous but firm and usually sways the father to her way of thinking.[86]

The distinction between the loudly proclaimed and carefully presented public authority of males in Italian Harlem, an authority we have seen was largely ceremonial, and the genuine private power of women needs to be emphasized here. The powerful women of the community were expected to show an absolute respect for their husbands and sons in public, even though everyone in the community knew that such subservience was theater. This contradiction is boldly expressed in a story collected by Covello:

> My brother who became head of the family (after the death of their father) had to take orders from her (the mother). But that was only in our home. On the street he tried to impress everybody that he was the boss of the family . . . also, as I remember, I could never make out why my mother would tell untrue things to other women in the street. She would always complain how strict our older brother was. She would say, "Oh, my Rocco thinks so-and-so," or "Oh, no, I must first ask Rocco." And so on. And she said these things while we knew perfectly well that the big bully Rocco would probably at the same time complain to my uncle saying how unreasonable, how impossibly crazy my mother was, and "Oh, if only I had the power, what I wouldn't do."[87]

The cultural demand that women show this deference to their men in public shaped the lives of women as wives and determined the styles of their exercise of power. Husbands and wives were expected not to show affection for each other in public, for example, partly out of modesty, but also because such a display would temper the public perception of hierarchical ordering within the household. Women were compelled to sit quietly through extravagant declarations of male power and supremacy, although they might share an ironic glance with other women present.

Although the power of women in Italian Harlem was private, they were not sheltered, and when it was necessary for the good of the domus they freely wielded their power outside the home. In the earliest history of Italian Harlem they confronted head-on the challenge of female Protestant home visitors who sought to enter their homes and rearrange them according to their standards of "hygiene" and "comfort."[88] They went out and yanked their children out of Protestant playgrounds and day-care centers. Mothers went to school to talk to officials about their sons and daughters, and, when it was called for, they went ahead and disciplined their children publicly. A young woman complained to Covello: "If it were up to my mother she would not hesitate to accompany me to the school and park herself right in the classroom. She is very unhappy about my work in high school, where, in her estimation, my contacts with bigger boys are loaded with danger."[89] Throughout the history of Italian Harlem, but especially in the 1940s and 1950s, women were better educated than men, so it seemed appropriate even on purely pragmatic grounds that they be the ones to take care of official public business outside of the home.[90]

Because women wielded the real power in the home, however subterranean its operation, this meant that they were the ones who needed to be cajoled, entreated, or manipulated when a member of the domus wanted to do something. Young men brought their dates home and gingerly introduced them to their mothers, knowing that there was no appeal from this judgment. The effort to secure maternal sanction could involve weeks, even months, of careful preparation and negotiation, and if these failed, an equally long time of pleading and argument. A young man hoping to marry his non-Italian sweetheart anticipated a protracted engagement, "It will take me probably a year to bring up the subject gently, and by that time I may have brought my mother to my point of view."[91] If young men and women decided to go ahead against the maternal will, which meant going against the will of the domus, then it was the maternal responsibility to express and embody the disapproval and anger of the domus.

The power and importance of women in the domus are exaggerated to heroic proportions in the memories of the men and women of Italian Harlem. People who can remember their fathers in only the vaguest terms cherish intimate and detailed memories of their mothers. Usually the memories preserve the public–private dichotomy. People always begin their recollections of their mothers by emphasizing their obedience to the domus, their subservient and self-sacrificing lives; but invariably and quickly this image gives way to a forceful memory of their mothers as powerful and strong women, the "bosses of the family."[92] One of my informants recalled his mother in ways characteristic of such recollections, and very revealing. He remembered her as huge and spoke of "all three hundred and fifty pounds of her" going about the chores on the streets of Italian Harlem. Although she was so big, he added, she was clean; and she did not have the odors usually associated with people her size. She was powerfully strong and "dominated" the life of the domus.[93] In this man's memory, and in the memories of other people who grew up in Italian Harlem, his mother *is* the domus. She is big, inescapably real—in other words, unavoidable, overpowering. The magnitude of these women's bodies in the memories of their children is a powerful testament to the perception of their strength and authority. And she is clean, all expectations to the contrary, just as Italian Harlem's tenements are clean despite expectations.

The identification between women and the domus shaped the lives and behavior of all men and women in Italian Harlem, of course, but it had particularly fateful consequences in the lives of young unmarried women. Their lot was not an easy one. All the community's fears for the reputation and integrity of the domus came to focus on the behavior of young women. A "good family" was one in which the young women behaved modestly and adhered strictly to the authority and demands of the domus. The reputation of young unmarried women was, without qualification, an obsession in the domus-centered society. In the imaginations and understanding of the community, older married women with children were the sources of authority and responsibility in the domus; their younger sisters and daughters, on the other hand, appeared alternately, and frequently simultaneously, as volcanoes ready to erupt or as lambs wandering in a world of wolves. In either case, the threat was the same: ineradicable vergogna for the domus.

It was the responsibility of all the members of the domus to insure the suitability of their women for marriage. A father boasted to Covello: "no one will point at our girl disapprovingly. She has a good reputation among the people here, and I know, even the boys respect her. She will marry someday, probably one of the local boys. And she will be a desirable bride."[94] One family decided it had to leave Harlem for the sake of its daughters because one of them, who had done "nothing serious . . . just fooling around with the boys," had become the subject of rumors, "and her reputation suffered." A comare of the domus, who had made the suggestion that the family move away, commented, "I am pleased that they moved; because M. [the girl] can still start a new life."[95] Family concern for the reputations of its daughters was not misplaced, clearly. Men and women in the domus-centered society realized all too well the dangers made explicit by a young man born in East Harlem but sharing completely the sexual perceptions of his parents from Campania: "A young girl's reputation can be easily damaged even though there is little that can be pinned on her. And a girl with a ruined reputation not only puts her family to shame, but destroys the opportunity to get a good husband."[96] Or, to put this another way, she destroys the opportunity of perpetuating the life of her domus, extending its reach into another generation and, by failing to acquire her own domus, of becoming a real woman.

As a result, the upbringing of Italian American girls in Harlem was exceedingly strict and fraught with anxiety and dread. They were kept very close to home, where they could be watched over by their fathers and brothers and initiated into the responsibilities and expectations of the domus by their mothers. According to an American-born father:

> Teaching a girl is not the husband's business but the wife's. . . . And because my wife still feels a great deal about Italian customs, our daughter is much more Italian than the boy. The girl, for instance, likes Italian cooking; she goes eagerly with my wife to see the Italian "comares" in Smithtown and once a month or so they go for a visit to my wife's family in Brooklyn.[97]

"Much more Italian" here should be read as "faithful to the domus." Young women were allowed out only in the company of chaperones, who were usually female relatives or comari, a group the young women of Italian Harlem found it difficult to avoid.[98] Dorothy Reed reported that when a young woman finally got permission to go out, her family extended its reach over her into the streets. "Many a girl is escorted to her club and her father or brother waits on the curb across the street until she is ready to be taken home."[99]

The world outside the domus, from the perspective of men and women determined to protect the honor of their daughters, was a very dangerous place where the unthinkable could occur at any time. Young women allowed to make occasional forays into this world were hastened back into the domus. When a time had been agreed upon for a girl's return, it was kept with extraordinary precision—lateness was not tolerated. Young women who flirted with hopes of greater freedom would be met with severe discipline. A third-generation woman from East Harlem summed up her education in the domus in the early 1940s this way:

> Italian girls are still very restricted in their social contacts. She is supervised and chaperoned on almost all occasions. Only at her place of work is she free from the vigilance of her parents, her brothers or relatives. But even so, her going to work and coming from work are watched by the mother, and woe to the girl who arrives several minutes later than the customary time. A real inquisition begins, and the girl must give a very good explanation lest a suspicion arises that she spent some time in the company of a man, without supervision.[100]

Some families eliminated the possibility of such encounters by forbidding their daughters to go out after dark.[101]

However complicated dating may have been for young men, it was infinitely more so for young women. They were under enormous parental pressure to get married, a reality that impinged upon all their dates. Their young men had to be approved by all members of the domus, and girls were encouraged to choose their companions from "the community in which one lives or the circle of family, relatives and friends."[102] Once a young man had appeared in the domus, and certainly if he appeared more than once, it was assumed that the couple was "practically engaged," in the words of a young woman uneasy with this pressure.[103] If this did not follow, the young woman's reputation, not the man's, was in danger. This system worked well at keeping the young women of Italian Harlem in line. One of Covello's sources emphasized the impossibility of escape: "So if she has a boy-friend, he will most likely be one of the local boys. And never can she keep it a secret from her family because rumors travel fast. And the first one who finds out is usually the brother. Therefore a girl knows that it is useless to hide, and the best thing is to tell it at home and have her boyfriend approved by the family."[104]

But a young woman's sexual troubles only began with her family; they continued, in a different form, on the date itself. A woman's repu-tation rested completely in the hands of the young men she went out with—the young woman herself was quite powerless to defend herself against rumor and insinuation, as the young men of Italian Harlem appreciated fully. The subject of young women's reputations was a frequent topic of street conversations among men who knew that in the hypersensitive domus-centered world of Italian Harlem the slightest word or gesture could spell doom for a young woman, en-dangering or destroying her chances to inhabit a respectable domus for herself.[105] And in a society dominated by women in the domus, this was one of the few opportunities men had to wield a truly terrible power of their own over women (who might soon be mothers and wives themselves) as a gesture of hostility against their own mothers or in retaliation for their own entrapment in the demands of the domus.

So young women were summoned to a dangerous dance by their men. The latter made their advances—and then watched to see if they would be resisted as they wanted and expected to be. A young man explained, "An Italian boy is very much pleased when the girl he courts refuses to be petted; he respects her all the more for this."[106] Another fellow, whose parents feared that his girlfriend was too weak physically to make a good wife, proudly reported: "She is a very de-cent girl; this I know for she gave me a mean wallop when I jokingly spoke of the beauty of her breasts. I felt that wallop good and proper, and no sick girl can deliver that punch."[107] This was called "manag-ing" one's boyfriend, and all well-brought-up women were expected to have this skill.[108] In the parks and hallways of Italian Harlem, boys drew their dates out to the limits of the domus-centered society to test them, to see if they would perform according to the expectations of the culture. This act of aggression and power was masked by the boys' perception of themselves as guardians of the domus. These moments were even further complicated; both young men quoted above insisted that they were modern, sophisticated people, free from the prejudices of their immigrant parents, unconcerned with the reputations of their dates. Their women were getting mixed signals, then; they knew that, at least superficially, their men did not want them to be old-fashioned. To be successful with men in Italian Harlem, young women had to know how to "manage" these complex male needs while remembering all the time that one false move would bring disaster down on them.

This drama is a further revelation of the nature and limits of women's power in the domus-centered society. The young women were being called to play, in these highly charged moments, the same role played by their grandmothers and mothers in the domus. But the challenge itself, the summons to power, was an act of aggression and hostility. Who had the real power here—the women who had to uphold the standards of the domus or the men who put them to the test? Again, women seem trapped by the power assigned them in the domus, their authority linked to an inescapable dialectic of aggression and resentment. Their power, although it is real, is also their powerlessness.

The challenge of the parks was repeated in daylight in other contexts. Young women in Italian Harlem were forever being called upon to demonstrate to their community that they had been well raised and were capable of assuming their roles at the center of the domus. Their families sought to prepare them, therefore, for their public roles as wives and mothers. They were kept constantly in the company of female relatives. From a very early age they were expected to share the burdens of housework and child-raising with their mothers. While their brothers went out to school or to play, girls labored prodigiously in their homes. They spent their Saturdays cleaning their apartments and their Sundays helping their mothers cook the family meal. Young women were expected to help support their families financially, and parents assumed that in their old age their daughters would take responsibility for them. Girls were frequently assigned unpleasant tasks outside the home, particularly those tasks it would embarrass the men to perform. Older sisters, for example, seem to have been the ones to go out and collect public support money during the Depression. All of this was meant to show the community in general, and young men in particular, that the girls would make good wives and mothers.[109]

The relationship between brothers and sisters in Italian Harlem was an especially complex familial bond. Both younger and older brothers expected, and seem generally to have received, the obedience and submission of their sisters. One young man mused: "Suppose [my sister] went out with the wrong fellow, and I told her not to. I would not have to beat her, she would follow my recommendation because I am her brother. Not listen to me? . . . I don't think that's possible."[110] The bravado here obscures the sense of mutual support between brothers and sisters that was valued in the community, but it does make explicit the foundation of these relations in male claims of power over the young women of the domus.[111] Covello noted that the young men expected their sisters to wait on them and anticipate their needs. They assumed that their sisters would obey them in the matter of dating, claiming the right to judge and approve or disapprove of their sisters' companions. Males saw all this as the expression of their duty to "protect" their sisters. But again, as many young women realized, the dynamics of brother–sister relations allowed men the opportunity publicly to dominate at least one of the women of their domus.[112]

The extent to which brother–sister relations were an occasion for the public expression of male power in the domus is clearly revealed in the bitter rivalries that invariably erupted between young men and their sisters' boyfriends. The following scenes were quite common in the streets and parks of Italian Harlem. A young woman came home one night and told her brother that her date had been teasing her unkindly. Her brother raged: "I just could not control myself. Immediately going downstairs, I met him (the fellow) on the corner and although he is about twice my size, I tore into him. The other boy received a very bad cut over his right eye and had to get two stitches."[113] Another young man accosted his sister's new boyfriend on the street and shouted at him, "You better keep away from my sister—you know, I don't like you!" Then he initiated a brutal fistfight with his rival, which ended with the latter running off yelling, "I hope your whole family drops dead!"[114] A boyfriend ran into his date's brother by chance in Central Park, and without saying a word the latter "tore into" him, "both arms flaying."[115]

Such stories constitute one of the various ways the people of Italian Harlem presented themselves and their community to themselves and to others. Young men came to have a heroic sense of their identity as their sisters' protectors and guardians. This domestic vigilantism, ostensibly directed toward preserving the purity of the domus, reveals the rage within it, the terrible anxieties attending its perpetuation, and the role that the submission of women played in enforcing its codes and demands. Women were the symbols of the domus; young women were the symbols of its continuity but also of its fragility. And fraternal violence, which was as much against their sisters as it was on their behalf, was one of the prices women paid for their centrality in the domus-centered society.

Young women often resented and sometimes resisted this pressure to obey all their male relatives and to conform to the expectations of the domus. Sometimes they imagined futures for themselves that included more than the replication of their mothers' and grandmothers' lives in the domus. Such fantasies became particularly worrisome in the 1940s and 1950s, as young women, better educated than their brothers and boyfriends, entered white-collar clerical positions. Their families valued their financial support and certainly did not keep them from such employment; but there is no indication that the culture adjusted itself quickly to this new reality. Marie Concilio's criticism of the rearing of women in 1940 expressed the frustration of this generation. Traditional expectations and attitudes remained the same. A strictly raised immigrant girl complained in 1939 that her parents were not allowing her the freedom to "find myself."[116] A schoolteacher complained in 1940 that, although young Italian American women now "go out to business," still their parents are insisting on traditional southern Italian attitudes toward women.[117] The fears of the older generation were expressed by one woman's mother, who felt that by going to school and getting a good job her daughter would "scare away good suitors who may not have that much schooling. On the other hand, the girl herself may get funny ideas of looking down on the average young man."[118] Her daughter went ahead and attended high school, but the tensions with her mother remained.

As a result, the lives of young women in Italian Harlem were awhirl with conflict. Dating, engagement, wedding plans, schooling, and work were all areas of struggle between young women and their families. There was little escape from all of this for young women. If they tried to meet their dates secretly, they were risking the terrible rages of their brothers, as well as the threat to their own reputations. One man's daughters, who fought continually for some freedom and space, were described by a friend as "always in fear of getting caught and of being subjected to humiliation in the presence of others."[119] Young women, often expected to sacrifice their own plans if they conflicted with either their brothers' aspirations or the intentions of their

*Little girls of Italian Harlem lined up in their first communion dresses during the July procession*

domus, frequently found themselves supporting their brothers through college or professional school. They were called upon to sacrifice their own plans to care for a sick relative or parent.[120]

There were severe limits to the possibilities for rebellion among young women in Italian Harlem. The demands and proprieties of the domus weighed more heavily on them than on their brothers. The latter might experiment with rebellion for a while, sleeping in cars or joining the army; but, shackled with their fragile reputations and unceasingly under the scrutiny of the community, young women did not have such opportunities. Rebellion would mean the end of their hopes to marry and have a domus of their own; it could bring scandal to the family, ruin to themselves. As a result of all this pressure, young women internalized the values and expectations of the domus even more completely than their brothers did. Although they may have often dreamt of greater freedom and independence, or at least some relief from the manifold expectations and demands made on them by members of their domus and by the community, young women, like their brothers, submitted to the domus-centered society. Their anger and resentment, too, would need to find other expression than rebellion and mutiny against the domus.

Older married women with children were the centers of power and authority in the private matriarchy of Italian Harlem, dominating the lives of the members of their domus, defining tradition, called upon to heal and condemn, to express anger and approval, making important decisions for their sons and daughters and grandchildren. These women, of course, began their lives unmarried and childless, so they had all already experienced the undercurrents of male anger against women in the culture, the subtle interrelationships between male power and the power of women in the domus, and the meaning of powerlessness. Our task now is to explore the consequences of the power of women in Italian Harlem, to go deeply into their power in order to find there the real nature of their powerlessness.

The story of Theresa, who sought me out eagerly one morning to tell me about herself, will serve as an introduction to this consideration of the complexities of women's lives in East Harlem. In an extreme form, Theresa's biography expresses the vulnerability of women in the community. Born in Italy, she emigrated as a child and settled in Harlem, where eventually she married another immigrant, not from her hometown. Her husband left her after their first child was born, came back and stayed only until she was pregnant again, and then left for good.

When they were together, Theresa had had to endure being told by her neighbors that her husband took women into her apartment when she was out; and yet, she told me, she tried all the while not to believe this evidence. She assessed her marriage: "I had a hard life. I got married, and it got worse." When her second child was born, she was so upset about her husband's leaving that she could not produce any milk for the baby. She was forced for the next few years to travel all over Manhattan every week to collect assistance from various charitable and public agencies, journeys lengthened by her worries about the children she had left behind in the care of neighbors. All her anxieties seemed to be encapsulated in the remembered dread that she would lose her place on line at these places—to do so would have meant staying away longer from her children and thus perhaps failing as a mother, as well as being longer away from the security of her apartment building in Harlem.

Theresa worked during these years, long hours for low wages. Her wages were so poor that she had to suffer another hurt later in life when she could not help her older daughter find the tuition to go to designer's school. She barely speaks English, yet she was in a position where her life and the lives of her daughters depended upon her making contact with American officials. Her anger and frustration about this emerged in an exchange with a police officer in the relief office in Lower Manhattan. He told her she should get down to the office earlier in the morning: "'I can't come earlier than this,' I said to him, 'you want me to bring my baby and sleep in the front of the door here?' He say, 'Don't be like that!' And I say, 'Well, don't ask me like that,' I say, 'because I have two small children home.'" Just after her second daughter was born, social workers in a local clinic suggested to Theresa, who was very sick, that she put her children into a home for a short while. She answered, "My children put away when I die."[121]

Theresa was a good woman of the domus. But the complex of meanings and expectations that constituted the definition of "the good woman" trapped and bound women. A good woman, in the understanding of the community, had little or no life outside the domus. She had no friends who were not either related to her or linked to her as comari. She stayed close to home; people always remember their mothers as homebound. The good woman was a hard and uncomplaining worker who slaved from morning to night in and on behalf of the domus; she rose long before everyone else and was still awake when the last male drifted off to sleep at night. A good woman felt uncomfortable outside the domus; an extreme statement of this isolation was the insistence among many male immigrants that their wives not learn English and the pride among many women at not having done so after many years in the United States. A good woman did not know how to leave the neighborhood and never learned anything about public transportation. A good woman was utterly loyal to her husband and children; she would sacrifice "everything" for them, as the popular expression put it. She overlooked and covered over her husband's faults. She was humble, submissive, obedient. And above all, she was silent; as men and women remember their mothers, these women are surrounded by a great and deep silence.[122]

This was the public definition of the good woman. The reality, of course, the private reality, was quite different: women were the powers to be reckoned with in the domus, the sources of authority and tradition. But men in Italian Harlem, who had little real power in the domus itself that was not connected to their mothers, sisters, or wives, did have great authority in defining and maintaining the meaning of the "good woman," as young women with endangered reputations knew all too well. The fragility of the reputations of young women was educational; it revealed to them and to us the fragility of their mothers' reputations.

So was Theresa a good woman of the domus? Her female neighbors thought so; they sympathized with her, left money on her kitchen table when she was not looking, took care of her children when she had to go out on errands. But the question is more complicated when it is looked at from the perspective of the public definition of the good woman. Like most of the women of Italian Harlem, Theresa had to leave her apartment often to go into other areas of the city. She had to develop enough skill in the English language to deal with public officials, a task assumed by other women in the community too. Clearly she knew the intricacies of New York's public transportation. Besides all the other difficulties of her life, Theresa's reputation, from the perspective of the public definition of the good woman, was quite fragile after her husband left her. Women were summoned to an ideal which, given the conditions of life in Italian Harlem, was impossible to conform to. Perhaps Theresa's insistence on telling her story reflects her desire to present a public *apologia pro vita sua*.

There was another way in which Theresa was trapped by the

public definition of "the good woman." While her husband was being unfaithful to her, Theresa bound herself by a domestic vow of silence, insisting to her neighbors that he was innocent. She was doing here what any good (and frightened) woman of the domus would have done: sacrificing herself for the good of the domus. Her fear, of course, was that she would be held responsible for the collapse of the domus if she acted too aggressively against her husband. But to do this, Theresa had to still her own anger, silence all her needs and emotions, which must have been powerful indeed, because they demanded expression fifty years later.

Although women were powerful in the domus (and although this power was very real), their power was also a cage, the bars of which were fashioned from the material of the public definition of the good woman. They were compelled to exercise only a certain kind of power in a certain way, as defined and maintained by the community by means of the normative ideal of the "good woman." This public ideal was available to men to wield against women in retaliation for or as a restraint on the power women exercised in the domus.

Childless married women—"childless" was a designation heavy with shame in the community—had less power than their sisters with children, and unmarried women had no authority at all. The treatment of young women again served as a kind of educational drama in the community: this is how women without children are treated. Theresa's lot would have been a hard one indeed if she had had no children to anchor her identity in the community. Without them, she most likely would have had to return in humiliation to her parents' domus, marked as a failure in the eyes of the community. The authority and power of women was contingent, then, as they knew, and depended on their success in the domus. The prospect of failure was terrifying because it could undermine their identities as women.

But within the domus itself, because of their assigned place in it and because of the kind of power they were compelled to wield, women were always at the vortex of conflict. Allocation of authority in the domus depended on the mother; her oldest brother and her favorite, usually oldest, son had power because of their relationship with her. This meant that she was at the center of the bitter conflict that inevitably developed between these males and the other men in the domus. She was the focus of jealousy and competition; her power to assign authority was resented. Young women bound to the older women of the domus turned their anger and frustration against them when their desires for greater freedom and space was thwarted. Because they defined and expressed the will of the domus, demanded its execution, and articulated its anger and disapproval, they bore the brunt of frustration, anger, and resentment. Struggles for autonomy within the domus frequently culminated in long periods of alienation between women and their children. When people wanted to rage against the claustrophobic demands of the domus, they raged against the women of the domus, "all three hundred and fifty pounds" of them; and when they wanted to escape the domus, they turned against its women.

What could women do when this happened? In their role as the central power in the domus, they were required to stay and fight fiercely, knowing that the eyes of the community were on them and dreading failure in the maintenance of a stable and obedient domus. But this is also where the emphasis on silence and sacrifice in the public definition of the "good woman" reveals its power and purpose: women were expected to be silent and long-suffering while their children and menfolk raged against the power they insisted their mothers wield. By breaking the silence, furthermore, women would bring shame down on the domus and on themselves for having failed to educate members of their domus properly into the communal canons of respect and obedience.

The particular kind of power women were compelled to exercise was also bitterly resented. One of the most important consequences of the public–private dichotomy in the realities of power in Italian Harlem was that it compelled women to exercise their authority and influence in subterranean ways. Italian women lived under the pressure of two dangerously conflicting demands: that they exercise their power in the domus and that they appear powerless. Their exercise of power, therefore, was frequently clandestine. They attained their ends by manipulation and indirect influence or they acted through a specially chosen surrogate, such as their oldest son or brother. This kind of power, however, generates bitter suspicion toward those compelled to wield it and provokes the fiercest resentment. The influence of women who had to be powerful in this way was hated; their power seemed dark, uncontrollable, unreachable for appeal. A suspicion arises that those who wield such power have a pervasive unseen influence, even if in fact they do not, and they are held responsible for dealing behind the scenes.

Women's power seemed capricious, favoring one son over another, insisting on the maintenance of traditions everyone else thought irrelevant or embarrassing. Women seemed willful and impossibly strong-minded. They held out against weddings, refused to enter the homes of children who had displeased them, demanded an end to romances for frustratingly illogical reasons, demanded that good jobs be turned down lest the tie to themselves and to the domus be severed. They acted in the domus by provoking their husbands or sons or brothers into action. The power of women seemed too great, too devious and intimate; but this was the only kind of power and the only way of exercising it that the culture allowed them.

To whom did women turn, then, in the times of their troubles? Usually to other women, to their comari and female relatives and friends. The heroes of Theresa's story were her female neighbors, to whom she repeatedly expressed gratitude during her autobiographical account. They were there to help her with her children, with housework when she was sick, and with food and money when her poverty was most extreme. The women of Italian Harlem were surrounded by comari living in the same apartment building or in the neighborhood to whom they could turn for physical and moral support. There seems to have been a real spirit of cooperation among women living in the same apartment building. Young women relied on their sisters for advice and for protection against the demands of their domus.

Yet in this culture dominated by strong but deeply vulnerable women like Theresa, one of the most serious and persistent points of domestic conflict was in relations among women. Mothers sat in judgment on their sons' prospective spouses, a trial that could end in years of bad feelings and bitterness. Young women came to resent the company of their female relatives and comari, which was forced on them as a restraint within the domus. The matrilocality characteristic of Italian Harlem was another source of conflict among women. The mothers of young men resented their daughters-in-law and *their* mothers for taking their sons away from the domus; this maternal anger, in turn, became a source of frustration and resentment among men forced to maintain a delicate balance between mothers, wives, and mothers-in-law. Relations between sisters-in-law were often troubled, particularly between the wife of an oldest son and his sister. In the context of matrilocality, women viewed each other as rivals for power and love. Although women did seek out the company of women for support and consolation, this area of their lives was also difficult and complex.

Women also went to church on 115th Street to talk to the Madonna. Church attendance and public participation in religious activities was left largely to women in Italian Harlem. As we will see, the religious experience of women in Italian Harlem was most complex. It restated and confirmed their roles in the community and the nature of their power; but it also offered them a chance to articulate their concerns, anxieties, and troubles to a divine woman they knew was sympathetic to them. In the domus of their divine mother on 115th Street, the women of Italian Harlem could unburden themselves and reveal the complexities of their lives.

## CHAPTER VI

# Toward an Inner History
# of Immigration

**T**HERE is a hidden history of immigration that needs to be studied in order to understand the immigrants themselves, however difficult it may be to locate the appropriate tools with which to do this. Immigration was as much a spiritual event as it was a political and social response to particular historical conditions; the outward journeying was matched by a changing inner terrain. Anticipation of their new life in America was powerful among the men and women preparing to emigrate. The United States was imagined as a "mythical land immense and magnificent, opulent with food and flowers."[1] One immigrant wrote that his picture of the United States was of "vast stretches of virgin lands and great, winding rivers," an image formed in southern Italian schools, where the story of Columbus was taught frequently and with a pride that expressed a sense of shared history with the new land.[2] Carlo Levi observed that New York was a mythical city for the peasants of Lucania, "an earthly paradise, Jerusalem the golden, it is so sacred as to be untouchable; a man can only gaze at it, even when he is there on the spot, with no hope of attainment."[3] Broughton Brandenburg, who traveled to Sicily in 1902, noticed there a "spirit which today stirs all Italy, all Greece, all Syria, all Hungary and Roumania, and has spread deep into the hearts of the people of the whole of southern Europe. The eyes of the poor are turned with longing fancy to 'New York.' That is the magic word everywhere. The sound of it brings light to a hundred million faces in those lands."[4]

The excitement of this anticipation mounted on the eve of departure and peaked on the journey over. In the town where Brandenburg was staying, a family's parting became a religious celebration: the little girls in the family were dressed in their white "*festa* dress" and the family itself, with all its relatives, marched through the town for a final blessing at the church. On the afternoon of this last day, the graves of family members were visited and a "sort of solemnity pervaded the household."[5] The domus, living and dead, was called upon to witness the departure of its emigrants, who may have had the intention of returning but did not know how long they would be gone, what changes and deaths would occur while they were away, and even whether for unforeseen reasons they might not return. It was a sad but also an exciting moment.

This spirit seems to have lasted the voyage over, despite persistent abuse, humiliation, and exploitation of the immigrants in Italian ports and by non-Italian crews—despite, as well, the awesome dislocation experienced by the people themselves, often women and children traveling alone and for the first time.[6] Garibaldi Lapolla writes that regional ties were affirmed during the crossing; the people played games of chance and sang folksongs.[7] The night before arriving in "la Batteria" was as solemn a moment as the parting. Brandenburg tells us, "The night before, the joy among the emigrants that they were reaching the promised land was pitiful to see, mingled as it was with the terrible dread of being debarred."[8] At midnight, the women woke sleeping children and dressed them in their best clothes to meet their fathers and then prepared themselves to meet their husbands, whom they might not have seen for a long time.

Though this was the moment of anticipation realized and sacrifice rewarded, it was also, as Brandenburg saw, an experience of profound anxiety and dread. It was a time of shattered expectations: the longed-for city of myth, with its fabled buildings of pure white stone, turned out to be gray and discolored.[9] The immigrants were terrified that some small overlooked requirement, a payment they had failed to make or a test they had not taken, would keep them out of the country, a fear that remained with many of the older immigrants as the fear of deportation until the Second World War.[10] They also feared separation in the port from family and friends.

One of Covello's students, Eugene Mazzola, in an essay written in 1939 and given the ringing title "Westward—to the Land of Opportunity," remembered the mixed emotions of his own arrival in New York nineteen years before.[11] After a "long, almost epochal" voyage, Mazzola got his first glimpse of the city of dreams: it was "dingy, drab" in comparison with the New York he had imagined for himself. It had "canyon-like streets" and "drab buildings." Was this "strange, cold city" the magnet that had drawn "not only the Mazzolas but thousands of other 'paesani' from the sunny fields of Italy?" Mazzola found that the frenzied and strange atmosphere of the port oppressed him with a feeling of "apathy." None of this was expected, neither the realities of New York nor the deadening of his emotions after the many excitements of his departure and crossing. He comments ruefully, "Of course, we had given little credence to the stories of golden towers and streets paved with gold, but we had believed implicitly the jubilant letters from relatives who had migrated before us." There was seemingly no end to the unpleasant surprises in store for Mazzola. His first sight of Italian Harlem was profoundly disorienting after the discomforts of the long journey. "There remains only a confused picture of hawking merchants, rows of pushcarts and open markets, and masses of people everywhere." The apartment his relatives escorted him and his family to seemed confining, claustrophobic: "The windows seemed too small and did not seem to permit enough sunlight to pierce those uninviting walls." He was unprepared for the mix of peoples on 114th Street. And he was also unprepared for the difficulties of life in the promised land, where children were undernourished, men and women were compelled to toil long and hard hours, people were poorly clothed, and the living conditions were very bad. Mazzola noted that this was his education. "Later I learned that very often [the people of Italian Harlem] were exploited by corrupt politicians or men of questionable enterprise and were helpless to protect themselves." It was all recognizable, of course—but the immigrants had not been expecting to see these things in the promised land.

Often the newly arrived expressed their disillusionment with the United States and their own feelings of dislocation in sensory terms. Italian parents in East Harlem in the 1930s were still attributing the unhealthy teeth of their children to bad American air. Immigrants in Roseto, Pennsylvania, told Carla Bianco that in America the flowers have no perfume, the sea is not salty, and the food is tasteless. As we have seen, the immigrants believed that the very air of America could corrode the strength of the domus.[12]

The lament that the food in the United States was tasteless recalls Mazzola's disturbing emotional apathy in port. The immigrants seemed to be distancing themselves from their new and confusing world. This gives an added dimension to the profusion of Italian food merchants in East Harlem: the people were surrounding and locating themselves with recognizable smells and tastes, compensating for their sensory confusion. Older Italians who have remained in Harlem since the transition to Spanish Harlem find it difficult to leave the familiar and identifiable world they succeeded in creating around themselves.

The immigrants experienced other dislocations with implications for the coherence and confidence of their knowledge and perceptions of themselves and of their world. They were men and women of severed memories: they remembered a time and a place they no longer even remotely inhabited. Of course, this is true of all people to some extent; but the fortunate will at least remain in the country of their birth, speaking their native language, eating foods they recognize as good and nutritious. Not so for the immigrants. They had left the familiar behind and were never able exactly to reproduce it, however hard they might try.

Personal integrity and stability depend on the ability to remember. Memory locates the individual in a community: individuals share memories with various groups—family, neighborhood, city, and so on—and this communion of memory is the foundation of their membership in these groups. Memory is also that which binds men and women together in their most intimate relations with their families. Older members of the family share their recollections, which are often part of a corporate memory they too had once been taught, with their younger kin, who in this way are invited and integrated into the generations. Memory finally helps shape personal identity: men and women discover who they are in their memories.

But the distance of the immigrants from their lives in Italy, their complex feelings toward their homeland, and their hopes for a new beginning for themselves and especially for their children made them unwilling or unable to share their memories with their American-born or -raised offspring. Conflicts in the domus between generations further exacerbated the failure to share memories. In many households, language was a barrier to such sharing. Covello discussed his perception of the drifting apart of memories that occurred in immigrant homes at a rally in East Harlem to encourage residents to become American citizens:

> There was a hunger of the spirit for something still denied us. The older people still clung to their memories of their native land and to the loyalties of mind, heart and spirit that are forever interwoven with the scenes of childhood. Their children—born in America—know nothing of the heritage of their mothers and fathers. Their loyalties were bound up with their birthright. When they would have become old men and old women, their memories would be, not of lands across the sea but of America, its traditions, its customs. They could not understand their parents. Their parents could not understand them.[13]

Covello was afraid of a deep and lasting anomie, a loss of vision and direction resulting from the loss of memory.

Confronted with this manifold threat of alienation, the immigrants dreaded the collapse of the moral order in their community. This is the meaning of the cry of one of Lapolla's characters when she calls New York "a strange land . . . where things are topsy-turvy." Covello's father greeted a bag of oatmeal, sent home by well-meaning Protestant home missionaries, with the denunciation: "They give us the food of animals to eat and send it home to us with our children. What are we coming to next!"[14] Constantino Panunzio writes that the pressure he felt to follow the American command of hasty assimilation, "Forget your native land, forget your mother tongue, do away in a day with your inherited customs," drove him to the brink of mental and physical collapse:

> For years I was obliged to drive with all my powers in order to earn a livelihood and to compete with the world around me. . . . Then, too, there was the tension of continuous loneliness, of grief, of struggle, of abuse,—all of which attacked my nervous system, while the intensive rush of American life drove the propellers of the heart until they could scarcely move.[15]

Italian immigrants seem to have feared the heady and unfamiliar wine of their material success in the new world, a drink that could make a man or woman dangerously giddy and confused. They had come with the explicit hope of breaking out of the poverty in which their families had been trapped by political conditions in the mezzogiorno. They wanted to put an end to *la miseria.* One of Covello's informants told him: "In Italy, we did not waste anything. If a crumb fell on the floor, we bent down, picked it up and kissed it, thanking God that we had it."[16] One of my sources phrased this in more Americanized terms, "Over there, it's hard to put a dollar away."[17] With these experiences and memories driving them, Italians came to Jerusalem the golden because they had heard they could make more money there.

The men and women of Italian Harlem made this quite explicit to Covello:

> My grandfather and his son, my father, came to America to make more money, which he succeeded in doing, but never with the intention of remaining in America. He looked upon America as a place or a heaven where one could make money which could help him live better in Italy.

> [My grandmother] and her four children came to America to make money.

> *Question:* What caused you to consider emigrating to America? *Answer:* Friends who had returned to Nicosia from America looked prosperous and well-dressed. They told tales of prosperity in America.[18]

The compulsion of this materialism—although this is not a precise enough word to convey the complexity of hopes the Italians nurtured—reflected in part the immigrants' expectation that by defeating their poverty they would achieve a new dignity. It was this dignity and self-respect that startled and impressed southern Italians when their paesani returned from America for a visit. Emigration held out the promise that they, too, could become Christians.

This ambition often necessitated a constant struggle, however, which the immigrant experienced either as a gnawing worry or a relentless obsession. The subtle and all-absorbing demands of "making America," which in the language of the immigrants meant to become a great financial success, could seduce the Italian into a new bondage as fearsome as the old. One of my sources, an eighty-six-year-old man who emigrated in 1910, illustrates the dangers of this preoccupation.[19] When this man retired, he left his son a prosperous hat and shoe repair shop, which he had built up from nothing, in New York's financial district. He owned his home in the Bronx, paid for in cash, in a neighborhood where he was well known and widely respected for his considerable business acumen.

He began our conversation by emphasizing the economic difficulties of his early years in New York City: "I never stopped looking for a job. If I lose one job, right away I look for another one." This established the necessary context for the main theme of his autobiography, "I made money." He used this phrase more than twenty times in an interview that lasted less than two hours. It was clear throughout our conversation that his determination to succeed in America had demanded a controlled and disciplined life that left little room for anything else. He told me that he never rested, especially not on Saturday night and Sunday morning, the times when Americans tipped most extravagantly. When I asked if he belonged to any social clubs or regional associations, he answered: "I didn't have time to go to clubs. I was busy with shoe repair. I had two places; I was doing some business down there." He proudly told me that he was too busy even to go on a honeymoon. When I asked him if he had ever gone back to Italy, he responded angrily: "Why should I go back there? I had nobody. And then I was too busy making money. I came here with the idea to make money here." The only story he would tell about his life in Italy concerned his shrewd management of a flock of goats, the sale of which just before he left provided him with some of the capital he needed for his new start in America.

This passion for money not only shaped this immigrant's time but, as might be expected, informed his whole understanding of personal value. He presented himself exclusively as a crafty money-maker. "I made money, I lost money . . . I knew how to finagle." He used money to differentiate himself within his domus and to indicate his authority over his brothers and brothers-in-law, "I made more money than all of them, *me*. . . . I used to make more than my father, too. . . . My brothers, they don't know how to make money." When he wanted to share his pride in the splendor of his wedding, he said, "I invited all the good people," and compared the place of his celebration, the Hotel de la France, with the "little hall" rented by his brother for his wedding.

This immigrant had come to see all accomplishment, worth, and value in terms of making more and more money, a task he applied himself to with monastic discipline. By "making America" he would make himself. He came from a society that would have denied him all the decency and dignity it had the power to deny him; seen against this possibility, his triumph is compelling, and all the immigrants knew its power. But many of them feared it as well. They realized that such desire could devour a person, could engulf families and endanger the moral order

Garibaldi Lapolla probed this compulsion and fear in his two novels of East Harlem life, *Fire in the Flesh* and *The Grand Gennaro*. Both novels have as their main characters immigrants who are enormously successful in America; in both, these men achieve this success ruthlessly and with explicit disregard for Italian values, particularly the moral centrality of the domus. The latter book is a severe examination of the ambivalence of the immigrants' desire for success and status, and we should pause to consider this moral tragedy more closely. All the men and women in the novel are trapped in the web of their greed and desiring. Lapolla makes it clear that the web-spinning began in the economic exploitation of the mezzogiorno, and this gives the tragedy that unfolds a quality of inexorable destiny, a sense that the smaller tragedies of these individuals and families echo inherited generations of suffering. Like the man discussed above, Gennaro remembers Italy bitterly and points to the deprivations suffered by his family there as the origins of his own acquisitive passion: "It was not like this, ever. . . . There's something grown up in me, a madness. I don't know, ever since I saw the farm in the old country going for taxes and falling always deeper in debt and no hope ahead, and I picked up without saying good-bye, owing everybody money. . . . It's a strength, but a bad strength."[20] Gennaro comes to East Harlem determined to make money for his family, vowing success as revenge for his humiliations.

He is indeed successful, but in his progress Gennaro violates the most deeply held values of the community. The catalyzing betrayal of the novel is Gennaro's double-crossing of Rocco, his friend and *compare*, an act that initiates the accumulation of his fortune but also sets in motion the forces of his destruction. Along the way, Gennaro rapes a nurturing surrogate-mother figure, sinks temporarily into a life of inventive sexual depravity, fails to mourn his son's death in which he is complicit, and marries his adopted daughter. Rocco's assessment of all this is a crisp declaration of Gennaro's expulsion from the domus-centered society: "You were born an American."[21]

This tragedy has its chorus: the community disapproves of Gennaro and laments his violations of the moral order. In the voice of Zia Anna, Gennaro's housekeeper, the people complain: "We should have stayed in our vineyards and suffered a little poverty. What of it. To come here for a living and to become beasts . . . '*nna vergogna*.''[22] The community knows that it is greed that entices Gennaro to the extremes he is willing to go to. The betrayed Rocco tells him: "The American fever is in you. The touch of gold in your hands has been too much. We peasants are not used to it. It does queer things to us—the good it makes mean, the mean it makes brutal.''[23] What the community really mourns, though, is the shattering of the moral order—by Gennaro, but also, more importantly, by the very fact of having come to America to make money. Zia Anna's confrontation with Gennaro's depravity causes her to regret her own ambitions. The husband of the woman Gennaro has raped tells him, echoing Panunzio's regrets:

> I hate this country. It turns us all into different sorts from what we are. The clodhopper apes the man of education and good family; the man of good family becomes timid, or he's too well brought up to break the law and loses out. The last are first and the first are last, and the whole world seems upside down and crazy. I'm going back where everyone knows his place and things are orderly and decent.[24]

This is the power of Lapolla's vision of immigrant material longing. The community, however much it despises Gennaro and brands him a cafone, envies and respects his success, because it sees there its own most intimately held desires. Who would not respect Gennaro's arrogant triumph over the degradations two nations sought to impose on him? Gennaro has taken the abuse heaped on him and turned it to gold. In his words: "These bills . . . see, I found them on the streets, rags that were once fine dresses on the backs of American ladies. . . . I piled them up, I tied them up, I put them on my back. I carried them like a donkey way downtown. I sold them. . . . See, there they are, two thousand rags, each one a *scuto*.''[25] When the community comes to welcome Gennaro's wife, who is arriving from Italy, their blessing on her is a benediction of Gennaro's pursuits: "The sweet saint bring you prosperity, Rosaria *bella*. . . . May you make America, she willing, the blessed one. . . .''[26] Gennaro becomes a community leader: he marches at the head of the great communal religious procession; he is known to leaders outside the community and organizes a huge festa to greet the American fleet returning from the Spanish-American War; he is consulted by the priest who wants to build an Italian sanctuary in East Harlem. Indeed, it is Gennaro's greed that makes this church possible. Furthermore, the very people who condemn Gennaro are as avaricious as he is: his children, his workers—even Rocco, who is finally driven by his greed to kill an older, benign, and repentant Gennaro. Gennaro understands this complicity in his guilt and exploits it. In particular, he uses it in his domination of several impecunious Italian aristocrats who are completely dependent on him in East Harlem, a reordering of hierarchies that is one of his deepest sources of retributive satisfaction.

Lapolla does not overlook the American contribution to the development of this excitement in the Italian colony. His critique of American values is cast as a scathing satire of Protestant missionary activity in East Harlem. The immigrants' cupidity is bitterly appropriate in a society which itself worshiped money as an indicator of individual worth and prestige. The Italians of Lapolla's Harlem are conscious of the opulence of the Protestant churches just beyond the boundaries of their own poverty, on Park and Fifth avenues. These Protestants, repelled by the thought of letting the immigrants into their sanctuaries, conduct an economically exploitative ministry among the Italian poor. According to Lapolla, they try to buy the immigrants. They will only allow into their churches Italians who have been recast in their image. "If a family seemed to be of some refinement," the children were given clothes and invited to attend Sunday school at the "big church," where they were taught English, given coal in the winter, and "on specified days sent home with bundles of clothing, food and even toys." Later on their parents would be invited to church, but only if they would "discard their native costume and wear with some measure of casualness the American clothes supplied them by the mission."[27] Gennaro implicitly recognizes the power of this community to define moral standards and indicates their success in doing so when he reveals his own aspirations for Italian Harlem: "A bank,—a big bank is going to open in that corner. By Saint Jerome and the Holy Calendar, the Italians in this part of New York will be showing the Americans a thing or two. Yes, sir, yes, sir. With my church up soon, a bank here . . . we'll have a showplace."[28]

In the ironic evolution of Gennaro from moral monster to community leader, Lapolla reveals the depths of this passion for money in immigrant life. However much they fear it, however much they stand aghast at the potential desecration of their morality, they desire this success not only for itself but because this act of possession might dignify them, might give them the status and respect they could not find in Italy. Lapolla even suggests, rightly, that this passion was essentially for survival in America: Gennaro is destroyed only after he has quieted its fires. Without this drive, the immigrant was vulnerable.

Immigrants also had ambivalent feelings about the extent to which they should belong to their new country: although they wanted some access to the new culture, they feared the hasty Americanization plans devised by officials because they felt that these threatened their central values. A sense of alienation from America was often very strong in Italian Harlem, and there is evidence that this persisted in the older immigrant generations well into the 1950s. As a result of these ambivalences, the people of Italian Harlem often put off the process of naturalization as long as they could or resorted to a technique they called "half-citizenship," filling out preliminary requests for citizenship but never taking the process any further.

This alienation was not a purely internal matter; it was also caused by American xenophobia. In Panunzio's words: "I have seen prejudice, like an evil shadow, everywhere." Panunzio knew from personal experience that Americanization was often a code word for racial hatred.[29] The nature and meaning of American anti-Italian sentiment in the late nineteenth and early twentieth centuries is too large and important a subject to be treated quickly, but a sketch of the anti-Italian sentiment directed specifically at the Harlem community and the people's awareness of it will be helpful. Covello observed that the American attitude toward Italians went from a romantic and sentimental vision of Italy before 1870 to a deep hostility following contact with the first southern Italians arriving in New York. He notes that, by 1870, "Even the familiar organ grinder and the vendor of religious images were replaced by an inarticulate stereotype of a pick-and-shovel laborer from Italy."[30] Nineteenth-century urban, post-Puritan America would find the worker more frightening than the retailer of idols. Americans and American Catholics distinguished the northern Italian racial type ("Germanic") from the southern ("African"), a tendency that may have contributed to the identification of East Harlem with West Harlem. In 1912, Norman Thomas admitted that American-born Protestants in Harlem did not appreciate the presence of Italians in their churches.[31]

Covello remembered his own early education in East Harlem elementary schools with great bitterness. In his autobiography he writes:

Throughout my whole elementary school career, I do not recall one mention of Italy or the Italian language or what famous Italians had done in the world, with the possible exception of Columbus, who was pretty popular in America. We soon got the idea that "Italian" meant something inferior, and a barrier was erected between children of Italian origin and their parents. This was the accepted process of Americanization. We were becoming Americans by learning how to be ashamed of our parents.[32]

Covello feared his fellow students and his teachers, who took it upon themselves to change his name, to the great surprise and anger of his parents.[33] He hated the silence and military discipline forced on him. The situation did not improve when he got to high school where, he recalls, "the greatest obstacle was to establish any feeling of identity with these new students." Covello told an interviewer later in his life that his early schooling made him think that to become an American "we had to forget the way of life of our people."[34] Mazzola's experience in East Harlem schools two decades later was the same as Covello's. The young man recalled that his fledgling efforts to speak English were greeted with "painfully evident amusement and laughter" at Galvani Junior High School on 110th Street. As a result, "I suffered fancied indignations which I could not explain or forget."[35]

Covello once chose to express his anger over this situation at, of all times, a public naturalization rally held in East Harlem in 1938. He so eloquently states the problem of immigrant ambivalence toward their new home that his reflections are worth quoting and studying at length: "I remember, as a child, how I resented everything 'American' because American children seemed hostile to all of us foreigners. At the same time, everything in me yearned to have a share in all that Americans [sic] seemed to mean to these other children." He wanted to play in the streets with these American children, but there was always a barrier. Later, as he got older, the territorial line vanished, but: "there was always between the immigrant and his children and the Americans a vague barrier. As children we felt it though we could not see it. It separated us still from all that America meant. It hurt us more deeply still to feel that we were living in a country where we were excluded from full participation in all that was going on."[36] He knew that he was becoming more and more American, but he also knew that he was being rejected by that society. Covello added that the immigrants themselves must take some responsibility for this distance, mentioning in particular their reluctance to become naturalized citizens and adding, "I remember how ashamed I used to be of the fact that my father was not a citizen."

In 1941, Italians in New York City and in East Harlem gathered to protest the illegal detention of Italians by officials in the grip of wartime panic. The handbill circulated to announce the protest meeting complained: "Those arrested and those interrogated are poor people who, with or without passport, came to the United States with the hope of finding a piece of bread however stale, for themselves and their loved ones, and instead have found themselves like they were at home, with a handful of crumbs."[37] "A handful of crumbs"—although this does not express the entirety of the immigrant experience, it does articulate an important part of it. Southern Italians came to the United States to work hard and found themselves exploited and overworked. They continued to feel like aliens there in northern Manhattan, although they had labored to build the city and although their children were more of this land than the other. At some point in their lives, the immigrants in Italian Harlem had to ask themselves whether or not their journey had been worth all the trouble.

So the inner history of immigration is a story of ambivalences. Excitement and fear, apprehension and expectation characterized the crossing. In their new home, the immigrants had to struggle with the conflict between their enormous and all-consuming desire to "make America" and the fear that their success would threaten their values and unbalance their lives. They wanted to be a part of their new country, but they also wanted to keep their distance. The inner history of immigration is also a story of complex needs: for success, stability, participation and autonomy, faithfulness to tradition and an openness to the new ways, the need to recreate the familiar while in the midst of change.

The procession bearing the image of the Madonna of 115th Street walked amid the many tensions and complexities of the immigrants' lives, an emotional context as dense as the street life of the festa. The people were celebrating and calling upon the Madonna to heal them. In the ways they prayed to and approached the Madonna, the men and women of Italian Harlem revealed the most about themselves, and it is to this self-expression that we must now turn.

## CHAPTER VII

# The Meanings of the Devotion to the Madonna of 115th Street

HE devotion to the Madonna of 115th Street existed in the interstices between anticipation and reality, between the old and the young, the individual and the domus, between the United States and Italy, severed memories and emergent aspirations, the fear of success and the longing for it, between the old moral order and the discovery of the new. The figure of the Virgin was a symbol at the center of a ritual, and both symbol and ritual were taken up into a communal narrative mythology. The Madonna was not a stationary icon to be worshiped, but the focus of a drama to be acted out. The symbol was the focus; the festa provided the context for expressing and experiencing the emotional and moral content underlying the meaning of the symbol. Symbol, ritual, and myth—the entire experience of Mount Carmel emerged from and referred back to the people's lives; the men and women of Italian Harlem shaped and found themselves in the density of symbolic meanings when they attended the festa of the Madonna of 115th Street. In turn, their experience of the Madonna shaped their American destiny. We must attempt now to read what the symbol opens and discloses to us about the people.

## THE DEVOTION AND THE COMMUNITY OF IMMIGRANTS

The devotion to the Madonna of 115th Street met the emotional and moral needs of a population that had emigrated. In the earliest period,

163

from its founding to the time of Dalia's pastorate, which paralleled the first period of Italian immigration to the closing of the gates, when men were coming alone to New York, participation in the cult assuaged the complicated guilt of the immigrants. The devotion allowed men to be faithful to a woman on these shores as a sign of their faithfulness to the women they had left in Italy. Attendance at their mother's house located the men in the familial strategy of immigration: they had come because of their families and they could remember and acknowledge this in the devotion. In the earliest writings extant at the shrine, the church is identified strongly as "mammà's house," and *la Madonna* is called by the familiar and childlike "*nostra mamma.*" By initiating and attending the devotion to the Madonna of 115th Street, the men were declaring their faithfulness not only to their women but also to the moral and cultural system signified and dominated by women. The dimly glowing vigil lights which the earliest male immigrants kept burning in their rooms before images of the Madonna and the saints recalled the men to their moral culture: each night, with the sound of the elevated train coming in through the open windows, the noise of the street and the glowing of the gas factory's stacks, the red lamps summoned the men to be faithful to the values of their people. The devotion and the festa confirmed this and allowed the men to act out their faithfulness.

The immigrants, first men and then women too, as they arrived from southern Italy went to their mother's house, which is described as a place of rest and stability amid all change and on life's difficult journey. In a 1928 parish souvenir journal, the emotions and needs of this earliest period were remembered:

> The Italians who at that time were flooding into the country in great numbers, arriving in this city, immigrants battered by the sufferings of the long voyage and grief-stricken for having abandoned their homeland, sought an Italian church and were directed there, to the church of 115th Street.
>
> In this church they must have found comfort and hope for they never forgot the Madonna of 115th Street, whether they finally settled in New York, in a distant city or in the remote countryside.[1]

Here and elsewhere, the church is seen as the end of the long journey of immigration, a secure port in the "tempest of human society."[2] What the immigrants explicitly sought in their mother's house at the end of their wanderings was peace, protection, and pardon. We read in the *Bollettino* for September 1930: "When the fog begins to thicken on the horizons of our lives, and the flash of lightning and boom of thunder announce the outbreak of the hurricane of our suffering, of grief, of sorrow, and of anguish, we turn our eyes and our thoughts to this sanctuary and we find here safety, relief and peace."[3] The immigrants were calling to the Madonna to heal them of the many and various pains of their migration.

There is a way in which the entire festa recapitulated the experience of immigration. The annual celebration also involved a journey: for one day every year, the Madonna's throne became a wandering shrine, as the immigrants and their protectress took an extended trip through the neighborhoods. Participants in the devotion repeatedly emphasized the difficulties encountered by the devout both in getting to the shrine and then in making their way to the front of the church. The 1928 souvenir journal, for example, described the "long and fatiguing journeys [*viaggi*]" to the shrine, trips that involved "enormous expense" for the devout.[4] All of my informants stressed the fact that faithful came from "all over" to the annual celebration, and they particularly wanted to call to my attention long trips that involved crossing water—from Brooklyn, Staten Island, New Jersey; in each case, it was emphasized that a bridge had to be crossed or a boat taken but that this did not deter the faithful. Finally, after the Second World War, as Italian Harlem dispersed, a new emphasis was placed on the journeys back to the shrine undertaken by those who had moved out of the community, usually the children of immigrants.

By the principle of "inverted magnitudes," the signification of great realities or events by the smallest symbols or objects, the difficulties encountered in getting to the shrine opened out in meaning for the immigrants and played out again the movement of their migration, ending, as we were told their migration had ended, at their mother's feet. The younger generations were invited to share in a very physical way the central event of their parents' histories both by participating in the annual procession as children and by undertaking their long journeys back to Harlem for the devotion in later years. The fact that processions like these existed in Italy should not obscure the importance of the immigrants' choice of making the procession such a central and lengthy part of their devotion in the new world; we should not be confused in our analysis by thinking that anything had to be the way it became in the Italian colony. By the late 1940s, the theme of the weary traveler had been formalized into the rather standard spiritual idea of the shrine as a resting place on life's journey, but what may have been a spiritual cliché for others would always have a special meaning for the immigrants.

The facts that pilgrims came from all over to attend the July festa at *la chiesa della 115ma strada*, and that when they left they carried this devotion with them to await another return, meant a great deal to the people of Italian Harlem. Distance is a reality in the hearts of immigrants: the place of their birth is far behind, they have come a long way. This theme of the faraway helped shape the meaning of Mount Carmel and the intensity of the people's participation. The parish bulletin repeatedly urged all Italians, wherever they might be, to look to the Madonna for protection. The July festa was often depicted as a great homing, with men and women drawn back to Harlem by the force of Mary's presence there.[5] The people of East Harlem insistently emphasized this power of the Madonna to summon. One of my informants told me that her family chose to immigrate to Italian Harlem because they had heard from paesani that la Madonna was there.[6] The Madonna was called a beacon light for all the Italians of the world.[7]

This theme of distance, the physical distances separating families, is also present in the accounts of graces bestowed by la Madonna. In 1949, a woman wrote from Miami that she had been worried because she had not heard for six months from her son, who lived in Brooklyn, though she had written often to him. She prayed to the Madonna "to bring peace to my mind by receiving news from my son." Soon after her appeal, her son got in touch with her, assured her that he was in good health, and "apologized for having caused such sorrow to my heart."[8] During the Second World War, appeals to this power of the Virgin over distance took on a special urgency. One mother wrote in 1946: "Many times in this long period of four years I was without word from my son and my heart suffered immensely. But for all this I never succumbed but always had recourse to prayer."[9] In the same year, another mother wrote to thank the Virgin for giving her signs that her son was safe even though he had been reported missing in action.[10] Yet another woman wrote that before the war she had left her sons in Italy to study and then could get no word of them after the war's outbreak. But in this bitter situation, she wrote, she put her sons in the care of the Virgin of Mount Carmel and happily had just received news that they had survived the war.[11] Through their devotion to the Madonna, these women could stay in touch with distant loved ones with whom they had no other means of communication.

The sense evoked throughout is that the Madonna could overcome these various distances. For many Italians, participation in the devotion on 115th Street meant entering into a realm where distance vanished in the shared worship of the Madonna. Like the man who worked far away from his homeland secure in the knowledge that his lonely, distant labor was strengthening his family back home and even bringing it closer, so the men and women who prayed to the Madonna knew that this same peasant woman watched over their absent relatives. One of my sources told me that she loved to light vigil candles because she knew, when she awoke in the night, that the candle was burning in the church. So it was with the Madonna: when the Italians of Harlem woke at night two blocks away from their powerful protectress, they could feel part of the larger universe taken up into the Madonna's care. This triumph over distance was celebrated in the May 1929 issue of the parish bulletin: "O you who live in distant lands, in countrysides far away, in remote regions, turn your eyes in this month to the Virgin of Mt Carmel of 115th Street who listens to all, helps everyone and comforts all."[12] The people of East Harlem could glory in the fact of their proximity to the Virgin; in this very important area of their lives, as they kept reminding themselves by dwelling on the distances others had to come to get to their Madonna, they had triumphed over the harsh reality of distance.

Finally, as their efficacious presence in the community indicated, the Madonna and the saints had immigrated to the new world with their people. This was one of the implications of the arguments Tofini made to Leo XIII in his efforts to secure the Madonna's coronation. The evidence of the many graces the Madonna had granted the people of Italian Harlem was surely a sign that she had come to the new world with them. Her presence in East Harlem gave divine and maternal sanction to the immigrants' decisions to leave southern Italy and served, together with the saints, as an expression of the continuity between the old world and the new that the immigrants were trying to achieve in other ways in their lives in Italian Harlem. Like a woman who left her paese to join her son or daughter and grandchildren in Harlem, the Madonna had left Italy and come to New York. Tofini's emphasis on the intensity of the people's devotion to their *mamma divina* was also a revelation of their faithfulness to their earthly families and to their Italian traditions—all of which is enclosed within the symbol of the Madonna. Her presence helped soothe the anxieties and guilts of the immigrants, the pain and fear of the thought that they had abandoned not only their families but something essential in themselves as well. In these days, the living presence of the Madonna and the saints in Harlem helped to maintain the psychic and cosmic integrity of the immigrants.

## THE DEVOTION AND THE PEOPLE'S FAITHFULNESS TO ITALY AND SOUTHERN ITALIAN TRADITIONS

The statue of the Virgin, imported from the old country, was a visible link between Italy and East Harlem. The parish journal devoted considerable space to various aspects of Italian culture and occasionally sought to establish the interrelatedness of faith in la Madonna and Italian patriotism.[13] The immigrants, of course, initially felt little emotion for the nascent Italian nation-state which they knew only as oppressor; but the fact that paeans to Italian culture, written by an educated middle-class resident of the community, appeared in a popularly read devotional journal may have contributed to the emergence in East Harlem of a love for Italy in addition to the people's regional loyalties. This Italian-American-made popular *italianità* may have contributed to the fondness many in East Harlem felt for Mussolini, not as a Fascist but as a symbol of the forceful presence they were still groping for in this country at the time. The journal also printed notices of local Italian cultural events, such as a concert given by "Le Figlie di Dante" at Wadleigh High School in 1929.[14]

For the most part, however, the continuity of faith and devotion which the parish journal made explicit was seen as a faithfulness to southern Italian traditions. The procession, we are told, recalled the great traditional religious processions of southern Italy, just as the Italian American societies consecrated to particular saints resembled those in Italy.[15] The people were urged to relive their Italian past, to reaffirm their Italian selves during the festa. They were told to recall the little shrines to Mary scattered all over Italy—in valleys, beside rivers, deep in forests—and in this way to travel again the spiritual geography of their youth as they worship at the shrine on 115th Street.[16] Though they could not actually be in southern Italy, they could behave as though they were there; indeed, there are times when the author of the parish bulletin actually confused the two places, so that it is occasionally difficult to tell whether he is writing about Italy or East Harlem.[17]

For one week a year, the immigrants could refresh themselves, reestablish their memories, and relocate their stability by returning to their hometowns in religious spirit. In the middle of New York City, in the midst of a grueling work-week, and in the context of fear and sensory confusion, the immigrants could return to the source of their memories and integrity. In the words of the official history, the devotion gave to these men and women "the illusion of still being in their hometowns and served as a parenthesis of joyous thoughtlessness [*spensieratezza*], once a year, in the midst of the crushing work which bore down on their shoulders and of the effort to survive in the face of countless difficulties."[18] The immigrant was able temporarily to reexperience the smells, tastes, and sounds of the lost world of his or her past. This annual moral reorientation and resituating could give the immigrants confidence and hope in the face of their fears that immigration had undermined their moral world. We have seen that immigration was often experienced as a disorientation of sense perception, that the immigrants suffered a genuine sensory dislocation after arriving in the new world. The festa served as a powerful antidote to this fundamental moral and sensory anomie, assuring the immigrants that the world still turned on its axis and that they were still human beings who could taste things and who could be good people.

When the immigrants entered this world, they brought their children with them. The identity of Mount Carmel as a multigenerational event has been emphasized throughout its history. We are told in a souvenir journal that even in 1884 participants in the devotion included the American-born children of recently arrived immigrants.[19] The official history of the devotion records that the second generation took part in the festa as something they had learned from infancy.[20] This integration of generations was considered a characteristic enough feature of the event to be included by a Puerto Rican observer in a brief description of it written in 1949.[21]

The multigenerational character of the festa, like its expression of faithfulness to Italy, assured Italians that they had not severed themselves completely from their tradition or from the possibility of sharing that tradition with their children. It provided the immigrants with a sacralized occasion to welcome their children into their morality and culture. The emphasis in the popular history of the cult was not on the mere participation of children in the devotion, but rather on a generational continuity expressive of a deep faithfulness to tradition. In July 1934, the editor of the parish journal urged: "Parents! See to it that your children take part in this great manifestation of faith, explain to them the significance of this great event, to them who are the living history of the future, they will be the faithful narrators of the glorious history of the sanctuary on 115th Street."[22]

The devotion not only provided the younger generation with a way of proclaiming their loyalty to their parents and of locating themselves in a tradition that was the inescapable basis of their identities, but also contained the experience for them so that they could leave Italian Harlem and seek out their own futures. In the words of the official history:

> Let us say here in passing that, to tell the truth, the basic outlines of this devotion have remained the same down to the present and that the second and third generations of Italians in no way have lost this filial devotion inspired in them by the example of their parents and by the accounts of the miracles worked here by the mother of God.[23]

Parents and children together fulfilled vows, usually made by the former, to the Madonna; together they prepared for and welcomed guests into the domus, shouldered the heavy burden of the family's pain, cleaned the apartments and streets of the community. Children accepted the responsibility of fulfilling the vows of their deceased parents.

This, indeed, is one of the secrets of the continuity of the devotion even after the passing of Italian Harlem: younger Italian Americans who had left the community for more prosperous Italian settlements in the Bronx and elsewhere returned yearly to East Harlem to participate in the devotion. Many of them came back regularly in any case to visit their elderly parents, and the devotion remained the occasion for a joining of generations in a celebration of memory and place. Perhaps the knowledge that the Virgin still watched over Italian Harlem soothed some of the guilt and anxiety felt over having left their parents behind in a troubled community. One of my informants told me that his family used to come from the Bronx to visit his grandmother in Harlem frequently; they would go first to her apartment, and then, while she was preparing the Sunday meal, his father would take him to the church of Mount Carmel for a visit to the Madonna.[24] The second and third generations, furthermore, kept coming to the festa even after their parents had died, and frequently accepted the responsibility of fulfilling the vows of their deceased parents.[25] The devotion thus provided for the communion of generations, the sharing of experience, and the moral location and integration of people separated first by different pasts, then by changing lives in the present, and finally by death.

## THE DEVOTION AND THE DOMUS

The domus of Mount Carmel drew its meaning from and found support in its identification with the domus; the domus drew its meaning from and found its support in its identification with the domus of Mount Carmel. In the presence of an all-powerful mother who was called upon to ratify and approve what was going on and to offer her protection, the festa displayed and summoned the people to participation in a ritualistic condensation of the domus-based values essential to the life of the community and its self-understandings and self-presentations. The members—living and dead—of the domus were brought together in all the moments and events of the festa, from the preparations in the homes of Harlem before the feast day to the *pranzi* that followed the great procession and the visiting that went on through the night. They also came together under the heavy burdens of wax candles carried in the procession and in the shared responsibility of fulfilling vows. There were plenty of opportunities during the many days and nights of the celebration to show rispetto to various members and branches of the extended family and to comari, to end old quarrels, to reestablish ties with relatives from outside the community. Young and old spent important time together during the festa. The living assumed the vows of the dead, and people found themselves recalling past feste and the faith and devotion of their dead kin. Bonds of reciprocity were exposed and blessed as people in the community shared each others' lives during the festa.

There was another primal and fundamental way in which the devotion sanctioned the domus-based values of the community. The festa of the Madonna of Mount Carmel recreated the primary and traditional environments of the Italians—the preverbal environment, on the one hand, and the remembered environment of Italy, on the other—in the presence of a quasi-omnipotent mother who healed or did not heal, depending on the behavior of the individual. For the older immigrants and their Italian-born children, the sense world of the festa was the sense world of their southern Italian childhoods; for the later generations in East Harlem, the sense world of the festa recalled the smells, sounds, and tastes of life in the domus. In both cases, the festa and the domus, the sense world was shaped and presided over by a powerful woman. The religious experience of July 16 had the power to evoke memories that were extraordinarily basic: the people seemed to be returning not only to their paese but, more profoundly, to their mothers. The festa was a time of regression, in other words, and the smells, tastes, and sounds of it helped to precipitate and sustain this regression. The devotion summoned people into the sacral domus and surrounded them with familiar tastes, smells, sounds, colors, and textures; in this way, in the presence of their "mamma," the people returned to the world in which they had first learned, from their mothers, what reality was, what was good and what bad, what their basic values were and the values of their community. The festa and the long-passed intimate moments of moral formation smelled, tasted, and sounded the same.

When we consider what was taking place at the festa—the integration of young people into the traditional values, the communal reaffirmation of these values, the establishment of the nexus between individual and family, family and community, and so on—and when we add the absorption of the stress-filled polarities of Italian psychosocial life into a healing ritual to this picture, we can see that the creation of this sense world as the environment in which all this occurred was an effort to structure a very basic point of orientation. It was an attempt to establish a context within which a multileveled resolution could take place and receive maternal sanction. The food, noise, and smells all established the necessary precondition for the absolution, resituation, and reintegration that took place at the festa.

This precondition was essential because it set the individual in the environment of maternal instruction, power, and comfort. Everyone was a child again during the festa. In this way, the men and women of Italian Harlem were prepared to receive what the festa taught and confirmed for them about themselves and their community. But it is the unique power of the festa of 115th Street that all of this took place on levels more powerful than the conscious. A man standing in front of his celestial mamma's house on 115th Street and smelling the aromas and hearing the sounds of his childhood would be resituated in the moral world of his culture by the smell of sausage sizzling in a pan or tomato sauce simmering or by the cracked voices of women chanting; these aspects of the festa, so troubling to American Catholic officials, bore as much of the religious or cosmological meaning of the celebration as the events that took place inside the church. *All* the smells, sounds, and tastes of the days and nights of the festa, in the context of the festa, reintegrated individuals into the totality of their culture.

The Italians ate a great deal during the days and nights of the festa. This centrality of eating, one of the ways in which the traditional and primary sense world was created and maintained during the celebration, referred to and depended on what took place in the domus. Eating was the sacrament of the home, and the Sunday meal was more important to the immigrants than regular attendance at mass. Eating expressed the ideal unity of the home and defined the real hierarchy of authority within the domus—the meal became a drama of authority and resistance, the context of reconciliation and the affirmation of tradition. The consumption of food at the festa established a deep structural link between the celebration with all its meanings, and the home with all its needs. A process of mutual ratification found secret support as the participants experienced the festa orally, as food in the homes and food in the streets. Food was symbol and sanction and sacrament, integrating the home, the streets, and the sacred.

The people who came to the festa took away a reminder of the day—and of what they had learned at the celebration—in the scapulars that were given out at the altar. Scapulars of the Madonna are said to protect—to guard the body and defend the soul. These scapulars were given to the people in their mother's house in return for the sacrifices they had made on that day; they would find their way into people's wallets and purses, bedrooms and kitchens. Children wore scapulars for protection; the sick wore them in hope of a cure; the old wore them for consolation and comfort. The scapulars became another expression of the ties that bound members of the community together, as well as of those that existed among the self, the domus, and the divine. A young man, for example, who carried a scapular of the Madonna in his wallet at his mother's request would know that he was part of the same world as his parents, who kept their scapular tied to their bedpost, and as his long-deceased grandmother, whose scapular was still kept by the family; and all these ties would have been authorized and sanctified by the fact that all the scapulars had been acquired at the festa of the Madonna of 115th Street. The scapular of the Madonna of Mount Carmel was an emblem of the people who declared themselves at the annual festa.

The devotion also served as a way of expressing and healing the intense familial and generational conflicts characteristic and disruptive of Italian American family life and of protecting the domus from the outside influences that seemed to threaten it. The pages of Mount Carmel's parish journal throughout its history are filled with accounts of domestic troubles into which the Madonna is either asked to come or already has and is being thanked. Most of these accounts were addressed directly to the Madonna, and the printed correspondence represents only a fraction of the huge volume of letters received at the church. People also described their needs to the Madonna during the festa, when they would call out their troubles to her in the streets or in church, in the presence of their neighbors.

The devout themselves asked to have these stories published, and this tells us that in the accounts of healing they saw something essential about themselves. The stories, almost always told by women, always had roughly the same three-part structure. First, the women told the Madonna about their trouble: sickness (either psychological or physical—or both), unemployment, family tension, unhappy relationships. These problems were never presented as only personal, as nothing was in Italian Harlem; the crisis always threatened the domus. In the first act of these popular dramas, the domus appears fragile and vulnerable, on the brink of collapse. Then the Madonna intervenes. She heals the suffering child or parent, finds work for the unemployed, comforts the emotionally troubled. In these ways she saves the domus, and the accounts conclude with the domus intact again, a reintegration sanctified by the Madonna's intervention.

At various times, to give only a glimpse of her activities, the Madonna saved a seven-year-old boy who had fallen out of a sixth-floor window, a little boy who was hit by a trolley car, and a little girl suffering from pneumonia.[26] In many cases, the Madonna was called on to intercede in a situation where the negligence of a parent was the (usually unexpressed) cause of near tragedy. A father who had been left to mind his infant daughter ("Beautiful, lively, a real treasure") watched in panic as she fell from her crib onto her head. He cried out to the Madonna and the baby escaped harm, as we learn from an account written by the child's mother.[27] In another case, a woman had allowed her seven-year-old daughter to go on a class outing. Late in the afternoon after the trip, the school bus left the girl off in an unfamiliar spot in the neighborhood and she lost her way. Her parents and their neighbors searched through the streets for her without success. Then the girl's mother prayed to the Madonna and the girl was found unharmed.[28] These stories and many others reveal a concern for the manifold threats of an urban environment, and all implicitly depict mothers and fathers distracted and preoccupied by a multitude of worries and anxieties. The Madonna's healing attention was also prayed for in cases of nervous breakdown, usually when the implied cause was either familial or sexual. Women who were suffering either the anxiety of the pressure to marry or the agony of being caught in unwanted relationships that the community would not have approved of their breaking off pleaded with the Madonna for help. She was called upon in cases of troubled pregnancy, in particular those in which the doctors had given up on the life of either the child or the mother. Often she was asked to intervene in instances of explicit family tension. In 1948, a woman wrote from Newark: "For a very long time there was no peace in my family. I made as many novenas as I possibly could but to no avail. However, from the time I turned to our Lady of Mt. Carmel, a change came over the family. Peace and reason was established and I know that it was only through Our Lady's intercession that this came about."[29] Another person wrote to thank the Virgin for resolving a struggle that had raged in her family for months.[30] After the war, the prayers sent to the Madonna from the newer and more prosperous areas of Italian settlement reflected the whole new set of anxieties plaguing these more upwardly mobile Italian Americans. Now the prayers were for a husband's business or a daughter's success in school. Daughters became the family members most often prayed for, reflecting the new precariousness of young women in the Italian community, better educated and better employed than their male counterparts.[31]

The Madonna's cures for the most part were not spectacular: most frequently she was called upon to heal very minor household accidents and common domestic maladies—dental problems, mild fevers, colds, the many dilemmas in the lives of the poor. One woman thanked the Madonna for healing her leg after she poured a little boiling water on it while she was cooking.[32] The Madonna was appealed to in cases of family separation, even those of limited duration and small distance.[33] Her assistance was sought by countless men and women, though mostly women, suffering from a multitude of unexplained maladies, fevers, convulsions, spasms, and seizures. The intimate dimension of these small catastrophes was eloquently stated by one of the Madonna's supplicants: "Please, Father, pray for me as I have been having many troubles through my life. Nevertheless, I always offer all my suffering to God: May it be his will."[34]

The intensity with which requests for help with these small problems was expressed reflects the precariousness of poor people's lives, lives in which an inflamed molar could be the beginning of a chain of consequences that could end in untold, if not unexpected, suffering. But this intensity—and the mysteriousness of many of the maladies—suggest another possibility. The Madonna was asked to intervene in crises in which sickness was only one component of a complex of familial and personal tensions: the many unexplained ailments and psychosomatic symptoms mean something besides illness.

Conflicts in the domus found expression in these many accounts of unnamed sickness and minor accidents. The stories expressed the anger many felt against the domus. They articulated the alienation that many suffered within it despite their feeling that this was the only genuine source of their identities, as well as the distance from it that many individuals in the domus wanted to attain but could not. When the healing stories are studied against the background of the troubled domus, it becomes clear that the healing that occurred is very complex. On one level, the illnesses themselves were healed; on deeper levels, the people were pleading with the Madonna to heal their rage and the guilt of it, to heal their longing to escape the confines of the domus and their anger at the futility of this longing. The Madonna was also asked to protect the domus—which, as we saw, was always perceived as extremely vulnerable, despite all the evidence to the contrary—from the destructive possibilities of this rage. The healing stories of Mount Carmel express the pain of the domus and its prayer to be healed.

The stories had meaning to two sets of people—those who told them and those who heard them. In the first case, they allowed the people who had suffered to express their confusion and sense of vulnerability. The stories, however, were even more important for those who heard them during the festa. Remember that these were people of the troubled domus listening to the accounts of healing; they knew how to read them, we can only guess at what they may have seen in them. In the account of the father left alone with his baby, for example, the story is about the baby, but it is also about male ineptitude in the domus, about the fears of the vulnerability of the domus amid the many threats and distractions of New York, about the father's guilt and his wife's anger. The story confirms the belief that the domus is threatened when the mother is not there. Behind the brief account of the woman scalded while cooking, the community might have seen a demanding domus that would not let the woman be for a moment, a threatened domus missing the care of a mother, a husband and children with many needs, or a woman's anger and loneliness.

For the audience reading and listening to these accounts, the healing stories enacted what Peter Brown has called a *psychodrame* of disintegration and reintegration, an enactment especially important in times of crisis or transition. In the accounts of healing at the shrine, the people experienced the breakdown of families at work and in the streets, a possibility they always dreaded, symbolized by the metaphor of sickness. They were also allowed to enjoy the spectacle of the threatened domus, the domus brought to the brink of collapse—which is where many unconsciously wanted to see it. What a relief it must have been for this population, locked into the domus, to see its fragility publicly displayed. And what a relief it must have been to experience this knowing all the while that the domus would triumph at the end, as it always did. In the familial balance inevitably regained by the end of these stories, the power and preeminence of the domus are revealed, its resilience and authority displayed. The healing stories were the sacred, cathartic theater of Italian Harlem: the community could derive a deep retributive satisfaction from the threatened demise of the domus while looking forward to the satisfactions of the domus' final triumph.

One of the central meanings of the annual festa, then, was the power and authority of the domus over the lives of individuals and its resilience to their anger. The custom of children sharing their parents' and grandparents' vows revealed the extension of the power of the domus over time and reminded the individual that his or her identity as an individual was subsumed into this larger identity. The most powerful and obvious symbol of the domus triumphant and of its authority to summon its members to submission was the practice of sharing the heavy burdens of the huge candles during the procession. Here the domus was shown to be intact despite its troubles: individuals sharing the responsibility for carrying the symbol of the domus' crisis were acknowledging their responsibilities in the domus. They were literally bowing down to its authority. When these men and women brought the candles into church, after carrying them through the streets of Italian Harlem in full view of their neighbors and the Madonna, and laid their burdens down at the feet of the Madonna, they were begging her to heal their pain and rage and suffering; but at the same time they were participating in and acknowledging the power of the domus over them. The people were thanking the Madonna for her safekeeping of the domus, but this was a most ambivalent gratitude.

## THE SHAPING OF *CARA HARLEM*

Just as the individual's experience of the devotion—the devout had private reasons and concerns that brought them to the shrine on 115th Street—was integrated into the devotion as a family event, so that individual devotion became, with or without the consent of the individual, an element of this larger context, so too the family event became part of a neighborhood experience. Here we come to one of the most important historical meanings of the devotion to Mount Carmel in Harlem. In Italy, the people had participated in the special devotion to the saint of their hometown, an affirmation of their belonging to a particular paese. Religious festivals were also linked to collective activities, such as the harvest or the time of sowing.[35] Feste symbolized, celebrated, and helped to achieve the integration of individual destiny with communal solidarity. Participation in the celebration of the festa and worship of the summarizing symbol of the Madonna became the nexus between the individual domus and the neighborhood in Italian Harlem.[36]

In the face of the many difficulties that troubled the poor, ill-housed, ethnically diverse, dirty, and dangerous community of Italian Harlem, the devotion to the Madonna of 115th Street helped shape *cara Harlem*. Religious solidarity, communion within the various expressions of popular religiosity, can precede social or communal soli-

*115th Street, facing west*

darity in poor communities. It seems that, once separated from the
hopeless poverty and mutual mistrust engendered by the conditions of
the mezzogiorno, which the people had already acted against in a
number of communal institutions and movements both on the peninsula and in Sicily during the late nineteenth and early twentieth centuries,[37] the men and women of Italian Harlem turned first to religious
solidarity as a way of expressing nascent community consciousness.
They transformed the devotion from a regional celebration in honor of
the protectress of Polla to a celebration in honor of the Madonna of
115th Street.

By 1928 at the latest, and probably much earlier, the church of
Mount Carmel was identified with 115th Street and the Virgin referred to as "la Madonna della 115ma strada."[38] This identification
was quite natural given the intense street life of the festa: it was a
spiritual event with a geography. The devotion absorbed the geography into itself so that no distinction can be made between the religious
event and the setting. This identification constituted a sacralization of
Italian Harlem. People considered 115th Street holy because the
Madonna resided there, and this attitude spilled out onto the streets:
during the days and nights of the festa the neighborhood was transformed, as people cleaned the streets, decorated their fire escapes,
washed their windows, and scrubbed the tenement hallways.

The devotion to Mount Carmel overcame southern Italian regional identities by absorbing them into the church. Although regional
societies continued to meet as long as the older immigrants survived,
many of them met in this country at the church of Mount Carmel. In
this way, their regional loyalties were deflected, and they entered the
constellation of stars over the Madonna's throne. The popular histories of the devotion are quite clear on the importance of this contribution. In the 1928 souvenir journal, it is carefully specified that no
regional or provincial distinctions were made at Mount Carmel.[39] The
story of the construction of the bell tower is cast as a triumph over
regionalism.[40]

The devotion to the Madonna also worked against neighborhood
isolationism: the feast of Mount Carmel was a central communal event
that mobilized the energies of all Italian Harlem and absorbed manifold local conflicts and identities into a shared task. It summoned
people out of their neighborhoods to participate in the life of Italian
Harlem: the devotion was a source of pride and responsibility in cara

Harlem. This can be compared to the people's feelings about other churches in Italian Harlem: though they might know about St. Lucy's, for example, or even feel that it was a beautiful church, unless men and women came from the neighborhood around the church they would not feel any special loyalty to it. But everyone was proud of the devotion to Mount Carmel. In 1941, the *East Harlem News* proudly told its readers that two hundred thousand people were expected in the neighborhood for that year's festa, adding, "This is one of the events in the life of East Harlem which you simply must experience."[41]

It is in this context of the relationship between the devotion and the community that we must understand what the people were saying when they took the clothes off their recently healed children on the day of the festa and donated them to the church for distribution to poor children in the neighborhood. By this gesture, they revealed their understanding of the intimate connection between private grief and joy and the claims and contributions of the community: the tremendous occasion of the healing of a child was not a time for celebration within the domus alone but also a moment to acknowledge the important sustaining bonds that existed between the domus and the community. Such times of powerful sadness or happiness were times not only to be shared with others, but were actually occasions of special connection between the individual domus and the community. The connection was one of mutuality and reciprocity: the Madonna's healing action created the requirement of social reciprocity and entailed a moral response. It did not isolate the affected domus but, rather, drew it back into society and exposed the ties that bound the domus and the neighborhood. The domus in its crises or joys included the neighborhood.

Sickness and health, which are in any case personal and potentially isolating realities, are especially dangerous in communities like Italian Harlem which have a shared history of oppression and a contemporary existence characterized by intense struggle and sacrifice. Sickness can be interpreted as a curse, as the work of jealousy and spite; and health—especially the health that follows sickness—could be angrily and anxiously guarded, attended by the fear of relapse, and could even be viewed as a triumph of the domus over the malicious intentions of neighbors. The exchange of clothes at the shrine offered another way of thinking about sickness and health as times of connectedness and mutuality between the domus and society. This, as we have seen, was in fact the way that sickness and health were experienced in Italian Harlem: people absolutely needed their neighbors to survive. So the exchange symbolized and sanctified the way life was lived there.

It is significant that the child was brought to church actually wearing the clothes that would soon be worn by another child; besides situating the recently healed child back in society, the exchange also expressed how the people understood the balance between domus and society in the definition of an individual's identity. It revealed a sense that each person's identity involved two inextricable domains, the public and the private. No one existed only in the domus.

Finally, the Madonna herself is revealed as the source of the connection between the self and the community. It is her act which entails the giving of the gift of clothing. The people here seem to be acknowledging the centrality of the Madonna of 115th Street in the shaping of their public world, their sense of mutual responsibility and concern. They were also acknowledging the importance of women in establishing this nexus. When people asked after each other's mothers on the streets of Italian Harlem, or watched out for each other's sisters, or chose where they were going to live on the basis of where their mothers or sisters lived, they were shaping a public world through the medium of women. The same thing seems to be happening in this ritual of exchange at the shrine: it was the community's sacred mamma who drew people out of the domus into the interconnecting world of social responsibility and reciprocity. In this way, the ritual reflected and affirmed the public role of women in shaping the social life of Italian Harlem.

In the earliest days of the community, before East Harlem had become an Italian colony, the festa was a brave declaration of presence, proclaiming to Irish and German Catholics and to American Protestants that the Italians had arrived and that they would do things their way. By celebrating the Madonna of 115th Street, the Italians claimed the neighborhood for themselves. The wealthy of West Harlem and the Catholics of East Harlem soon knew where the Italians lived. The procession emphasized this claim by marking the boundaries of Italian Harlem each year and giving those boundaries divine sanction. Later in the history of East Harlem, when the Puerto Ricans began arriving in the 1940s and 1950s, the procession and the devotion intimidated the newcomers. A Puerto Rican woman told me that when the procession came down into the emergent Puerto Rican neighborhoods at the lower end of East Harlem, the people there adopted a very cautious and wary attitude toward it, understanding that this was an expression of local Italian prominence. They knew, furthermore, that they were not welcome to join the procession at that early date.[42]

The sense experience of the festa, and in particular the food consumed, also marked out what was Italian and what was not in the ethnically dense world of northern Manhattan. This is illustrated by a story told by a young Puerto Rican man to a high-school English class in the late 1940s.[43] One afternoon he wandered by mistake into Italian Harlem, not always a pleasant experience for young Puerto Rican men at this time. When he tried later to set down what he thought and felt about the experience, he centered his description almost exclusively on tastes and smells. He defined the Italian community by the strong smell of the old men's cigars, by the different taste of the coffee, the aroma of tomato sauce, and the smell of wine. The young Piri Thomas called the neighborhood around Mount Carmel "spaghetti country" and Italians "spaghetti benders."[44] Just as the procession defined the boundaries of the community during the festa, so did its strong smells and tastes.

As the procession mapped out and gave a divine sanction to the borders of Italian Harlem, it also, together with the street life of the festa, sacralized the streets. Within the consecrated context of the festa, the people claimed the streets for themselves. We have seen that the men and women of Italian Harlem had deeply ambivalent feelings toward the streets of their community: they feared the crime that took place there and abhorred the filth and danger of the streets; but at the same time they needed the streets and were compelled to spend much of their lives in them. Italians also brought a love of the streets with them from Italy, where they had lived as urban agriculturalists in densely populated towns. And it was in Italy that they had learned to claim the streets by blessing them.[45]

The street was thus a theater of extremes in Italian Harlem, a carnival alternately beckoning and frightening. The devotion to Mount Carmel responded to this tension: it was the annual blessing and reclamation of the streets, the urban equivalent of the Mediterranean custom of carrying the statue of a town's protector out into the threatening but inescapable and necessary sea. Furthermore, precisely because the streets were an extension of the home, they too had to be gathered beneath the moral canopy. It is significant in this regard that New York's Italians quickly acquired a reputation for cleaning up the neighborhoods they inhabited.[46] Like the statues in the home, the Madonna in the streets was proclaiming and promising the people's moral authority over the gutters, helping to incorporate them into the domus-centered society and recreating them as the scenes of rispetto—toward the Virgin, among neighbors, families, and friends. As the Madonna was asked to heal persons and families, so she was asked to touch the streets, where the hurt was deep. The devotion was a neighborhood event, and in a dense, often divided, always outcast neighborhood, this annual communion was a healing simply by the fact of the gathering at the maternal shrine.

The devotion, the church, and the monthly parish bulletins (especially the souvenir issues) also helped to define and legitimate the local power structure. Prominent neighborhood doctors and lawyers advertised their services in the pages of the parish bulletin, just as they marched at the head of the procession on July 16, claiming for themselves an authority in the community at a time when they were not welcomed into the American elite.[47] Local merchants contributed to the devotion in a bid for greater prestige. The Italian savings bank, located in the neighborhood, occupied a prominent place in the pages of the parish journal into the early 1930s. Funeral directors took out large advertisements in the various souvenir journals. Notices of political parties and the endorsements of local Democratic and Republican clubs also appeared in these souvenir editions, together with advertisements of Italian firms, particularly food concerns, in East Harlem and other Italian American settlements. Local restaurateurs took out space, local bakers promised beautiful Italian cakes for marriages, baptisms, and other *grandi occasioni*, food importers announced their genuine Italian products.[48]

The souvenir journals had obviously become prestigious occasions for displaying status and proclaiming faithfulness to the Virgin, a faithfulness that also meant loyalty to the community and to tradition despite wealth or American-bestowed rank, when the latter came.[49] All of these advertisements and notices were grouped like a wreath around what was ostensibly the main concern of the periodical, the publication and celebration of the Madonna's healing graces. The preoccupations of Italian Harlem—money, food, proper funerals, the prestige of the local elite, and the stories of healing—all found expression together in the church and the devotion. Mount Carmel thus became the integrating center for the life of the whole culture, under the benign gaze of the Madonna. If Italian American culture seemed nowhere else to cohere, if elsewhere there was tension between money and devotion, anxiety over the chances of a dignified death in the new world, a distaste for American food and a desire to be part of a new culture, all these came together and found articulation in the church on 115th Street.

Finally, the Madonna and the devotion provided a point of stability in the midst of constant transience and upheaval, both in the early life of the community, when men and women came and went according to their fortunes and expectations, and at the end of the community's life, as younger people left for better homes elsewhere. Frequently in the descriptions of the devotions it was emphasized that the Madonna would always be there on 115th Street waiting for her children, regardless of where they had gone. Although men and women might leave the community temporarily or move around within it, they could take comfort from the stable residence of the Madonna on 115th Street. Italian Harlem seemed like a place of stability and security to many of its residents, and one of the reasons for this was that at the center of the community was the divine domus presided over by the divine mother. When men and women who had left the community came back to Harlem, they always stopped in to visit the Madonna, whom they knew would always be there. As one of my informants expressed this, "Where else do you go when you come back, but to your mother's house?"[50] This sense of security shaped people's feelings about cara Harlem.

As cara Harlem began to disappear in the 1950s and 1960s, what continued to exist of it, in reality and in memory, existed in relation to the Madonna. She was there at the center of people's recollections of their community, she determined what people took away with them when they left, and she was there to welcome them back to a very changed but, because of her presence, still recognizable community when they returned to visit or bury aging parents and relatives. Continued participation in the devotion, even from a distance, offered the people who had moved away some continuity and stability in the context of their own geographical and social mobility. During one of my interviews in North Arlington, New Jersey, with a family that had moved from East Harlem first to the South Bronx and then, much later, across the river, I was taken into the master bedroom and shown an old and faded scapular of the Madonna tied to the bed. The family had been given the scapular some twenty years before at the annual festa at Mount Carmel. By means of this relic, these people had remained in touch with their protectress, and through her with cara Harlem, even after any physical connection with northern Manhattan had been severed. The scapular had become a symbol of the values and faith first nurtured in the homes of Italian Harlem.

The creative and constitutive power of the Madonna of 115th Street is still in evidence today. What is left of Italian Harlem seems to be clustered around the Madonna. East Harlem, now Spanish Harlem, remains a troubled community. The people express profound anxiety over the problem of street violence and easy availability of drugs. But as always in the history of East Harlem, there is enormous popular effort and hope there, a resistance and resilience strong in the face of official neglect. For some, this hope is focused on and sustained by the Madonna of 115th Street. A very old Jamaican woman summed up this continuing confidence in the Madonna, "The Neighbor[hood] change, but Mt Carmel is still outstanding."[51]

## THE COMMUNITY REVEALS ITSELF TO ITSELF

The people of East Harlem beautified the church on 115th Street always one step beyond their means: with every new addition to the church, the popular history describes the sacrifice and generosity of the faithful despite their difficult circumstances.[52] The construction of the church and its many remodelings in this way became an external symbol for the pride, self-respect, and aspiration of the Italian people of Harlem. Their beautification of the church was the people's statement of the integrity of their values and the depth of their faithfulness despite their poverty.[53] In this way, Mount Carmel did not just mirror the changing fortunes of East Harlem; rather, it anticipated them and became a symbol of the people's potential. Beyond this, the very development of the devotion can be seen as a paradigm of the destiny of the immigrants in the United States—from the humblest origins and against considerable odds to unheard-of triumphs. Mount Carmel served as beckoning symbol of what the immigrants wanted for themselves and what they believed themselves capable of.

This interpretation is suggested by the way the story of the devotion is told. The origins of the church are presented in an early account as a great dream realized against formidable obstacles. "The profiteers," we are told, "and those who did not know how much the soul of the Italian people was capable of when it concerned la Madonna, smiled sceptically and urged prudence." Then a dialogue is described between the people and their detractors:

> Don't venture upon the unknown. Gauge yourselves according to your economic conditions.
> [The people reply:] We want a temple for the Madonna!
> But you'll need money! How will you pay the workers?
> We'll be the workers. We'll work for nothing, after we get out of work at the factory.[54]

This can be read as a mythical restatement of the entire endeavor of immigrants in the United States: with our own hands we will accomplish this work!

This same theme underlies the story of the bell tower, which was completed in 1927.[55] As this tale is told, the people are shown looking at the face of the church after the completion of the tower, and exclaiming "We never thought we could have succeeded like this!" The people are seeing what they are capable of by looking at what they have accomplished for the Madonna and the community. In 1928 the front of the church was cleaned. Once again, this is portrayed as a popular triumph—this time of the people, through their folk hero, Dalia, who "knew neither the word 'enough' nor the word 'obstacle.'"[56] Finally, we are told in 1933 that the people were especially proud of the remodeling work done on the sanctuary during the hard and financially troubled years of the Depression.[57] At the time of evictions in the community, the people showed their self-respect by beautifying the Madonna's house.

Pride in this demonstration of faithfulness and loyalty in hard times echoes a similar pride expressed by several of my informants who told me that even during the Depression the people of East Harlem cared for each other, sharing whatever they had. Again the history of Mount Carmel parallels and uncovers the inner history of Italian Harlem, the history of the people's values, of what they considered their deepest quality. By participating in the devotion to the Madonna of 115th Street, the people were participating in the symbolic recapitulation of their own American destinies; the devotion revealed the meaning of their hopes and confidence, reminding them of these realities when they lost sight of them. It was on this deepest level that the men and women of Italian Harlem celebrated themselves when they celebrated the Madonna.

The festa also educated the people of Italian Harlem. The totality and cultural power of the symbol of the Madonna had an identity apart from any individual participant; although (and because) the Madonna was of the people, she still confronted any individual or family as a separate reality over which they had little conscious control. Every individual who took part in the devotion was thereby taught and integrated into the community's values. Once a year the entire community left its houses and stores and places of work—left, in other words, the normal structure of their lives—took their Madonna off her throne, and, together with her, poured into the streets. The community on these days was given the opportunity to see itself acting as a community. The essential and complex structures of the social life of a community in transition were bodied forth in a highly visible manner, in the people's relations with each other and with the Madonna. As Peter Brown has written: "the festival of a saint was conceived of as a moment of ideal consensus on a deeper level. It made plain God's acceptance of the community as a whole: his mercy embraced all its disparate members, and could reintegrate all who stood outside in the previous year."[58] Everyone who talks about the devotion to the Madonna of 115th Street takes care to mention that even those people who would not set foot in church faithfully attended the festa.

This is the dialectic of the encounter between a religious symbol and an individual (or a family or a community). The symbol emerges in a complex manner as the summation and universalization of the community's inherited tradition and moral wisdom. Symbol and individual encounter each other and an integration occurs. The individual is resituated in the community. This is why it was so important for the event to be multigenerational. The event and the symbol existed for those who observed it, as well as for those who participated in it.

## THE DEVOTION AND THE LARGER COLLECTIVITIES
## OF THE CITY AND NATION

The devotion to the Madonna of 115th Street was like a nest of Russian dolls, each doll encased by a larger one: the devotion had private meanings for each of the devout; meanings in the domus and the neighborhoods; and meaning also, as the people saw it, in the city of New York and in the history of the nation. Carla Bianco knew an immigrant woman in Brooklyn who kept a small replica of the Statue of Liberty on her night table next to the image of the protectress of her paese. The women called the madonna of the harbor "Santa Liberata."[59] This can stand as a symbol for one of the struggles confronting the immigrants in their new home, that of finding a way of connecting themselves to their new land—and of establishing this connection, furthermore, in a way that would not violate their values. Indeed, the self-location of the immigrants in the United States, if it was to be profound enough to be successful, had to work through their deepest beliefs. The American Catholic church could not serve this function, at least not initially: its cultural distaste for the immigrants amounted to an existential rejection of their whole value system. For the Italians of Harlem, the attempt at rootedness in the new land took place, at least in part, through the central religious event of the colony, the devotion to the Madonna of 115th Street.

The devotion allowed the immigrants to claim a part of American space and American time. The annual festa took place in New York and the people of Italian Harlem asserted that the July celebration was an important moment in the annual life not just of their community but also of the city. In 1934, for example, the parish bulletin proudly noted, in Italian, "The City of New York in general and the great and ancient [antico] section of Harlem in particular will participate [on the coming July 16] in a demonstration of faith which will long be remembered in the history of this great city."[60] The claim is, of course, that Italian Harlem and New York have a common experience and history, a claim the city itself rarely acknowledged.

The devotion was also used to lay claim to a place in the history of the nation. The earliest and most important example of this was the argument that Father Tofini made to Leo XIII in supporting the popular request for a crown for the Madonna. His arguments offer us a glimpse into the people's needs and self-perceptions in the early years of the community. Tofini began his presentation to the pope by documenting the numerous graces which the Madonna had granted the people of Italian Harlem. He emphasized that her generosity not only revealed her love for the Italian people but also signaled her new concern for the United States. The official historian of the devotion ratifies this argument when he adds that all three new world Marian devotions were recognized at about the same time, "as though all of a sudden, Mary, Queen of Heaven, desired officially to take under her mantle this land discovered by Columbus in the name of the most Holy Savior."[61] There is a hidden message in this argument: Mary had become concerned for the United States because something new had happened in its history—her beloved Italian people had arrived. East Harlem's faith in Mary's loving nearness to the streets of Upper Manhattan gave Italians a special role in American history. Mary had come to the new world because they had come there—she had emigrated with them. Henceforth, from the time of Italian immigration, this land discovered by an Italian would know the love of the Madonna.

Tofini's most powerful, difficult, and crucial argument was the one he offered to overcome the obstacle of the requirement that the cult be of recognized antiquity.[62] This demanded subtlety, since at the time Tofini was making his arguments the devotion was all of twenty years old. Tofini rose to the challenge. History is different in the United States, he told the pope. In Europe, where history is older, antiquity is measured in centuries; but in the new world, the meaning of time is "psychologically different." Here twenty years is the equivalent of the centuries required by Rome.

There was something else at stake here besides the crown. In 1904, the Italians of Harlem had only been in America about twenty years—as long as the Madonna herself. By arguing through Tofini the antiquity of the cult of the Madonna of 115th Street, the people of Italian Harlem were laying hold of a place in American history for themselves, a place in American time. They had been in Harlem only twenty years—but it seemed much longer than that: and it was much longer, if time is measured in changes. The immigrants in their perception of the age of the cult were dealing with their own sense of the long time they had been from Italy, as well as claiming America for themselves.

Local historians and commentators continued to make this claim throughout the history of the devotion, bidding for American time through the devotion by seeing the latter as being of long duration. Very early in its history, the devotion on 115th Street was presented as a venerable Italian tradition to be shared by Italians of all generations and a patrimony to be passed on to the future.[63] In later years, young Italian Americans were told to share in the great history of Italians in America by participating in the ancient cult of the Madonna del Carmine.[64] The official historian of the devotion reminded his readers in 1954 that America had always been a land of immigrants, so that they should not feel shy about claiming their rightful place in its story. Then he went on to suggest that the coronation of the Madonna in 1904 represented the fulfillment of the plans of Providence for the United States. Italian Harlem, then, with its Madonna, could not simply claim a place in American history: it could claim to be the telos of that history. It is possible that the men and women of the community did not completely share this sense of the importance of their neighborhood, but their pride in the devotion constituted for them an important link with the larger collectivities of city and nation.[65]

The dignity and age of the Madonna was thought to be shared by the neighborhood as well. By the early 1930s, at least, Harlem was refered to as the "antico" Italian quarter of New York, and the devotion was being called evidence of the ancient faithfulness of Italians to the Madonna on these shores. The local funeral directors, merchants, and professional people who advertised in the annual souvenir journal sought, by associating themselves with the Madonna, to claim some of the status of age for themselves, suggesting that dignity and tradition accrued to those who played some role in the devotion.[66]

All of this was a way of announcing that the Italians had been in Harlem much longer than it seemed. Their traditions there were venerable and ancient: one should not be mislead by the brevity of their actual years there. In their reflections on the place of the devotion to the Madonna in the new world, Tofini and the mythmakers of the *Bollettino Cattolico* created a special, ageless time for the devotion and assured the Italians of Harlem of their long presence in American destiny.

## SUCCESS

We have seen that there was among the immigrants a fear of material success and achievement in the new world as well as a longing for it: the people were afraid that success could make a man into a cafone and turn the world upside down. At the same time, they understood that without this drive to succeed, the voyage to America would be useless and they would never succeed in becoming cristiani. This ambivalence was a source of tension in the community. In the late 1920s, after the Italian American community had attained some confidence and self-respect, after the golden gates had closed and the younger generation had emerged as American, and before the Great Depression reminded the Italians of Harlem that they were still among the poorest, the editor of the *Bollettino* began a series of articles that seemed to respond to this tension and fear. Throughout 1929, Salvatore Vigorito published little biographies of local *prominenti*—druggists, doctors, lawyers—describing in great detail their professional qualities, their education, their domestic arrangements and contentments. He even described the ways they had arranged the furniture in their offices.[67]

These stories, appearing where they did, in a journal dedicated to the devotion to the Madonna, had meaning on several levels. Vigorito was defining professionalism as Americans understood it, responding perhaps to the community's aspirations by holding out these paradigms of financial and professional success for emulation. He was defining success for the community, naming the ambitions of some of the parents of Italian Harlem for their children. To this extent, he was making public the kind of advice once given Covello by his father: "Nardo. . . . In me you see a dog's life. Go to school. Even if it kills you. With the pen and with books you have a chance to live like a man and not like a beast of burden."[68] Vigorito was performing a practical service for the people of the community: he gave them clues as to what *bella figura* was in their new home, an essential service of translation.

More important, however, is the fact that these accounts appeared alongside the more usual stories of healing in the domus and the fervent prayers of the people to the Madonna. A healing by association was taking place here: Vigorito's stories were healing stories too. He was assuring the people that their dreams of making America need not turn the world upside down and turn them into cafoni. The men and women he described remained good people, faithful to tradition and to the Madonna. Vigorito encouraged and legitimated the aspirations of his readers, even if these were not cast precisely in the terms he outlined. The juxtaposition of these stories with the accounts of the Madonna's graces, finally, suggested that there need be no ultimate tension between such material goals and Italian and Italian American identity and faithfulness. It was as though Vigorito were telling the people of the community not to be frightened by their aspirations or those of their children. And he held out the promise that the Madonna would heal this tension too.

## HEALING AND THE SENSE WORLD OF THE FESTA

Creation of the proper primary environment was also essential to the healing that was hoped for at the festa. Here we must anticipate our later discussion of women and the feast of Mount Carmel. The healing took place in the context of a devotion to a woman. It will be recalled that women were responsible in this culture, as they are in many others, for maintaining and defining traditional norms and mores. In Anna Ruddy's disturbing phrase, women were the "burden bearers" of Italian Harlem,[69] and among the burdens they bore was sickness—their own and that of members of their families. The festa and the healing aspect of the devotion must be understood against the background of the old-women healers who were important figures in the first generation of immigrants and of the importance of the comare tradition in the community.

Anna Ruddy describes a scene of healing in her fictionalized memoir of Italian Harlem, *The Heart of the Stranger*.[70] An Italian woman is sick, near death; the American doctor has come and gone—he has done what he could but offers little hope. This is a persistent theme in the healing stories of the shrine as well: the American doctors in these stories always say the situation is impossible and that the loved one is going to die. Sometimes the doctor is depicted as urging the necessity of a long and complicated cure that would have the effect of taking the loved one away from the family for a considerable period of time. It is always at this moment that the individual or his or her family turns to the Madonna (not right away: this is the devotion of immigrants who are tempted to try new things, not of the people who remained behind in Italy), and this turning is always cast as a protestation of a faith that is total and, it is cautiously emphasized, has never been lost. The immigrants almost seem to be pleading with the Madonna not to misunderstand their prior appeal to American medicine.

The summoning of the female healer or the Madonna is analogous to the immigrants' preference for Italian midwives and funeral directors. At these important transitional moments in the history of an individual and his or her relations to the community, the Italians wanted the transition supervised by one of their own people, in particular a woman of their culture. (Farenga Funeral Home was introduced into East Harlem by a woman, Signora Farenga, who for many years, contrary to all public expectations of the community, did most of the private work of undertaking, such as preparing the body.)[71] This, in turn, recalls the insistence that primary rituals take place at Mount Carmel. We are thus alerted to interpret healing as high drama, shaped by the tension between the old world and the new, between the new moral and cultural universe and opportunities and the tradition.

This is certainly the hidden meaning of Ruddy's healing story, for after the doctor leaves the neighbors call in Donna Rosina, the local (often this meant that the woman lived in the same apartment building) matriarchal guarantor and arbiter of traditional norms. The first thing she says upon entering the sickroom is, "It's a mercy I came in or she would certainly have died from taking that filthy stuff." She accuses the doctor of trying to poison the sick woman with his medicines. The fear in this case was of pollution: the sick woman was threatened with defilement by the doctor, a figure who represented a frequent source of tension in the immigrants' lives as well as a symbol of the new culture. Donna Rosina then criticizes the doctor's ignorance of Italian, saying "a man who can't speak a word of Italian is no good to cure the Italians when they're sick." She insists on a complete change in the environment of the sickroom, in all her commands ordering the exact opposite of what the American doctor had required. She says: "I know them . . . they're all alike, ordering the windows to be opened in the sickroom and keeping people's friends away from them, as though anyone wanted to be alone when they are sick. . . . How can anyone get well without good wine and strong food to strengthen them, and the company of their friends to cheer them up?"

To be deprived of traditional food is to be deprived of deeper sources of nourishment. What Donna Rosina was saying here was that the healing environment was all wrong, that the patient was being separated from communal sources of healing.[72] Ruddy called Donna Rosina a "presiding judge" who adjudicated important matters of moral deportment and convention, and she tells us disapprovingly that Donna Rosina was "strictly conservative" and that the "little village in Calabria where she was born set her standards for manners and morals." Donna Rosina defined the proper healing environment, however, and in the definition revealed and transmitted, in the appropriate sensory context for such transmission, certain traditional values. She reaffirmed the centrality of communal participation in healing: neighbors, friends, and family are part of the healing environment, along with good food and wine. The individual must be so ecologically located as a precondition of both healing and moral instruction. Food, people, drink, well-defined boundaries (the closed windows)—Donna Rosina describes here not only the healing environment but also an Italian festa and a family meal. The healing that took place at the festa was a microcosm of the whole ecology of the event, recapitulating and encapsulating the meaning and movement of the whole.

## THE ITALIAN WAY OF BEING HUMAN

The festa was a declaration, affirmation, and sacralization of the Italian way of being human and of expressing their humanity. In particular, it was an announcement to any who cared to listen—and many heard, including Protestant social workers, Irish Catholics, the police, and other representatives of the surrounding culture—that all this emotion, color, noise, food, and rispetto was Italian. It is clear that one of the things Catholic and Protestant social workers tried to teach Italians was to restrain their emotions. They tried, as part of their campaign to defuse what they saw as the dangers of the inner city, to induce or coerce the immigrants to adopt another way of being human than the way the immigrants claimed as theirs. This was both a class and a cultural issue.

Anna Ruddy reveals this cultural attitude in her self-defined role as Protestant observer at the deathbed scene discussed earlier. She views with icy condescension the "noisy demonstrations of affection" in the sickroom, the playful rousing of the patient, which was really a serious attempt to keep her from slipping away into unconsciousness, the crowding round the bed. Garibaldi Lapolla has a very bitter scene in *The Grand Gennaro*.[73] After a crisis in the family, three Italian children are made to enter a children's asylum on the suggestion of a somewhat satirically drawn character that is unmistakably Anna Ruddy.[74] As Lapolla constructs the scene, the children are made to wear institutional clothes, to eat institutional food, and are taught to hold back their emotions, even toward their rather desperate family. Lapolla intends here to depict a total stripping away of the Italian personality, and the scene is drawn with sharp contrasts between the American and the Italian women present. The Protestant nurse who takes charge of the children says to them, "say goodbye [to your family] and don't forget . . . nobody cries in the J.P.A." Covello's memories of the Soup School on 116th Street and Second Avenue confirm Lapolla's picture of the kinds of existential pressure Italians were under in Harlem. The Protestant teachers there, all women, expected strict decorum from their Italian charges. Covello remembered hours spent at disciplinary attention either before the American flag, singing three cheers for the "Red Watzam Blu," or before the Bible. He recalled: "Silence! Silence! Silence! This was the characteristic feature of our existence at the Soup School. You never made an unnecessary noise or said an unnecessary word."[75]

In 1948, Covello received a rather sad letter from an Italian American woman who had been adopted by Ruddy's female American organist.[76] The woman begins by saying that Covello probably does not recognize her name. She married a non-Italian and then changed her first name from Concetta to Constance, because "my two children were annoyed whenever they were questioned about their mother's name by the teachers." This woman then went on to assess Ruddy's influence on her: "Miss Ruddy certainly changed the course of my life. . . . sometimes I wonder if for the best or not. Certainly I received a religious training which I never would have received otherwise." Yet now, she adds, she is living alone—she has separated from her husband; her children have married and left home. She concludes, "there is the point where I wonder if it was for the best that my life should have been so changed—for perhaps had I married someone of my own nationality I might have been happier."

It is in this context that we must understand what it was that the Italian community was proclaiming in such a vivid way in its feste. The festa of the Madonna of Mount Carmel announced that the entire texture of Italian humanity was good, that these people's needs and styles of organizing their inner and outer lives were good. This is one of the reasons why the immigrants used the festa to connect themselves with the United States: it established the connection on their own terms. There was more than a small element of defiance in this proclamation, coming as it did from the poor, despised, and feared community of Italian Harlem.

The festa was also a disciplining of the members of the community in the ways that Italians were supposed to carry themselves in the world. The days and nights of the festa offered the people of Italian Harlem experiences of widely differing moods and emotions, from the penitential submission of fulfilling difficult vows in the procession, to the delight of the parties and rounds of visits, to the excitement of competition and chance in the bazaar games. In this way, the festa was an opportunity for the people to remind themselves, teach their children, and enforce in the community how they thought a human being should behave.

Consider two examples of this: the difficulty of getting to the front of the church, so emphasized in all accounts of the festa; and the preparations made in the homes of the community for guests. In the first case, the people were demonstrating the value they placed on endurance; in the second, they were revealing the norms of rispetto. In both cases, the education was complex and complete: the participants demonstrated how to hold their bodies, how to treat other people in contrasting times of discomfort and pleasure, how a person should compose his or her face at such times, whether humor was appropriate or not and if so what kinds of humor, how physical discomfort should be borne, whether one should complain or not, and so on. In other words, in all these nuances of appropriate deportment they were demonstrating what they meant by "cristiano," and under the watchful gaze of the Madonna they gave flesh to this idea for themselves and their children.

## THE FESTA AND THE WORLD OF WORK

The festa must also be understood as a working-class redemption of time, the immigrants' claiming of time for themselves. Here again we enter the realm of interstices and disharmonies. Italians, even in New York, liked to live near their work both for economic and social reasons; but this created the problem of finding a way to distance themselves from the world of work, of establishing a private life apart from the demands of the "giobba."[77]

The immigrants had expected to improve the conditions of their employment in the United States, and yet they often found themselves doing the meanest work under constant threat of frequent, if temporary, unemployment. The manifold pressures and tensions of the worlds of work and unemployment were experienced in a particularly acute way by Italians, because labor was considered an integral part of an individual's responsibility, affection, and commitment to his or her domus. The earliest immigrants suffered deeply from the difficulties of finding and keeping work because unemployment prolonged their separation from their families and threatened to brand them as failures in the quest to become "Christians" that had inspired their departure from Italy in the first place.

The history of Italian labor in New York City, extending down to the 1930s and early 1940s, is a history of hard wage labor at grueling jobs under the supervision of other ethnic groups. In the earliest days of Italian Harlem, Italians worked as rag-pickers, junk and bottle collectors, bootblacks, newsboys, beer sellers, candy makers, sign makers, barbers, and pushcart vendors; some worked on New York's docks. During periods of economic prosperity, Italian men worked construction over in West Harlem, as well as in East Harlem, where cheap tenements were erected in the late nineteenth and early twentieth centuries, or on New York's expanding rapid transit lines. Italian women worked at home making artificial flowers or in factories as dressmakers, in addition to the immense amount of work they did for their families.[78]

Although there was some improvement over time, change was severely limited by Italian Harlem's marginal economic position. In 1932, a high percentage of East Harlem parents were doing menial labor, and salaries were correspondingly low.[79] East Harlem always suffered first and hardest in times of general economic decline and always made the slowest progress back. In 1940, 78.9 percent of New York's work force was employed, whereas in East Harlem the figure stood a full ten percentage points below that.[80] The real figure was probably lower still, since the financial position of the Italian home depended on the work of all members, including those who might not be surveyed in official studies. Economic hardship in Italian Harlem was intensified by regular, periodic unemployment. Although the oldest generation of immigrants were well acquainted with this reality from their years in Italy, this should not be taken to mean that the situation was any easier for a family to bear. Italians knew and feared their dependence on work, and the Italian rispetto for labor is in part an acknowledgment of its power over the lives of men and women.

In order to understand how the festa provided, for a brief period, an enclosed alternative world to the world of work, and to understand what it was about their labor that needed healing, we must pause to emphasize several outstanding features of Italian American work from 1880 until the late 1940s. First, there was the fact of their utter dependence on regular employment: when there was no work, people went hungry. As Lapolla writes of one of his characters, Giovanni, "He lived too near the sort of life that depends upon day-to-day labor not to have a keen sense of the importance of work."[81] The subject of work was all-absorbing and a source of guilt and anxiety.

Second, local and national forces attempted to assert their authority and control over Italian labor for a number of reasons. Locally, there was a fierce conflict between Italians and the longer-established Irish, who controlled the distribution of work and served as foremen and supervisors in Harlem's industries. This hostility between Irish and Italian workers found expression in the Catholic church and left wounds so deep that it is remembered to the present. Immigrant work was also the subject of national concern and fear. At the first convention of the National Conference of Catholic Charities in 1910, a Franciscan priest from Ohio expressed this concern in these words: "The factories and other places that give employment to the poor are often the veriest hotbeds of rank socialism and naturalism, of open hostility to every positive religious creed and rule of morality." The priest observed that this danger was particularly acute in the immigrant population because of their "dense ignorance" and the "absence of those motives which in their European homes did much to maintain them in their religious allegiance, such as universal custom, immemorial family tradition, deference to the demand of the public, and so on." The immigrants are thus rendered "easy marks for the propagators of socialistic, anarchistic and nihilistic doctrines and agitation."[82]

The immigrants had the misfortune to enter the country just as time-management studies were becoming common and as employers, guided by the advice of the developing social sciences, became more sophisticated and thorough in their efforts to reorder and coopt their workers' culture. The totality of the effort to structure the immigrants' lives at home and at work is revealed in the fantasies of management theorists of the period. The Welfare Secretary of the Iron and Steel Institute, for example, urged careful tutelage of the immigrant in the:

> regulation of his meals, the amount, the character and the mastication of them, the hours of rest and sleep, the ventilation of rooms . . . washing of hands before meals, daily washing of feet, proper fitting of shoes, amount and kind of clothing, care of the eye, ear and nose, brushing of the teeth, and regularity of the bowels. Cultivation of cheerful thoughts has much to do with the body. Another thing that the workman should be taught is that the first condition of health is fruitful toil. We are made to labor.[83]

This cultural attack is similar to those leveled by the Protestant and Catholic social and religious workers who entered the Italian colonies. Every detail of immigrant life became the object of anxious scrutiny and criticism—and concerted efforts to change them.

The festa constituted a challenge to and offered freedom from the world of work in a number of ways. The time of the festa was fluid, uncontrolled: remember that estimates of its duration varied widely. It was a celebration that knew no time clock, so that here at least, the immigrants were temporarily free from this daily pressing constraint. The festa was sacred time in which the immigrants could affirm their communal and familial values. The personal and communal emphasis during the festa was on reciprocal relations—with the Madonna, with neighbors and friends—so that the festa served in this way as an annual confirmation and celebration of the economic reciprocity that characterized business and social relations in Italian Harlem. It was a time of mutual responsibility, not wage alienation. Genuine interpersonal relations were affirmed. Sympathetic American employers might call Sicilians good "raw material" for industry, but during the festa this raw material showed it had a face.[84]

The festa offered an occasion for the display of energy and enthusiasm not appropriate or possible in the work place; it was as though the people of Italian Harlem were declaring: See! We are still alive! During the festa men and women worked at freely assumed chores on behalf of their families, their community, and the Madonna. The festa was explicitly a time of community-oriented and personally fulfilling labor. It is in this way that the people present the history of the church as well: recall that the men and women of Italian Harlem are said to have built the church of the Madonna with their own hands after days of exhausting labor. Again, the devotion offered the opportunity for self-affirmation and freedom in contrast to the world of work.

The two popular histories of the devotion to Mount Carmel are aware of this aspect of the celebration. We have seen that the official historian considered the festa "a parenthesis of joyous thoughtlessness, once a year, in the midst of the crushing work which bore down on their shoulders and of the effort to survive in the face of countless difficulties."[85] The editor of the parish bulletin in 1934 urged: "Italians of Harlem! Let us abandon our daily places of work, in our hearts and in our minds. Let us form no thought that does not turn to HER who in every moment covers us with her loving care."[86]

The Italians of Harlem also declared their freedom from the world of work in a custom related to the festa of the Madonna of 115th Street.[87] At any time during the year, but especially during the celebration, a person could promise the Madonna that if she granted a particular request, he or she in return would wear a sky blue robe tied around the waist by a white sincture for a specified period of time. To keep this promise, people had to wear the robe on the streets of the community, on public transportation, and even on their jobs. The custom disappeared from the community in the late 1930s and 1940s. While it lasted, however, it was a striking symbol of the people's determination to declare their own values and worth and the priority of their own culture in environments where these might not have been recognized.

The Madonna was also asked specifically to heal many different kinds of pain the Italians suffered on account of the work they did. Every year, a work-weary population trooped to 115th Street carrying wax replicas of its hurt. In 1928, a young worker in Brooklyn was traumatized by an industrial accident and in the months following the incident became suicidal. He was cured, we are told by his wife, after she prayed to the Madonna; now, she concludes, she and her husband go every year to the shrine.[88] This scenario was repeated throughout the years, as the Madonna was called upon to heal work-related suffering. The accounts are always given by women. In 1947, a woman's husband was hurt in a fall at work. He was taken to the hospital and given the last rites. But his family gathered around him, praying for a cure; and when he regained consciousness his first thought was of the Madonna. As a result, we are told, he was healed.[89] In another story, someone's brother (the sex of the correspondent is not clear), seriously burned on the job, was taken to a hospital, where doctors told his family that he would not survive. "With all my faith," the correspondent turned to the Madonna and now, the story ends, this man is on his way to complete recovery.[90]

The Madonna was also asked to heal the inner hurts associated with work, such as the anxiety of unemployment and the preoccupations of poverty. The festa was defined as a time of unburdening "worries and disappointments," and for the people of Italian Harlem these always included the deep fear of unemployment.[91] In 1946, a woman wrote in to the church: "Two months ago my husband was laid off after having worked in the same place for nine years. I was so worried I didn't know what to do." Turning to the Madonna in her distress, she made a novena and happily she was able to report that her husband got his job back.[92] Another woman wrote in 1948 that the Madonna had helped her son find work after he had been fired and that his new job was better and paid him double. As a sign of her gratitude and relief, this woman promised to attend the weekly novena from that moment on and every week to light a candle to the Madonna.[93]

The Madonna was asked, finally, to bless the very fact of working itself. In a prayer printed in the parish journal in 1930, the Madonna was implored to bless the homes of the devout, their children, their elderly relations, and then, finally, after this context had been thus established, to pronounce her benediction on their work.[94] This prayer reminded the Italians that the proper setting for their labor was the happiness and stability of their domus. Besides serving as additional evidence of the ways in which the devotion was used to instruct people in the values and priorities of the community, this prayer indicates another level on which the world of the festa stood against the world of work. The sacral environment of the festa confronted the materialism of the immigrants and reminded them to set their goals in the larger moral context of the family. The devotion to the Madonna annually, and daily by means of the scapulars that the people took away with them, reaffirmed the primacy of other values and reminded the people of the meaning of work and of the real nature of their mutual obligations.

## FROM SUFFERING TO SACRIFICE

In their prayers to the Madonna, in the promises they made to her, and in their behavior on the day of the festa, the men and women of Italian Harlem attempted to transform their suffering into sacrifice and so redeem it and subtly triumph over it. Religious sacrifice is freely chosen: unlike the many burdens which poor people must bear in their daily lives, suffering assumed in a sacral context is freely assumed. The devotion to the Madonna of 115th Street offered the men and women of Italian Harlem many opportunities to choose suffering, usually on behalf of their families. They could participate in the penitential practices associated with the shrine, such as walking barefoot through the streets of Italian Harlem. Most of the vows made to the Madonna involved the assumption of suffering on the part of the person making the vow; indeed, the purpose of the vows often seems to have been to trade one suffering for another, to replace unbidden pain with discomfort freely promised.

By means of this religious alchemy, the people of Italian Harlem attempted to assert their superiority over the suffering they had to endure in their everyday lives. Religious sacrifice allows men and women to believe that they have some control over their destinies even when they fear that they are otherwise bound by severe social and economic constraints. By freely assuming suffering, as opposed to merely enduring pain, the men and women of Italian Harlem were declaring something of their pride and sense of self-worth. In this way, religious experience becomes a realm of relative freedom in the midst of lives ruled by necessity.

The question arises, however, whether this religious behavior is not, or does not become, masochistic, a desperate infliction of punishment on the self in a frustrated rage against the perception of powerlessness. At least with regard to one area of the lives of the people of Italian Harlem, this conclusion seems unavoidable. Almost all the suffering assumed in the vows made to the Madonna was assumed on behalf of the domus. Given the inescapable power and authority of the domus over the lives of individuals and the constant but frustrating and futile rebellion within it, it could be that the devotion to the Madonna of 115th Street encouraged people to repress their rage against the domus by turning it inward. The vows made at the shrine also confirmed the value and importance of sacrificing the self to the domus, blessing one of the most troubled aspects of Italian American culture in Harlem. Although the devotion offered an outlet for the expression of anger toward the domus, allowing people to experience its collapse in the stories of sickness told at the shrine, still, the solidarity of the domus expressed and enacted during the festa was celebrated in the context of a devotion in which the individual was called upon to suffer on behalf of, and instead of, the domus. In the masochism that constituted one of the meanings of the vows made to the Madonna of 115th Street, the festa confirmed and gave divine sanction to the power of the domus in Italian Harlem.

But religious sacrifice also provides for a kind of triumph and resolution, and these two possibilities of sacrifice—entrapment and resolution—cannot really be separated. Let us return to the example of the woman who promised the Madonna that because her son found

work, she would go every week to the shrine and light a candle in the
Virgin's honor. Sacrifice here has many meanings and functions. First
of all, by means of her weekly chore, the woman remained an intimate
part of her son's life, whether or not he was still living at home. Undoubtedly, the young man knew that his mother was sacrificing at
least a morning of her week, every week, on his behalf; this knowledge
served as an additional bond between the young man and his domus. It
made rebellion on his part against the domus much more difficult.
Second, by this weekly sacrifice on behalf of her son, the woman identified herself with the *mater dolorosa*, the faithful, long-suffering, and
self-sacrificing mother so dear to Italian religious tradition. In this
way, her weekly journey itself became a living link between her and
the divine mother and a sanctification of the quotidian in her own life.
On the other hand, it also bound her tightly to the tradition which
insisted that women must suffer on behalf of their families; in this
way, she contributed to maintaining the culture that bore down on
her. Third, in her promise, by the assumption of suffering in return for
the cessation of her son's suffering (over which neither she nor her son
could have any control—suddenly the young man was fired), she
moved from a position of total powerlessness, in which she was forced
to stand by helplessly as an anxious observer, to a context in which she
could be the agent of change and good. Finally, her weekly sacrifice
also had a Christian meaning: in making this sacrificial pilgrimage,
which could have involved walking across the street or just as easily
could have required three hours on public transportation into a changing and threatening neighborhood, this woman affirmed the redemptive centrality of sacrifice and acknowledged the authority of
divine figures over her life. Both of these are truths which Christianity
seeks to teach; this woman participated in them in an intimate and
existential way, deriving meaning for her life from the Christian perceptions and endowing them with meaning out of the circumstances of
her life.

## WOMEN AND THE DEVOTION TO THE MADONNA
## OF 115TH STREET

The devotion to the Madonna of 115th Street was a women's devotion,
both in the sense that women were the main participants in it and in
the sense that it emerged out of and reflected the special role and

position of women in Italian culture. The devotion articulated and sanctified the many complex realities of women's lives in Italian Harlem. The Madonna offered women great support and consolation in their difficult lives there: they were able to identify with this divine woman and draw strength from the identification. But at the same time that the devotion offered women this consolation, it reaffirmed those aspects of the culture which oppressed them: the source of their comfort was also the source of their entrapment. The devotion revealed the power of women in the culture, but it also allowed men and women to express their anger toward and fear of that power. Furthermore, the power of women as revealed in the devotion and in the figure of the Madonna was defined in such a way that the power itself became another form of constraint. The devotion to and the figure of the Madonna represented the apotheosis of women in Italian Harlem; but this was a most constricting apotheosis. Women found the Madonna's azure cloak, so ceremoniously draped over their shoulders, a heavy one indeed.

Women outnumbered men in the devotion since the time of the earliest available documents, although they were not included in its organizational life. They have always been the primary economic support of the devotion.[95] With only about two exceptions, women wrote in to report the graces granted by the Madonna even when the grace had been bestowed on a man. Women were also the central figures in the life of the church. The church's chorus, founded in 1928 under the direction of the composer and conductor Casimino Dello Joio, was made up of unmarried women. Their debut was a performance of Dello Joio's "Ave Maria" in April 1928.[96] The choir was still composed exclusively of young women after the Second World War.[97] The Parent-Teachers Association of Mount Carmel consisted only of married women, although not necessarily only those with children: married, childless women were also encouraged to participate in the life of the PTA.[98] (This official domination of the parents' group by women was not typical of Italian Harlem: across the street at Franklin, and earlier at Clinton, men and women both were involved in their sons' education.)[99] For young women in Italian Harlem, the church was one of the few places where they could socialize and enjoy themselves away from parental scrutiny.[100] In 1930, the sisters of the church, together with the young unmarried women of the Children of Mary, organized a club at the church-sponsored Saint John's Settlement House for girls ten to

fourteen years old. Their intention, according to a little notice written
by a Child of Mary and published in the parish journal, was to relieve
the mothers of the parish of some of their worries and to help the girls
grow into good young women.[101] In 1931, the sisters organized and
supervised an embroidery club for young women, for both their material and spiritual benefit; there is no indication that the sort of unemployment workshops held for men at Union Settlement or at Haarlem
House were ever organized at Mount Carmel.[102]

The special place accorded women at Mount Carmel also found
sacramental emphasis at the church. During First Communion ceremonies, for example, for both boys and girls, little girls held the communion cloth for the communicants. In the annual procession, women
marched right in front of and around the Madonna. At the church's
Good Friday service in 1946, the Children of Mary, dressed in their
blue robes in imitation of the Madonna, were given the privilege of
carrying the cross up and down the aisles.[103] Local women served as
hostesses at their mother's house during the yearly celebration. Finally, the church celebrated Mother's Day with great solemnity and joy.

Women felt a profound sense of identity and a special closeness to
the Madonna, as they reveal in their letters to her requesting graces or
thanking her for favors granted. When their sufferings as mothers and
wives were most intense, as these women tell their stories, when they
felt that no one else could understand their particular agonies, they
turned to the one who long ago had appealed to the masses of Europe
because of her evident participation in humanity's trials. The mothers
and grandmothers of the women of Italian Harlem had contributed to
the evolution and popularity of this image, which now found an urban
restatement. The Madonna to whom these women were so attached
was not a distant, asexual figure, but a woman like themselves who
had suffered for and with her child.[104] Her power was located precisely in those areas where the power of Italian women, in all its
complexity, was located: the domus. Like Italian women, the Madonna was expected to hold families together. She was also asked to for-
give and to protect, suggesting a complex and considerable power—
and one that could be wielded capriciously.

The church on 115th Street was repeatedly identified in the pages
of the parish bulletin as the home of the immigrants' mamma. For
older immigrants, this was meant to remind them of their mothers'
houses in Italy, reinforcing the already powerful resonances that exist-

ed among memory, mother, and the divine, interlocking identifications that carried moral and psychological responsibilities. The men and women of Italian Harlem made this identification with a detailed and articulated imaginative precision that kept it from becoming a spiritual cliché. They imagined the church, as literally as they could, as their mamma's house, with all the nuanced affection and understanding with which they might have recalled their earthly mothers' homes. For example, one of the impulses behind the community's support for the renovation of the church school in 1935 was: "The opening of the school [after renovation] was imperative: the parents demanded it with the insistence that the house of their Mamma of Carmel, without the echoing voices of countless children, seemed abandoned and without joy."[105] Men were identifying their wives and sisters, and men and women were identifying their mothers, aunts, and comari, with a very powerful woman.

The devotion had another and private meaning for women, however. All the stories of graces reveal the limits of women's control in the culture and in the domus: the temporary breakdown of family life in times of sickness and unemployment, children's sometimes bitter assertions of independence against their mothers, the difficulties young women experienced in extricating themselves from socially sanctioned but personally unwanted relationships, the agonies of the pressures to marry and bear children, and so on. In these cases, which offer us a glimpse into the kitchens and living rooms of Italian Harlem, if a woman was to fulfill her role as protectress of the family, she needed the assistance of her own, more powerful and private protectress, to whom she could confide the difficulties she would inevitably experience. The Madonna's participation was essential if these women were to fulfill, in their own understanding, the roles and responsibilities assigned to them. The Madonna helped them nurture and succored them when they failed.[106] The graces derived part of their meaning, then, from the gap between the expectations of women's power and the realities of it. As all the accounts of graces reveal, women turned to the Madonna out of an awareness of the severe limitations of their power and a sense of desperation over their ultimate powerlessness in the community. The local tradition eloquently recorded the gratitude and need of these women.

As we have seen, the women needed a protectress: the cultural, social, and psychological pressures they were under in the culture

*The annual procession, ca. 1938*

were often extreme and rendered them most vulnerable. So women turned to the Madonna for help and consolation and strength. It was into lives more or less like Theresa's that the Madonna was asked to come. Sometimes she was asked to provide the strength that women, bound by the terrible fragility and power of their reputations as men defined them, needed to free themselves from dangerous cultural constraints. In 1946, a woman from the Bronx wrote that she had prayed fervently to the Madonna that a young man, the only one she thought could make her happy, would propose to her. He did, and she was grateful to the Madonna. But then she discovered that he behaved in ways she could not approve of. Now, of course, this young woman was trapped: there was no culturally sanctioned way to break off an engagement. So, "I put myself under the guidance of the Madonna, asking help in making a decision in this matter. Finally I decided to break the engagement." She concluded by promising always to attend the weekly novena.[107] In this case, the Madonna provided the essential ratification for this very difficult action, which would have found approval nowhere else in the community, while the young woman's attendance at the weekly novena gave her the chance to demonstrate her constancy to the community, and especially to other suitors.

In the following year, a young unmarried woman reported that she had been suffering from chest pains for several years. She prayed to the Madonna to give her the courage to go to the doctor, who told her that it was "all my imagination." Then she added, "With the help of Our Lady of Mount Carmel I have been able to forget everything and I am certain that without her I would never have had the courage to help myself."[108] We know little about what was plaguing this woman's imagination, but we do know that she chose to call attention to the fact that she was not married right at the beginning of her story, and we also know the pressure to marry placed on young women in the community. It is perhaps not too much to suggest that it was the anxiety arising from this situation that this women was asking the Madonna to heal. Both of these healings shed some light on the many cases of undefined maladies for which women turned to the Madonna for help.

The Madonna also helped women deal with the distancing from their culturally sanctioned, intimate power which, as we have seen, was an essential moment in the dynamics of Italian American family life: children who moved away, daughters seeking to define their own lives. The rebels invariably turned against their mothers, who expressed and symbolized the power of the domus; then these women turned to the Madonna. The Madonna's intervention provided relief for both parties in this dilemma: for the older women, comfort for their confused sense of hurt; for the children, the devotion was a contained context in which they could express their own sense of familial loyalty and commitment. The Madonna was called up to salve the consequences of a sometimes pathologically intense family life which, when it exploded, usually exploded against the women of the domus.

Finally, the devotion defused tensions among women, opening the way for the solidarity that was essential if the beleaguered women of Italian Harlem were to survive. It allowed women to share in a mutual celebration of a figure who understood and sanctified their lives. It brought young and old women, usually compelled to spend so much difficult time together, before the throne of a woman who, understanding them both, would heal them both, and together. One of the ritual expressions of this integration was the custom of young women holding onto white ribbons extending from the wedding-cake structures of candles carried by older women on their heads during the procession. The white ribbons symbolically anchored the young women to these matriarchs, representing tradition and cultural conservatism, providing them with an annual occasion for reestablishing ties with the significant females in their lives. The Mount Carmel PTA offered childless women the opportunity to share in some of the responsibilities of child-raising, an outlet for what might otherwise have become a most destructive source of intimate competition and private agony. The Madonna was a divine comare, blessing and approving that traditional source of solidarity among Italian American women. By gathering round the figure of a woman, the women of Italian Harlem could rediscover their common sisterhood, a discovery that was essential if they were to find the support they needed, not only from the woman waiting for them at the end of their annual pilgrimage, but especially from the woman who lived cross the hall.

The public–private dichotomy that characterized male and female identities and relations in Italian Harlem was reproduced and sanctioned by the devotion and festa on 115th Street in the ritual inversion of the normal ordering of this relationship. The festa was a public celebration and acknowledgment of the power and authority of women: all those people, men and women alike, had gathered to worship an omnipotent woman. The private power of women in the domus was manifest to the community in the figure of the Madonna. Women came out of their homes and, walking behind the symbol of their power, took over the streets of Italian Harlem on July 16. Once a year, then, the realities of familial and cultural authority were publicly acknowledged and strengthened in the celebration, and the power of women, usually expected to be kept hidden, was publicly proclaimed.

On the other hand, the socially approved concealment of women's power was also sanctioned by the nominal male control of the event. The *congregazione* that was ostensibly responsible for the practical details of the annual celebration was all male throughout the period we are considering. A woman's auxiliary appeared in the late 1920s, but this group seemed inessential and was composed mainly of upwardly mobile, socially successful women already accustomed to some social presence. The grand marshals of the procession were always locally prominent males. Men were also the authoritative figures in the life of the church.

The annual festa of Our Lady of Mount Carmel revealed to the culture the socially and morally normative and stabilizing power of women as the culture believed it to exist, while at the same time it legitimated the authority of the public–private dichotomy of power. But just as the devotion and the festa publicly acknowledged the power of women, it was also an opportunity for the community to define that power and bind women by the definition. During the days and nights of the festa and in their devotion to the Madonna, women were taught what their appropriate sphere was, what a wife and a mother were—and they learned this in the presence of a most powerful woman, who was nevertheless limited in the geography of her power.

In March 1930, the editor of the *Bollettino Cattolico Mensile*, Salvatore Vigorito, wrote a long piece in strikingly and unavoidably lyrical prose, entitled "Madre."[109] His purpose was to sing the praises of Italian mothers; and in doing so he defined in no uncertain terms what a mother should be. A mother, we are told, is the "sorrowful creature" whose life "has its beginnings in pain and end in love." Nothing in the created order is more beautiful than "a young woman with a baby in her arms." Vigorito continues:

Hers is the deepest and most feeling nature in this world of cold hearts and frantic steps, and it is in this way that to her gentle spirit the first cry of the new newborn seems like a chord from the center of eternity, music of the spheres. She will never forget the son whose first steps she guided with such genuine solicitude. Whether he becomes a prince or a prodigal son, the sound of his steps will always cause his mother's heart to leap in the quiet night.

A mother finds her comfort in the "monotony of service and strength of heart that come to her under the weight of the race which she bears." Her wisdom is infinite, Vigorito tells us, and then goes on to enunciate just what it is that a mother knows: "She is wise enough to know that there is more joy in the smile of her baby boy than in the cheers of the crowd and that the sweet drama of her children at their innocent games is preferable to the tinsel scattered by society." Possessed of this secret truth, she has accepted Christ's witness of greatness—to be a servant. "With a patience that does not know irritation and a love which never diminishes, a mother pours out her inexhaustible spirit in suffering and the sacrifice of herself for her children. . . children who may be the most base in this world of egoism and pleasure." He concluded: "The gentle grace of a mother can give peace to this unquiet world."

Vigorito, speaking for the culture, laid an awful weight on women already bent low from the physical and emotional cares of raising children and working in Italian Harlem. Theresa's laconic comment is relevant here again: "I had a hard life. I got married and it got worse." Women are here enclosed by this apotheosis, trapped by emotionally claustrophobic expectations and demands, denied any genuine outlet for the complex emotions they suffered in a constantly changing and always challenging environment—an environment, moreover, in which they were expected to bear the conflicting responsibilities of tradition and change. As Vigorito presented their lives to them, women were deprived even of the relief of anger, even toward children who might despise or hurt them. With a calm that seems callous and lyricism that seems pernicious, Vigorito assigned women to their suffering. The identity of Italian American women was to suffer. Well indeed might women carry their heavy burdens of wax to the altar at Mount Carmel, to leave them there at the feet of one whom they had been taught would assume them.

Vigorito and other writers at the shrine returned continually to the theme of women and quiet suffering from 1928 to the Second

World War.[110] Another example of this constraint by definition appeared in what was ostensibly an obituary notice for a young man in the parish. The solemn and culturally vulnerable moment of death is exploited to instruct women in their duties. The focus of the obituary was kept relentlessly on the boy's mother:

> Let us incline our heads now to the inconsolable mother, the Signora R. N. [I have omitted the name], keeping silent in the presence of her immense grief, certain that this exemplary mother of a family will be fortified [or inspired] by the more blessed resignation to be always guide and advisor to her sons, R. and G., who have established themselves in the commercial life, and for the Doctor, A., who, although he is still young, has already so established himself in the vast field of medicine and surgery that he is enormously valued by his colleagues and admired and venerated by his numerous and affectionate Italian American clientele.[111]

Throughout the obituary, the author uses suffocatingly lyrical prose: there is an aesthetic of entrapment, a lyricism so ornate that it becomes difficult to extricate oneself from it. What began, but only briefly, as an obituary for a dead youth, becomes a lesson on the responsibilities and nature of motherhood—sorrow, resignation, and strength. The presentation of this identity is nestled in a paragraph that begins with the community ("Let us incline our heads") and ends with the mother's grief being swallowed up by the activities of the males in the domus—for whom, she is reminded, she is responsible.

This journal was read as devotional literature by many, a monthly spiritual guide. These definitions of women, therefore, appeared in a sacral context, always authorized with reference to the Madonna. Vigorito locked women into their homes and into the confines of their emotions. The graces of the Madonna had the same effect. One woman wrote, in 1946, that her mother's hand had become infected but because of the intervention of the Madonna did not have to be amputated, with the result that now, "thanks to the Madonna, she can do housework like sewing, cooking, etc."[112] A woman who spilled boiling water on her leg was quickly enabled by the Madonna to return to her household chores.[113] In one of the rare stories told by a man, a young widow who lived with her father (the correspondent) and her children suffered either from a bloodclot or was coughing up blood. She was taken to the hospital, where they discovered and operated on a tumor in her stomach. Her father says, "Imagine the anxiety of her family, of her poor father, and her five children!" On the day of the operation, he telephoned the hospital continually. Told of the gravity of his daughter's condition, he lit two candles to the Madonna and gathered his grandchildren together to recite the litany, at the end of which he was moved to cry out, "Holy Virgin, give me back my daughter and restore the mother of these innocent ones!" His daughter returned home after only fifteen days.[114]

These stories have several meanings. They reflect first of all the difficulties of life in the struggling Italian American communities, where even the temporary loss of a spouse or a homemaker could cause profound anxiety, arising out of a sense of hopelessness and of being overwhelmed by too many of life's demands. This reality was stated eloquently by Sidney Mintz's informant, Taso, after his sister's death, "And after she died we had to solve problems."[115] These accounts also remind us of a fact that is obvious in economic terms but often undervalued in its human meaning: the families of Italian Harlem, and those of other poor communities as well, worked and survived together as a unit, a necessity that intensified their intimacy and increased their power to compel submission and restrict independent growth.

In every case, furthermore, the Madonna restores a woman to the center of her family, a clear divine approbation of the ordering of the life of the domus. Those who read these accounts, in particular those women who had a special devotion to the Madonna, could hardly mistake the lesson that this was where women belonged. Women, therefore, experienced a specific *psychodrame* within the larger drama of disintegration and reintegration of the festa. Vicariously, they experienced the separation from the domus expressed in the stories, depicted in terms of sickness and death, and then experienced the reintegration of women into the domus at the end of the accounts. The entire devotion then—the stories of healing, the penitential practices of the women on the day of the festa, the identification of women with the sorrowing mother—all defined and constrained women as patient, silent sufferers, located inescapably in the home and within the confines of their emotions. Perhaps, and simply, this explains the hysteria of women at the shrine.

Vigorito did not make life any more pleasant for the unmarried women who read his journal. These women, as we have seen, were threatened with serious anomie in the Italian American community. The church and the devotion, consequently, labored particularly to instruct young girls in the proper ways of being a woman. Young unmarried women, from the age of seventeen, were encouraged to join the church's Children of Mary, the purpose of which was stated by one of its members in 1932: "As children of Mary we have a high ideal found in God's own precious Mother, in the Queen of Heaven and earth and of May. To show our great affection we must strive to imitate the virtues of Mary; to plead with her to obtain for us all the graces we need; to keep our souls fixed on the holy example of Mary."[116] This identification must not be interpreted in narrowly sexual terms. Imitation of Mary would primarily mean integrating oneself into the realities of the ambivalent power of Italian American women, choosing a model that specified suffering as the boundaries of personal identity and power, and preparing oneself for the complex location of women in the culture. The patron saint of the society was Saint Agnes, a woman honored as much for her patient suffering as for her defense of her purity.[117]

Unmarried women marched closest to the Madonna during the procession. The Children of Mary were given the responsibility of instructing the children who were candidates for First Communion. This association reinforced the ideal of feminine purity, since these young innocents are a special symbol of the unspotted life in Italian popular understanding; but it also gave the young women practice in dealing with children, a sacralization of the role already assigned them in the culture and a credential available to them to indicate their worthiness as spouses.[118] Events at the church put young women in frequent and hierarchically ordered contact with married women. On Mother's Day in 1951, for example, the mothers of the parish, together with single women, attended a special mass at which "the presence of God was sensed by all as these good women received Holy Communion while their children sang hymns of praise and thanksgiving."[119] After mass, the mothers of the parish were treated to breakfast, during which they were waited on by the unmarried women. In all these ways, the church and the devotion prepared younger women for the only role that the culture publicly would tolerate for them—marriage and child-raising.

The church continued to play this pedagogical role after World War II, as Italian American women stepped out into new social and economic roles. Fertility rates among young Italian American women born between 1915 and 1925 were lower in the postwar period than for women of any other ethnic group.[120] Perhaps the men associated with the shrine felt a new urgency to maintain the traditional position of young women. Italian American women in this period dreamed, albeit subtly, larger dreams than they had before, and although there is no indication of outright rebellion—indeed, just the opposite—the voices of middle-aged Italian American women today are often edged with bitterness or sadness over lost hopes.[121] It is frequently insisted that the Italian American family remained intact in this period, that young Italian American working women stayed close to home. The devotion to the Madonna of Mount Carmel contributed to the shaping of the lives of young women in this period, introducing them to the styles and consequences of their power.

Finally, the festa reproduced characteristic modes of relationship in the community between powerful women and those subject to them. Though the people loved the Madonna, they also feared her enormous and potentially capricious power. They propitiated a deity that could be, as one of the men quoted above claimed his mother was, "how unreasonable, how impossibly crazy." This was, of course, the same kind of power men and women claimed that the significant women in the community—their mothers, married aunts, the healers, and comari—wielded; it was the domus-centered and absolute power which these women were compelled (and taught by the devotion) to wield. One man told me that if men did not behave at the festa as their women wanted them to behave, the latter would withhold nourishment in the domus. He used this as a symbol of the kind of power women possessed and revealed on the day of the festa. Once a year, women were educated into the nature and limits of their power at a celebration of a woman of power.

At the same time, however, women were also expected to atone at the festa and before the symbol of their power precisely for the power the community claimed was theirs. Women almost exclusively bore the penitential burden of the devotion. They alone bartered their suffering to free a member of their domus from pain or misfortune. They alone were dragged down the main aisle of the church, licking the stones that paved the way to the throne of the Madonna. The festa was the time of the exaltation but also of the degradation of the women of Italian Harlem; given the structure of the life of the domus and the assumptions of the community about the role of women, degradation and exaltation could not be separated. Even as it was affirmed and revealed in a sacred setting, women were called upon to pay for their possession of the power which they had no choice but to accept.

Women, then, were both the center and the victims of the annual celebration on 115th Street. The devotion summarized and sanctified all the complexity of the lives of the women of Italian Harlem. It revealed the kind of power the community wanted women to possess, bound women to this power, and then offered the community a way to express its anger against women. At the same time, the Madonna offered women a refuge from, and a source of consolation for, the very order the devotion was sustaining.

## POWER

The immigrants feared the irrationality and incomprehensibility of power. From the moment of their arrival they revealed their concern: recall their anxiety that they would unknowingly do something wrong and so be excluded or deported from the country. Centuries of political oppression and colonization in the mezzogiorno had left their mark. Distant and self-serving authority, in their eyes, took sons away and sent them to wars that would profit only the wealthy, denied or granted them assistance, built housing projects in the neighborhood from which they were then excluded on the basis of apparently unreasonable regulations designed to defeat them. Successful politicians of the people, like Marcantonio, knew that they had to remain close and accessible to the community if they were going to be trusted. Even so, their success in this was limited by popular suspicion. Marcantonio, for example, is widely held responsible for what is perceived as a self-serving or willful—or even just completely irrational—encouragement of Puerto Rican migrants to settle in Italian Harlem.[122]

The festa drew on the anxious energies of this multileveled dread of power. Annually, the people immersed themselves in their anxiety regarding the forces of the world that surrounded them by bringing themselves before a symbol of such power. They expressed and purged themselves in the hysteria at the shrine. They attempted, by their suffering and their faithfulness, to come to terms, at least emotionally, with the existence of such power. They tried to adjust their attitude toward a world in which such power seemed to flourish on every level—familial, local, national, and cosmic. As American-born and -raised young people came to adulthood during and after World War II and claimed more of a place for themselves in American society, it seemed less necessary to propitiate this kind of power. Perhaps their participation in the war, their longer residence in the United States, or their upward mobility gave them a different understanding of the nature of power and the individual's relation to it. Changes in this most fundamental perception contributed to the passing of the devotion to Mount Carmel in the late 1940s and 1950s.

At the annual festa, the men and women of Italian Harlem were morally and psychologically reintegrated into the whole of their culture. On the day of the celebration in honor of the Madonna, the people were recalled to the communal values by the culturally established resonances in their consciousnesses and memories between their mothers' houses and the house of their *mama celeste*. For the older immigrants, as they aged in their new world, the festa was the annual occasion for returning to their old villages, in the presence of their mother; there they lived out in a condensed and vivid form and in a sacral context the entire moral structure of their community. They were able to take their children into this world. Throughout the life of the community, the annual festa was a point of moral reorientation for the Italians of Harlem.

The devotion existed at the center of Italian Harlem. It articulated and revealed the community's deepest and essential values and educated all the members, all the generations, of Italian Harlem into those values. The Madonna, emigrating with her people, consoled them during the trials—both physical and spiritual—of immigration. The devotion ratified the complex structures and legitimated the demands of the domus as it offered a way of expressing anger toward it and even of distancing oneself from it. The festa served to regenerate the culture itself in the tense dynamic of death and rebirth which found expression both in the stories of the collapse and salvation of the domus recorded in the parish journal and in the degradation and exaltation of women that occurred during the celebration. It helped shape the community of cara Harlem and offered the immigrants a self-respecting way to find some link with their new home. The devotion was the heart of Italian Harlem, the expression and sanctification of its inner life in all its complexities. And the festa was an arena in which all the deepest struggles of the people would be expressed, acted out, and then finally contained in the presence of the divine mother. The people were right: the Madonna had come to live with them on 115th Street.

## CHAPTER VIII

# The Theology of the Streets

OUTHERN Italian popular religion gave voice to the despair of men and women long oppressed— oppressed with peculiar, sadistic ingenuity—and reinforced attitudes of resignation and fear, as well as a sense of the perversity of reality. All of this was certainly present in the devotion to the Madonna of 115th Street—but this is not the whole story. The immigrants were people strong enough to leave southern Italy and to struggle with the many hardships of migration to secure "Christian" lives for themselves and their families; their religious vision expressed both fear and courage, exile and security, submission and defiance. Every July 16, the soul of a people was revealed in East Harlem. In the devotion to Mount Carmel, as it spilled out of the homes and onto the streets of Italian Harlem, we are offered a unique opportunity to read the theology of a people.

There are problems with such an effort, of course. The theology of the men and women of Italian Harlem would be implicit only, evident for the most part in gestures and attitudes, and so difficult to systematize. But it would simply not be true to say that these people were silent about such things or that their theology was merely a corruption or a poor assimilation of Catholic doctrine. They thought and talked about God and the saints constantly, they wondered about the meaning of their lives, they pondered their place in the scheme of things. Having set the festa in its proper place at the center of Italian Harlem, it becomes possible to understand popular theology critically, in the context of the total life of the community. Theology has a full context now; what is known of the whole life of the culture will inform and restrain what can be said about its theology.

This popular religious thinking was strongly shaped by a Catholic sensibility, although not necessarily by the Catholic church, Italian or American. The immigrants and their offspring were resolutely Catholic, a Catholicism woven deep into the fabric of their family lives. One not wholly sympathetic Protestant pastor noted in 1917 that the immigrants could not bear being accused of disloyalty to the Catholic church.[1] Other observers concurred: whether or not the immigrants went to church regularly or sent their children to parochial schools, they were clear in tenaciously understanding themselves as, and calling themselves, Catholics.[2]

This Catholicism, however, had little to do with the church, which in the mezzogiorno was known as part of the system of oppression and in the United States seemed eager, though unable, to reproduce the caste system the people had known in Italy. The anger of the immigrants toward the American Catholic church is clear in the history of Italian Harlem. The people greatly resented being compelled to worship their Madonna in the lower church. An old Italian resident of East Harlem told Marie Concistre in the early 1930s:

> In 1886 the Italians in East Harlem lived within a radius of about a quarter of a mile. There was only one church to go to and that was what we used to call the "American Church" at East 115th Street (now the renowned Madonna of Mount Carmel Church). In those days we Italians were allowed to worship only in the basement part of the church, a fact which was not altogether to our liking. But the neighborhood became more and more Italian—Now Our Lady of Mt. Carmel Church is our very own.[3]

In another souvenir journal, published in 1927, it was noted that Italians who came to East Harlem from all over the United States found "everything good, everything beautiful," with one great exception: "that venerated image for which you have labored so much should not be in the lower church, but on high, in the upper church." The author of this little sketch concurred, "The observation was just, the lament reasonable."[4] Elsewhere the lower church is described in angry terms as "without light and air, small and with an inconvenient entrance, without a bell tower, the glass case [enshrining the Madonna] set upon weak little walls under a cover of zinc, corroded by time."[5]

The people knew, of course, that the leaders of the American church downtown frowned upon their devotion, upon this public display of a Catholicism that was viewed as pagan and primitive. There is a spirit of defiance in popular spirituality. Dalia was revered in the neighborhood for showing the Madonna and her people the rispetto they had come to America to secure and for putting an end to the humiliation of *la chiesa inferiore*. This spiritual defiance is essential if religious experience is to serve, as we saw it did in Italian Harlem, as a mode of popular self-expression: it allows the people to claim their religious experience as their own and to affirm the validity of their values.

The troubled history of the mezzogiorno and the complex problems of the Italian American domus left their marks on popular religiosity in Italian Harlem. The vows made to the Madonna could at times (though not as often as people think) be little more than a crude bartering with the divine, an attempt at bribing destiny. There are instances where the people mechanically checked off a list of payments to the various divine figures, always careful to give the Madonna a little more. In such cases, the relationship with the divine became a mere patron–client relationship, and the Madonna a kind of divine enforcer to be treated respectfully out of fear alone. Furthermore, the manipulation of suffering to gain the attention of the divine and secure special favors often seemed, and may have been, pathological in its origins and consequences. At times the people seemed to want to bind themselves to the divine with a covenant of pain.

The gambling that invariably took place at Italian American feste vividly expresses this side of the devotion. The people of Italian Harlem played games of chance in the presence of the Madonna. They also made deals with her, wagering their pain and discomfort to win some prize they had long been hoping for. At these moments the Madonna became the symbol of fate, of the powerful forces which southern Italians saw pressing down on them and their families, and the festa became a sacred bazaar at which the people anxiously watched the wheel of fortune spinning, literally and spiritually, in the streets.

The street theologians had much more to say than this, however. Most clearly they proclaimed that suffering and sacrifice were the essential links between themselves and the divine. Their own suffering was used to create a deep bond of sympathy with the redemptive suffering at the heart of Christianity. Each July, in a distant recapitulation of Calvary, the immigrants marched through East Harlem bearing heavy burdens of wax. Churches throughout Italy, and the Church of the Madonna on 115th Street, display in small corner niches the *ecce homo*, a bust of the suffering Christ, so that people can see the suffering of the man and sense the commonality of their pain with his. In the summons "Behold this human being," Italians recognized the truth of their own lives, and this recognition became the ground of their religious experience. Identification with the suffering of Christ and the Madonna became the people's way of participating in the central mystery of the Christian faith.

In the Church of Saint Ann, which was (and still is) one of the major stops on the pilgrimage route of the procession through East Harlem, there is a striking statue of the Madonna. Dressed in a real and heavy black dress identical to those worn in mourning by the older Italian women of Harlem, Mary stands at the railing of the side altar. She is easily mistaken for a woman at prayer. She is at the foot of the cross, and her face wears an expression of great and violent grief. Dark circles are painted around her eyes and her mouth is open in sorrow. This statue was a favorite shrine for men and women, but especially for women, during the festa. The Madonna is close enough to be touched, so that people bringing their sorrows to this image of the suffering divine could reach out and clutch her dress in their fists. In this way, the people of Italian Harlem and the Madonna appeared to be clinging to each other in their troubles.

This kind of devotion enjoys a considerable heritage. For centuries Catholic Europe had known the tradition of the intimately portrayed and experienced suffering divine, expressed most forcefully in Spanish gothic crucifixes, Italy's sorrowing *pietà*, and the stigmata of Francis and most recently of Padre Pio. In the devotion to the Madonna of 115th Street, which takes its place in this tradition, the people used the facts and trials of their lives as their way of faith. It was a faith of the quotidian sanctified: the people's own lives became the way of faith; their suffering, the nexus with divine suffering and, through that, the way to the hope of redemption.

The people's awareness of and participation in the great Christian dialectic of suffering and redemption was strikingly revealed in a ritual popular at Mount Carmel in the period under consideration.[6] On Good Friday, the figure of Jesus was taken down from the huge and special cross used for the occasion and carried around the church on the shoulders of young women, recalling Anna Ruddy's comment that these were the burden-bearers of Italian Harlem. Once again the divine, in this case the suffering divine, was in motion among the people. On Easter Sunday, this same Christ, hands outstretched and nail pocked, not a special Resurrection figure, was displayed in glory on the altar. The people were expressing here an intimate sense of the movement from suffering to triumph.

As we have seen, the movement from suffering to sacrifice during the festa was a movement toward freedom: by embracing suffering on the day of the festa and on behalf of their families and the Madonna, the men and women of Italian Harlem were declaring their human freedom and dignity. The Italians in Harlem and elsewhere respected suffering and acknowledged its inescapable place in their lives. In the words of one of my sources, the people believed "they had to suffer. They'd be surprised if they didn't have to suffer."[7] The people's ritual sacrifice was usually a literal reenactment of their real suffering. In a broader sense, the very atmosphere of discomfort and suffering on the day of the celebration paralleled the conditions of la miseria. The official historian of the devotion equated the early conditions of the immigrants' lives in New York with la miseria and located the origins of the devotion and its emphasis on sacrifice in this continuity of experience. But significantly, in this new-world document sacrifice means triumph—it was what was required of the immigrants if they would prevail in their struggle against adversity in their new home, a struggle which, it is emphasized, they undertook themselves.[8] In the devotion, the people recapitulated and sanctified this central dynamic of immigration, and as they did so they entered into the essential Christian mystery of the movement from suffering to redemption. Their own suffering thus undertaken became the pathway to the encounter with the divine. And through transformed suffering, the people articulated their acceptance and transcendence of suffering. Religious sacrifice, as observed earlier, is the human claim of self-respect in the face of suffering.

Sacrifice was also a demonstration of rispetto for the Madonna. It was as though the people were saying to her: "This is what we are willing to do for you." They offered their sacrifices as gestures of gratitude for the Madonna's care and as expressions of a deep and abiding faith, a faith which still has the power to challenge those who remember it. According to one of my sources: "Most of them came on foot, barefoot, from Brooklyn. They walked over the bridge, all night long, or during the afternoon. They had some faith. I mean, whether you have faith or not, God had to give them something, because the sacrifices they did . . . I couldn't do it."[9] Sacrifice was thus a display and a celebration, an expression of the people's love for the Madonna—although, according to the inner meanings of rispetto, this was a love that was never far from fear. The people approached the holy, then, in fear and with love.

The sacrifice assumed at the devotion was also a discipline. The people learned faithfulness and patience in suffering and saw that this was how their community defined the good man or the good woman. They were taught the importance of a stoic fortitude in the face of the nature of things—but they also revealed that they could rebel against their fates, that there were limits to what they would accept, and that this rebellion was also part of the way in which they understood their humanity. These people could reach a point where they would call the divine to account for what they considered too dreadful a fate.

It was important to show the divine that they could be patient and respectful because the people at the same time held the divine responsible for what happened in their lives. They expected a reciprocal relationship; they would show their anger if the saints or the Madonna did not show proper rispetto in return. One woman who had been going to the festa since 1928 explained her relationship with the Madonna to a reporter from *Il Progresso* during the celebration in 1949: "I have received many graces but now I want another one, and I'm sure the Madonna will listen to me, because I fight with Her, I get angry with Her, and then I always ask her pardon—this is the best system."[10] As we saw earlier, one of my sources spoke with fierce hostility against Saint Anthony because, she said, he had watched while her mother, who had a special devotion to him, died a slow death. This was a bitter anger of love and trust betrayed, as intense as the love demonstrated to the Madonna in the devotion each year on 115th Street. That these people could express so much anger against figures they believed had power over their lives and could demand just treatment from these sacred persons reveals an important aspect of this popular spirituality and, in turn, of the nature of the community. In their religious experience, the immigrants in Harlem and their children rebelled against the victimization that might have seemed their lot. They asserted their subjectivity against these personifications of the forces that would objectify them. When the limits of what they considered tolerable were reached, they reacted with intense outrage and anger. In their religious experience, then, a sense of cosmic indignation was nurtured, and this could have political consequences. It is in the context of what we see here about the inner life of the community that we can better understand why the Italians of East Harlem kept sending the angry and very vocal Vito Marcantonio to Congress: he expressed their outrage too.

The people seemed to be saying during the festa that although the Madonna and the saints were to be held responsible for what happened in their lives, they were also loved in the sufferings of the people, who knew that the divine figures suffered as well. Perhaps the reciprocity expected by the people during the festa included a mutual forgiveness. The roots of sympathy lie deep in the capacity to feel an identity between one life and another. We have seen that in the domus-centered society the connections and sense of mutual responsibility among people were established either by imagining others in the context of one's own family or by seeing them (or including them) in one's home. Italians cast their relations with the divine in the same context. They brought the holy into their homes, filling their rooms with the familiar figures of saints and the Madonna. They performed careful rituals of rispetto toward these figures and included them in the life and decisions of the domus. In this way, the divine was further involved in mutual responsibilities with the people. This was not a contract or a patron–client relationship; rather, it was a domus-centered bond.

In this context, the ecce homo tradition takes on another meaning. Blood bound the members of the domus together; blood established bonds of responsibility and affection among people. The face of the man-god in the ecce homo tradition is bathed in blood—redemptive, life-giving blood, according to the beliefs in which these immigrants had been raised. This divine blood was the foundation of the covenant that existed between the divine and the domus. Just as blood ties demanded reciprocity and responsibility in the domus, so this image of a bleeding God established a profound intimacy between the people, who knew the meanings of blood, and the divine. Son and mother, brother and sister were bound by deep ties of blood, and so were the human and the divine.

The divine, in the figures of the Madonna and her suffering son, was not distant from the lives of the people of Italian Harlem but was there in the streets and in the domus. Italians lived intimately with the saints: they wore their clothes, told funny and affectionate stories about them. They would not be exiled from the sacred. *Giornalieri* (day laborers), the lowest class of workers in southern Italy, were known popularly during the nineteenth century as "saints," both a celebration and a gentle mocking of saint and worker alike. In a Sicilian ballad, to cite another example of this intimacy, Jesus, urged by Mary to save a lusty woman's soul, goes to her in the dark disguised as her lover. The song proclaims, "The Knight went to the bed of the sinner / Jesus Christ went to that bed."[11] In Italian Harlem, the people wrote letters directly to the Madonna and spoke familiarly and colloquially of their closeness to her.

The saints and the Madonna had responsibilities within the domus-centered structure of Italian American life. The communion of saints and people took place in the domus and in the sacred domus on 115th Street; home- and family-based mores were extended to heaven. The saints were expected to be faithful according to the standards of the domus, and just as it rendered the divine intimate, this extension of moral responsibility sacralized Italian ethics. It is pointless to look for Italian American faith apart from the domus: as with all other aspects of their lives, God and his mother and the saints were real to these people only in relation to it; they existed in the world of the domus and not apart from it. The world of the sacred was not entered only, or even mainly, in churches: it was encountered and celebrated through family life, hospitality, and friendship, as well as in the daily trials of the people. It was experienced in the same way, in the same places, and with the same responsibilities and frustrations as these other aspects of their lives. That is why the Italians of Harlem went faithfully to church for baptisms and weddings but not for Sunday mass. People always imagined the divine in relation to the domus: the divine figures most important in the religious life of Italian Harlem were people in domus relationships—la mamma celeste, her son, the brothers Cosmos and Damian, and Saint Anthony, who was a popular, sacred *compare*.

Italians also show us in their faith how personal their God was. Mary was called "mamma," Jesus was thought of as a loving son. In this intimacy, the people seemed to live out quite naturally Jesus' pronouncement of a new relationship with the divine. Italian American faith, in other words, was an incarnational faith. Heaven was close to the people. Although they made a distinction between themselves and the sacred, the people never set the two worlds completely apart. They had brought their Madonna with them across the ocean and every year they took her out into the streets where they lived. They would not allow religious officials, in this country or in Italy, to alienate them from the sacred.

The people believed that God took a hand in shaping and guiding their lives. One of my sources spent a long time tracing for me the twisting paths she and her husband had taken before, as she understood it, God brought them together at Mount Carmel. This woman was convinced, in very specific terms, that her life reflected God's plan. Another woman wrote to the Madonna, "I always offer all my suffering to God: May it be his will."[12] The men and women of Italian Harlem believed that this same nurturing providence shaped the development of the devotion to Mount Carmel and, in particular, brought Dalia to the parish.[13] The graces which people sought from the Madonna, finally, are also evidence of a trust in the participation of the divine in the concerns and crises of the people's everyday lives.

As they insisted on a personal God who could know the hidden sorrows of their lives, the Italians of East Harlem revealed a sense of the insufficiency of a male God. Women seemed to doubt that a male God could understand their needs and hopes and so they turned to another, complementary divine figure whose life was one of suffering for her child, a story that resonated deeply with the economy of Italian American family life. There was a popular Mariology in Italian Harlem that was quite different from official versions but consistent with a long European popular tradition: the women in the community believed that Mary had suffered the pains of childbirth, that she had menstruated, and that she worried constantly about her child.[14] They felt that she could understand and help them because she had shared their most private experiences and because she was as powerful—and as powerless—as they were. Furthermore, the community knew the power and authority of women, and they expected to see this reflected in the ordering of the divine. The arrangements of Italian Harlem's heaven were similar to the arrangements of its life on earth.

The divine had many faces for the people of Italian Harlem. The Madonna's gaze was sometimes warm and maternal, welcoming her children into their mamma's domus to find peace and rest; but the

Madonna was also an unpredictable and fierce woman who had to be propitiated with pain. Jesus, who seems a much less complex divine figure than his mother in the popular theology of Italian Harlem, was a suffering and dutiful son. Saint Anthony and other saints, like Ann, Cosmos and Damian, and Joseph, were familiar figures who behaved much the way one's earthly relations and comari and compari did— sometimes they seemed to have power and be dependable, at other times they showed no respect and so deserved none in return.

For all their intimacy with the divine, the Italian immigrants of Harlem and their children also knew the sense of a *mysterium tremendum*. This was clearly indicated by their behavior in the sanctuary on the day of the festa, by the various penitential disciplines they undertook during the celebration, and by the spirit of rispetto—love–fear— which permeated the July days. In these ways the people expressed a profound sense of guilt and sinfulness, an intimate sense of the troubles of Adam and Eve's children, and a real awareness of the otherness of God. When I asked one of my informants why the devout performed such arduous penances as walking barefoot on the hot streets of Manhattan, he said it was because they knew the truth of the Ash Wednesday blessing, that they had come from dust and would return to dust.[15] In the 1946 parish journal following that year's celebration, it was noted that many people confessed their sins before and during the day of the festa so that they would be worthy to go before the Madonna and ask her help.[16]

The Italian sense of the holy is expressed in the idea of rispetto. Rispetto indicated a general attitude toward life, affirming the dignity of the person respected as well as the person respecting. The concept was complex, as we have seen, weaving together love and fear, intimacy and distance. But at its most basic, rispetto was a humbling and humble acknowledgment of things as they are, a recognition of what is. Work, time, and other people were all to be respected because they were all inescapably real. The idea also carried connotations of reciprocity, an insistence on shared responsibility and mutually recognized dignity. It is profoundly indicative of Italian faith that this rispetto was used to describe all meaningful relations in Italian Harlem and was at the same time the most appropriate term for the community's and the individual's relationship with God. There was not one kind of respect for the Madonna and another for the community and domus; the posture was the same in both cases, and this was recognized and blessed during the celebration.

The people of East Harlem willingly acknowledged their dependence on the divine and accepted the responsibilities this entailed. The vows made before and during the festa expressed their awareness of this dependence, their fear of it, and their gratitude for it. The people cherished these vows, held intimately as signs of their "love and devotion," as one woman told me, as well as of their responsibility and faithfulness. The souvenir journal of 1926 records: "They came to the great throne of the Blessed Virgin driven by the immense desire to fulfill the ardent vows which for an entire year they jealously guarded in their hearts and to give a new vigor and hope and faith in their souls in this Sanctuary and to find support in the misfortunes of life."[17] The seriousness with which the vows were taken indicates that the people valued the qualities they revealed in making and keeping them. This annual festa of vow-making mirrored the reciprocity-oriented economy of East Harlem: again the people's relations with the divine paralleled and so ratified and authorized their social relations. At the festa, the community's commitment to reciprocity was announced and blessed.

The vows also served as a way for the living and the dead of the domus to remain in relation. The dead were part of the total community of the domus in Italian Harlem. Their images stood alongside those of the saints and the Madonna in people's homes. Men and women went faithfully to the cemeteries in the Bronx and Queens where the dead of Italian Harlem reposed to demonstrate their continuing love and respect. And the living assumed the vows of the dead, perpetuating in this way the latter's presence in the domus. This was a most intimate communion between the living and the dead.

Finally, the festa revealed something of what Italians thought about destiny and the human place in it. The men and women of the mezzogiorno are usually portrayed as fatalistic, isolated by intense amoral familism, and suffocated by their belief in a predetermined universe. The world of Italian Harlem certainly included such sentiments. Popular belief in the evil eye, for example, was fatalistic, expressing the fear that what happened in one's life could be the result of a curse. Italian Americans from southern Italian backgrounds will sometimes not acknowledge or anticipate good things lest they tempt fate to punish them for such evident satisfaction and contentment. A people so long deprived of a share in the responsibility for their history and so long subjected to the psychosocial consequences of colonialism might well be fatalistic.

The undifferentiated focus on this aspect of southern Italian inner life, however, has been responsible for an overemphasis on the crudely magical aspects of Italian spirituality. But, again, this is not the whole story. In the proper circumstances fatalism could be replaced by a deep sense of God's determining presence. Indeed, in the context of what has already been said about the personal God of the people and the rispetto shown at the festa, we can state this popular sensibility more forcefully: the people of Italian Harlem would not believe that Jesus, Mary, and the saints would refuse to enter their lives. What others have seen as fatalism we are now in a position to realize was, in its positive expression, an abiding respect for things as they are, a humility before the givenness of reality.

The festa, moreover, articulated, celebrated, and confirmed the people's belief that destiny, however terrible it might be, was a shared destiny. It confirmed the communion of people and saints, living and dead, present and absent, that Italians viewed as so essential to the good life. As one of my sources proudly told me when explaining why elderly Italians insisted on remaining in East Harlem even after it had become "dangerous" in the eyes of their upwardly aspirant children, "Italians need people."[18] If there was one thing the festa of July 16 gave Italian Harlem it was people.

So the street theologians proclaimed that divine and human are in a relationship of mutual responsibility and reciprocity; that the divine needs the human as the human needs the divine; that Christ's redeeming blood established an intimacy between heaven and the domus; that the power of the divine is awesome, not always comprehensible from the perspective of the human and to be approached with love and fear; that the divine is bound to behave with rispetto toward the human; that living and dead, holy and human exist together in the communion of saints; that what God proposes men and women must respect, though they are also free to entreat the divine for help and support; that reality is communal, not individual, and destiny shared; that suffering can become triumph. The Italians brought an ancient religious heritage to the community along the East River; and the American Catholics of the downtown church, dazzled by the prospects of success at last in the United States and embarrassed by this Mediterranean spirituality spilling onto the streets and into the awareness of Americans, might have learned from listening to the voices of the streets.

   The fusion of sacred and profane, of the serious and the apparently trivial, troubled observers of the festa, who were offended by the noise and food and emotion in the presence of the sacred. Yet as we back off from the festa and see it in all its lived intensity, in the conflict and tension as well as the hope and reverence of the people's new lives, hear the prayers and cries and laughter, and smell the steam of sausage and peppers cooking under colored lights, we sense that this sustaining of opposites is probably the epiphany of the entire meaning of the festa. These people took all the pain and hope of their lives and brought them to a divine mother, who lived not only in the faith of their present but in the faith of their past as well, as she merged in their memories with their own mothers. They carried all this into her house, which they had built. On the streets they claimed and in the homes they sanctified, they prayed to be healed of the hurts they knew would come on those streets and in those homes. They begged to be nurtured through another year. And they knew that the path to the divine was the same dense and trying and joyous and painful path that they trod every day.

*Brilliant*

# A Note on Abbreviations

In citing my interviews, I used a number and letter notation system to protect the source's privacy and to give the reader essential information about the source. For example, the code PM-M-2-50 means:

PM   = Fictional initials for the source, but consistent throughout so that the reader will know who is saying what
M    = Sex (Man; W = Woman)
2    = Raised and lived in East Harlem for many years, but no longer resident there
50   = Age

The variations in the third category above, Residential Status, are:

1    = Still living in East Harlem
3    = Never lived in East Harlem
½    = Works in East Harlem but does not live there any more
4    = Worked in East Harlem for many years but no longer works or lives there

Other symbols used are:

R    = Priest or brother
PR   = Puerto Rican

For brevity's sake, I have called all the interviews found in the Covello Papers, with the exception of those clearly marked as having been conducted by someone else, "Covello Interview." This is not quite fair to all the people who helped Covello over the years, but in most cases the interviewer is not identified. I have listed all the significant information about these sources the first time they appear; after that, I have used a shortened form for convenience.

I have also used abbreviations for the different titles of the Mount Carmel parish bulletin, which was called by many names over the years though it remained the same journal. I have abbreviated these titles as follows:

BCM   = *Bollettino Cattolico Mensile*
LVMC = *La Voce del Monte Carmelo*
RCM   = *Revista Cattolica Mensile*

Archives have been abbreviated as:

CP      = Covello Papers
LaGP  = LaGuardia Papers, New York Municipal Archives
MCA   = Mount Carmel Archives
NTP   = Norman Thomas Papers
NYAA = New York Archdiocese Archives
USA   = Union Settlement Archives

# Notes

INTRODUCTION

1. Bernard J. Lynch, "The Italians in New York," *The Catholic World* 47 (April 1888): 67–73.

2. Gabriel A. Zema, "Jottings in Italy," *The American Ecclesiastical Review* 129 (August 1953): 95–99.

3. John V. Tolino, "The Priest in the Italian Problem," *The Ecclesiastical Review* 109 (November 1943): 321.

4. Ibid., p. 326.

5. Henry J. Browne, "The 'Italian Problem' in the Catholic Church of the United States, 1880–1900," *United States Catholic Historical Society, Historical Records and Sketches*, vol. 35 (New York: The United States Catholic Historical Society, 1946).

6. Silvano M. Tomasi, *Piety and Power: The Role of the Italian American Parishes in the New York Metropolitan Area, 1880–1930* (Staten Island, N.Y.: Center for Migration Studies, 1975).

7. Rudolph J. Vecoli, "Prelates and Peasants: Italian Immigrants and the Catholic Church," *Journal of Social History* 2 (Spring 1969).

8. Emmanuel LeRoy Ladurie, *Montaillou: The Promised Land of Error* (New York: Vintage Books, 1979), pp. 352–53.

9. Ibid., p. 250.

10. See Shawn Weldon, *Register of the Leonard Covello Papers, 1907–1974*, MSS Group 40. Published by The Balch Institute for Ethnic Studies, Philadelphia, Pennsylvania, 1982.

CHAPTER 1

1. "Souvenir Program. Our Lady of Mt. Carmel. 1939," no pagination (the title is in English but the text is in Italian), MCA; "La Congregazione del

Monte Carmelo della 115ma Strada," no pagination, MCA; Domenico Pistella, *La Madonna del Carmine e gli Italiani d'America. Storia del Santuario della Madonna del Carmine, 115ma Strada in New York City* (New York: n.p., 1954), p. 62; interviews with PR-M-R-1-60, WS-M-2-70, and FS-M-2-75.

2. "Souvenir Program. Our Lady of Mt. Carmel. 1939," MCA.

3. Interviews with PR-M-R-1-60, AS-W-2-55, PM-M-2-50; also "Mt. Carmel Parish Bulletin" 15, no. 3 (July–August 1954): 1–2, MCA.

4. Interview with FS-M-2-75.

5. Christian McLeod [Anna C. Ruddy], *The Heart of the Stranger: A Story of Little Italy* (New York: Fleming H. Revell Co., 1908), p. 62. This is always mentioned in the articles in *Il Progresso*.

6. Garibaldi Marto Lapolla, *The Fire in the Flesh* (New York: The Vanguard Press, 1931), pp. 150–52.

7. Interviews with AA-M-3-86 and PR-M-R-1-60; *Il Progresso Italo-Americano*, July 17, 1937; "Numero Ricordo. 5mo anniversario della Fondazione della Chiesa di Maria SS. del Monte Carmelo. 1884–1935." For a good description of a similar scene in Brooklyn, see Antonio Mangano, "Italian Tent Work in Brooklyn," *The Baptist Home Mission Monthly* 28 (October 1906): 370; Garibaldi M. Lapolla, *The Grand Gennaro* (New York: The Vanguard Press, 1935), p. 47; *BCM* 4, no. 5 (July 1931): 12, MCA.

8. Interviews with PM-M-2-50, FS-M-2-75, MS-M-1-78; on the drinking that took place at feste, see Mangano, "Italian Tent Work," p. 370; on gambling in Italian Harlem, see Norman Thomas to Captain Brady, Police Precinct, 104th Street, New York City, June 30, 1917, NTP.

9. Interview with BS-W-1-80.

10. "Religion of Lucky Pieces, Witches and the Evil Eye," *World Outlook* 3 (October 1917): 25; Norman M. Thomas, "Six Years in Little Italy," originally published in *The Assembly Herald* 24 (March 1918). Reprinted in *Protestant Evangelicalism in America* (New York: The Arno Press, 1975), pp. 149–51. My citation is to this volume, p. 149.

11. Interviews with PR-M-R-1-60 and BS-W-1-80; for a good catalogue of these objects, see Carla Bianco, *The Two Rosetos* (Bloomington and London: Indiana University Press, 1974), pp. 106–07.

12. Interview with MS-M-1-78.

13. Interview with PR-M-R-1-60.

14. *BCM* 2, no. 3 (June 1929), front cover, MCA. In 1937, to cite just one example, 18,000 pounds of candles were donated to the church during the festa. *Il Progresso Italo-Americano*, July 17, 1937.

15. Interviews with PR-M-R-1-60, DP-M-R-2-75, and MS-M-1-78.

16. *Il Progresso Italo-Americano*, July 17, 1923; interview with BS-W-1-80 and MS-M-1-78.

17. This is powerfully evoked in Pietro DiDonato's fierce novel of Italian-American life, *Christ in Concrete* (Indianapolis and New York: The Bobbs-Merrill Company, 1939), pp. 248–49.

18. McLeod [Ruddy], *Heart of the Stranger*, p. 69; Lapolla, *Fire in the Flesh*, p. 150; Lapolla, *Grand Gennaro*, p. 47.

19. Interview with PR-M-R-1-60; *BCM* 2, no. 5 (August 1929), MCA.

20. Ibid. See also interview with NL-W-1-55; Pistella, *La Madonna del Carmine*, pp. 83–84.

21. A clear picture of Irish and Italian tensions in East Harlem emerges from the following sources: Amedeo D'Aureli, "Study of a Typical Patriarchal Italian Family" (unpaginated, 1936, handwritten manuscript prepared for Leonard Covello), which sketches the life and reminiscences of a family in Italian Harlem, CP; Orlando Guadalupe, "My Community," 1939, paper prepared for Leonard Covello by New York University student, CP; interviews with PR-M-R-1-60 and ZS-M-½-45; Lapolla, *Grand Gennaro*, p. 3; W. A. Swanberg, *Norman Thomas: The Last Idealist* (New York: Charles Scribner's Sons, 1976), p. 38. The subject is also discussed in Antonio Mangano, *Sons of Italy: A Social and Religious Study of the Italians in America* (New York: Missionary Education Movement of the United States and Canada, 1917), p. 102, and Virginia Yans-McLaughlin, *Family and Community: Italian Immigrants in Buffalo, 1880–1930* (Ithaca and London: Cornell University Press, 1977), pp. 112ff. The primary material that evidences this apparently implacable antagonism in New York City is voluminous. On the subject of Jews in East Harlem, see Jeffrey S. Gurock, *When Harlem Was Jewish, 1870–1930* (New York: Columbia University Press, 1979), passim, and Lapolla, *Grand Gennaro*, pp. 47–58. Information on blacks and Irish at the celebration from *BCM* 2, no. 5 (August 1929) and interviews with NL-W-1-55 and PP-M-1-65; see also Mangano, "Italian Tent Work," p. 370.

22. "La Voce del Monte Carmelo" 9, no. 7 (July 1948): 4–5 (another title for the parish bulletin, first used in 1945), MCA. There were actually several processions during the time of the festa, including one on the 15th, one on the morning of the 16th (which was sometimes in honor of Saint Anthony), and then the big procession on the afternoon of the 16th.

23. Interviews with PF-M-2-45, IM-W-1-50, and MS-M-1-78; *Il Progresso Italo-Americano*, July 17, 1951. On girls and women surrounding the Madonna, see McLeod, *Heart of the Stranger*, pp. 67–68; this is also clear from the collection of photographs at Mount Carmel. It is still the practice at the shrine.

24. Interview with MS-M-1-78; "Fede e Cultura" 6, no. 6, (July 1934): 9; "La Voce del Monte Carmelo" 9, no. 7 (July 1948): 4–5, MCA; Norman Thomas, "Six Years," p. 149; the segregation of the sexes is also evident in the pictures at the church.

25. Interview with PF-M-2-45; also "La Voce del Monte Carmel" 10, no. 7 (July 1949): 5, MCA; *Il Progresso Italo-Americano*, July 18, 1902.

26. Lapolla, *Grand Gennaro*, pp. 45–47.

27. Ibid.; also interviews with WS-M-2-70, MS-M-1-78; Lapolla, *Fire in the Flesh*, p. 151.

28. Ibid., p. 46.

29. In 1896, for example, donations totaled over two thousand dollars (*Il Progresso Italo-Americano*, July 17, 1896). On the subject of contributions, see McLeod, *Heart of the Stranger*, pp. 69–70; Thomas, "Six Years," p. 149; interview with PR-M-R-1-60; Antonio Mangano, "The Associated Life of the Ital-

ians in New York City," originally published in *Charities* 12 (May 7, 1904), pp. 476–82; reprinted in Francesco Cordasco and Eugene Bucchioni, eds., *The Italians: Social Backgrounds of an American Group* (Clifton, N.J.: Augustus M. Kelley, 1974), pp. 143–51. My citation is to this volume, p. 149.

30. Interview with WS-M-2-70; Lapolla also specifies that women walked barefoot, *Grand Gennaro*, p. 47.

31. Interview with PR-M-R-1-60; Laurence Franklin, "The Italian in America: What He Has Been, What He Will Be," *The Catholic World* 71 (April 1900): 77–78.

32. McLeod, *Heart of the Stranger*, pp. 67–68; interview with AJ-M-2-30.

33. Interview with PR-M-R-1-60 and MS-M-1-78; Pistella, *La Madonna del Carmine*, p. 62.

34. Interview with WS-M-2-70 and SS-M-2-65.

35. All my sources emphasized this aspect of the festa.

36. Italians also fired off guns on New Year's Eve, a custom that could be deadly: one of my informants' mother was killed as she stood by a window. Interview with DD-M-3-55.

37. Interview with NL-W-1-55.

38. "Souvenir Program. Our Lady of Mt. Carmel. 1939." See also "Numero Ricordo" (1928), p. 6, MCA.

39. Pistella, *La Madonna del Carmine*, p. 84.

40. "Souvenir Program. Our Lady of Mt. Carmel. 1939."

41. Interviews with BS-W-F-1-80 and MS-M-1-78.

42. Interview with NL-W-1-55.

43. John S. Gaynor, *Memoir of Father Dolan* (Buenos Aires: n.p., 1958), pp. 13–14. Gaynor learned of this custom from an article written in 1904 and preserved among Dolan's papers in Argentina. Dolan was pastor of Mount Carmel from 1898 until 1908. MCA.

44. For some indication of the importance of the scapular, see "La Voce del Monte Carmelo" 6, no. 11 (November 1945): 4; *BCM* 2, no. 5 (August 1929), MCA.

45. Gaynor, *Father Dolan*, p. 13.

CHAPTER 2

1. "Interviews on East Harlem Development": John Kane, interviewed by S. Busaca, CP; and Amedeo D'Aureli, "Study," under the heading, "Occupational Adjustment," CP; see also Thomas Kessner, *The Golden Door: Italian and Jewish Immigrant Mobility in New York City, 1880–1915* (New York: Oxford University Press, 1977), pp. 129–33.

2. Covello Interview, "Italian Family in America," P.M.-Bu-I, CP; "Interviews on Development," Guiseppe Perricano, interviewed by S. Busaca, CP; Pistella, *La Madonna del Carmine*, pp. 36–37; Workers of the Federal Writers Project, Works Progress Administration in the City of New York, *The Italians of New York: A Survey* (New York: Random House, 1938), p. 21; "Union Settlement: Seventy-one Years of Concern for Human Needs," historical sketch

prepared at Union Settlement, 1966, USA; Anna C. Ruddy, "True Little Stories at Mulberry Bend," autobiographical sketch prepared for Covello, ca. 1940, CP; Edward Corsi, *In the Shadow of Liberty: The Chronicle of Ellis Island* (New York: The Macmillan Company, 1935), p. 22; Perricano Interview, CP.

3. "Interviews on Development," Reverend Pietro Campo, Pastor of the Jefferson Park Italian Methodist Episcopal Church, interviewed by S. Busaca, CP; Lapolla, *Grand Gennaro*, pp. 3–5; "History of East Harlem. East 108th Street," L. Parziale, interviewed by A. D'Aureli, October 28, 1935, CP; Perricano Interview, CP; see also George Enrico Pozzetta, "The Italians of New York City, 1890–1914," (Ph.D. diss., University of North Carolina, 1974), pp. 76–78.

4. Covello Interview, "Italian Family in America," P.M.-Bu-I, CP; "Interviews on Development," Michael G. Pasca, CP; Italian thrift is noted, for example, in Lynch, "The Italians in New York," pp. 67–68; also in research document, F. J. Panella, January 24, 1936, "C. Family Life," CP; also Pozzetta, "Italians of New York City," p. 164.

5. Perricano Interview, CP.

6. Research note, "Regionalism in the Italian Community," which cites as source an article by William Engle in *The World-Telegram*, December 31, 1935, CP; Perricano Interview, CP; Guadalupe, "My Community," CP. Memories of this arrival of the Calabresi are preserved in Lapolla, *Grand Gennaro*, p. 7.

7. Interview with PR-M-R-1-60; "Commitment to People," interview with Ruth Atkins, Coordinator for the East Harlem Project for Comprehensive Health Planning, in "Listen What People Say," a brochure of interview transcripts prepared for Union Settlement, 1973, USA.

8. Gurock, *When Harlem Was Jewish*, p. 147.

9. Parziale Interview, CP. On the local Tammany Club in East Harlem, see Swanberg, *Norman Thomas*, p. 38. See also Pozzetta, "Italians of New York City," p. 157, and Arthur Mann, *LaGuardia: A Fighter against His Times, 1882–1933* (Philadelphia and New York: J. B. Lippincott Company, 1959), p. 156; Gaynor, *Father Dolan*, pp. 13–15.

10. Gurock, *When Harlem Was Jewish*, pp. 143–44; also, "Living in East Harlem," interview with Adelaide Loehrsen, in "Listen What People Say," USA; City Planning Commission, Department of City Planning, "Community Renewal Program," Raymond and May Associates. East Harlem Planning Area #308. (ca. 1960), p. 4.

11. "Hard Times," interview with Helen M. Harris, Headworker at Union Settlement, 1930–1940, in "Listen What People Say," USA.

12. Leonard Covello, *The Social Background of the Italian American School Child* (Leiden: E. J. Brill, 1967), p. 1; interviews with PM-M-2-50; FS-M-2-75; PF-M-½-45.

13. William B. Shedd, "Italian Population in New York," Casa Italiana Educational Bureau, Bulletin no. 7, Columbia University, no date, no pagination. Shedd's data is from the 1930 census. This publication dates from about 1932. Covello supervised this project.

14. For example, in the 1920s and 1930s, the neighborhood around 100th Street and Third Avenue was primarily Irish, Jewish, and Slovak; 114th Street and First and Second avenues were a mixed Irish, Italian, and Jewish community throughout the history of Italian Harlem. "Life of a Boy in a Non-Italian Community" (Paul Allongi—BFHS-Bu.), CP; Eugene Mazzola, "Westward—to the Land of Opportunity," January 14, 1939 (term paper written for Covello), CP; "A Portrait of East Harlem," January 1960 (no author cited), p. 1, CP.

15. Interview with PM-M-2-50.

16. Corsi House Interviews, February 26, 1981.

17. Pistella, *La Madonna del Carmine*, p. 33; Pozzetta, "Italians of New York City," pp. 131, 173–75; Kessner, *The Golden Door*, pp. 28–29.

18. I have been helped here by Virginia Yans-McLaughlin's analysis in *Family and Community*, pp. 81–82, and passim; and by Sydel F. Silverman, "Agricultural Organization, Social Structure, and Values in Italy: Amoral Familism Reconsidered," *American Anthropologist* 70, no. 1 (February 1968).

19. Covello Interview, "Personal Interview. Man, 58 years of age. Came to America about 1908, married here. Location: Girgenti, Sicily. Class: Landless Workers," CP.

20. D'Aureli, "Study," CP; see also Pozzetta, "Italians of New York City," pp. 84–85.

21. Corsi, *Shadow of Liberty*, p. 22.

22. This is how it appears in Broughton Brandenburg, *Imported Americans: The Story of the Experiences of a Disguised American and His Wife Studying the Immigration Question* (New York: F. A. Stokes Company, 1904), pp. 199ff. My intention is not to rewrite history here. Ellis Island was a place of great suffering, loneliness, and trial for most of the immigrants, as Edward Corsi, among many others, has vividly described in *Shadow of Liberty*, pp. 61–87. But I want to emphasize this other possibility of the immigrant experience at the point of entry.

23. Mazzola, "Westward," CP.

24. Interview with FS-M-2-75; also Covello Interview, "Family Bonds," A.C.S.—S.B.—39, CP; Covello Interview, "Assimilation and Family Establishment. Story of an Assimilated Family," Francesco Armato, S.B.—NYU—1938, CP.

25. Covello Interview, "Family Solidarity and Ties with Italy," N.G.—S.B.—1939, CP.

26. "Personal Interview" (cited in note 19 above), CP; D'Aureli, "Study," CP.

27. Covello Interview, "Family solidarity," L.B.—S.B.—II, CP.

28. D'Aureli, "Study," CP; Covello Interview, "Thrift," from case study: The Tiano Family—S.B.—NYU—1938, CP; "Personal Involvement," interview with Leonard Covello, USA; Research Document, F. J. Panella, January 24, 1936, "C. Family Life," CP; Mangano comments upon Italian thrift in *Sons of Italy*, pp. 113–14; Covello Interview, "Family solidarity," L.B.—S.B.—II, CP; interviews with NL-W-1-55 and WS-M-2-70.

29. Corsi, *Shadow of Liberty*, pp. 23–24.

30. Covello Interview, "Emigration," Ch.P.—By—II, CP; Covello Interview, "Attitude toward formal education," from case study: A.C.—S.B.—NYU—1940, CP.

31. D'Aureli, "Study," CP; Covello Interview, "Health and Magic," case study: G.R.—EHYS—'43, CP; Covello Interview, "Probable causes of immigration," Life History—C. Bono, CP; interview with PM-M-2-50.

32. Circular letter, The Italian American Students League, February 13, 1936, CP.

33. Covello dissertation note, "Family and Community in America," 11, CP; Interview with NL-W-1-55; "Service Boys' Fund of East 104th Street, New York," periodical printed in East Harlem for the servicemen from St. Lucy's Parish 4, no. 1 (June 1945): 4, CP; see also File Folder 227, Box 2554, "Italy—American Relief For," LaGP.

34. John H. Mariano, *The Second Generation of Italians in New York City* (Boston: The Christopher Publishing House, 1921), p. 25; Pozzetta, "Italians of New York City," p. 161.

35. Research document, F. J. Panella, January 24, 1936, "C. Family Life," CP.

36. On the practice of taking in boarders: interview with GO-W-3-83; Lynch, "Italians in New York," p. 68; Mariano, *Second Generation*, p. 29; McLeod, *Heart of the Stranger*, p. 127; Mangano, *Sons of Italy*, p. 24. On the fancied moral abuses of this practice, see John Ryan's comments in "Tuesday, September 27th. The Dependent Family," in National Conference of Catholic Charities, *Proceedings* (Washington, D.C.: Catholic University of America, 1910), pp. 88–165; Panella, Research document, CP.

37. G. S. Plumley, "Report of Calvary Church. Worth Street, Near Centre," New York City Mission and Tract Society, *55th Annual Report* (New York: 50 Bible House, 1882), p. 46.

38. Jacob A. Riis, "Feast Days in Little Italy," originally published in *The Century* 58 (August 1899): 491–99; reprinted in Wayne Moquin, ed., *A Documentary History of the Italian Americans* (New York: Praeger, 1974), pp. 314–16. My reference is to the latter, p. 316.

39. Brandenburg, *Imported Americans*, pp. 119–20; see also Lapolla, *Grand Gennaro*, pp. 4–5.

40. Brandenburg, *Imported Americans*, pp. 140–41; "Religion of Lucky Pieces, Witches and the Evil Eye," p. 25.

41. "Calabria bella, dove t'hai lasciate?" Italian Folk Music Collected in New York, New Jersey, and Rhode Island, volume 2: Calabria, recorded and edited by Anna L. Chairetakis (Ethnic Folkways Library, FES 34042).

42. Covello Manuscript Diary, Friday, July 8, 1921, between Potenza and Napoli, unpaginated, CP.

43. Interview with WS-M-2-70.

44. Interview with NL-W-1-55.

45. Interview with SS-M-2-65.

46. Yans-McLaughlin, *Family and Community*, p. 71.

47. D'Aureli, "Study," CP.

48. "Personal Involvement," interview with Leonard Covello, "Listen What People Say," USA; see also Bianco, *Two Rosetos,* p. 51, and Yans-McLaughlin, *Family and Community,* p. 222.

49. E. Lyell Earle, "Character Studies in New York's Foreign Quarters," *The Catholic World* 68 (March 1899): 787.

50. Bianco, *Two Rosetos,* p. 92.

51. Lapolla, *Grand Gennaro,* pp. 92–93.

52. D'Aureli, "Study," CP; Panella, Research document, CP.

53. Brandenburg, *Imported Americans,* pp. 244–45.

54. Marie A. Lipari, "Interview with Vincent Scilipoti," April 5, 1934, CP; F. J. Panella, "K. Attitudes and Behavior in Relation to Early Settlers," January 31, 1936, CP; see also Pozzetta, "Italians of New York City," pp. 320–29.

55. For example, Mary Van Kleeck, *Artificial Flower Makers* (New York: Survey Associates, 1913), pp. 67ff.

56. See Miriam Judith Cohen, "From Workshop to Office: Italian Women and Family Strategies in New York City, 1900–1950" (Ph.D. diss., University of Michigan, 1978), p. 160; Pozzetta, "Italians of New York City," p. 341; Edwin Fenton, *Immigrants and Unions: A Case Study. Italians and American Labor, 1870–1920* (New York: Arno Press, 1975), passim.

57. Marie A. Lipari, "Interview with Vincent Scilipoti," CP.

58. *New York Times,* July 4, 1880, 12:1; on infant mortality as indicator of general health, see Kenneth B. Clark, *Dark Ghetto: Dilemmas of Social Power* (New York: Harper & Row, 1967), p. 31.

59. *New York Times,* July 4, 1880, 12:1, "The Terrible Death Rate."

60. "Proceedings of Preliminary Meeting to Consider Measures for Protecting Financial and Civic Interests in East Harlem, held at the East Harlem Health Center, 158 East 115th Street," mimeographed minutes, no date (ca. 1938–39), CP; also "Speakers Kit. From Weingast's Report," ca. 1935, CP; "The Protestant Churches of East Harlem. Report of a Survey by the Pathfinding Service for the Churches, with Recommendations by Local Protestant Ministers," June 1947, pp. 15–16, 18, mimeographed copy in CP; "Haarlem House and the Neighborhood," souvenir yearbook, 1930, CP.

61. For the years 1935 to 1940, "Speakers Kit. From Weingast's Report," ca. 1935, CP; also Pozzetta, "Italians of New York City," pp. 108–09; Mann, *LaGuardia,* p. 231.

62. McLeod, *Heart of the Stranger,* p. 127; this density is also emphasized in Joseph H. Adams, "The Italian Quarters of New York City," *The Baptist Home Mission Monthly* 31 (September 1909), pp. 379–84.

63. Dorothy Reed, *Leisure Time of Girls in a "Little Italy"* (Portland, Ore.: n.p., 1932), p. 23.

64. Gurock, *When Harlem Was Jewish,* pp. 139ff.; Pozzetta, "Italians," p. 116; Mann, *LaGuardia,* p. 231; Covello, "The Community of East Harlem," typescript sketch prepared in about 1940. Covello here was working from the report of the Mayor's Commission on City Planning, 1936, CP. "Report—East Harlem." A sketch of the community, working from census data and city re-

ports, prepared under Covello's guidance in about 1948, p. 5, CP. George Metcalf, "Metro North Moves Mountains," *The Reporter*, November 17, 1966, p. 2; Ellen Lurie, "A Study of George Washington Houses, Conducted by the Union Settlement Association, 1955–56," sec. 1, pp. 1–2, USA.

65. Ibid., pp. 141–42.

66. D'Aureli, "Study," CP.

67. In 1938, for example, there was a mass meeting for better housing at Benjamin Franklin High School (Handbill: "Who Wants Better Housing?" March 22, 1938, CP). In 1939, members of the East Harlem Housing Committee, which was composed of members of the community and students and faculty from Franklin, circulated a petition in the community demanding improved housing. "Petition. East Harlem Tenants," 1939, CP.

68. Interviews with FS-M-2-75, PM-M-2-50, WS-M-2-70; Metcalf, "Metro North," pp. 1–2; "The Protestant Churches of East Harlem," 1947, pp. 1–2; "A Description of Union Settlement and Its Relation to East Harlem," 1885–1960, no author, no date, p. 4, USA; "A Portrait of East Harlem," January 1960, p. 3; City Planning Commission Report, 1960, p. 40.

69. Norman Thomas to Harold, December 6, 1915, NTP.

70. "Early On," interview with Sophie White Wells, daughter of Gaylord S. White, Settlement Headworkers, 1901–23, in "Listen What People Say," USA; on the "Black Hand," see Pozzetta, "Italians of New York City," pp. 181–230.

71. Swanberg, *Norman Thomas*, pp. 37–38; *Harlem Home News*, December 22, 1911; *Harlem Home News*, July 31, 1913.

72. Interviews with FS-M-2-75, PM-M-2-50. East Harlem was the birthplace of Frank Costello: see George Wolf, with Joseph DiMona, *Frank Costello: Prime Minister of the Underworld* (New York: William Morrow & Company, 1974), pp. 19–21; *Harlem Home News* for July 31, 1913, notes, "Nearly every corner in 'Little Italy' was crowded with loafers, many of them recognized as criminals."

73. Leonard Covello, chapter outline, no date, CP; see also Mann, *LaGuardia*, p. 231; "Haarlem House and the Neighborhood," 1930, p. 4; "New York City Housing Authority. East River Houses. Public Housing in East Harlem," July 1941, p. 8, CP.

74. "Boys' Club Study at New York University," unpublished section of Covello's autobiography, CP.

75. Reed, *Leisure Time*, p. 19.

76. Interview with WS-M-2-70, PM-M-2-50, MR-W-1-PR-30, FS-M-2-75; on gang tensions in a later period, see "Contributing," interview with Rafael Flores, Youth Worker at Washington Houses Community Center, in "Listen What People Say," USA.

77. Interview with FS-M-2-75.

78. Covello Interview, "Role of Brother," interview with Tony the Cleaner, BF-I, CP; interview with PR-M-R-1-60; see also Mangano, "Associated Life," p. 144; Pozzetta, "Italians of New York City," pp. 96, 176; Mann, *LaGuardia*, p. 251.

79. Interviews with FS-M-2-75, WS-M-2-70, SS-M-2-65.

80. Mariano, *Second Generation*, p. 9.

81. Interview with NL-W-1-55; also *BCM* 2, no. 1 (April 1929): 6–7; *BCM* 2, no. 2 (May 1929): 6; *BCM* 2, no. 3 (June 1929): 9–10.

82. Index to New York Italian Societies, copied from NYC newspapers of 1934, CP.

83. Interviews with PM-M-2-50 and FS-M-2-75.

84. Interview with PM-2-M-50.

85. Interviews with PF-M-2-45, PM-M-2-50, NL-W-1-55, FS-M-2-75, MS-M-1-78; Mazzola, "Westward," CP.

86. Interview with FS-M-2-75.

87. Report by Marino on Committee on Neighborhood Councils, November 17, 1936, CP.

88. "Life of a Boy in Non-Italian Community," CP; "Confidential Copy #2. Preliminary Report of the Boys' Club Study, New York University, March 15, 1929. By Frederic Thrasher, Director," University Archives, New York University, Brown Papers; Mazzola, "Westward," CP; interview with Sal Sala, "Listen What People Say," USA; on high rates of residential mobility among New York Italians, see Pozzetta, "Italians of New York City," p. 108–09, and Donna R. Gabaccia, "Houses and People: Sicilians in Sicily and New York, 1890–1930" (Ph.D. diss., University of Michigan, 1979), pp. 272–73. Gabaccia notes of the downtown community, "Writing about her Elizabeth Street neighbors, Betts conveyed a picture of migrants who moved often and nonchalantly, perhaps even irrationally."

89. Antonio Arrighi, "The Calvary Italian Evangelical Church. 155 Worth Street, New York," New York-City Mission and Tract Society, *61st Annual Report* (New York: 50 Bible House, 1888), pp. 72–73; Antonio Arrighi, "Italian Evangelical Church of the City Mission. 150 Worth Street, New York," New York City Mission and Tract Society, *62nd Annual Report* (New York: 50 Bible House, 1889), p. 70. Arrighi noted this throughout the 1890s in successive reports. Virginia Yans-McLaughlin issues an important warning on interpreting this population flux, in *Family and Community*, pp. 78–79.

90. *New York Times*, June 2, 1880, 8:5; Lapolla, *Grand Gennaro*, pp. 99–100; interview with MS-M-1-78; "Interviews on East Harlem Development," John Kane, interviewed by S. Busaca, CP. The slaughterhouse on 112th Street remained an obnoxious problem in the 1940s (Vito Marcantonio to LaGuardia, June 5, 1945, LaGP). On the terrible conditions of Italian Harlem, see: East River Houses Report, 1941, p. 8; Covello sketch, "The Community of East Harlem," ca. 1940; Mayor's Commission Report, "Certain Characteristics of Health Areas in East Harlem District," ca. 1935, p. 51, CP; also Pozzetta, "Italians of New York City," p. 116.

91. Robert A. Caro, *The Power Broker: Robert Moses and the Fall of New York* (New York: Vintage Books, 1975), pp. 516–18, 715, 912–13; East River Houses Report, 1941, p. 8.

92. Leonard Covello, *The Heart Is the Teacher* (New York: McGraw-Hill Book Company, 1958), p. 21; also Lapolla, *Grand Gennaro*, pp. 104, 153, 279.

93. Covello, *The Heart Is the Teacher*, p. 56.

94. Corsi, *Chronicle*, pp. 23–24; also Lapolla, *Grand Gennaro*, p. 104.

95. Reed, *Leisure Time*, p. 18.

96. "Haarlem House Report, 1930–1931," mimeograph, CP; Piri Thomas, *Down These Mean Streets* (New York: Vintage Books, 1974), pp. 26ff.; Bernice Burroughs, "And Who Is My Neighbor?" sketch of East Harlem, prepared for Methodist Board of Missions, February 1948, p. 1; Metcalf, "Metro North," p. 2; "The Protestant Churches of East Harlem," 1947, pp. 4–6; "The Protestant Churches and Puerto Ricans in New York City," report prepared by the Pathfinding Service for the Churches, ca. 1946, p. 5, CP.

97. "Proceedings of Preliminary Meetings to Consider Measures for Protecting Financial and Civic Interests in East Harlem. . ." (full citation, n. 60 above), CP; "Italian Health in U.S. Report on Conditions in Manhattan, 1921–1925," CP. (This report was based largely on Haven Emerson, "Significant Differences in Racial Susceptibility to Measles, Diphtheria, and Scarlet Fever," *The Journal of Preventive Medicine* 5, no. 5 (September 1931).

98. Covello, *The Heart Is the Teacher*, pp. 251–52.

99. "Haarlem House Report, 1930–1931," CP.

100. "Hard Times," interview with Helen M. Harris, Headworker of Union Settlement, 1930–40, "Listen What People Say," USA; on the conditions of New York's Italians in general during the Depression, see Ronald H. Bayor, *Neighbors in Conflict: The Irish, Germans, Jews and Italians of New York City, 1929–1941* (Baltimore and London: The Johns Hopkins University Press, 1978), pp. 10–11, 18–19.

101. Corsi House Interviews, February 26, 1981.

102. Interviews with PM-M-2-50, WS-M-2-70; also "Hard Times" Interview, USA.

103. "Hard Times" Interview, USA.

104. "Speakers Kit. Our East Harlem Community, Its Needs and the Role of the School in Helping to Solve These Needs," ca. 1935, CP.

105. *New York Times*, May 16, 1893, 9:5.

106. *Time*, November 4, 1946.

107. On LaGuardia's Congressional career, see Howard Zinn, *LaGuardia in Congress* (New York: W. W. Norton & Co., 1969); Corsi discussed his Haarlem House career in his autobiography, *In the Shadow of Liberty*, pp. 27–31; see also Mann, *LaGuardia*, pp. 154, 158, 198, 231. Mann notes that LaGuardia's election as East Harlem's Congressman in 1922 was an expression of "self-conscious ethnic pride" among Harlem's Italians, a pride that took shape partially in response to aggressive theories of Anglo supremacy that characterized the "tribal Twenties."

108. Interview with WS-M-2-70; see also Pozzetta, "Italians of New York City," p. 166.

109. Interview with PP-M-1-70.

110. Interview with PF-M-2-45.

111. "Annual Dinner Dance and Entertainment of the Alumni Associates of Haarlem House. Hotel Pennsylvania," May 25, 1946, printed program, C.P.

112. "Service Boys Fund of East 104th Street. The Committee for the Armed Forces," vol. 2, no. 1 (July 1943): 4, CP.

113. "Commitment to People," interview with Ruth Atkins, "Listen What People Say," USA.

114. Guadalupe, "My Community," CP.

115. Interviews with FS-M-2-75, WS-M-2-70, AS-W-2-55, PM-M-2-50.

116. Mazzola, "Westward," CP.

117. Thomas, *Down These Mean Streets*, p. 350.

118. Interview with NL-W-1-55.

## CHAPTER 3

1. This discussion of mutual aid societies in Italian Harlem is based on: Covello Interviews: "Change of Status of Women. Mutual Aid Society," A.M.I.—S.B.—1940; "Mutual Aid Societies," interview with "Italian—2nd Generation. Lawyer—42 yrs," IA-By—III; "Mutual Aid Society as Social Center," interview with "2nd Generation Female College Student," E. Locquanti—S.B.—1940—all in CP; Margaret A. Harrington, "The Stiglanese Mutual Aid Society of Yonkers," term paper for Covello NYU course, January 1940, CP; Covello dissertation notes: "Changes in Cultural Patterns of Italians in America"; "Assimilation of Men and Women,"—both in CP; "Italian Societies," S. L. Testa, WPA worker, "1st Generation Italo-Am." This is a short autobiography collected by Covello, CP; "Italo-American Societies cultural changes. Reported by Miss Buongiorno," S.B.—NYU—1941, CP; "Change in Status of Women in Mutual Aid Societies," J.B.—S.B.—1939, CP; "Italo-Americans in the American Small Towns," survey by "3 Italo-American Girls," 1939, CP; interview with PR-M-R-1-60; *BCM* 4, no. 5 (July 1931), MCA; Lapolla, *Grand Gennaro*, pp. 114, 192, 242. See also Pozzetta, "Italians of New York City," pp. 243–45.

2. Covello Interview, "Mutual Aid Societies," interview with "Italian—2nd Generation. Lawyer—42 yrs," IA-By—III, CP.

3. This sketch of the founding of the devotion to Mount Carmel in East Harlem is based on: Pistella, *La Madonna del Carmine;* John S. Gaynor, *The English-Speaking Pallotines* (Rome: Gregorian University Press, 1969); interviews with PR-M-R-1-60 and DP-M-R-4-70; Covello Interview, "Interviews on Development. Informant: Reverend Father Enrico Mizzatesta, Rectory—448 East 116th Street," CP; "XVI Luglio, Il Venerabile P. Vincenzo M. Pallotti. L'Ordine dei Pallottini. Il Santuario della 115ma strada in New York," an account prepared in 1926 or 1927 for a parish souvenir journal and published in the parish bulletin, MCA; [Souvenir Journal to Celebrate the New Bell Tower], May 17, 1927, printed by Napoli Press, 444 East 115th Street, NYC, MCA; "Numero Ricordo. 5mo. Anniversario della Fondazione della Chiesa di Maria SS. del Monte Carmelo. 1884–1935," MCA. Other sources used for particular details will be cited when necessary.

4. Father Kirner to Pallotine General House, May 30, 1884. (A photocopy of this letter, which is in the Archives of the Pallotine Order in Rome, was given me by Father Barry Bossa in New York.)

5. Franklin, "The Italian in America," p. 77.

6. Earle, "Character Studies in New York's Foreign Quarters," p. 790; on feste, see also Pozzetta, "Italians of New York City," pp. 289–93.

7. Pistella, *La Madonna del Carmine*, p. 43. Other regional societies at Mount Carmel also had such images sent from Italy; see *BCM* 2, no. 3 (June 1929): 9, MCA.

8. Kirner to Pallotine General House, May 30, 1884.

9. "La Congregazione del Monte Carmelo della 115ma Strada," historical sketch prepared for souvenir journal, 1926 or 1927, MCA. This was the first year that an article on the devotion and the community appeared in the pages of *Il Progresso Italo-Americano*, July 17, 1884.

10. Robert Emmett Curran, *Michael Augustine Corrigan and the Shaping of Conservative Catholicism in America, 1878–1902* (New York: Arno Press, 1978), pp. 70–71.

11. Pistella, *La Madonna del Carmine*, pp. 45–47: also *BCM* 5, no. 7 (July 1932): 6–9; Gaynor, *English-Speaking Pallotines*, pp. 148–49; *Il Progresso Italo-Americano*, July 17, 1884. On Corrigan's interest in New York's Italian immigrants when he was the city's archbishop, see Pozzetta, "Italians of New York City," pp. 279–80, and Richard M. Linkh, *American Catholicism and European Immigrants, 1900–1924* (New York: Center for Migration Studies, 1975), pp. 53, 68–70. However, as we will see, Corrigan was quite ambivalent about these immigrants in his city.

12. Pistella, *La Madonna del Carmine*, p. 42; "La Congregazione del Monte Carmelo," MCA.

13. The first members were Luigi Marazita, Antonio Canero, Antonio Botta, Giuseppe Ferro, Vincent Barbo, and Donato Grabbamonte.

14. Curran, *Michael Augustine Corrigan*, p. 98.

15. Pistella, *La Madonna del Carmine*, pp. 56–58; also bell tower commemorative journal, MCA; Gaynor, *English-Speaking Pallotines*, p. 150; interview with DP-M-R-4-70.

16. Gaynor, *English-Speaking Pallotines*, p. 149; interviews with PR-M-R-1-60, NL-W-1-55, and IM-W-1-50. Kirner's nephew, in a commemorative article written for the Pallotines in 1928, mentions a resident of East Harlem, James Maguire, as the "first and generous" benefactor of the new church (Aemilian Zepf, "Rev. Aemilian Kirner—The First Pallotine Missionary in the United States," *The Pallotine News* 1, no. 6 [June 1928]). In a financial report he submitted to the archdiocese for the period 1884–January 1886, Kirner lists the Italian contribution to the building of the new church at $496.50. He differentiates this from the plate collection ($3,242.40), "drawing of prizes" ($1,105.00), "various donations" ($630.00), and assorted fund-raising efforts, suggesting that all of this money came from sources other than the very poor Italians living in East Harlem. (He has a separate entry for "Italian laborers," $800, which may have been his computation of the labor costs saved by donated work.) Financial Report, Father Kirner, Our Lady of Mount Carmel Church, NYAA. Finally, Kirner was assisted in his fund-raising drive by influential friends of his among the New York clergy.

17. Gaynor, *English-Speaking Pallotines*, p. 150. Gaynor here is working from an article in the *London Tablet*, November 8, 1884.

18. Pistella, *La Madonna del Carmine*, p. 66.

19. Ibid., p. 62. Kirner may also have been able to exploit a bitter feud

that had divided the regional society into warring factions. Kirner to Pallotine General House, May 30, 1884.

20. Gilbert Osofsky, *Harlem: The Making of a Ghetto. Negro New York, 1890–1930* (New York: Harper & Row, 1971), pp. 82–83.

21. Antonio Mangano, "Italian Tent Work," p. 370.

22. Lynch, "Italians in New York," pp. 69–73.

23. H. J. Hillenbrand, "Has the Immigrant Kept the Faith?" *America* 54 (November 23, 1935): 153.

24. D. Lynch. S.J., "The Religious Conditions of Italians in New York," *America* 10 (March 21, 1914): 559.

25. On the cultural assumptions of conservative prelates in this period, see Linkh, *American Catholicism*, pp. 7ff.; on Corrigan, see Curran, *Michael Augustine Corrigan*, pp. 98ff.

26. Linkh, *American Catholicism*, pp. 38ff.; for Italians' perception of Irish attitudes toward them, see, for example, Albert R. Bandini, "Concerning the Italian Problem," *The Ecclesiastical Review* 62 (March 1920): 278–85; Nicola Fusco, "A Catholic Priest's Work," *Il Carroccio* 20 (September 1924): 281–84; LaMartinella, "Italian Catholics in America. Apropos of Archbishop Canevin's Pamphlet," *Il Carroccio* 18 (October 1923): 355–56. Vecoli comments on this tension in his well-known article, "Prelates and Peasants," p. 227.

27. John Farley to Cardinal Girolamo M. Gotti, Prefetto della Propaganda, January 4, 1903, Vatican Archives, Archivio del Capitolo di San Pietro, Madonne Coronate, vol. 20, 1898–1903.

28. Interview with PR-M-R-1-60.

29. Interview with PR-M-R-1-60; *Il Progresso Italo-Americano*, July 17, 1950, also mentions the new prohibition against candles, noting its conspicuous lack of success.

30. For feste as a challenge to clerical authority see: Mangano, *Sons of Italy*, pp. 16–17, and Bianco, *Two Rosetos*, p. 120.

31. Yans-McLaughlin, *Family and Community*, p. 92; also interviews with FS-M-2-75 and WS-M-2-70.

32. Jacob A. Riis, "Feast Days in Little Italy," originally published in *The Century* 58 (August 1899): 491–99; reprinted in Wayne Moquin, ed., *A Documentary History of the Italian-Americans* (New York: Praeger, 1974), pp. 314–16. My citation is to this volume, p. 315.

33. Bandini, "Concerning the Italian Problem," p. 282; Aurelio F. Palmieri, "The Contribution of the Italian Catholic Clergy to the United States," in *Catholic Builders of the Nation*, vol. 2 (Boston: Continental Press, 1923), p. 143; Pistella, *La Madonna del Carmine*, pp. 40–41. *Il Progresso Italo-Americano* faithfully recorded the sums donated in the early years of the devotion. By 1896, the figure was over two thousand dollars. *Il Progresso*, July 17, 1896.

34. Interviews with NL-W-1-55 and PR-M-R-1-60.

35. W. H. Agnew, "Pastoral Care of Italian Children in the United States," *The Ecclesiastical Review* 48 (March 1913): 259–60.

36. Pistella, *La Madonna del Carmine*, pp. 40–41; also, interview with PR-M-R-1-60.

37. Citation from NYU Ph.D. dissertation by Marie Concistre, "Establishment of Italian Churches in America. Protection by divinities—Non-Canonic Concepts vested in primitive aleatory concepts," p. 232, CP. This dissertation is no longer available.

38. Kirner to General House, May 30, 1884.

39. Pistella, *La Madonna del Carmine*, p. 38; for an example of this in another Italian American community, see Bianco, *Two Rosetos*, pp. 120–21.

40. Untitled Souvenir Journal to commemorate bell tower; see also *Numero Ricordo* (1928), pp. 6–10, MCA.

41. This account is based on interviews with DP-M-R-4-70, PR-M-R-1-60, and BB-M-R-1-35. A more precise dating seems impossible: there are no court records of this case, and the Pallotine order retained no files on it.

42. Pistella, *La Madonna del Carmine*, p. 63; Nels Anderson, "The Social Antecedents of a Slum: A Development Study of the East Harlem Area of Manhattan Island, New York City" (Ph.D. diss., New York University, 1930), chap. 7, p. 8, CP; *New York Times*, October 19, 1887.

43. Souvenir Journal, "XVI Luglio. Il Venerabile P. Vincenzo M. Pallotti. L'Ordine dei Pallottini. Il Santuario della 115ma Strada in New York," no pagination, no date, MCA.

44. Pistella, *La Madonna del Carmine*, pp. 69–71; on the growth of the devotion in these years, *Il Progresso Italo-Americano* reported in 1892 that "thousands and thousands" of Italians made their way to Harlem for the celebration; by 1902, the crowd was estimated at between fifty and one hundred thousand men and women; in 1905, ten thousand people tried to attend the high mass on the sixteenth of July. *Il Progresso Italo-Americano*, July 17, 1892; July 18, 1902; July 18, 1905.

45. Pistella, *La Madonna del Carmine*, pp. 69–71; Scipione Tofini to Leo XIII, Vatican Archives; The Canons of Saint Peter to Michael Farley, Archbishop of New York, May 12, 1903. The latter is the official announcement of the decision of the chapter (full citation in n. 27 above). Gaynor, *Father Dolan*, pp. 12–14.

46. Pistella, *La Madonna del Carmine*, p. 96; Leo granted a special indulgence to New Yorkers celebrating the feast of the Madonna of Carmel at churches in her name in 1892; in 1894, he granted a plenary indulgence to participants in the devotion on 115th Street. *Il Progresso Italo-Americano*, July 14, 1892, July 17, 1894.

47. I am heavily dependent in this presentation on Emmett Curran's excellent study, cited in note 10 above, especially pp. 58–155.

48. Cited in Curran, *Michael Augustine Corrigan*, p. 98.

49. Ibid., p. 117.

50. Ibid., p. 324. Curran notes that the Irish American prelates suspected the Germans of having "an almost preternatural influence in Rome," p. 141.

51. Ibid., p. 324; also Robert D. Cross, *The Emergence of Liberal Catholicism in America* (Chicago: Quadrangle Books, 1968), p. 93; and Sydney E. Ahlstrom, *A Religious History of the American People* (New Haven and London: Yale University Press, 1972), pp. 830–41.

52. Texts in John Tracy Ellis, ed., *Documents of American Catholic History* (Milwaukee: The Bruce Publishing Company, 1955), pp. 514ff. and 553ff.; see also Cross, *Emergence of Liberal Catholicism*, pp. 194–96, 200–01.

53. Ellis, *Documents*, p. 517.

54. Cross, *Emergence of Liberal Catholicism*, p. 200.

55. Curran, *Michael Augustine Corrigan*, p. 81.

56. Cross, p. 179; Curran, pp. 407–20.

57. This sense of a special relationship with the papacy is indicated also in a joke rather bitterly told by an Italian priest in 1923: "Once a gang of laborers were repairing a street-car track under the direction of an Italian boss. Father O'Toole of the neighboring Catholic church, passing by, discovered one of his parishioners among these laborers. He approached him, and with a sneer in his eye and a fling in his voice said, 'Pat, how do you like your dago boss?'

'Pretty good, father, pretty good,' answered Pat, and also with a sneer in his eye and a fling in his voice, he added, 'And how do you like yours, Father?'" from LaMartinella, "Italian Catholics in America," p. 356.

58. This is discussed in Marco Caliaro and Mario Francesconi, *John Baptist Scalabrini: Apostle to Emigrants* (Staten Island, N.Y.: Center for Migration Studies, 1977), pp. 115–252; I also profited from Arturo C. Jemolo, *Church and State in Italy, 1850–1950*, trans. David Moore (Oxford: Basil Blackwell, 1960); and S. William Halperin, *Italy and the Vatican at War: A Study of Their Relations from the Outbreak of the Franco-Prussian War to the Death of Pius IX* (Chicago: The University of Chicago Press, 1936).

59. Pistella, *La Madonna del Carmine*, pp. 104–06; Gaynor, *Father Dolan*, p. 13.

60. Ibid., pp. 107–08.

61. Again the annual articles in *Il Progresso Italo-Americano* are helpful: in 1932, the paper noted that 250,000 people attended the festa; in 1937, 10,000 marched in the late-afternoon procession alone. The celebration in 1938 was the biggest ever. *Il Progresso Italo-Americano*, July 17, 1932, July 17, 1938.

62. For an example of this, see Taso's autobiographical reflections in Sidney Mintz, *Worker in the Cane: A Puerto Rican Life History* (New York: W. W. Norton & Co., 1974), p. 30.

63. *BCM* 3, no. 6 (July 1930): 2; also, interview with NL-W-1-55.

64. Untitled Souvenir Journal to commemorate bell tower.

65. Ibid.

66. Interviews with NL-W-1-55 and IM-W-1-50.

67. Interviews with PF-M-½-45 and SS-M-2-65.

68. See reference to solemnization of engagement in *BCM* 2, no. 2 (May 1929): 8, MCA.

69. "La Voce del Monte Carmelo," 6, no. 11, (November 1945): 10.

70. Ibid.

71. *LVMC*, 7, no. 3 (March 1946): 6, MCA.

72. Ibid., no. 1 (January 1946): 6, MCA; *Il Progresso Italo-Americano* captures the mood of these war years well, July 17, 1943, and July 17, 1944.

73. *LVMC* 6, no. 11 (November 1945): 4, MCA.

74. Interview with BB-M-R-1-35.

75. *LVMC* 7, no. 8 (August 1946): 8, MCA.

76. Interview with NL-W-1-55; this event is also described in *Il Progresso Italo-Americano*, July 17, 1944. *Il Progresso*'s account of the devotion in the previous year, before the Italian surrender, noted that people prayed that the war which had brought their two beloved countries into conflict would soon end, and that at the next festa the tricolor and the stars and stripes could once again fly together (July 17, 1943).

77. Interviews with IM-W-1-50, BB-M-R-1-35, and PF-M-½-45.

78. *LVMC* 7, no. 8 (August 1946): 13, MCA.

79. Ibid., no. 5 (May 1946): 12, MCA.

80. Ibid., no. 4 (April 1946): 5, MCA.

81. For example: *LVMC* 8, no. 6 (June 1947); *LVMC* 9, no. 12 (December 1948); *LVMC* 8, no. 2 (February 1947). On this period in American history, see Marty Jezer, *The Dark Ages: Life in the United States, 1945–1960* (Boston: South End Press, 1982), pp. 18ff.

82. *LVMC* 7, no. 6 (June 1946): 10, MCA.

83. *LVMC* 8, no. 6 (June 1947): 9, MCA.

84. *LVMC* 9, no. 12 (December 1948): 5, MCA.

85. *LVMC* 10, no. 11 (November 1949): 9; "The Parish Bulletin" 12, no. 3 (June–July 1951): 11; *LVMC* 8, no. 6 (June 1947): 16; *LVMC* 8, no. 8 (August 1947): 10–11; *LVMC* 9, no. 8 (August 1948): 12; *LVMC* 8, no. 11 (November 1947): 12, MCA.

86. *LVMC* 8, no. 2 (February 1947): 9–10, MCA.

87. *LVMC* 10, no. 4 (April 1949): 8, MCA.

88. *LVMC* 7, no. 11 (November 1946): 14; *LVMC* 8, no. 8 (August 1947): 14, MCA.

89. "Mt Carmel Parish Bulletin" 15, no. 4 (September–October 1954), MCA.

90. My understanding of these years of the ending of Italian Harlem has been helped by: Metcalf, "Metro North"; Lurie, "George Washington Houses"; 1960 City Planning Commission Report (see chap. 2, n. 10, for full citation); "The Protestant Churches of East Harlem," 1947 report; East Harlem Protestant Parish Report, ca. 1964–1965, CP; "New York City's Puerto Ricans: Asset or Liability?" A Statement Relating to the Program and Needs of the Union Settlement, 1952, CP. Also important to my understanding of these years were the interviews collected by Andrew Iacovacci for an unpublished paper, "The Decline of Italian Harlem," Fordham University, 1983.

91. "Mt Carmel Catholic Apostolate Society" 1, no. 3, (May–June 1953): 9, MCA.

92. *LVMC* 8, no. 2 (February 1947): 12; *LVMC* 8, no. 6 (June 1947): 12; *LVMC* 8, no. 8 (August 1947): 9, MCA.

93. *LVMC* 9, no. 8 (August 1948): 10, MCA. Also, interview with PR-M-R-1-60.

94. "Mt Carmel Catholic Apostolate Society," 1, no. 3 (May–June 1953): 3, MCA.

95. *LVMC* 8, no. 11 (November 1947): 14.

96. *Il Progresso* put the number at the festa in 1949 at 250,000; by 1952, this had dropped to 100,000; in the next year, the pastor is quoted as estimating the crowd at 50,000. The number climbs to 100,000 again in 1956, although the police estimates are lower; in 1957, a crowd of 20,000 is reported on the day of the procession. After this, there are no more articles on the annual celebration until 1972, when a special report on the festa recalls it as the "grandmother of all the Italian festivals in New York." *Il Progresso Italo-Americano*, July 17, 1949, July 17, 1952, July 17, 1953, July 17, 1956, July 17, 1957, July 17, 1972.

97. *LVMC* 8, no. 9 (September 1947): 3, MCA.

98. "Mt Carmel Catholic Apostolate Society," 1, no. 3, (May–June, 1953): 3, MCA.

99. "Mt Carmel Parish Bulletin," 15, no. 3 (July–August 1954): 1–2, MCA.

100. *LVMC* 8, no. 8 (August 1947): 4 and 6, MCA.

101. "Catholic Apostolate and Association of Mt Carmel," 2, no. 1 (January–February, 1954), MCA. The frequent changes in the name of the parish bulletin throughout the postwar period seem to reflect the changes in the identity of the church.

102. The church on 115th Street still receives hundreds of letters addressed by the faithful to the Madonna, and the priests there still faithfully acknowledge them. But the letters come now from far away and from the old and sick, according to a priest who read many of them. Many of the letters come from Florida. Written directly to the Madonna in simple Italian, the tone and content of these letters is indicated by the following excerpts: "I have need of many graces and I have great faith in the Madonna. I am eighty-six years old and I used to come to the festa as often as I could. But now I am very old; I can't leave the house; I have great need of the Madonna. I listen with great pleasure to the Novena." "My mother loved the festa, she would always go. Pray for her." "Pray that I will have a safe trip to Italy, where I will be settling down." "I can no longer come to the festa because of my age; hold me under your cloak and bless me." All of these excerpts appeared in F.A., "Regina degli Apostoli," *Bollettino Trimestrale* 42, no. 3 (September 1980): 27–28.

CHAPTER 4

1. Louis M. Giambastiani, "In the Melting Pot: The Italians," *Extension* 7 (September 1912): 9–10, 20–21.

2. EZS, "The Family and Some." Treatment of novel in preparation, submitted to a publisher, 1976. By permission of the author.

3. Interview with PM-M-2-50.

4. Th. DeStefano, "Preservation of Italian Traditions," term paper, SB. 1941, CP.

5. Covello Interview, "La Famiglia in America" (L.C.), CP.

6. See also the Covello Interview entitled "Preservation of Italian Traditions," CP.

7. Covello Interview, "Establishment of Life in America," interview with "First Generation. 42 years—from Baiano, near Naples. American lawyer." This interview was clipped by Covello from Stefano Miele, "America as a Place to Make Money," *World's Work*, December 1920, CP; see also D'Aureli, "Study," CP.

8. Covello Interview, "Cultural Changes" (V.M.-B.F.-II), CP; Covello Interview, "Family," C.G., CP; "Preservation of Italian Traditions," CP.

9. Covello Interview, "Marriage concept Italo-American father (dentist) living in a town about 5,000 people—50% Italian origin," CP.

10. "La Famigila in America."

11. Covello Interview, "Prestige of Family Size. Third Generation. Female. 26." (M.R.—8B—39), CP; Covello Interview, "Role of Oldest Brother in US," L.H.—18 (age 16), CP.

12. Covello Interview, "Marriage Concepts of Italian Girls, Italo-American. 42 years old. Came to US as boy of 3. Father of 5 girls, 1 boy," CP.

13. Covello Interview, "Case Study," R.M.—E.H.Y.S.—1943.

14. Covello Interview, "Family Bonds. First-generation male, from near Naples. 45 years. Bringing up Girls," CP.

15. Covello Interview, "Persistence of Italian Family Tradition," CP.

16. "La Famiglia in America," CP; interview with GO-W-3-83.

17. Covello Interview, "Family Cohesion. Discipline. 2nd Gen—HS student—boy—16½ years—father from Sicily—mother born in America," RC-BFHS-Bu, CP.

18. "Family," C.G., CP.

19. Interview with PM-M-2-50.

20. Covello Interview, "Friends etc. in America. 2nd Generation," Lois Pesce-B-38; Covello Interview, "Family (Concept of Friends) (America). 2nd Gen. Female. College Grad," C.V.-B-62, CP.

21. Covello Interview, "Illiteracy of parents, as factor in attitudes toward formal education (school)," C.P.-BFHA-Bu, CP; interview clipped by Covello from National Commission on Law Observance and Enforcement, "Report of Causes and Crime," Washington, D.C., 1931, vol. 2, no. 3, p. 4, CP; Covello dissertation note, "Some basic mores in family life," CP.

22. "Some basic mores in family life," CP.

23. Covello Interview, "Italian Family in US. In rural district," S.B.—NYU—1941, CP; Covello Interview. "Retention of old customs," J.T.—S.B.—NYU—1938, CP.

24. Covello Interview, "Family. Position of Women," CP.

25. Covello Interview, "Health and Magic" (Case Study.—G.R.—EHYS—'43), CP; account of dream in *La Voce del Monte Carmelo* 10, no. 11 (November 1949): 3, MCA.

26. Interview with AA-M-3-86; on anticlericalism in Italian New York, see also Pozzetta, "Italians of New York City," p. 269.

27. Norman Thomas met a particularly unsavory wandering priest in 1916 in East Harlem and even used the services of eight ex-priests in his work among Harlem's Italians. Norman Thomas to Rev. Edward Niles, Baltimore

(1916); NT to Theodora Finks, March 30, 1916, NTP. See also Gabriel A. Zema, "Jottings in Italy," *The American Ecclesiastical Review* 129 (August 1953): 98; also interview with DP-1-R-4-70.

28. See Richard Gambino, *Blood of My Blood: The Dilemma of Italian Americans* (Garden City, N.Y.: Doubleday & Co., 1974), p. 238.

29. Palmieri, "The Contribution of the Italian Catholic Clergy to the United States," p. 131.

30. Ibid., p. 132.

31. Covello Interview, "Italian family and family tradition. 2nd Generation. 39 years—father of one daughter and one son. Lake Ronkonkoma," CP.

32. Covello Interview, "Retention of Family Tradition in the 3rd Generation." (Life History—T.B.—S.B.—NYU—1938), CP; "Some basic mores in family life," CP; Covello Interview, "Economic Role of Children," L.B.—S.B.—II, CP; interview with PR-M-R-1-60.

33. "Marriage concept Italo-American father (dentist) . . ." (see n. 9 above), CP; "Italian Family and family tradition" (n. 31 above), CP.

34. Covello Interview. "Dowries among Italo-Americans. 2nd Generation man, 22 years" (T.N.-B.F.-I), CP.

35. Covello Interview, untitled interview note, CP.

36. "Family. Position of Women," CP.

37. "La Famiglia in America," CP; Covello Interview, "Rearing of children demands a proper social milieu. 2nd Generation—36 years, female. Parents from near Avellino, Campania," R.C.-S.B.-1939, CP.

38. "Family. Position of Women," CP.

39. Covello, *Social Background*, p. 199.

40. Interview with AS-W-2-55.

41. Both quotes are from Covello, *Social Background*, pp. 80–81.

42. Interview with PM-M-2-50 and NL-W-1-55.

43. Covello, *Social Background*, pp. 160ff.; see also, for example, Anthony H. Galt, "Carnival on the Island of Pantelleria: Ritualized Community Solidarity in an Atomistic Society," *Ethnology* 12, no. 3 (July 1973): 325–39. The perception of Italian "amoral familism" was, of course, popularized by right-wing social theorist Edward Banfield.

44. Covello, *Social Background*, p. 163.

45. Leonard Covello to the Students of Benjamin Franklin High School, Wednesday, October 26, 1938, CP.

46. Leonard Covello, WOV Radio Broadcast Transcript, October 6, 1945 (in Italian), CP.Virginia Yans-McLaughlin has made a similar observation to the one I am making here, in *Family and Community*, p. 232.

47. "Mutual Aid Societies," interview with "Italian-2nd Generation. Lawyer. 42 years," CP.

48. Covello Interview. "Concept of 'family.' 2nd Generation HS Student. 15. Father from Apulia, mother American-born," P. Ludovico—BFHS—Bu, CP.

49. Joseph Leopold, typed account of East Harlem Italian funeral, July 6, 1934, 113th Street, CP.

50. AS-W-2-55; SS-M-2-65; PM-M-1-50; IM-W-1-50.

51. Interview with PM-M-2-50.

52. Interviews with PM-M-2-50 and FS-M-2-75.

53. Interview with NL-W-1-55.

54. Covello, *Social Background*, pp. 88–89; Covello Manuscript Diary, Friday, July 8, between Potenza and Napoli. Unpaginated, CP; Covello Interview, "Health" (A.J.S.-B.-III), CP.

55. Interview with LCL-W-½-65.

56. Interview with PM-M-2-50.

57. Interviews with WS-M-2-70 and FS-M-2-75.

58. Interview with FS-M-2-75 and LCL-W-½-65; Covello dissertation note, "2nd and 3rd Generations. In describing Italo-American Backgrounds," CP.

59. Interview with FS-M-1-75.

60. Covello Interview, untitled quotation, CP.

61. Interview with WS-M-1-70; Covello Interview, "Family Interaction in U.S. Family Cohesion," A.J.S., CP.

62. Interview with PR-M-R-1-60.

63. Interview with FS-M-2-75.

64. Interview with AS-W-1-55.

65. Interview with PR-M-R-1-60.

66. Interview with FS-M-1-75.

67. Interview with SS-M-2-65; Leonard Covello, WOV Radio Broadcast Transcript, CP.

68. Covello Interview, "Family. Ital. in America," (P.M.-Bu-I), CP; Covello Interview fragment, "Family," L.C., CP; Student Autobiography, "Mother's concern over family prestige." (A.J.B.-S.B.-1939), CP; Covello Interview, "Economic basis of friendships. 2nd-Generation school-teacher, female," C.L.T.-S.B.-1940-II, CP; On the understanding of labor as an expression of rispetto: Lapolla, *Fire in the Flesh*, p. 61; Covello Interview, "Marriage among Italo-Americans," interview with "Tony the Cleaner—BF-I," CP; Mariano, *Second Generation*, pp. 252ff. See also *BCM* 3, no. 7 (August–November 1930): 10, MCA.

69. Covello Interview, "Attitude of brother toward older brother. 2nd Generation. High School Student, boy, 16 yrs. Parents from Sicily," CP.

70. Covello unpublished reminiscence, "Social Distance between Father and Son," ca. 1936, CP.

71. Covello Interview, untitled fragment, "C.G. 1st Generation. Came to America at age of 30," CP.

72. Covello Interview fragment, "Italians in U.S. 2nd Generation. Family Control," CP.

73. Interviews with EZS-M-½-45, LCM-M-½-65.

74. Lapolla, *Grand Gennaro*, p. 58.

75. Mazzola, "Westward," CP.

76. Interview with GO-W-3-83.

77. "La Famiglia in America," CP.

78. Alan Schaffer, *Vito Marcantonio: Radical in Congress* (Syracuse, N.Y.: Syracuse University Press, 1966), p. 12.

79. Interviews with FS-M-2—75, WS-M-2-70, PF-M-½-45, Corsi House Interviews, February 26, 1981.

80. Covello Interview fragment. "Close proximity by Italian villages in Italian American communities," OL-15, CP; "Family Interaction in U.S."; Family History, "Story of an Assimilated Family," J.B.—S.B.—NYU—1938, CP; "La Famiglia in America," CP; this is also mentioned in Daisy H. Mosely, "The Catholic Social Worker in an Italian District," *The Catholic World* 114 (February 1922): 618–28; reprinted in Cordasco and Bucchioni, *The Italians*, pp. 439–48. My reference is to this volume, p. 443; see also Kessner, *The Golden Door*, p. 154.

81. Covello Interview fragment, untitled, CP.

82. "Some basic mores in family life" (see n. 21 above), CP.

83. Earle, "Character Studies in New York's Foreign Quarters," p. 786.

84. Prominent in this school of interpretation are Virginia Yans-McLaughlin, Richard Gambino, and Thomas Kessner.

85. Stephen Steinberg, *The Ethnic Myth: Race, Ethnicity and Class in America* (New York: Atheneum, 1981), pp. 100ff.; Cohen, "Workshop," chaps. 4 and 5.

86. Interviews with FS-M-2-75, AS-W-2-55, LCL-W-½-65.

87. Reed, *Leisure Time*, p. 37; Covello Interview fragment, "Family," C.G. L.C., CP.

88. Covello Interview, "Community Life. 1st Generation male, 52 years old, from near Avellino. In South Orange, New Jersey," (R. Chase—S.B.—1939), CP.

89. Covello Interview fragment, untitled, CP. See also "Family Cohesion. Discipline," CP; "Family (concept of friends) (America)," CP; Covello Interview fragment, "Family," D. L.C., CP; "Some basic mores in family life," CP; Covello Interview fragment, untitled, CP.

90. Reed, *Leisure Time*, p. 45; Mariano, *Second Generation*, pp. 252ff.; interview with AS-W-2-55; Covello Interview, "Family Cohesion. 2nd Generation HS. student—boy—16 years old—parents from Sicily—20 years in America," M.S.—BFHS—Bu, CP; "Retention of family tradition in the 3rd Generation," CP; Covello Interview fragment, "Family," L.C., CP; family history, "Family. Ital. in America," P.M.—Bu—I, CP; Mangano, *Sons of Italy*, p. 34; Panunzio, *Soul of an Immigrant*, p. 20.

91. Covello Interview, "Italo-Americans—Cohesion of," from Autobiography, AJB-SB—1939, CP.

92. Untitled interview fragment, "Family." L.C., CP.

93. "Family. Ital. in America," CP; interview with AS-W-2-55.

94. Interviews with FS-M-2-75, PM-M-2-50; George Stautz, Jr., "Observation of a Street Festival on 105th Street between First and Second Avenues," September 21, 1929, typewritten student paper, CP; account of family reaction of conversion to Protestantism in "Italian Young People and Their Church," The New York City Mission and Tract Society, *Annual Report*, January 1907, p. 22.

95. My thinking on this has been shaped by David E. Stannard, *The Puritan Way of Death: A Study in Religion, Culture and Social Change* (Oxford: Oxford University Press, 1979), and Phillipe Ariès, *The Hour of Our Death* (New York: Alfred A. Knopf, 1981).

96. Lapolla has drawn a powerful scene of death among the early immigrants, in *Grand Gennaro*, pp. 114ff.

97. Covello Interview, "Eating. 2nd Generation woman, school teacher." CLT-SB-1940, CP.

98. Leopold funeral account, CP.

99. Interview with PF-M-½-45.

100. Interview with PF-M-½-45; Leopold funeral account, CP.

101. "Eating," CP.

102. Interview with BS-W-1-80; "Study of a Family," typescript account of family history, undated (ca. 1935), pp. 12–13, CP; Covello interview fragment, untitled, M.T.-By-II, CP; Covello, *Social Background*, pp. 89–90.

103. Research document, F. J. Panella, January 24, 1936, "C. Family Life," CP.

104. Covello Interview fragment, "Family," LC, CP; Account of family crisis, "Role of Father. (Rebellious attitude of daughter). 2nd Generation Italo-American school teacher, female," CLT-SB-40 II, CP; "Friends etc in America," CP; Clipping from *Il Progresso Italo-Americano*, "Risposte brevi," February 27, 1941, CP; Covello Interview fragment, T. diB.—By—II, CP; "Family (concept of friends) (America)," CP; untitled interview fragment, "Family," LC, CP.

105. Interview with EZS-M-½-45; this is commented upon also in Margaret Carlyle, *The Awakening of Southern Italy* (London: Oxford University Press, 1962), p. 92.

106. An example of this are the prayers women sent the Madonna begging her to keep their sons out of the army; in many cases, the women seem a little embarrassed at what they are doing. *LVMC* 10, no. 4 (April 1949), MCA.

107. "Study of a Family," CP.

108. Covello Interview fragment, "Honor of the Italian Girl," T.G.—By—II, CP.

109. Interviews with FS-M-75, SS-M-2-65, MB-M-2-75, PM-M-2-50; the story about the Madonna's crown comes from MS-M-1-78.

110. Interview with PM-M-2-50.

111. Interview with WS-M-2-70.

112. Interview with WS-M-2-70.

113. Interview with MB-M-2-75.

114. Interviews with PM-M-2-50, AS-W-2-55, WS-M-2-70; Giacobbe Interview, Ugo Cavallo, "Regionalism in America. Community," 1930, CP; Ercole Cantelmo, "Usi, Costumi e Feste degli Italiani negli Stati Uniti," in *Gli Italiani negli Stati Uniti D'America* (New York: Italian American Directory Co., 1906), p. 159; Covello, *Social Background*, p. 75.

115. Interviews with SS-M-2-65, PM-M-2-50, LCM-M-½-75.

116. Interviews with PM-M-2-50 and EZS-M-½-45.

117. Interview with PM-M-2-50.

118. Covello Interview. "Mores relevant to Italian girls. 2nd Gen. school teacher, female," LCT-SB-1940 II, CP; Covello Interview fragment, "Family-child relations," L.H.-17, CP.

119. "Study of a Family," CP.

120. Covello Interview, "Two Documents. Girl-Boy Relationships," CP.

121. Interviews with BS-W-1-80 and PR-M-R-1-60; Lapolla, *Fire in the Flesh*, p. 96.

122. Interviews with BS-W-1-80 and MS-M-1-78; Stautz, "Observation of a Street Festival," CP.

## CHAPTER 5

1. Covello Interviews: "Personal Interview, Man, 58 years of age. Came to America about 1908, married here. Location: Girgenti, Sicily. Class: Landless workers"; "Family," C.G.; "Italians in U.S. 2nd Generation Family Control," CP.

2. Covello Interview, "Retention of caste system in an Italian family in a non-Italian Community. 2nd Generation Female, 24 years old, parents from Sicily. Elmsford, N.Y.," CP.

3. Th. DeStefano, term paper fragment, "Preservation of Italian Traditions," SB 1941, CP.

4. Life history (fragment), "Retention of Family Tradition in the 3rd Generation," T.B.—S.B.—NYU—1938, CP; also Covello Interview, "Cultural Changes," V.M.—B.F.—II, CP.

5. Family history, "Three Generations of an Italian Family." Fragment: "Criterion of Assimilation. Italo-American Father. 62 years. From Calabria," F.A.—S.B.—NYU—1938, CP.

6. Excerpts from Donna Lydia's advice column, various years, typed on index cards, CP. See also on Donna Lydia, Covello Interview, "Family (concept of friends). (America)," CP.

7. Quoted in Reed, *Leisure Time*, p. 35, from an unpublished address at Haarlem House, 1929.

8. Ibid., p. 31. This is also apparent in Cantelmo, "Usi, Costumi e Feste . . ." (chap. 4, n. 114 above), p. 157; Grace O'Brien, "Catholic Social Settlements," National Conference of Catholic Charities, *Proceedings*, 1910, pp. 143–44; Mariano, *Second Generation*, pp. 93ff.; and Cimilluca, "Natural History," p. 87.

9. "Family (concept of friends). (America)," CP; also "Life of Boy in Non-Italian Community," Paul Allongi—BFHS—Bu, CP.

10. Covello Interview fragment. "Family Interaction in the U.S. Family cohesion," A.J.S, CP.

11. Interviews with FS-M-2-75, PM-M-2-50, EZS-M-½-45; also Frederic Thrasher to E. E. Brown, October 10, 1928, University Archives, NYU.

12. Citation from National Commission on Law Observance and Enforcement, "Report of Causes of Crime," Washington, D.C., 1931, CP.

13. Covello Interview, "Second Generation's Attitude Toward Marrying

Non-Italians," interview with "2nd Generation H.S. Student. Boy. 16½ years. Parents from Sicily. Poor Student, Truant," CP; "Study of a Family," CP; Covello Interview, "Mores Relevant to Girls. 2nd Generation School Teacher. Female," L.C.T.—S.B.—1940. II, CP; Extract from Children Court Case Record, 1923, NYC, CP; Covello Interview, "Two Documents. Girl-Boy Relationships," CP; "Personal Interview. Man, 58 years of age . . . Girgenti, Sicily," CP; Minutes and statement, Conference on Attendance and Truancy, Friday, May 5, 1944. Present: Mr. Covello et alia, CP; term paper fragment, Ida Altman, "Education of Italians. Impressions by non-Italians," School for Social Research, 1940, CP; Covello Interview fragment, "Illiteracy of Parents as factor in attitudes toward formal education (school)," C.P.—BFHS—Bu, CP; family history fragment, "Italian Family in U.S. (in rural district)," S.G.—S.B.—NYU—1941, CP; from case study, "Attitude toward Education," J.T.—S.B.—NYU—1938, CP; from case study, "Attitude toward Formal Education," A.C.—S.B.—NYU—1940, CP; Handwritten Student Responses to Covello Question, New York University, Rose LoCascio, 120–203, Mon. 608, CP; interviews with PR-M-R-1-60 and PM-M-2-50.

14. "Second Generation's Attitude toward Marrying Italians," CP.

15. Covello Autobiographical Statement, handwritten, no date, CP.

16. Covello dissertation fragment, "Family," CP; DeStefano, term paper fragment, "Preservation of Italian Traditions," CP; Covello Interview, "Family (concept of friends)," CP; Guadalupe, "My Community," CP.

17. "Two Documents. Girl-Boy Relationships," CP.

18. Covello reminiscence, "Social Distance between Father and Son," C. 1935–6, CP.

19. Covello autobiographical fragment, unpaginated, untitled, CP.

20. Austin Works (chairman, BFHS English Department), Handwritten Response to Questionnaire on Behavior Problems, BFHS, 1935, CP.

21. C. L. Tepedino, autobiographical fragment, "Americanization of Italian Children through the School," CCS—NYU—1941, CP.

22. Term paper, Alice C. Kraus, "The Italians and Dentistry," prepared for Covello course, NYU 120.81, no date, CP; also Covello Interview fragment, "Assimilation—Parent—Child," P. Filloramo, CC School—NYU—1941, CP; term paper fragment, V. Bono, "An Assimilated Italian Family," fragment title: "Language in the Home and Community," S.B.—1938, CP.

23. On the cramped quarters of Italian Harlem, see interviews with PM-M-2-50 and AS-W-2-55; "Ugo Cavallo," CP; Covello Interview fragment, "Home Education of Girl. Italo-American. 2nd Generation Female. Marie Concilio," SB—1940, CP; Covello Interview fragment, "Girls. Miss S.—20 years. Born in Italy. Came to U.S. at age of 7," CP; Covello Interview fragment, "Dowry Among Italo-Americans. Male. 36 years. Born in USA of Sicilian Parents," (??—BF—I), CP; Mazzola, "Westward," CP; "Second Generation's Attitude toward Marrying Non-Italians," CP.

24. "Some basic mores in family life," CP.

25. "Social Distance between Father and Son," CP.

26. "Mores relevant to Italian girls," CP.

27. Covello Interview fragment, "Family life in US," L.H.—23 (age 20), CP.

28. Interviews with FS-M-2-75, PM-M-2-50, Corsi House Interviews, LCL-W-½-65, EZS-M-½-45; also "Study of a Family," CP.

29. Autobiographical fragment, John DiVietro, "Italo-Americans from Basilicata. (Family). After 1940," CP.

30. "Dowry among Italo-Americans," CP; also Covello dissertation note, "Disorganization of the family," CP.

31. Covello Interview fragment, "Endogamy among Italo-Americans. Old man, born near Bari, Apulia," (??—B.F.—I), CP.

32. From Case Study, "Retention of old customs," J.T.—S.B.—NYU—1938, CP.

33. "Mores relevant to Italian girls," CP.

34. "Study of a Family," CP.

35. Interviews with PR-M-R-1-60, AS-W-2-55, FS-M-2-75, PM-M-2-50; also autobiographical fragment, "Cultural changes" (V.M.—B.F.—II.), CP; "Some basic mores in family life," CP.

36. Covello Interview fragment, "Honor of Girl. 2nd Generation. Par. from Campania," G.T.—B.F.—I., CP; Covello Interview, "Concept of Health in marital relations. 2nd Generation. 16. BFHS. Student. Both parents from Calabria," C.P.—BFHS-Bu, CP.

37. Covello Interview fragment, "Family," D., CP.

38. Interviews with PM-M-2-50, FS-M-2-75, AS-W-2-55; also "Study of a Family," CP.

39. "Concept of Health in marital relations," CP.

40. Covello Interview fragment, "Raping Girls. 3rd Generation. 19 years." (Paul ?—By—II), CP; Covello Interview, "Raping Girls," interview with "Italo-American Policeman. 2nd Generation," P.P.—By—II, CP.

41. Interviews with FS-M-2-75 and PM-M-2-50; also Covello Interview fragment, "Family," D., CP; "Study of a Family," CP; "Raping Girls," interview with "Italo-American Policemen," CP; Covello Interview, "Boy Friends and Girl Friends," interview with "Several Italo-American girls at NYU," CP.

42. Covello Interview fragment, "Bringing Up of Girls. Reaction of boys to Non-Italian girls. 2nd Generation. Par. from Sicily. Rationalization," (T.G.—By-II), CP.

43. "Raping Girls," interview with "Italo-American policeman," CP.

44. Interview with PM-M-2-50.

45. Covello Interview fragment, "Role of oldest brother in U.S.," L.H.—18 (age 16), NYU, CP; also Covello Interview fragment, "Brother–Sister Relationship," (M.D.P.—BFHS—Bu), CP; Covello dissertation fragment, "Girl's Conduct," CP; "Some basic mores in family life," CP; Covello Interview fragment, untitled, CP.

46. "Life of Boy in Non-Italian Community," CP.

47. Covello Interview fragment, "Family Cohesion. Discipline. 2nd Generation. H.S. student. Boy. 16½ years. Father from Sicily. Mother born in America," R.C.—BFHS—Bu, CP; see also "Role of Brother," interview with "2nd Generation. Tony the Cleaner," BF-I, CP.

48. Interview with PM-M-2-50.

49. "Study of a Family," CP; interview with PM-M-2-50.

50. Covello Interview, "Attitude of Brother toward older brother. 2nd Generation. High School Student. Boy. 16½ years. Parents from Sicily," P.L.—BFHS—Bu, CP.

51. Memo, Office of the Principal, October 22, 1942, CP.

52. Covello Interview, "Father's position in the attitude of children. 2nd Generation H.S. Student. 15. Father from Apulia. Mother American born," Patsy Ludovico. BFHS—Bu, CP.

53. The public–private split in male–female relations and identities is also commented upon in Cohen, "Workshop," and Covello, *Social Background;* on southern Italian attitudes toward male authority, see "Social Distance between Father and Son," CP; Covello dissertation note, "Role of Brother in America," CP; Covello Interview, "On Paternal Authority. Family from Apulia," (P.R.—III—28), CP; Covello dissertation note, "Assimilation of Men and Women," CP; "Study of a Family," CP.

54. Term paper fragment, "Attitude Toward Italo-Americans. Italian Family," Jane McDonald. S.B.—1941, CP.

55. Covello Interview, "Role of Father. Rebellious Attitude of Daughter. 2nd Generation Italo-American School Teacher. Female," CLT-S.B.—40-II.

56. "Italian Family Discipline. Family Discipline in America," CP; from case study, "Retention of old customs," J.T.—SB—NYU—1938, CP.

57. Covello Interview fragment, "Italian Family Discipline. Family Discipline in America," B.H.—31. John Fazio, CP.

58. Covello Interview, "Italian family in America. Domination of Father," Elizabeth Locquanti. S.B.—1941, CP.

59. Interview with PM-M-2-50.

60. Interviews with EZS-M-½-45 and WS-M-2-70; see also "Concept of Health in marital relations," CP; Covello dissertation note, "Assimilation of Men and Women," CP.

61. Covello Interview, "On Paternal Authority," CP; "Retention of a caste-system in an Italian family in a non-Italian community," CP.

62. "Study of a Family," CP.

63. "Personal Interview," CP.

64. Interview with WS-M-2-70.

65. "Study of a Family," CP.

66. Covello Interview fragment, "Italian Solidarity," L.H.—5. Age 24, CP; also Covello Interview fragment, "Friendship, (boys)." L.H.—22. Age 22, CP.

67. Covello Interview fragment, "Parental Discipline in U.S.," L.H.—34—Age 21, CP; also Reed, *Leisure Time*, pp. 48ff.

68. "Girls," CP; Reed, *Leisure Time*, p. 52.

69. "Study of a Family," CP.

70. Thomas, "Six Years," p. 151, in *Protestant Evangelism.*

71. "Retention of family traditions in the 3rd Generation," CP.

72. Covello Interview and family history, "Italian family and the family

tradition. 2nd Generation. 39 years. Father of one daughter and one son. Lake Ronkonkoma," (?p—By—II), CP.

73. Covello Interview, "Marriage among Italo-Americans," interview with "Tony the Cleaner," BF—I. CP.

74. "Girls," CP.

75. "Attitude of brother toward older brothers," CP.

76. EZS, "The Family and Some."

77. "Home education of girl," CP.

78. "Italian family and the family tradition," CP.

79. Covello Interview fragment, "Family Bonds," A.C.S.—SB—39, CP; also interview with AS-W-2-55; Corsi House Interviews; LCL-W-½-65; also Covello Interview and family history, "Cultural Changes" (V.M.—BF—II), CP; "Girl's Conduct," CP.

80. Family history, "Story of an Assimilated Family. The family as a social world in America," J.B.—S.B.—NYU—1938, CP; also "Family Bonds," CP.

81. Interviews with BS-W-1-80, WS-M-2-70, AS-W-2-55, PR-M-R-1-60; also case study, "Health and Magic," G.R.—EHYS—'43, CP; EZS, "The Family and Some."

82. Interviews with PF-M-½-45, FS-M-2-75, AS-W-2-55, PR-M-R-1-60; also Lapolla, *Grand Gennaro*, p. 259ff.; account of funeral, Joseph Leopold, Friday, July 6, 1934, 113th Street, CP.

83. Interview with PM-M-2-50.

84. Mazzola, "Westward," CP.

85. Interview with PM-M-2-50; also "Attitude of Brother toward older brother," CP; Minutes and statement, Conference on Attendance and Truancy, CP; "Mores relevant to girls," CP; "Marriage among Italo-Americans," CP; Untitled Covello Interview fragment, "Family," L.C., CP; "Some basic mores in family life," CP; Covello autobiographical fragment September 1957, CP; Reed, *Leisure Time*, pp. 35ff.; "Concept of Health in marital relations," CP.

86. "Attitude toward Italo-Americans," CP; interview with LCL-W-½-65.

87. Quoted in Cohen, "Workshop," p. 54; also "Some basic mores in family life," CP.

88. For example, McLeod [Ruddy], *Heart of the Stranger*, p. 29ff., and passim.

89. Covello Interview, "Contact of girls with males. Miss Marchisella. School Teacher. 3rd Generation. Italo-Americans," CP; also "Study of a Family," CP; List of Names and Addresses, Parents Association Executive Council, 1943–44, CP.

90. Interviews with PM-M-2-50 and Corsi House Interviews.

91. "Second Generation's Attitude Toward Marrying Non-Italians," CP

92. Interviews with PM-M-2-50, AS-W-2-55, NL-W-1-55, PR-M-R-1-60; Covello Interview, "Endogamy among Italo-Americans. Old man, born near Bari, Apulia," (??—B.F.—I), CP.

93. Interview with PM-M-2-50.

94. "Italian family and family traditions," CP.

95. "Honor of Girl," CP.

96. "Honor of Girl," CP; also "Study of a Family," CP; case study, "Italian Family Mores," B.F.—S.B.—NYU—1941, CP; Reed, *Leisure Time*, pp. 37–38; *LVMC* 9, no. 4 (April 1948), MCA.

97. "Italian family and family traditions," CP.

98. Covello dissertation note, "Position of Girl," CP; also "Contact of girl with males," CP.

99. Reed, *Leisure Time*, p. 31.

100. "Contact of girl with males," CP.

101. Covello Interview fragment, "Parental Control of girl in U.S. Going to Movies," A.H.—14B, CP; also "Raping Girls. 3rd Generation. 19 years," CP; "Study of a Family," CP; interviews with IM-W-1-50, AS-W-2-55, LCL-W-½-65, NL-W-1-55.

102. "Contact of girl with males," CP.

103. "Boy Friends and Girl Friends," CP.

104. "Role of Brother," CP; also Reed, *Leisure Time*, p. 37.

105. Interview with PM-M-2-50. According to my informant, "A girl's reputation was really made on the guy." Also interview with FS-M-2-75.

106. "Honor of Girl. 2nd Generation. Par. from Campania," CP.

107. "Concept of Health in marital relations," CP.

108. "Italian family and family traditions," CP; also untitled interview fragment, "Position of Women. Family," L.C., CP.

109. "Two Documents. Boy-Girl Relationships," CP; Covello autobiographical statement, CP; Reed, *Leisure Time*, pp. 36–39; interviews with IM-W-1-50, NL-W-1-55, AS-W-2-55, LCL-W-½-65, PM-M-2-50; Untitled Covello Interview fragment. "Family," L.C., CP; also Th. DeStefano, term paper fragment, "Preservation of Italian Traditions," CP; Corsi House Interviews.

110. Covello Interview fragment, "Brother-Sister Relationship," S.C.—BFHS—Bu, CP; see also interview with EZS-M-½-45.

111. On the spirit of cooperation, see "Some basic mores in family life," CP.

112. Covello autobiographical statement, CP; "Role of Brother," CP; "Father's position in the attitude of children," CP.

113. Covello Interview fragment, "Brother-Sister Relationship," L.H.—31—(Age 19), CP.

114. Fragment from Motion Picture Study, Thrasher and Cressey, Life Histories, "Older Brother in the Role of Protector of Sister," CP.

115. Covello Interview fragment, "Brother as Protector in the U.S.," L.H.—34, CP.

116. Covello Interview, "Accommodation in America," T.C.—S.B.—1939, CP.

117. "Mores relevant to Italian girls," CP.

118. Covello dissertation note, "Position of Girl," CP.

119. "Study of a Family," CP.

120. Interview with AS-W-2-55; untitled interview fragment, "Family," L.C., CP.

121. Interview with T-W-1-70.

122. "Italian family and the family tradition," CP; untitled interview fragment, "Family," D. L.C., CP; Citation from Nizzardini and Joffe, "Italian Food Patterns," with commentary by Covello, "The Italo-American housewife," CP; also Covello dissertation note, "Assimilation of Men and Women," CP; "Life of a Boy in a Non-Italian Community," CP; Covello Interview fragment, "Marriage concept," CP; untitled autobiographical fragment, C.G., CP; autobiography fragment, "Language Adjustment," ATB—SB—1939, CP; also interviews with SS-M-2-60, FS-M-2-75, and Corsi House Interviews.

## CHAPTER 6

1. Bianco, *Two Rosetos*, p. 35.

2. Panunzio, *Soul of an Immigrant*, pp. 59–60.

3. Carlo Levi, *Christ Stopped at Eboli*, trans. Frances Frenaye (New York: Farrar, Straus and Giroux, 1947), p. 126.

4. Brandenburg, *Imported Americans*, pp. 96–97.

5. Ibid., 123–24; Lapolla draws a similar scene of parting in *Grand Gennaro*, p. 135.

6. On the subject of this mistreatment, see Brandenburg, *Imported Americans*, pp. 135–46; for excitement on ship, see ibid., pp. 199ff.; Lapolla, *Fire in the Flesh*, p. 21. One of my informants emphasized the terrors of being in Naples for the first time, interview with NL-W-1-55.

7. Lapolla, *Fire in the Flesh*, pp. 20ff.

8. Brandenburg, *Imported Americans*, p. 199.

9. Pauline Barrese, "Southern Italian Folklore in New York City," *New York Folklore Quarterly* 21 no. 3 (September 1965), p. 184.

10. Brandenburg, *Imported Americans*, pp. 40, 145; interview with AA-M-3-86.

11. Mazzola, "Westward," CP; see also Covello, *The Heart Is the Teacher*, p. 141. Covello observes, "How devastating must be the disillusionment to the average immigrant, how difficult to face up to the facts of reality."

12. Kraus, "The Italians and Dentistry," CP; Bianco, *Two Rosetos*, p. xiii.

13. Leonard Covello, Naturalization Rally Address, Julia Richman High School, Wednesday evening, June 1, 1938, CP.

14. Lapolla, *Grand Gennaro*, p. 153; Covello, *The Heart Is the Teacher*, p. 25.

15. Panunzio, *Soul of an Immigrant*, p. 187.

16. Covello Interview, "Thrift," C.G., CP.

17. Interview with AA-M-3-86.

18. Covello Interview with L.B.—S.B.-II, CP; Covello Interview with AJB-SB-1939, CP; Marie A. Lipari, "Interview with Vincent Scilipoti," CP.

19. Interview with AA-M-3-86.

20. Lapolla, *Grand Gennaro*, pp. 22–23.

21. Ibid., p. 12.

22. Ibid., p. 81.

23. Ibid., p. 18.

24. Ibid., p. 37.

25. Ibid., p. 91.

26. Ibid., p. 151.

27. Ibid., p. 174; one cannot avoid this conclusion after reading Ruddy's East Harlem memoir.

28. Ibid., p. 223.

29. Panunzio, *Soul of an Immigrant*, pp. 82, 103ff.

30. Covello, *Social Background*, p. 22.

31. Norman Thomas to Mr. Adriance, May 19, 1912, NTP.

32. Covello, *The Heart Is the Teacher*, p. 43.

33. Ibid., p. 30.

34. Transcript copy of interview with Leonard Covello, sent by Joseph Lederer, Editor of *The Urban Review*, December 4, 1968, p. 3, CP.

35. Mazzola, "Westward," CP.

36. Covello Naturalization Rally Address, 1938, CP.

37. Circular. "Italo-Americani protestate contro l'istituzione di campi di concentramento in America. Oggi a me, domani tocca a te!" 1941, CP.

## CHAPTER 7

1. "Numero Ricordo" (1928), p. 6, MCA.

2. *LVMC* 8, no. 8 (August 1947): 4; also "Numero Ricordo" (1928), pp. 6–8; *BCM* 3, no. 6 (July 1930): 2, MCA.

3. *BCM* 2, no. 6 (September 1929): 2, MCA.

4. "Numero Ricordo" (1928), p. 6; see also "Souvenir Program. Our Lady of Mt Carmel. 1939," MCA.

5. For example, "La Congregazione del Monte Carmelo della 115ma Strada" (ca. 1926–27), MCA.

6. Interview with NL-W-1-55.

7. *BCM* 2, no. 2 (May 1929), MCA.

8. *LVMC* 10, no. 3 (March 1949): 7, MCA.

9. Ibid. 7, no. 1 (January 1946): 6, MCA.

10. Ibid., no. 2 (February 1946): 5, MCA.

11. Ibid., no. 1 (January 1946): 5, MCA.

12. *BCM* 2, no. 2 (May 1929): 4; also interview with AO-W-3-55.

13. *RCM* (Another title for the parish journal, *Revista Cattolica Mensile*) 1, no. 2–3 (March–April 1928); *BCM* 2, no. 3 (June 1929): 9, MCA.

14. *BCM* 2, no. 1 (April 1929): 15, MCA.

15. This is commented upon in "La Congregazione del Monte Carmelo della 115ma Strada"; "Numero Ricordo" (1928), pp. 6–8; *BCM* 2, no. 7 (October 1929): 2; *BCM* 3, no. 6 (July 1930): 2, MCA.

16. *BCM* 3, no. 6 (July 1930): 2, MCA.

17. For example, *BCM* 2, no. 7 (October 1929): 2, MCA.

18. Pistella, *La Madonna del Carmine*, p. 37; see also Bianco, *Two Rosetos*, pp. 50ff.

19. "La Congregazione del Monte Carmelo della 115ma Strada," MCA.

20. Pistella, *La Madonna del Carmine*, p. 40.

21. Guadalupe, "My Community," CP.

22. "Fede e Cultura," 6, no. 6 (July 1934): 2, MCA.

23. Pistella, *La Madonna del Carmine*, p. 69.

24. Interview with AS-M-4-27.

25. Interviews with NL-W-1-55, BS-W-1-80.

26. *BCM* 3, no. 6 (July 1930): 13; *LVMC* 7, no. 7 (July 1946): 6, MCA.

27. *BCM* 2, no. 6 (September 1929): 6, MCA.

28. *LVMC* 9, no. 6 (June 1948): 5. See also *LVMC* 8, no. 9 (September 1947): 13; "The Parish Bulletin" 12, no. 2 (April–May 1951): 61, MCA.

29. *LVMC* 9, no. 2 (February 1948): 4, MCA.

30. Ibid. 8, no. 3 (March 1947): 5, MCA.

31. Ibid., p. 13, MCA; for this period in the history of Italian American women, see Cohen, "Workshop to Office," pp. 266ff.; Judith Smith, "The Immigrant Family and Cultural Change: Two Generations of Italians and Jews in Providence, Rhode Island," paper presented at the Joint Conference of the American Italian Historical Society and the American Jewish Historical Society, March 27, 1977; and Judith Smith, "Italian Mothers and American Daughters: Changes in Work and Family Roles," paper presented at the American Italian Historical Association Conference on the Italian Immigrant Woman in North America, Toronto, Canada, October 1977.

32. *BCM* 2, no. 6 (September 1929): 6; another example of this is found in *LVMC* 6, no. 11 (November 1945): 10, MCA.

33. For example, *LVMC* 8, no. 1 (January 1947): 5, MCA.

34. *LVMC* 8, no. 6 (June 1947): 12, MCA.

35. Ladurie, *Montaillou*, p. 279; Panunzio, *Soul of an Immigrant*, p. 7; Peter Burke, *Popular Culture in Early Modern Europe* (New York: Harper Torchbooks, 1978), pp. 178–204.

36. This is certainly implicit in the way Anna Ruddy presents her picture of the *festa* (see McLeod, [Ruddy], *Heart of the Stranger*, pp. 64ff.).

37. John Briggs, *An Italian Passage: Immigrants to Three American Cities, 1890–1930* (New Haven and London: Yale University Press, 1978), pp. 5–36; E. J. Hobsbawm, *Primitive Rebels: Studies in Archaic Forms of Social Movement in the 19th and 20th Centuries* (New York: W. W. Norton & Company, 1965), pp. 30ff.

38. "Numero Ricordo" (1928), p. 6; *BCM* 2, no. 5 (August 1929): 1–9, MCA.

39. "Numero Ricordo" (1928), p. 8, MCA.

40. Souvenir Journal to celebrate the new bell tower, May 17, 1927, MCA.

41. "East Harlem News" 1, no. 4, June, 1941, p. 7, CP.

42. Interview with MR-W-PR-1-33.

43. Guadalupe, "My Community," CP.

44. Thomas, *Down These Mean Streets*, p. 41.

45. Ellen May, "Why Italians Need the Gospel," *The Missionary Review of the World* 12 (November 1909): 817–18.

46. This is mentioned in D. Lynch, "Religious Conditions," p. 558.

47. For example, *BCM* 2, no. 1 (April 1929), front cover, MCA.

48. Lapolla, *Grand Gennaro*, p. 47; *BCM* 3, no. 12 (December 1930); *BCM* 4, no. 12 (December 1931), MCA; "Numero Ricordo. 5mo Anniversario della Fondazione della Chiesa di Maria SS. del Monte Carmelo. 1884–1935," MCA.

49. For example, "Souvenir Program. Our Lady of Mt Carmel Church. 1939," MCA.

50. Interviews with NL-W-1-55 and AS-W-2-55.

51. Interview at Our Lady of Mt Carmel Church, October 1980.

52. See, for example, *BCM* 5, no. 7 (July 1932); also Souvenir Journal to commemorate bell tower.

53. Compare the symbolic meaning of this expense with that paid by the working class in industrial England for funerals, as studied in Eric J. Hobsbawm, *Pelican Economic History of Britain*, vol. 3: *Industry and Empire* (New York, 1970), p. 39.

54. Souvenir Journal to commemorate bell tower.

55. Ibid.

56. "Numero Ricordo" (1928), p. 10, MCA.

57. *BCM* 5, no. 8 (July 1933): 13, MCA.

58. Peter Brown, *The Cult of the Saints: Its Rise and Function in Latin Christianity* (Chicago: The University of Chicago Press, 1981), p. 100.

59. Bianco, *Two Rosetos*, p. 89.

60. "Fede e Cultura," 6, no. 6 (July 1934): 11, MCA.

61. Pistella, *La Madonna del Carmine*, p. 43.

62. Ibid., pp. 85–87.

63. Untitled Souvenir Journal to commemorate bell tower, MCA; and *BCM* 2, no. 2 (May 1929): 2, MCA.

64. "Fede e Cultura," 6, no. 6 (July 1934): 2 (the Mt. Carmel Parish Bulletin had been renamed in 1934), MCA.

65. Pistella, *La Madonna del Carmine*, pp. 15–16.

66. *BCM* 3, no. 7 (August–November 1930): 10, MCA.

67. Ibid. 2, no. 2 (May 1929): 9, 16; ibid., no. 3 (June 1929): 10; ibid., no. 5 (August 1929): 14; ibid., no. 6 (September 1929): 7, MCA.

68. Covello, *The Heart Is the Teacher*, p. 41.

69. McLeod [Ruddy], *Heart of the Stranger*, p. 97; also interviews with AS-W-2-55 and PM-M-2-50.

70. McLeod [Ruddy], *Heart of the Stranger*, pp. 156ff.

71. Interview with PF-M-½-45.

72. This is subtly akin to Covello's idea of the community school where not just the child but the whole family is welcomed and taught.

73. Lapolla, *Grand Gennaro*, pp. 171–74.

74. Lapolla was one of Ruddy's young students at the Home Garden Settlement House. "Memo to Dr. Covello from Gari Lapolla, November 3, 1948," CP.

75. Covello, *The Heart Is the Teacher*, p. 27.

76. Constance M. to Leonard Covello, no date [1948], CP.

77. This is mentioned by Antonio Arrighi, "The Calvary Italian Evangelical Church, 151 Worth Street, New York," The New York Mission and Tract Society, *60th Annual Report* (New York: 50 Bible House, 1887), p. 62. It is given scholarly attention in Kessner, *Golden Door*, pp. 127ff.

78. Kessner, *The Golden Door*, chaps. 3 and 4; Pistella, *La Madonna del Carmine*, pp. 29–30; Lapolla, *Fire in the Flesh*, p. 102.

79. Reed, *Leisure Time*, p. 24; Kessner, *The Golden Door*, pp. 129–33; "Report. E.H." (ca. 1946), CP.

80. "Report. E.H." (ca. 1946), p. 3, CP.

81. Lapolla, *Fire in the Flesh*, p. 61; also interview with PP-M-1-65.

82. A Father of the Franciscan Province of Cincinnati, Ohio, "Loss of Faith among the Poor," in National Conference of Catholic Charities, *Proceedings*, 1910, p. 370.

83. David Montgomery, *Workers' Control in America: Studies in the History of Work, Technology and Labor Struggles* (Cambridge: Cambridge University Press, 1979), p. 36.

84. The reference to raw material comes from Brandenburg, *Imported Americans*, p. 85.

85. Pistella, *La Madonna del Carmine*, p. 37.

86. "Fede e Cultura" 6, no. 6 (July 1934): 2; also *LVMC* 7, no. 7 (July 1946): 8, MCA.

87. Interviews with PR-M-R-1-60 and BS-W-1-80.

88. *BCM* 2, no. 5 (August 1929): 11, MCA.

89. *LVMC* 8, no. 1 (January 1947): 5, MCA.

90. Ibid. 8, no. 4 (April 1947): 5, MCA.

91. Ibid. 9, no. 7 (July 1948): 9, MCA.

92. Ibid. 8, no. 3 (March 1947): 5, MCA.

93. Ibid. 9, no. 5 (May 1948): 5; "The Parish Bulletin" 13, no. 3 (May–June 1952): 6, MCA.

94. *BCM* 3, no. 6 (July 1930): 2; see also the prayer published at the end of "La Congregazione del Monte Carmelo della 115ma Strada" (1926–27).

95. On donations, see *BCM* 3, no. 2 (February 1930): 11; ibid., no. 4 (April 1930): 10; *LVMC* 10, no. 2 (February 1949): 15, MCA.

96. *RCM* 1, nos. 2–3 (March–April 1928): 11, MCA.

97. *LVMC* 7, no. 1 (January 1946): 12, MCA.

98. Ibid., no. 11 (November 1946): 13, MCA.

99. Covello, *The Heart Is the Teacher*, pp. 129ff.

100. Covello Interview, "Contact of girl with males. Miss Marchisella. School Teacher. 3rd Generation Italo-American," CP.

101. *BCM* 3, no. 2 (February 1930): 12, MCA.

102. *BCM* 4, no. 5 (July 1931): 7; also interview with PP-M-1-65.

103. *LVMC* 8, no. 5 (May 1947): 16; *LVMC* 7, no. 5, (May 1946), p. 13, MCA. Interview with PR-M-R-1-60.

104. An old woman in Lapolla's novel, *The Grand Gennaro*, prays, "Oh, Virgin Mary . . . thou who has had the agony of a suffering child, thou wilt understand when we pray thee to be merciful, to go before they glorious son and tell Him to be kind to our Carmela" (p. 343).

105. "Numero Ricordo. 5mo Anniversario della Fondazione della Chiesa di Maria SS. del Monte Carmelo. 1884–1935." See also *LVMC* 8, no. 8 (August 1947): 4; *LVMC* 9, no. 7 (July 1948): 3, MCA.

106. For example, *LVMC* 7, no. 12 (December 1946): 5, MCA.

107. Ibid., no. 7 (July 1946): 6, MCA.

108. Ibid. 8, no. 9 (September 1947): 6, MCA.

109. *BCM* 3, no. 3 (March 1930): 7, MCA.

110. Ibid. 2, no. 6 (September 1929): 6; 3, no. 1 (January 1930): 14, MCA.

111. Ibid. 3, no. 1 (January 1930): 14, MCA.

112. *LVMC* 7, no. 5 (May 1946): 7, MCA.

113. *BCM* 2, no. 6 (September 1929): 6, MCA.

114. Ibid., no. 7 (October 1929): 8, MCA.

115. Mintz, *Worker in the Cane*, p. 43.

116. *BCM* 5, no. 7 (July 1932): 10, MCA.

117. *The Hours of the Divine Office in Latin and English* (Collegeville, Minn.: The Liturgical Press, 1963), 1: 1700, 1730.

118. *BCM* 3, no. 4 (April 1930): 6, MCA.

119. "The Parish Bulletin" 12, no. 3 (June–July 1951): 12–13, MCA.

120. Ira Rosenwaike, "Two Generations of Italians in America," *International Migration Review* 7, no. 3 (Fall 1973).

121. See, for example, Sharon Hartman Strom, "Italian American Women and Their Daughters in Rhode Island: The Adolescence of Two Generations, 1900–1950," in Betty Boyd Caroli, Robert F. Harney, and Lydio F. Tomasi, eds., *The Italian Immigrant Woman in North America* (Toronto: The Multi-Cultural Historical Society of Ontario, 1978). Also interview with AS-W-2-55.

122. This was uniformly maintained by my informants, but some expressed particular bitterness: PF-M-½-45, FS-M-2-75, PM-M-2-50.

CHAPTER 8

1. Mangano, *Sons of Italy*, p. 150.

2. Franklin, "The Italian in America," pp. 70–71; Daisy M. Mosely, "The Catholic Social Worker in an Italian District," originally published in *The Catholic World* 114 (February 1922); reprinted in Cordasco and Bucchioni, *The Italians*, pp. 439–48. My citation is to the latter, p. 45.

3. Marie Concistre Interview, "Religious discriminations," CP; also Lapolla, *Fire in the Flesh*, pp. 278–79.

4. Souvenir Journal to commemorate bell tower, MCA.

5. "Numero Ricordo" (1928), p. 10.

6. Interview with PR-M-R-1-60.

7. Ibid.

8. Pistella, *La Madonna del Carmine*, p. 33.

9. Interview with PR-M-R-1-60.

10. *Il Progresso Italo-Americano*, July 17, 1949.

11. Bianco, *Two Rosetos*, pp. 179–80.

12. *LVMC* 8, no. 6 (June 1947): 8, MCA.

13. Ibid. 9, no. 7 (July 1948): 3, MCA.

14. Maria Hartman-White, Interviews with Italian-American Women from East Harlem and Brooklyn, unpublished research, Fordham University, 1983.

15. Interview with PR-M-R-1-60.

16. *LVMC* 7, no. 8 (August 1946): 7, MCA.

17. "La Congregazione del Monte Carmelo della 115ma strada"; also *BCM* 2, no. 3 (June 1929): 9, MCA.

18. Interview with PR-M-R-1-60.

# Selected Bibliography

ARCHIVAL MATERIALS

Elmer Ellsworth Brown Papers. University Archives, New York University. New York.
The Leonard Covello Papers. The Balch Institute for Ethnic Studies. Philadelphia.
Fiorello LaGuardia Papers. New York Municipal Archives. New York.
Vito Marcantonio Papers. New York Public Library. New York.
Norman Thomas Papers. New York Public Library. New York.
Parish Archives, Our Lady of Mount Carmel Church. East 115th Street. New York.
Union Settlement Archives. 237 East 104th Street. New York.
Vatican Archives, Archivio del Capitolo di San Pietro. Rome.

MISCELLANEOUS DIRECT SOURCES

"The Reminiscences of Mrs. Marie LaGuardia." Columbia University Oral History Project. New York.

PUBLISHED PRIMARY SOURCES

Adams, Joseph H. "The Italian Quarters of New York City. *The Baptist Home Mission Monthly* 31 (September 1909): 379–84.
Agnew, W. H. "Pastoral Care of Italian Children in America." *The Ecclesiastical Review* 48 (March 1913): 257–67.

Arrighi, Antonio. "The Calvary Italian Evangelical Church, 151 Worth Street, New York." The New York City Mission and Tract Society. *60th Annual Report* 62. New York: 50 Bible House, 1887.

Bandini, Albert R. "Concerning the Italian Problem." *The Ecclesiastical Review* 62 (March 1920): 278–85.

Boville, Robert G. "Italian Evangelization." *The Baptist Home Mission Monthly* 29 (April 1907): 134–35.

Brandenburg, Broughton. *Imported Americans: The Story of the Experiences of a Disguised American and His Wife Studying the Immigration Question.* New York: F. A. Stokes Company, 1904.

Cantelmo, Ercole. "Usi, Costume e Feste degli Italiani negli Stati Uniti." *Gli Italiani negli Stati Uniti D'America,* 156–63. New York: Italian-American Directory Co., 1906.

*Catholic Builders of the Nation.* 2 vols. Boston: Continental Press, 1923.

"Catholic Italian Losses." *The Literary Digest* 47 (October 11, 1913): 636.

Cerrati, Michael. "Pastoral Care of Italian Immigrants." *American Ecclesiastical Review* 64 (March 1921): 279–84.

Chivers, E. E. "Our Baptist Mission Work." *The Baptist Home Mission Monthly* 27 (May 1905): 187–200.

Cirigliano, D. "Protestant Attitudes in Our Parish." *Woodstock Letters* 48 (1919): 222–31, 340–49; (1920): 216–22, 335–40.

Corsi, Edward. *In the Shadow of Liberty: The Chronicle of Ellis Island.* New York: The Macmillan Company, 1935.

Covello, Leonard. *The Heart Is the Teacher.* New York: McGraw-Hill Book Company, 1958.

Cushing, Richard J. "Italian Immigrants." *The Catholic Mind* 52 (October 1954): 604–09.

DiDomenica, Angelo. "The Sons of Italy in America." *The Missionary Review of the World* 41 (March 1918): 189–95.

———. "Conditions among Italians in America." *The Missionary Review of the World* 58 (February 1935): 71–73.

Dixon, John. "Our Church and the Foreigners." *The Assembly Herald* 14 (January 1908): 30.

Earle, E. Lyell. "Character Studies in New York's Foreign Quarters." *The Catholic World* 68 (March 1899): 782–93.

Eliot, Ada. "Two Italian Festivals." *Charities* 8 (1901): 321–22.

Fidelis. "Nationalism and Catholicity of the Clergy in the United States." *The Ecclesiastical Review* 70 (March 1924): 295–98.

Franklin, Laurence. "The Italian in America: What He Has Been, What He Shall Be." *The Catholic World* 62 (April 1900): 67–80.

"From an Immigrant's Logbook: Some Experiences of an Unknown in the Steerage—a Narrative of Fact, Not Fiction." *The Baptist Home Mission Monthly* 30 (January 1980): 15–21.

Fusco, Nicola. "A Catholic Priest's Work." *Il Carroccio* 20 (September 1924): 281–84.

Giambastiani, Louis M. "In the Melting Pot: The Italians." *Extension* 7 (September 1912): 9–10, 20–21.

Ginger, Mina C. "In Berry Field and Bog: The Seasonal Migration of Italian Pickers to New Jersey, Its Profit, Its Cost, Illiteracy and Disease." *Charities* 15 (November 1905): 162–70.

"Hear the Voice of Children from Sunny Italy. Ages from Nine to Eighteen." The New York City Mission and Tract Society. *Annual Report* (January 1907): 7–11.

Hillenbrand, H. J. "Has the Immigrant Kept the Faith?" *America* 54 (November 23, 1935): 153–55.

Hodges, Leroy. "The Church and the Immigrants: A Record of Failure and the Remedy." *The Missionary Review of the World* 25 (March 1912): 167–72.

*Gli Italiani negli Stati Uniti d'America.* New York: Italian American Directory Company, 1906.

"The Italian Problem." *Extension Magazine* 12 (September 1917): 3–4.

"The Italians and Evening Mass." *The Ecclesiastical Review* 45 (September 1911): 340–42.

"The Italian Young People and Their Church." The New York City Mission and Tract Society. *Annual Report* (January 1907): 21–22.

Jones, Henry D. *The Evangelical Movement among Italians in New York City. A Study.* New York: For the Comity Committee of the Federation of Churches of Greater New York and the Brooklyn Church and Mission Federation, 1933–34.

Kelley, Francis C. "The Church and the Immigrants." *The Catholic Mind* 13 (September 8, 1915): 471–84.

Lagnese, Joseph C. "The Italian Catholic." *America* 44 (February 21, 1931): 475–76.

Lapolla, Garibaldi M. *The Fire in the Flesh.* New York: The Vanguard Press, 1931.

———. *The Grand Gennaro.* New York: The Vanguard Press, 1935.

LaMartinella. "Italian Catholics in America. Apropos of Archbishop Canevin's Pamphlet." *Il Carroccio* 18 (October 1923): 355–56.

Lynch, Bernard J. "The Italians in New York." *The Catholic World* 47 (April 1888): 67–73.

Lynch, D. "In the Italian Quarter of New York." *The Messenger of the Sacred Heart of Jesus* 36 (February 1901): 115–26.

_____. "The Religious Conditions of Italians in New York." *America* 10 (March 1914): 558–59.

McLeod, Christian [Anna C. Ruddy]. *The Heart of the Stranger: A Story of Little Italy.* New York: Fleming H. Revell Co., 1908.

McSorley, Joseph. "The Church and the Italian Child. The Situation in New York." *The Ecclesiastical Review* 48 (March 1913): 268–82.

Mangano, Antonio. "The Associated Life of Italians in New York City." *Charities* 12 (May 7, 1904): 476–82.

_____. "Evangelism among the Italians." *The Baptist Home Mission Monthly* 27 (October 1905): 374–75.

_____. "Italian Evangelization in Brooklyn." *The Baptist Home Mission Monthly* 31 (November 1909): 465–67.

_____. "Italian Tent Work in Brooklyn." *The Baptist Home Mission Monthly* 28 (October 1906): 370–71.

_____. "Italian Work in Barre, Vermont." *Missions* 7 (June 1916): 476–77.

_____. *Religious Work among Italians in America.* Philadelphia: The Board of the Home Missions and Church Extension of the Methodist Episcopal Church, 1917.

_____. *Sons of Italy: A Social and Religious Study of the Italians in America.* New York: Missionary Education Movement of the United States and Canada, 1917. Reprinted New York: Russell and Russell, 1972.

_____. "A Successful Mission for Italians." *The Baptist Home Mission Monthly* 31 (July 1909): 338–40.

_____. "Thirty Years of Work with the Italians of Buffalo." *The Baptist* 6 (December 28, 1925): 1318–19.

Mariano, John H. *The Second Generation of Italians in New York City.* Boston: The Christopher Publishing House, 1921.

Moseley, Daisy H. "The Catholic Social Worker in an Italian District." *The Catholic World* 114 (February 1922): 618–28.

Nardi, Michael. "The West Side Italian Church. 34–36 Charlton Street." The New York City Mission and Tract Society. *Annual Report* (January 1909): 12–13.

National Conference of Catholic Charities. *Proceedings.* Washington, D.C.: Catholic University of America, 1910.

O'Brien, Grace. "Catholic Settlement Work in Brooklyn." *Survey* 17 (May 7, 1910): 203–04.

_____. "Catholic Social Settlements." National Conference of Catholic Charities. *Proceedings,* 138–45. Washington, D.C.: Catholic University of America, 1910.

Palmieri, Aurelio F. "Il clero italiano negli Stati Uniti." *La Vita Italiana* 8 (February 15, 1920): 113–27.

———. "Italian Protestantism in the United States." *The Catholic World* 107 (May 1918): 177–89.

Panunzio, Constantine Maria. *Immigration Crossroads*. New York: The Macmillan Company, 1927.

———. *The Soul of an Immigrant*. New York: Macmillan, 1921.

"Pastoral Care of Foreign Catholics in America." *The Ecclesiastical Review* 70 (February 1924): 176–81.

"Pastoral Care of Italian Immigrants." *The Ecclesiastical Review* 68, no. 5 (May 1923): 506.

Petty, A. Ray. "120,000 Italians in the Back Yard." *The Baptist* 3 (February 25, 1922): 107.

Plumley, G. S. "Report of Calvary Church. Worth Street. Near Centre." New York City Mission and Tract Society. *55th Annual Report*, 38–48. New York: 50 Bible House, 1882.

———. "Report of Calvary Church. Worth Street, Near Centre." The New York City Mission and Tract Society. *56th Annual Report*, 20–24. New York: 50 Bible House, 1883.

Price, Willard. "What I Learned by Traveling from Naples to New York in the Steerage." *World Outlook* 3, no. 10 (October 1917): 3–5.

*Protestant Evangelism among Italians in America*. New York: Arno Press, 1975.

"Religion of Lucky Pieces, Witches and the Evil Eye." *World Outlook* 3 (October 1917): 24–25.

Reynolds, Minnie J. "The Italian and His Church at Home." *The Missionary Review of the World*, 34 (August 1911); 597–603.

Riis, Jacob A. "Feast Days in Little Italy," *The Century* 58 (August 1899): 491–99.

———. *How the Other Half Lives*. New York: Hill and Wang, 1957. Originally published 1890.

S. Congregatio Concilii. "Epistula Circularis ad Episcopos Italos et Americanos, Relate ad Sacerdotes Italos, qui ad Americanas Regiones Emigrant." *American Ecclesiastical Review*, 18 (February 1898): 193–95.

Sartorio, Henry C. "Work among Italians." *The Churchman*, September 1, 1917, 273.

"Scenes in the Steerage." *The Baptist Home Mission Monthly* 30 (February 1908): 48–54.

"Scenes in the Steerage. The Treatment That Makes the Passengers Desperate." *The Baptist Home Mission Monthly* 30 (March 1908): 96–104.

Senner, Joseph. "Immigration from Italy." *North American Review* 162 (June 1896): 651–59.

"Settlement Work among Italians." *St. Vincent DePaul Quarterly* 13 (May 1908): 210.

"A Short History of the Mission of Our Lady of Loreto, New York." *Woodstock Letters* 46 (1917): 172–87.

Skinner, Lilian M. "Our Italian Neighbors." *Neighbors. Studies in Immigration from the Standpoint of the Episcopal Church,* 85–108. New York: Domestic and Foreign Missionary Society, 1920.

Sorrentino, Joseph M. "Religious Conditions in Italy." *America* 12 (October 17, 1914): 6–7.

Testa, Stefano L. "For the Italian. A Ministry of Christian and Patriotic Appeal." *The Assembly Herald* 17 (January 1911): 11.

_____. "Strangers from Rome in Greater New York." *The Missionary Review of the World* 31 (March 1908): 216–18.

Thomas, Norman M. "Six Years in Little Italy." *The Assembly Herald* 24 (March 1918): 149–51.

Thomas, Piri. *Down These Mean Streets.* New York: Vintage Books, 1974.

Tolino, John V. "The Church in America and the Italian Problem." *The Ecclesiastical Review* 100 (January 1933): 22–32.

_____. "The Future of the Italian American Problem." *The Ecclesiastical Review* 101 (September 1939): 221–32.

_____. "The Priest in the Italian Problem." *The Ecclesiastical Review* 109 (November 1943): 321–30.

_____. "Solving the Italian Problem." *The Ecclesiastical Review* 99 (September 1938): 246–56.

Walsh, James J. "The Irish and the Italians." *Il Carroccio* 27 (January 1928): 114–16.

"Work among the Italians." *The Baptist Home Mission Monthly* 24 (August 1902): 223–24.

"A Young Italian's Story." *The Baptist Home Mission Monthly* (March 1909): 123–25.

Zarrilli, John. "Some More Light on the Italian Problem." *The Ecclesiastical Review* 79 (September 1928): 256–68.

_____. "A Suggestion for the Solution of the Italian Problem." *The Ecclesiastical Review* 70 (January 1924): 70–77.

Zazzara, Jerome N. "Pastoral Care of Italian Emigrants." *The Ecclesiastical Review* 64 (March 1921): 279–81.

Zema, Gabriel A. "The Italian Immigrant Problem." *America* 55 (May 16, 1936): 129–30.

_____. "Jottings in Italy." *The American Ecclesiastical Review* 129 (August 1953): 95–99.

OTHER SOURCES

Abel, Theodore. *Protestant Home Missions to Catholic Immigrants* New York: Institute of Social and Religious Research, 1933.

Alba, Richard D. "Social Assimilation among American Catholic National Origin Groups." *American Sociological Review* 41 (December 1976): 1030–46.

Anderson, Nels. "The Social Antecedents of a Slum: A Study of the East Harlem Area of Manhattan Island, New York City." Ph.D. diss., New York University, 1930.

Banfield, Edward C. *The Moral Basis of a Backward Society*. New York: The Free Press, 1958.

Barrese, Pauline J. "Southern Italian Folklore in New York City." *New York Folklore Quarterly* 21 (September 1965): 181–93.

Bell, Rudolph. *Fate and Honor, Family and Village: Demographic and Cultural Change in Rural Italy since 1800*. Chicago: University of Chicago Press, 1979.

Bianco, Carla. *The Two Rosetos*. Bloomington and London: Indiana University Press, 1974.

Briggs, John W. *An Italian Passage: Immigrants to Three American Cities, 1890–1930*. New Haven and London: Yale University Press, 1978.

Brown, Peter. *The Cult of the Saints. Its Rise and Function in Latin Christianity*. Chicago: University of Chicago Press, 1981.

Browne, Henry J. "The 'Italian Problem' in the Catholic Church of the United States, 1880–1900." United States Catholic Historical Society, *Historical Records and Studies*, vol. 35. New York: The United States Catholic Historical Society, 1946.

Bushnell, John. "La Virgen de Guadalupe as Surrogate Mother in San Juan Atzingo." *American Anthropologist* 60 (1958): 261–65.

Caliaro, Marco, and Mario Francesconi, *John Baptist Scalabrini: Apostle to Emigrants*. Staten Island, N.Y.: Center for Migration Studies, 1977.

Carlyle, Margaret. *The Awakening of Southern Italy*. New York: Oxford University Press, 1962.

Caro, Robert A. *Power Broker: Robert Moses and the Fall of New York*. New York: Vintage Books, 1975.

Caroli, Betty Boyd, Robert Harney, and Lydio Tomasi, eds. *The Italian Immigrant Woman in North America*. Toronto: The Multicultural Historical Society of Ontario, 1978.

_____. *Italian Repatriation from the United States, 1900–1914*. New York: Center for Migration Studies, 1973.

Christian, William A. *Person and God in a Spanish Valley*. New York and London: Seminar Press, 1972.

Cimilluca, Salvatore. "The Natural History of East Harlem from Eighteen Eighty to the Present Day." M.A. thesis, New York University School of Education, 1931.

Clark, Kenneth B. *Dark Ghetto: Dilemmas of Social Power*. New York: Harper & Row, 1967.

Cohen, Miriam Judith. "From Workshop to Office: Italian Women and Family Strategies in New York City, 1900–1950." Ph.D. diss., University of Michigan, 1978.

Cordasco, Francesco, ed. *Studies in Italian American Social History: Essays in Honor of Leonard Covello*. Totowa, N.J.: Rowan and Littlefield, 1975.

_____, and Eugene Bucchioni, eds. *The Italians: Social Backgrounds of an American Group*. Clifton, N.J.: Augustus M. Kelley, 1974.

Cornelisen, Ann. *Torregreca: Life, Death, Miracles*. New York: A Delta Book 1970.

_____. *Women of the Shadows*. Boston: Little, Brown and Company, 1976.

Covello, Leonard. "Cultural Assimilation and the Church." *Religious Education* 39 (July–August 1944): 229–35.

_____. *The Social Background of the Italian American School Child*. Leiden: E. J. Brill, 1967.

Curran, Robert Emmett. *Michael Augustine Corrigan and the Shaping of Conservative Catholicism in America, 1878–1902*. New York: Arno Press, 1978.

Davis, J. "Morals and Backwardness." *Comparative Studies in Society and History* (July 12, 1970), 340–59.

DiDonato, Pietro. *Christ and Concrete*. New York: The Bobbs-Merrill Company, 1937.

Dolan, Jay P. *The Immigrant Church: New York's Irish and German Catholics, 1815–1865*. Baltimore and London: The Johns Hopkins University Press, 1975.

Dore, Grazia. "Some Social and Historical Aspects of Italian Immigration." *Journal of Social History* 2, no. 2 (Winter 1968): 95–122.

Federal Writer's Project, New York City. *The Italians of New York*. New York: Random House, 1938.

Femminella, Francis X., and Jill S. Quadagno. "The Italian American Family." In Charles H. Mindel and Robert W. Habenstein, *Ethnic Families in America*, 61–88. New York: Elsevier, 1976.

Fenton, Edwin. *Immigrants and Unions: A Case Study. Italians and American Labor, 1870–1920*. New York: Arno Press, 1975.

Foerster, Robert Franz. *The Italian Emigration of Our Times*. New York: Russell and Russell, 1968. Reprint of 1919 edition.

Forster, Robert, and Orest Ranum, eds. *Food and Drink in History. Selections from the Annales*. Baltimore and London: The Johns Hopkins University Press, 1979.

Franchetti, Leopoldo, and Sydney Sonnino. *I Contadini in Sicilia*. Florence: Vallechi Editore, 1925.

Fucilla, Joseph G. "Anglicanization of Italian Surnames in the United States." *American Speech* 18 (1943): 26–32.

Gabbacia, Donna R. "Houses and People: Sicilians in Sicily and New York, 1890–1930." Ph.D. diss., University of Michigan, 1979.

Galt, Anthony H. "Carnival on the Island of Panterelleria: Ritualized Community Solidarity in an Atomistic Society." *Ethnology* 12, no. 3 (July 1973): 325–29.

Gambino, Richard. *Blood of My Blood: The Dilemma of Italian Americans*. Garden City, N.Y.: Doubleday & Co., 1974.

Gans, Herbert J. "Some Comments on the History of Italian Migration and on the Nature of Historical Research." *The International Migration Review* 50, no. 3 (Summer 1967): 5–10.

———. *The Urban Villagers: Group and Class in the Life of Italian Americans*. New York: The Free Press, 1962.

Geertz, Clifford. *The Interpretation of Cultures*. New York: Basic Books, 1973.

Ginzburg, Carlo. *The Cheese and the Worms: The Cosmos of a Sixteenth-Century Miller*. Translated by John and Anne Tedeschi. Baltimore: The Johns Hopkins University Press, 1980.

Gurock, Jeffrey S. *When Harlem Was Jewish, 1870–1930*. New York: Columbia University Press, 1979.

Handlin, Oscar. *The Uprooted*. New York: Grosset & Dunlap, 1951.

Hélias, Pierre-Jakez. *The Horse of Pride: Life in a Breton Village*. New Haven: Yale University Press, 1978.

*Italians in the United States. A Repository of Rare Tracts and Miscellanea*. New York: Arno Press, 1975.

Jemolo, Arturo C. *Church and State in Italy, 1850–1950*. Translated by David Moore. Oxford: Basil Blackwell, 1960.

Kessner, Thomas. *The Golden Door: Italian and Jewish Immigrant Mobility in New York City, 1880–1915*. New York: Oxford University Press, 1977.

Ladurie, Emmanuel LeRoy. *Montaillou: The Promised Land of Error*. New York: Vintage Books, 1979.

Levi, Carlo. *Christ Stopped at Eboli.* Translated by Francis Frenaye. New York: Farrar, Straus and Giroux, 1977.

Lewis, Oscar. *A Death in the Sánchez Family.* New York: Vintage Books, 1970.

_____. *La Vida.* New York: Vintage Books, 1965.

Linkh, Richard M. *American Catholicism and European Immigrants, 1900–1924.* Staten Island, N.Y.: Center for Migration Studies, 1975.

Lopreato, Joseph. *Peasants No More: Social Class and Social Change in an Underdeveloped Society.* San Francisco: Chandler Publishing Company, 1967.

MacDonald, John S., and D. Leatrice. "Chain Migration, Ethnic Neighborhood Formation and Social Networks." *The Millbank Memorial Fund Quarterly* 41, no. 1 (January 1941).

Mangione, Jerre. *Mount Allegro.* Boston: Houghton Mifflin Company, 1942.

Marcantonio, Vito. *I Vote My Conscience.* New York: The Vito Marcantonio Memorial, 1956.

Mintz, Sidney. *Worker in the Cane: A Puerto Rican Life History.* New York: W. W. Norton & Co., 1974.

Montgomery, David. *Workers' Control in America: Studies in the History of Work, Technology and Labor Struggles.* Cambridge: Cambridge University Press, 1979.

Moquin, Wayne, ed. *A Documentary History of the Italian-Americans.* New York: Praeger, 1974.

Moss, Leonard W., and Walter H. Thomson. "The South Italian Family: Literature and Observation." *Human Organization* 18, no. 1 (Spring 1959): 35–41.

Muraskin, William. "The Moral Basis of a Backward Sociologist." *American Journal of Sociology* 79, no. 6 (1974): 1484–96.

Nelli, Humbert S. *Italians in Chicago, 1880–1930: A Study in Ethnic Mobility.* New York: Oxford University Press, 1970.

Odencrantz, Louise Christine. *Italian Women in Industry: A Study of Conditions in New York City.* New York: Russell Sage Foundation, 1919.

_____. "Why Jennie Hates Flowers." *World Outlook* 3, no. 10 (October 1917): 12–13.

Osofsky, Gilbert. *Harlem: The Making of a Ghetto. Negro New York, 1890–1930.* New York: Harper & Row, Harper Torchbooks, 1971.

Parsons, Anne. *Belief, Magic, and Anomie: Essays in Psychological Anthropology.* New York: The Free Press, 1969.

_____. "The Pentecostal Immigrants: A Study of an Ethnic Central

City Church." *Journal for the Scientific Study of Religion* 4 (Spring 1965): 183–95.

Pitkin, Donald S. "Land Tenure and Family Organization in an Italian Village." *Human Organization* 18, no. 4 (Winter 1959–60): 169–73.

Pozzetta, George Enrico. "The Italians of New York City, 1890–1914." Ph.D. diss., University of North Carolina, 1974.

Reed, Dorothy. *Leisure Time of Girls in a "Little Italy."* Ph.D. diss., Columbia University, 1932. Published Portland, Ore.: no publisher cited, 1932.

Rose, Philip M. *The Italians in America.* New York: George H. Doran Company, 1922.

Rosenzweig, Roy. *Eight Hours for What We Will: Workers and Leisure in an Industrial City, 1870–1920.* Cambridge: Cambridge University Press, 1983.

Rozewicz, A. J. "Another Problem Like the Italian." *The Ecclesiastical Review* 70 (April 1924): 381–86.

Sasuly, Richard. "Vito Marcantonio: The People's Politician." In Harvey Goldberg, ed., *American Radicals: Some Problems and Personalities.* New York: Monthly Review Press, 1957.

Schaffer, Alan. *Vito Marcantonio: Radical in Congress.* Syracuse, N.Y.: Syracuse University Press, 1966.

Sennett, Richard, and Jonathan Cobb. *The Hidden Injuries of Class.* New York: Vintage Books, 1973.

Sexton, Patricia Cayo. *Spanish Harlem.* New York: Harper Colophon Books, 1966.

Silverman, Sydel F. "Agricultural Organization, Social Structure and Values in Italy: Amoral Familism Reconsidered." *American Anthropologist* 70 (1968): 1–20.

Suttles, Gerald D. *The Social Order of the Slum: Ethnicity and Territory in the Inner City.* Chicago: University of Chicago Press, 1968.

Swanberg, W. A. *Norman Thomas: The Last Idealist.* New York: Charles Scribner's Sons, 1976.

Thompson, E. P. "Time, Work Discipline and Industrial Capitalism." *Past and Present* 38 (1967): 56–97.

Tilly, Louise A. "Comments on the Yans-McLaughlin and Davidoff Papers." *Journal of Social History* 7, no. 4 (Summer 1974): 452–59.

Tomasi, Lydio F., ed. *The Italian in America: The Progressive View, 1891–1914.* New York: Center for Migration Studies, 1972.

Tomasi, Silvano M. "Italian Catholics in America." In Robert Trisco, ed., *Catholics in America, 1776–1976.* Washington, D.C.: National

Conference of Catholic Bishops Committee for the Bicentennial, 1976.

———. *Piety and Power: The Role of the Italian American Parishes in the New York Metropolitan Area, 1880–1930*. Staten Island, N.Y.: Center for Migration Studies, 1975.

———, ed. *Perspectives in Italian Immigration and Ethnicity*. Proceedings of the symposium held at Casa Italiana, Columbia University, May 21–23, 1976. New York: Center for Migration Studies, 1977.

———, and Madeline H. Engel, eds. *The Italian Experience in the United States*. New York: The Center for Migration Studies, 1970.

Van Kleeck, Mary. *Artificial Flower Makers*. New York: Survey Associates, 1913.

Vecoli, Rudolph J. "Contadini in Chicago: A Critique of the Uprooted." *The Journal of American History* 51, no. 3 (December 1964): 404–17.

———. "Cult and Occult in Italian American Culture. The Persistence of a Religious Heritage." In R. M. Miller and T. D. Marzik, *Immigrants and Religion in Urban America*. Philadelphia: Temple University Press, 1977.

———. "Prelates and Peasants: Italian Immigrants and the Catholic Church." *Journal of Social History*, vol. 2 (Spring 1969): 217–68.

Wakefield, Dan. *Island in the City: The World of Spanish Harlem*. Boston: Houghton Mifflin Company, 1959.

Walsh, James J. *Our American Cardinals: Life Stories of the Seven Great American Cardinals*. New York and London: D. Appleton and Company, 1926.

Ware, Caroline. *Greenwich Village, 1920–1930*. New York: Harper & Row, 1965.

Williams, Phyllis H. *South Italian Folkways in Europe and America*. New Haven: Published for the Institute of Human Relations by Yale University Press, 1938.

Wolf, George, and Joseph DiMona. *Frank Costello: Prime Minister of the Underworld*. New York: William Morrow & Company, 1974.

Wylie, Laurence. *Village in the Vaucluse*. Cambridge, Mass.: Harvard University Press, 1974.

Yans-McLaughlin, Virginia. *Family and Community: Italian Immigrants in Buffalo, 1880–1930*. Ithaca and London: Cornell University Press, 1977.

Zaretsky, Eli. *Capitalism, the Family and Personal Life*. New York: Harper & Row Publishers, 1976.

Zinn, Howard. *LaGuardia in Congress*. New York: W. W. Norton & Co., 1969.

# Index

Abitini, 8

American-born generations, conflicts with elders. *See* Domus, conflicts between generations and the

Americanist crisis, 62

Americanization, 160–62

Anticlericalism, 83–84

Authority: of the domus, 113, 114, 178; of men, 117–18, 120–22; of fathers, 121–22; of women, 131–35, 147–48, 216; of mothers, 132–34; of men over women, 138–39, 145; of brothers over sisters, 139–41; fear of, 217–18

Bell tower, significance of the, 65–66, 180, 187

Benjamin Franklin High School, 31

Bianco, Carla, 189

"Black Hand, The," 31

Blacks: at the festa, 6; settlement of, in Harlem, 16, 17; and conflicts with Italians, 33, 95

Blood bonding, 82, 225

*Bollettino Cattolico Mensile,* 165, 191, 192, 211

Boys' Club, establishment of, 31, 33

Brandenburg, Broughton, 150, 151

Brown, Peter, 177, 188

Browne, Henry, xvi

*Cafone:* definition of, 87

*Campanilismo,* 34

Candles: significance of the weight of, 3–4; used in homes, 105; as symbol of the domus's authority over its members, 178

Cappella dei Soldati, 67, 69

Catholicism, American: Vatican's views on Italian immigrants and, 61–63; Italian views on, 220

Catholicism, Marian, 63

Catholics, American: views of, on feste, xv, 55, 56; Italians as, xvi; Saint Raphael societies and, 62

Catholic War Veterans of Italian Harlem, 69, 70

*Catholic World, The,* 55

Charms, sold at the festa, 3

Children: in the festa, 2, 7, 10; education of, by the domus, 82–83; raising of, 92; conflict with parents over companions, 110; conflict with parents over sports, 110–11; punishment of, 114; participation in the festa, 169–70; fulfilling of vows by, 170, 177

Christian, definition of a, 18, 85–86, 195–97

Church: distinction between religion and, xvii, 57, 220–21; erection of the church on 115th Street, 54, 186–88; 115th Street synonymous with, 180; as a place for women to socialize, 205–06

Church of Saint Ann, 222

Clothing: for the festa, 2, 6, 8; as a contribution, 11, 181–82; vows and certain types of, 201; symbolism of, 210

Cohen, Miriam, 98

283

*Comari/compari*, 90, 131, 226

Community: effects on, of devotion to the Madonna, 178, 180–86; meaning of the church to the, 186–88; its ways of dealing with tension over success, 191–92

Contributions: made during the procession, 8; made in the sanctuary, 10–11

Corrigan, Bp. Michael Augustine, 53, 54, 61–62

Corsi, Edward, 20, 37, 42, 45, 110

Covello, Leonard: his views of Italy, 21; pain of separation and, 23, 24; views on crime in Harlem, 31; first impressions of New York City, 37; list of problems in the community of Harlem, 43–44; principles of the domus, 83; values of the domus and the world outside the domus, 88–89; generational conflict and, 110–12; importance of memories and, 154; views on racial hatred, 160–62

Crime: in Italian Harlem, 31, 44; the domus and, 103–04, 127–29; street gangs, 123

Dalia, Gaspare, 54, 60, 65

Dating and courting, 115–17; for women, 137–39

Depression, the, effects on Italian Harlem of, 43–44

Diseases: of early immigrants, 28; meaning of the exchanging of clothing and views on, 181–82

Distances: traveled by pilgrims, 166; the Madonna and the ability to overcome, 166–67; importance of establishing distance from one's place of work, 197–202

Domus: definition of, xix–xx, 75, 77; and American-born generations, 77, 79, 102, 108, 109; immigrant memories of Italy, 78; marriage, 78, 79–80, 99–100, 109, 111, 114, 125–26; individuality and, 81, 82, 98, 99; blood bonding, 82; education and, 82–83; expulsion from, 83; principles of, 83; priests and, 83–84; nuns and, 84–85; its definition of a Christian, 85–86; holy figures and, 86–87; *cafone* and, 87; and life outside, 87–89, 92–93, 95, 102–03; relationships among domuses, 89; concept of hospitality, 90–91; and apartment houses, 91–92; funerals, 92, 101–02; *rispetto*, 92–94, 101; *vergogna* (shame), 95; politics, 96; job mobility, 98; fami-

ly gatherings, 100; crime, 103–04; religious articles, 105; importance of the devotion to, 171–78

Domus, conflicts between generations and the, 108; over marriage, 109, 111, 114; companions chosen by children, 110; sports, 110–11; conflicts among the youth, 111, 112, 125; relationships between fathers and sons, 111–12, 115, 118–19; relationships between parents and children, 113–15, 119, 122; dating and courting, 115–17; male authority, 117–18; relationships between mothers and sons, 118, 119–20, 125; relationships between fathers and daughters, 119, 120; relationships between husbands and wives, 119–20; dominance of fathers, 120–22; ways to escape the, 122–23, 125; examples of giving in to the domus, 125–27; ways of dealing with rage and violence, 127–29; relationships between mothers and daughters, 131, 136; relationships between sisters and brothers, 131, 139–41; sharing memories of the old country and, 153–55; importance of Mount Carmel to, 174–78; illness based on, 176

*East Harlem News*, 181

Economics of Italian Harlem: interdependence of generations and, 112; marginal position of, in the 1930s and 1940s, 198

Education: by the domus, 82–83; of women, 134; and the immigrant community, 196

Emigration, reasons for, 18, 154–55

Employment: problems of, 25–28, 197–98; for women, 28, 98, 198; job mobility and the domus, 98; for men, 114; effects of the festa on, 197–202; time-management studies, 199; requests made to the Madonna about, 201–02

Ethnic groups: established in Harlem, 16–17; attitudes of, toward Italian workers, 25–26; street gangs and, 33; values of the domus and, 102

Family: definition of, xx; ties to Italy, 19–20; early immigrants and, 21–22, 23–25. *See also* Domus; Relationships

Farley, John, 56

Fatalism, 229–30

*Feste:* American Catholics' views on, 55, 56; bans on, 57; Italian devotion to, 57;

difference between views of the clergy and the people on, 58; types of, 59. *See also* Our Lady of Mount Carmel, festa of

*Fire in the Flesh* (Lapolla), 157

Fireworks, use of, 6, 7, 10

Food: served at the festa, 4; Italians' views of American, 153; significance of, 172–73, 183

Funerals: mutual aid societies and, 51–52; the domus and, 92, 101–02; role of women at, 132

Gambling, 3, 221

Generational conflict, 109–12

Germans: as spectators at the festa, 6; settlement in Harlem of, 16

Giambastiani, Louis, 75

*Grand Gennaro, The* (Lapolla), 157–59, 195

Gurock, Jeffrey, 29

Haarlem House, 45, 46

"Half-citizenship," 160

Harlem, Italian: development of, 14, 16; relationships with other ethnic groups, 16–17, 89; second generation in, 20–21; housing in, 29, 31; juvenile delinquency in, 31, 33; crime in, 31, 44; regionalism in, 34–35; physical description of life in, 37, 42; effects of the Depression on, 43–44; after World War I, 45–48; during the 1940s and 1950s, 70–72

Healing aspects of devotion, 10, 132, 181–82, 193–95, 209–10; by the Madonna, 176

*Heart of the Stranger, The* (Ruddy), 193–95

Holy figures and the domus, 86–87

Horton, Robin, xx–xxi

Hospitality: importance of, to the domus, 90–91

Housing: in Italian Harlem, 29, 31; the domus and apartment, 91–92

Human nature, Italians' views on, 195–97

Immigrants, early: religious views of, xv, 163–65; communities of, 14; established in Harlem, 16; reasons for emigrating, 18, 154–55; ties to Italy of, 19–20, 150–51; men as, 21–22; effects of separation on, 23–25; employment problems for, 25–28, 197–98; health of, 28–29; first views of this country,

150–53; shared memories of the old country, 153–55; effects of American money on, 156–60; Americanization of, 160–62

Irish: as spectators at the festa, 6; settlement in Harlem of, 16; conflicts with Italians, 16–17, 56–57, 199

Irish American Catholics, views on Italian popular devotion, 55, 56

Italian American Students League, 21

Jews: as spectators at the festa, 6; settlement in Harlem of, 16; relationships with Italians, 95

Joio, Casimino Dello, 205

Juvenile delinquency, effects on the community of, 31, 33

Kirner, Emiliano, 53, 54, 58–59

Ladurie, Emmanuel LeRoy, xix–xx

LaGuardia, Fiorello, 45, 96

Lapolla, Garibaldi, 2, 22, 151, 157, 195

Leo XIII (pope), 60, 61, 62–64

Levi, Carlo, xvii, 150

*Longinqua oceani* (papal encyclical), 62

Love and *rispetto*, 93

Lucerne Memorial, 62

Lydia, Donna, 109–10

Lynch, the Reverend Bernard, 55

Madonna del Carmine, statue of: for the procession, 6; description of, 12; arrival in Harlem, 23, 50, 53; location in the church, 55, 57; crowning of, 64; moved to the main altar, 65; examples of requests made to, 174–76, 209, 213; fear of, 216; power of, 217–18; description of her statue in the Church of Saint Ann, 222

Mafia: outsiders' views of, 44; and the domus, 103–04, 127–29

Marcantonio, Vito, 44, 45, 96, 217

Marriage: the domus and, 78, 79–80, 99–100, 109, 111, 114, 125–26; blood bonding and, 82; attempts to escape the pressures of the domus and, 125; pressure of, 209

Materialism and success: preoccupation with, 155–57; discussed in the novels of Lapolla, 157–60; tension about and fear of, 191–92

Matrilocality, 148

Men: as early immigrants, 21–22; dominance of, 35, 119–20, 121–22; marriage and, 99–100, 111, 114;

Men (*continued*)
  employment for, 114; dating and, 116–
  17; how they escaped the pressures of
  the domus, 122–23; role of, in the
  festa, 211
Money: preoccupation with, 155–57; discussed in the novels of Lapolla, 157–60
Mother: authority of, 13–34; definition
  of, 211–12
Mount Carmel Catholic Apostolate Society, 71
Mount Carmel festa. *See* Our Lady of
  Mount Carmel, festa of
Multigenerational character of the festa,
  169–70
Music: at the festa, 12; church's choir,
  205
Mutual aid societies, functions of, 51–52,
  123

National Conference of Catholic Charities, 199
Neighborhood: feelings of solidarity in,
  46–48; as an extension of the domus,
  92; isolationism and, 180–81
New York Archdiocese: views on Italian
  popular devotion, 55–57
*New York Times*, 28, 44
Nuns and the domus, 84–85

Our Lady of Guadalupe, 60
Our Lady of Mount Carmel, devotion to:
  the war years and, 46–47, 67–69, 166–
  67; origins of, 52–53, 163–65; erection
  of the church on 115th Street, 54, 186–
  88; steps toward a universal devotion,
  58; Pope Leo XIII and the, 60, 61, 62–
  64; elevated to the status of a sanctuary, 60–61; renovation of the church,
  65; significance of the bell tower, 65–
  66, 187; rites of passage and, 66–67;
  effects of patriotism on, 69–70; postwar years and, 70–74; distance and,
  165–68; ties to old country and traditions and, 168–71; importance to the
  domus, 171–78; significance to the
  community, 178, 180–88; effects on
  regionalism, 180; effects on New York
  City, 188–89; effects on America, 189–
  91; healing aspects of the, 193–95,
  209–10, 214; role of women in, 204–07,
  209–17
Our Lady of Mount Carmel, festa of:
  preparations for, 1–2; length of time
  of, 2, 200; religious articles sold at, 3;
  pilgrimages to, 4; food for, 4, 172–73;

description of the procession, 6–8; at
  the sanctuary, 10–12; origins of, 52–
  53, 163–65; radio and, 71, 72; postwar
  years and changes in, 72–74; meanings
  of, 165, 177–78, 195, 210–11, 218, 229–
  30; effects on work, 197–202; significance of white ribbons, 210; role of
  men at, 211; unmarried women and,
  215
Our Lady of Perpetual Help, 60

Padrone system, in Harlem, 25
Pallotines, 53
Panunzio, Constantino, 154, 160
Paolucci, Girolamo, 60
Parish clubs and societies and effects on
  the devotion of la Madonna, 70–71
Patriotism: American, effects of, on the
  devotion of la Madonna, 69–70; Ital-
  ian, effects of, on the devotion of la
  Madonna, 168–71
Penitents, requests made by, 8, 10, 174–
  76
*Piety and Power*, xvi
Politics and the domus, 96
Polla (town), 52, 53
Power. *See* Authority
Priests and the domus, 83–84
*Propaganda Fide*, 61, 62
Protestants, American-born: views on
  Italians, 159–60, 220
Puerto Ricans: settlement in Harlem of,
  16; and conflicts with Italians, 33, 95;
  views on the festa of, 182–83

Racial hatred, 160–62
Regionalism, 34–35, 180
Relationships: between children and
  parents, 105, 110–11, 113–15, 119, 122,
  153–54; fathers and sons, 111–12, 115,
  118–19; mothers and sons, 118, 119–
  20, 125; among brothers, 118–19; fathers and daughters, 119, 120; husbands and wives, 119–20, 134;
  dominance of fathers, 120–22; among
  young men, 123; mothers and
  daughters, 131, 136; sisters and brothers, 131, 139–41; between women,
  148–49
Religion: definition of popular, xiv, xvi–
  xviii; Italians' views on, xv, 163–65,
  220–30; definitions of, xvii; distinction
  between church and, xvii, 57; how defined in this work, xvii–xviii
Religiosity: Italian Americans' views on,
  xv–xvi, 221–30

Religious articles: types of sold at the festa, 3; in homes, 105
Religious solidarity, 178, 180
Requests, made to the Madonna: types of, 10, 67–68, 74, 166–67, 174–76, 201–02, 209–10
Respect. See *Rispetto*
Riis, Jacob, 22, 57
*Rispetto* (respect): importance of, 92–94, 101, 120, 228
Rites of passage, 66–67
Ruddy, Anna, 193, 195–96

Sacrifices, religious, 202–04, 223–24
Saint Agnes, 215
Saint Anthony, 85–86
Saint Raphael societies, 62
Saints: statues of, sold at feste, 3; role of, 22, 57, 86, 105–06, 224–25, 226, 228
Saint Vincent Pallotti, 54, 74
Sanctuary, contributions made at the, 10–11
Scapulars, meaning of, 173–74, 186
"Service Boys' Fund of East 104th Street," 46
Sex: conflicts between generations over dating and courting, 115–17; role of unmarried women, 135–39
Shame (*vergogna*) and the domus, 95
Shrines, importance of, 22–23, 105
Social clubs, 34–35, 122
Souvenir journals: importance of, 184
Sports: effects of, on the devotion of the Madonna, 70–71; conflicts between generations over, 110–11
Steinberg, Stephen, 98
Street gangs, 33–34; used to escape the pressures of the domus, 123
Suffering, importance of, 21–23, 202–04

Third Plenary Council of American bishops, 54, 61
Thomas, Norman, 31, 123, 160

Thomas, Piri, 47, 183
Time-management studies, 199
Tofini, Scipioni, 60, 61, 167–68, 189, 190
Tomasi, Silvano, xvi
Traditions, faithfulness to, 168–70

Vatican: American Catholicism and the views of the, 61–63
Vecoli, Rudolph, xvi
*Vergogna* (shame) and the domus, 95
Vigorito, Salvatore, 192, 211–12
Vows made to the Madonna, 8–10; candles and, 3; children and the responsibility of fulfilling the, 170, 177; wearing of certain type clothing and, 201; types of, 202–03; meaning of, 229

Wartime, and devotion to la Madonna, 46–47, 67–69, 166–67
Wax body parts: sold at the festa, 3; presented to the Madonna, 10
Women: dragging of, xiv, 11; in the procession, 8, 206; employment for, 28, 98, 198; marriage and, 78, 79–80, 99–100, 109, 114; dating and, 116, 137–39; role of, in the domus, 129, 131–32, 135, 141, 143, 146–48; in conflicts between sisters and brothers, 131, 139–41; authority of, 131–35, 147–48, 216; at funerals, 132; as healers, 132, 193–95; subservience and, 133–34; education of, 134; position of unmarried, 135–39, 141, 143, 214–15; position of older married, 143–46; definition of good, 144–45; childless married, 146; role of, in the devotion, 204–07, 209–17; socializing of, 205–06, 215; closeness to the Madonna, 206, 207, 209, 227; fertility rate of, 215–16

Yans-McLaughlin, Virginia, 24
Youth of Italian Harlem: conflicts with elders, 111–12